Nortel Networks:
A Beginner's Guide

ABOUT THE AUTHORS

Jim Edwards, Billerica, MA, is a senior network engineer and is a member of the Premium Services Staff at Nortel Networks. He has supported numerous enterprise environments and is the key point of contact for multiple premium-services customers. Mr. Edwards has taken most of the Nortel Networks certification examinations and continues to work with most of the technologies that are introduced throughout this book. Mr. Edwards is the author of several technical documents, publications, and training manuals. Along with his networking experience, he has spent several years as a senior PC software technician, technical trainer, and help desk manager. He holds many networking and computing certifications. He can be reached at jedwards@nnabg.com.

Matt Jensen, Omaha, NE, works as a senior network engineer in the Global Customer Care Services group at Nortel Networks. He provides capacity planning, network design, implementation, and support services for multiple customers throughout the Midwest. Prior to coming to work for Nortel, Matt worked as a sales manager for a regional ISP, a customer service and sales manager at a national ISP, and a network analyst at a major IT outsourcer. Matt holds multiple vendor certifications and enjoys teaching what he knows at any community college that will let him. He can be reached at mjensen@nortelnetworks.com or mjensen@nnabg.com.

About the Technical Reviewer

Hang T. Lau is an adjunct professor of the Computer Science Department at Concordia University in Montreal, Canada. He has worked as a system engineer for Nortel Networks for the past 20 years in areas including network planning, speech recognition applications in telecommunication, and transport access radio network systems.

Nortel Networks:
A Beginner's Guide

JAMES **EDWARDS**
MATTHEW S. **JENSEN**

Osborne/**McGraw-Hill**

New York   Chicago   San Francisco
Lisbon   London   Madrid   Mexico City
Milan   New Delhi   San Juan
Seoul   Singapore   Sydney   Toronto

Osborne/**McGraw-Hill**
2600 Tenth Street
Berkeley, California 94710
U.S.A.

To arrange bulk purchase discounts for sales promotions, premiums, or fund-raisers, please contact Osborne/**McGraw-Hill** at the above address. For information on translations or book distributors outside the U.S.A., please see the International Contact Information page immediately following the index of this book.

Nortel Networks: A Beginner's Guide

1234567890 CUS CUS 01987654321

ISBN 0-07-213089-x

Publisher	**Copy Editor**
Brandon A. Nordin	Rachel Lopez
Vice President & Associate Publisher	**Indexer**
Scott Rogers	Valerie Robbins
Acquisitions Editor	**Computer Designers**
Francis Kelly	Kelly Stanton-Scott, Lauren McCarthy
Project Editor	**Illustrators**
Pamela Woolf	Beth E. Young, Michael Mueller
Acquisitions Coordinator	**Series Design**
Alexander Corona	Peter F. Hancik
Technical Editor	**Cover Series Design**
Hang Lau	Amparo Del Rio

This book was composed with Corel VENTURA™ Publisher.

This book is dedicated to my wife, Denise, and our four children:
Natasia, Shaun, Nick, and Emily. They are the reason for everything I do.
—Jim Edwards

To the best friends a man could have, Dr. Steve Jensen, Tim Cich, and Jesus Christ.
I owe you all so much more than I'll ever be able to repay.
And to my Mom: a finer mother there has never been...
—Matt Jensen

AT A GLANCE

CONTENTS

ACKNOWLEDGMENTS

This book was a challenge to all of us and there are many people that were involved in the success of its completion. I would like to first thank my co-author, Matt Jensen, for being there and putting forth the same effort that I did to see this dream become a reality. I would also like to thank the following individuals for the role each one of them have played, both directly and indirectly, which enabled me to complete this project (in alphabetical order): Fred Barone, Darnell Champen, Joe Chartier, Paul Galipeau, Jason Golden, Mike Hill, Peter Knoops, Phil Kubat, Paul Lane, Mike Leary, Eddie O, Bridget O'Rourke, Patrick Ryan, Joe Strasser, Andy Wayne, and Bogdan Wisloki. Thanks goes out to Steve Carr and Steve Gauger for the encouragement and advice each of them gave to me during this project. I also want to thank Ragho Mahalingam for introducing me to this opportunity. A special thanks goes out to Jim Unsworth for providing me with advice and sharing experiences of the past year and a half. I also appreciate Jim for allowing me to use his analogy of the MIBs in the book.

Kudos to everyone that was involved with this project from Osborne/McGraw-Hill. Special thanks to Pamela Woolf, Alex Corona, and Beth Young for the role each of them played in seeing this project completed. To Franny Kelly, thank you for giving me this opportunity and for providing me encouragement throughout this process.

My heart-felt appreciation also goes to Jason Towley, who encouraged me to pursue my love of writing. I also want to thank my mom for supporting me over the years and making me realize that if you put your mind to it, you can accomplish anything. To TaVaree, who always said "suffer what there is to suffer and enjoy what there is to enjoy," for teaching me to take each day and accept what cards I am dealt, I thank you.

Most importantly, I want to thank by beautiful wife, Denise, for not only providing the wonderful figures in Chapter 1, but mainly for supporting me in all my endeavors over the past few years. Denise, thanks for putting up with all the long hours and for being there each and every time I needed you. I could not have accomplished any of it without you, starlight. I love you and do appreciate all you have done for the kids and me.

—Jim Edwards

This book would have been impossible to complete without the foundation laid by four of the greatest people in the world, P.J. and Jerry Schnecker, and Steve and Cathy Jensen, thank you from the bottom of my heart for *everything*.

Thanks to Jim Edwards for all his time and dedication to this project and to Nortel, and to Hang Lau for keeping us honest. I'd like to add my thanks to the project team that Jim mentioned above. Especially to Alex Corona, a more humble man you will not meet.

Thank you Ms. Gnam for putting me on the right track so many years ago.

Mr. Getz, thank you for your sterling example and for not giving up on me.

Thanks to Patrick Mulvehill for teaching me that who I represent is so much more important than who I am.

Mr. Gothard, there would be no room for technical content in this book if I tried to express all that I am grateful to you for, so I'll just say this: Thank you for my sisters.

Without the support and understanding of my colleagues and superiors at Nortel this project would have been impossible to complete, so:

Thanks to Jeff Kovalik and Lee Orr, the best bosses an engineer could hope to have, Erich Krueger for showing me the ropes and proving that he is a man of boundless patience, and Sathy Ganesh for answering more silly questions than I care to remember.

Thanks also to the team at Compaq Direct, Ahmed Yeldram, Bruce Thiebauth, Chico Miranda, Vernon Gill, and Jeff Friesen, for their flexibility and respect (it means more than you know). I'd especially like to thank Jeff Busch and Wayne Brown for giving me time to get the answers they need.

—Matt Jensen

INTRODUCTION

The job of the average computer professional is tough, but network professionals are forced to deal with infrastructures that can change 100% in as little as one year. Keeping up with these changes requires almost constant study. Until recently, the only way to learn Nortel Networks technologies was to take a class (always an expensive proposition), read documentation at Nortel's Web site, or train on the job. None of which can strike the fine balance between cost and efficiency that self-study books can.

This book is intended to provide an overview of Nortel Networks' major Enterprise Data products and solutions, as well as networking in general. In no way should the reader expect to become a Nortel expert after completing this book. However, you can expect to know which Nortel product to use in a given situation and how to perform basic configurations. This book is the first of many from Osborne/McGraw-Hill that should be read to gain a more complete picture of what Nortel Networks has to offer networking professionals.

WHO SHOULD READ THIS BOOK

Nortel Networks: A Beginners Guide was written with two groups of people in mind: the network administrator just starting out in his career and the experienced network engineer that would like to get current on Nortel technologies and pursue Nortel's valuable certifications. To that end the first few chapters provide a general networking overview that a long-time engineer might want to skip over, while providing enough background information to allow the networking novice to keep up.

We highly recommend that those familiar with Nortel Networks' competitor's products read this book. Many Cisco certified engineers have been surprised by the reliability, power, flexibility, and ease of use of Nortel's data products. One of the authors of this book was once rather closed-minded about Nortel's products until he was forced to evaluate them by his employer. He was so impressed that it wasn't long before he was interviewing with Nortel Networks.

WHAT'S IN THIS BOOK

This book is written for individuals who are interested in learning about networking as well as those who just are looking for an introduction to networking with Nortel Networks products. We have attempted to go into enough detail to make this a very practical resource for you, without overwhelming you.

▼ **Chapter 1** provides a brief overview of networking, from the basics of how computers operate and send information, to some of the standards that allow different networks to communicate with one another. Various networking technologies both past and present are also discussed.

■ **Chapter 2** discusses the company that makes this book possible, Nortel Networks. Nortel as a company is changing each and every day, so some of the information that is introduced in this chapter will probably change along with Nortel. The products in this chapter are mainly provided to give the networking beginner an idea of the products used in today's networks, but in no way represent all Nortel Networks product offerings.

■ **Chapter 3** covers the certifications that Nortel Networks currently offers. These Nortel certifications are important and should be seriously considered by anyone that currently works with, or will be working with, Nortel Networks products.

- **Chapter 4** focuses on Nortel Networks Layer 2 switching technologies. From discussing the difference between hubs and switches to how to identify and configure the various switches, this is a must read for anyone that supports a LAN.

- **Chapter 5** focuses on the Nortel routing platform, BayRS. This chapter begins by discussing the types of bridging that are available, goes into the various router product lines, and concludes with an overview of the software that is used on Nortel routers.

- **Chapter 6** uses the information that is introduced in Chapter 5 and expounds upon it. It covers the various methods of obtaining access to the Technician Interface (TI) in order to configure and manage a Nortel router. The file system is discussed as well as the various commands that are available. This chapter is a handy reference guide for any network that contains Nortel routers.

- **Chapter 7** discusses the protocols that are supported by the Nortel Networks routers. From Apple Talk to TCP/IP and its applications, this is a nice introductory chapter for the networking beginner.

- **Chapter 8** provides an overview of network management. The advantages of the Simple Network Management Protocol (SNMP) are discussed. The Optivity application is also introduced in this chapter. This chapter is an excellent resource to obtain a general understanding of network management.

- **Chapter 9** delves into the up-and-coming technology known as *wireless networking*. The differences between traditional Ethernet and wireless Ethernet are discussed. Wireless networking is where many companies are moving, making this chapter a valuable resource.

- **Chapter 10** covers another popular trend: the VPN and its relationship to the Contivity Extranet Switch. This chapter is a must for any networking professional, both novices and seasoned veterans.

- **Chapter 11** provides a troubleshooting information. Anyone involved with networking knows, or soon will, that understanding how to reach the cause of a problem is one of the most challenging and rewarding parts of an engineer's job.

- **Appendix A** is a glossary of terms that are used in this book.

- **Appendix B** contains many of the commands that are available for the Passport routing switches.

- ▲ **Appendix C** contains many of the commands that are available in the Technician Interface on the Nortel Networks routers.

We expect that you will find this book to be a useful first step toward a full understanding of Nortel Networks and their data product lines. Working on this project has been a wonderful experience. We hope you enjoy reading it as much as we enjoyed writing it.

CHAPTER 1

Networking Basics

To grasp the concepts and technologies presented in this book, it is necessary to cover the basics of networking. Because the basics of networking could be a whole book in itself, we have not attempted to go into extensive details in this first chapter. Instead, this chapter serves as an overview of networking terminology and concepts. It is intended to introduce you to networking without being overwhelming. The foundation you develop as you read this first chapter will give you enough background information to understand the detailed concepts introduced later. This chapter covers internetworking and the architectures that enable you to communicate through the Internet.

INTRODUCTION TO NETWORKING BASICS

For many of us, just two short decades ago, networking was simply a grouping of dumb terminals that were linked to a mainframe. Most applications were built around this platform, whereas other applications were being built without networking in mind at all. It did not take long for employers to realize the need for computers in the workplace. As this need grew, the need to connect the computers for business purposes grew as well.

As the electronic age developed, the need to share data in an electronic format became increasingly important. Countless hours were spent printing, copying to disk, reformatting, and duplicating data. If data was to be shared between users, it usually was copied to a floppy disk. The floppy disk then would be passed around between users in the office; remote users would receive a copy by fax or a delivery service. Because of this practice, there was no standard way to ensure all copies on all workstations were updated when changes were made. For example, the multiple files were being shared with multiple users, who made multiple changes. The files were then exchanged with other users who made other changes, and forgot to tell the third and fifth users of the changes, and… well, you can see what a nightmare this was. It was mainly because of this inefficiency that networks evolved to what they are today.

At its most elementary level, a network consists of two or more computers connected to each other with a cable, allowing them to share information. All networking is based on this simple concept. An example of a basic network is shown in Figure 1-1. Computers that are part of a network can share data, messages, printers, fax machines, copy machines, modems, plotters, and many other hardware devices. New ways of sharing data and communicating through computers are being developed daily.

Most of us are familiar with the Internet and how graphical interfaces have made it so easy to use. With the powerful search engines, "click-here" links, and Internet addresses, we have all transformed into technical dependents. One of the major forms of communication in use today is e-mail, a communication mode that allows us to send an electronic letter thousands of miles away in seconds with just one simple click. There also are a multitude of programs that enable us to create our own Web sites, allowing a world full of

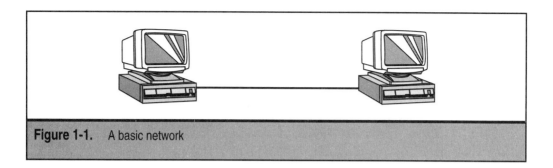

Figure 1-1. A basic network

opportunities to young entrepreneurs. We use it, we love it, and we all look forward to seeing what is next.

It is important to understand that the Internet is not one huge physical network. Instead it is a way to connect multiple physical networks and establish rules that allow the devices they reach to communicate. The hardware that connects to networks is an integral part of the network, but would be completely useless without software and the rules of engagement.

Behind the bells and whistles we enjoy while surfing the Web; using chat programs, playing games, shopping, and e-mailing (just to name a few); are many devices linking each of us to one another. But what makes these devices communicate? What types of devices are there? These and other questions will be discussed in detail throughout this book.

ELECTRONIC COMMUNICATION

To understand how information is passed through a network, we first must understand the basic concepts of how electronic communication works. All networking devices are similar to normal computer platforms except they are developed with the sole purpose of transporting and moving data and not storing it. Although networking devices do not have disks, which are used by computers to store data, they do have processors, require memory, and have operating systems.

Computing Basics

When a user first turns on a computer, it might appear to him or her that not much is happening. In actuality, there is a tremendous amount of processes running. The computer is performing what is called the Power On Self Test (POST). During the POST, the computer is performing a complex array of operations that ensure everything is working correctly. The computer can even warn you if there is something wrong, and in many cases provide an avenue to help solve and fix the problem.

The POST generates a small electrical signal, followed by a pre-programmed path to the microprocessor. The signal then cleans out leftover data that is in the computer's memory and resets the program counter to a number that represents the beginning address for the computer's boot program. The CPU uses this address to find and invoke the boot program, which invokes a series of system tests. The first thing that it checks is the microprocessor and the POST program. The processor then sends electrical signals through the system bus to check and verify that the hardware is intact and is operational. The system clock then is checked. The clock is very important because it is responsible for ensuring that signals are paced during operation so that they are sent and received in an orderly fashion.

You probably are thinking that this is quite a bit, but the user still has not seen anything appear on the monitor yet. The next step is when the POST tests video memory and ensures that the video adaptor is part of the basic input/output system (BIOS). Once it has confirmed this, the user will begin to see data arrive on his or her display monitor. Now the POST will write, read, and verify information to the system's random access memory (RAM).

The results of all this testing are verified with a chip in the CMOS, which is the official record keeper of installed components and their settings. When the computer is turned off, the CMOS retains its information through signals trickling from a battery. Once these tests are confirmed, the POST continues the boot process by checking and verifying that the installed disk drives are available and operational. The processor now checks and verifies that there is a keyboard installed and checks to see if there have been any keys that have been depressed.

You might be wondering at this point why we went into such depth in the computer's startup process. It is important to understand the functions and operations of a computer, as many of the networking devices that you will learn about in this book utilize similar boot-up diagnostic processes.

Let's take a look at what happens when a computer wants to process information. Computers take electronic information, determine what processes to use, and electronically send data to a determined hardware component. These electronic signals are transferred through transistors inside the CPU or memory and travel inside the computer over wires embedded in a circuit board. The transistor is the basic component from which all microchips are built. It can create only binary information: a 1 if current passes through or a 0 if current does not. These 1s and 0s are called bits and are the basic operation in electronic communication.

Data files and program files are stored in *binary code*. Binary data is a collection of bits that are stored on disks and are transferred over cables through an internetwork. Binary data might appear overwhelming to us, but it is the way computers and networking devices communicate. A *byte* is a collection of eight consecutive bits (see Figure 1-2). This not only enables systems to transfer information faster and more reliably, it makes debugging much simpler. Technically, the term *byte* refers to a hardware-dependent character size. Networking professionals use the term *octet*, referring to an 8-bit quantity on all computers.

01001100 - 8 bits or 1 byte

Figure 1-2. An example of a byte

Operating Systems

When operating systems first were developed, they were intended to handle the job of communicating with multiple types of disk drives. It did not take long for operating systems to evolve from that one basic task to become a mediator for all communications between the computer and the software that is run on it.

An operating system performs common tasks for different applications, so these tasks do not have to be rewritten for every application. If you did not have an operating system, or at least one that handles common tasks, you probably would not be able to store similar files on the same disk, would have to reconfigure print directives for every application you are running, and many of the functions we all take for granted would become painful routine tasks.

Networking devices use operating system software that performs very similar tasks to those used by operating systems for computers. The operating system used by Nortel Networks routing platforms is Gate Access Management Entity (GAME). GAME is discussed in more detail in Chapter 5.

THE OSI REFERENCE MODEL

Modern computer networks are designed in a very structured manner. To ensure design simplicity, most networks are organized in a series of layers.

The International Standards Organization (ISO), an international body that specifies standards for network protocols, is best known for its Open Systems Interconnection (OSI) seven-layer reference model (see Figure 1-3). The OSI reference model describes the conceptual organization of network protocols. You can subdivide the seven layers into two categories: The lower three layers deal with network functions and the upper four layers provide application-related functions.

A set of rules used to develop and arrive at the layers are as follows:

▼ A layer needed to be developed at each point where a different level of thought was needed.

■ Each layer had to perform a function that was well defined.

■ Each layer's function had to be developed with a standardized protocol in mind.

■ Boundaries between layers had to minimize information flow between interfaces.

▲ The number of layers had to be enough to perform separate and distinct functions, but not so many as to defeat the purpose.

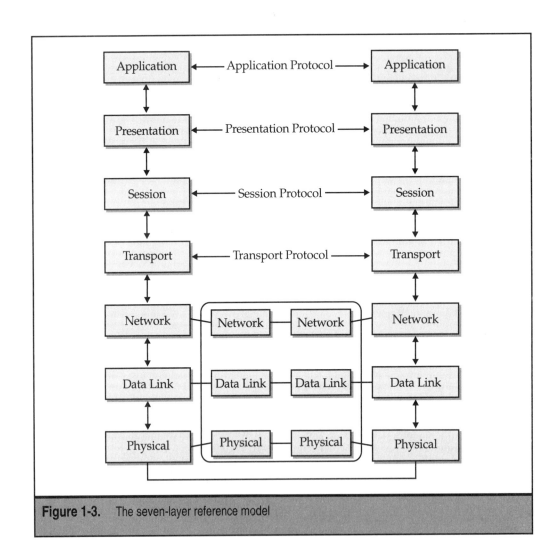

Figure 1-3.   The seven-layer reference model

The Lower Three Layers

Layer 1, the physical layer, specifies the physical connection as well as procedures to transfer packets from one machine to another. Types of devices operating at this layer are repeaters, concentrators, and hubs.

Layer 2, the data-link layer, is responsible for ensuring that the received data is checked for problems before being passed on to higher levels. The data-link layer is divided into two sublayers: the Media Access Control (MAC) layer and the Logical Link Control (LLC) layer. Types of devices operating at this layer are layer 2 switches and bridges.

Layer 3, the network layer, contains the functionality that defines the basic concepts of routing and destination addressing. The network layer ensures the completion of the connection between a host and network. Various protocols are associated with this layer. Routing protocols include OSPF and RIP; the IP protocol and IPX protocol also are included. These protocols are discussed in detail in future chapters. This layer is the layer that separates the network- and application-related functions previously mentioned.

The Upper Four Layers

Layer 4, the transport layer, determines packet size, amount of data used, networking architectures being used, and error acknowledgement and recovery. The transport layer breaks down long messages into smaller packets and correlates the smaller packets into an order to be easily reassembled on the receiving end. Protocols at this level include UDP and TCP.

Layer 5, the session layer, allows two or more remote agents to communicate. The session layer ensures that the flow of data is regulated by establishing and enforcing rules associated with the flow of data. Some protocols included at this layer are AppleTalk, Net BIOS, and NETBEUI. Using the connection-oriented services provided at this layer are FTP, SMTP, and Telnet; all of which are IP-related protocols.

Layer 6, the presentation layer, takes data received from the application layer (layer 7) and performs data compression, encryption, and file translation among different file formats. In other words, it is concerned with the syntax of data messages that are transferred between various application processes.

Layer 7, the application layer, is the highest level of the seven-layer reference model. It represents the actual applications used by users on a network.

In the OSI reference model, each layer acts as if it is communicating with the corresponding layer at the other side. Actually, data is being passed from one layer down to the next layer until it is finally transmitted onto the network medium by the physical layer (layer 1). While the data is being passed from layer to layer, each layer adds information to the message, so at the receiving end, the message will be sent up each layer until the corresponding layer is discovered.

TCP/IP

The Transmission Control Protocol/Internet Protocol (TCP/IP), also known as the TCP/IP protocol suite, is an industry standard that allows for communication among different vendors. TCP/IP is the most widely used and widely accepted protocol suite used today, and probably will remain the most popular for some time to come. As we have mentioned, TCP/IP is a suite of protocols, not just one protocol. It is the world's most implemented protocol suite, used by most businesses and individuals, although many people do not realize that is what they are using; all that most people realize is that they do have a connection to the Internet and that is enough for them.

In business applications, TCP/IP is becoming more and more the protocol of choice, seconded by the Novell NetWare protocol, which is discussed in more detail in Chapter 7 of this book. To explain the impressive influence TCP/IP has had in recent years, consider that Novell NetWare was the number one protocol used for client/server applications in most business networks until the early 1990s. One of the main reasons that TCP/IP became so popular was that it interfaced very nicely with Internet browsers and Web programming languages. As corporate intranets and applications that were Java-based became more popular, it just made more sense to use a protocol that interfaced with these types of applications.

TCP/IP also is very popular because it is portable. This means that you can easily access the network from home using a dial services application, move to other workstations on your network, and move your workstation throughout the network. With TCP/IP, you have the potential to access any network throughout the world. This is because TCP/IP addressing is a global addressing scheme.

TCP/IP originally was used by the Advanced Research Project Agency (ARPA) and has become a networking standard in multiple computing environments. TCP/IP allows for access to the Internet and its vast resources.

As most networks accept TCP/IP as a protocol, it has become the standard for interoperability for different types of computers and network devices. There have been various protocols that were written for TCP/IP; simple mail transfer protocol (SMTP), simple network management protocol (SNMP), and file transfer protocol (FTP) are some of these.

TCP/IP REFERENCE MODEL

The TCP/IP Reference Model was developed as a reference model used for ARPAnet. ARPAnet was a research network sponsored by the U.S. Department of Defense. Using leased telephone lines, it connected hundreds of universities and government installations. Eventually, satellite and radio networks were implemented and had trouble utilizing the existing protocols. The need to connect networks in a seamless way became a big goal, and the TCP/IP Reference Model was born. It is not important at this time to go further in depth on this subject, but it is helpful to understand how the OSI and TCP/IP reference models interrelate. Figure 1-4 shows an example of this.

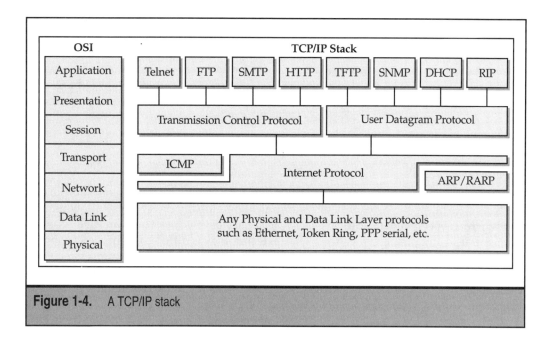

Figure 1-4. A TCP/IP stack

WAN AND LAN TECHNOLOGIES

Networks that span large geographical distances are much different, both physically and logically, from those connected on a more local level. Wide area networks (WANs) are the networks that provide communication over great distances. Most WANs are not limited in the distance they can travel. A WAN can be a network connecting New York to Chicago, or it can connect the United States to Japan. On the other hand, a local area network (LAN) spans a much shorter distance. LANs typically span a small building or a small campus.

LANs and WANs are terms that are used loosely by various networking professionals, as there are no written limitations on where one ends and another begins. A key difference is that WANs typically operate at a slower speed than do LANs. For example, a WAN speed normally will range from 56 Kbps to 155 Mbps, whereas a LAN will range from 10 Mbps to 2 Gbps. Additionally, LANs cover shorter distances and therefore are able to offer lower delay rates than WANs.

In LAN technologies, each computer is connected to a physical medium (for example, coaxial cable, twisted-pair cable, or fiber optics), through a network interface device. With WAN technologies, a network usually is a series of complex computers (switches) that are connected by communications lines and modems. Adding another switch extends the size of the network and the distance it travels. Users are connected to the switches, which allows them to send and receive data throughout the WAN. Bear in mind, however, that the larger a WAN gets, the longer it takes to route data through it.

Overview of a LAN

As we mentioned before, it is hard to establish a definition of exactly what a LAN is. Simply put, LANs allow the electronic exchange of information between users and peripherals on a network segment. A LAN can be as simple as two computers connected together or can be a more complex, high-speed network supporting multiple attached peripherals and users (see Figure 1-5). Determining what type of network to use depends on the requirements of the LAN.

Overview of a WAN

A WAN essentially is a LAN on a much grander scale. Figure 1-6 shows an example of a WAN. WANs allow the capability of communicating globally. WANs also allow remote access, which is becoming more and more necessary every day. There are two types of WANs: dial-in and direct connections. Dial-in technology is different from direct connections in that the connection is not permanent; once you have completed your session your connection is terminated. Direct connect technology usually connects offices, buildings, cities, countries, and so forth. WANs can be considered a vehicle that connects users of different LANs.

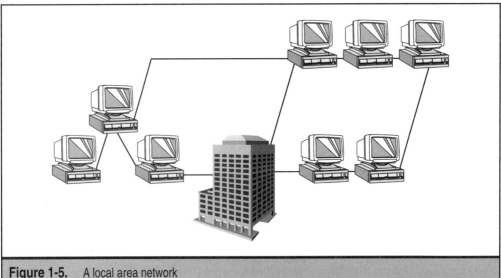

Figure 1-5. A local area network

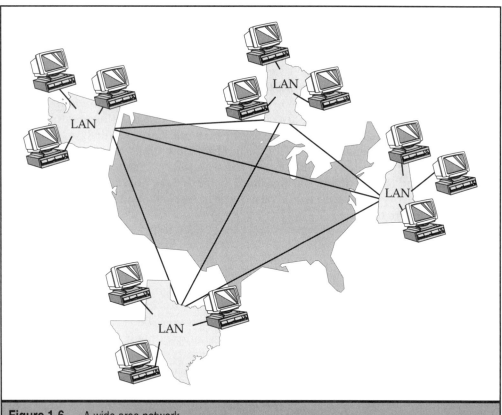

Figure 1-6.   A wide area network

TOPOLOGIES

A topology is the way devices in a LAN or a WAN are physically connected. A topology typically is represented in a drawing, which represents the devices and the cabling used to connect these devices. Some LANs represent multiple types of topologies, whereas others must adhere to specific topologies. The type that is used is dependant on the type of LAN chosen for your needs.

The two different types of topologies are physical and logical. *Physical* topologies represent devices and the interconnections between the devices. *Logical* topologies cover the methods, as in Ethernet, token-ring, FDDI, and ATM.

Star Topology

The *star* topology (see Figure 1-7) has end stations, or nodes, that are connected to a central point. The central point normally is a hub that is connected by cables to the nodes. An important thing to remember when configuring a star topology LAN is the amount of cabling used, as each node is on a point-to-point link.

An advantage to this type of topology is that there is no single point of failure within the cabling that would affect the entire network. A disadvantage to the star topology is that the hub can be a single point of failure for the network. This is unlikely, as most hubs have fault-redundancy, enabling availability and little downtime. This means that in the event of a hub/switch failure, a replacement can be installed in minutes.

Another disadvantage to the star topology is that it does not offer any redundancy options. Redundancy in this case would be a duplicate cable that would forward traffic if the main cable were to fail.

Bus Topology

The *bus* topology is a simple topology design, using a single cable that connects to multiple nodes (see Figure 1-8). The endpoints on the cabling segment are known as *terminating points*. Because this is a simple design, it also is very inexpensive to implement. However, managing this type of topology can be expensive. Because all nodes are connected to a single segment of cable, there is a possibility of having problems if a cable breaks, as there will be two separated segments; therefore, stations connected to one segment will not be capable of communicating with stations connected to the other segment.

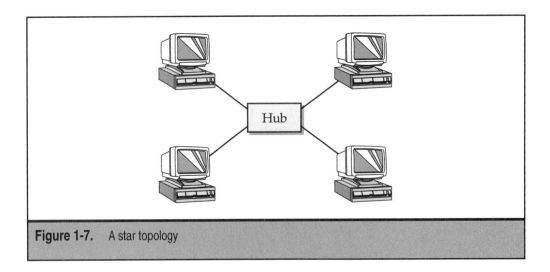

Figure 1-7.   A star topology

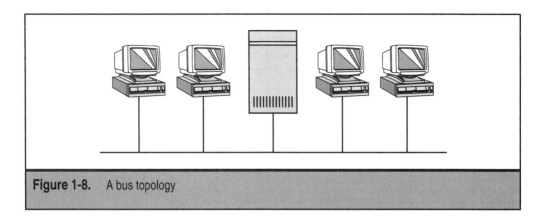

Figure 1-8. A bus topology

Ring Topology

The *ring* topology (see Figure 1-9) connects all nodes together in a loop, with each node acting as a repeater. The repeater can be considered the controller board in the node. Each node will receive a transmission and will repeat that transmission to the next node. Data is communicated in one direction and is received by the next node in the loop.

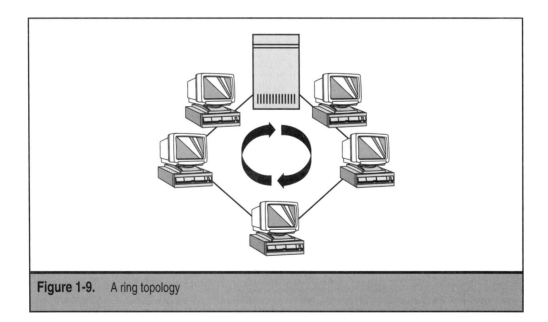

Figure 1-9. A ring topology

The term "ring" does not mean that the network is physically connected in a ring. As a matter of fact, in most cases, a ring topology is physically cabled in a star pattern. Each node is connected to its own cable. A major advantage of the ring network is that it is predictable. A disadvantage is that if one node breaks down, or if a network adapter card becomes inoperative, all the nodes in the ring go down.

Ethernet

Ethernet is a popular packet-switched LAN technology used by most medium- and large-sized corporations. Because it is so popular, there have been some revisions to Ethernet, so we will discuss the original design as well as some of the current revisions.

Properties of an Ethernet Network

Ethernet has been called a best-effort network because the hardware provides no information to the sending devices confirming that a packet was or was not delivered. TCP/IP protocols, discussed in Chapter 7, address and accommodate this type of hardware.

Ethernet has no authority to grant access; therefore, it uses an access scheme called Carrier Sense Multiple Access with Collision Detection (CSMA/CD). It is CSMA because multiple devices can access the Ethernet at the same time, and each device senses whether the Ethernet is being used. When an interface has a packet it wants to send, it listens to see if anything is being transmitted on the ether. If it does not detect anything being sent, it transmits the information it wants to send. If it does detect a current transmission, it will wait until it does not detect anything. This is why it is called "carrier sense." Figure 1-10 has an example of how CSMA/CD works.

When a transceiver sends data, the information does not reach all parts of the network at the same time. Therefore, it is possible for more than one transceiver to sense that the ether is not busy and to send information at the same time. When this occurs, the signals become scrambled, and a collision occurs. Because of this, each transceiver will monitor the cable it is transmitting on to see if there are any foreign signals interfering with its transmission. If it senses an interruption in transmitting, it stops transmitting, waits for the ether to clear, and then resends its data.

Fast Ethernet

Ethernet was invented with the intent to run minicomputers connected to terminal servers in a LAN environment. Now most user workstations are high-powered PCs that run intense applications on the network, interconnecting with multiple network devices. Not only is standard data being transmitted; video, graphical, and digital audio is being shared as well.

Workplace connection to the Internet is much more common than once anticipated. The numbers of users and nodes on a LAN have more than doubled in the last 10 years. With all these changes, and the need for quick and accurate networks, Fast Ethernet was developed. Fast Ethernet was a cost-effective way to enhance an already known protocol and bring networks up to speed. Fast Ethernet quickly became more commonplace. At 100 Mbps, it was 10 times faster than Ethernet, and was less than double the cost to implement.

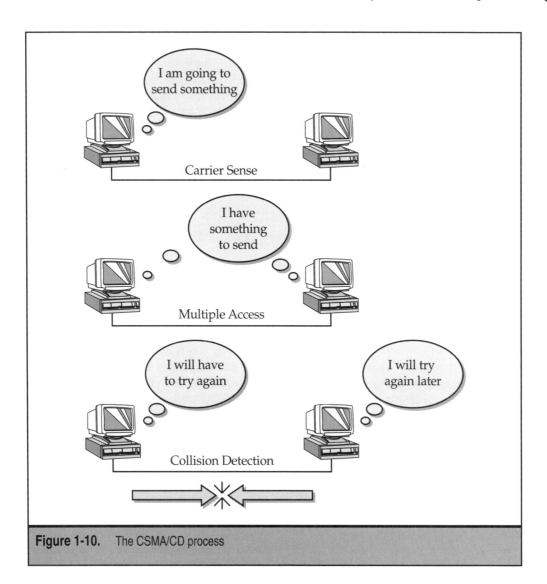

Figure 1-10.   The CSMA/CD process

Fast Ethernet easily can be made to interface with Ethernet transparently, so it is very popular and is used on many LANs around the world. Moving from a standard Ethernet environment to Fast Ethernet is a decision that must be thought out, as it does require a considerable investment. Client and server network interface cards (NICs) and new hubs must be purchased. Some older-style cabling also must be upgraded to support the Fast Ethernet network. One also must keep in mind that the desktop computers might not add to the speed of the transmission due to the age of the computer. Fast Ethernet is a worthwhile investment for businesses that need to transmit lots of data in short time spans.

Gigabit Ethernet

A committee was formed in November of 1995 to examine and determine if Gigabit Ethernet warranted a standard. The committee was known as The Gigabit High-Speed Study Group. This group accepted and reviewed technical submissions until 1996, and in November of that year, it met to establish the following objectives:

▼ To develop a 1000 Mbps Ethernet that allows both half- and full-duplex operation. Half-duplex means that a device is allowed to transmit or receive but not both. Full-duplex offers the capability to transmit and receive simultaneously.

■ To use the IEEE 802.3 Ethernet frame format.

■ To continue to use the CSMA/CD access method.

▲ To develop backward compatibility to Fast Ethernet and Ethernet technologies.

Gigabit Ethernet is a much newer technology than all the other technologies and is used mainly by network managers to support their backbone needs.

Token-Ring

IBM developed the Token-Ring protocol in the early to mid-1980s. The method for accessing the network is by intercepting a passing token. In token-ring, the computers are connected in a logical ring. An electronic token then is passed from one computer to another until it returns to the starting point. If a computer has information it would like to send, it will accept the token and attaches the data it would like to transmit. If the computer does not have any data to transmit, it will simply pass the token to the next workstation. If a computer accepts a token that already has data, the computer first will check to see if it is the destination node and will pass the token on. Token-ring networks generally are more expensive to maintain than Ethernet networks are and require additional processing power and time to handle the token passing functions. Because of the increasing popularity of Ethernet, token-ring use is decreasing.

FDDI

Fiber Distributed Data Interconnect (FDDI) is used primarily to connect two or more LANs over large distances. The access method of FDDI is usually token passing. FDDI is a dual ring topology, with transmissions occurring on one ring and the second ring acting in a redundant fashion. Because FDDI operates over fiber cabling, its major advantage is speed.

FDDI is a data transmission standard for a LAN environment. Data is transmitted across fiber-optic cables. FDDI is based on token-ring technology on a much grander scale. FDDI easily can support thousands of users.

A FDDI network has two token-rings, one primary and one backup. This redundancy makes FDDI a very desirable standard. The backup ring is used to increase capacity when it is not needed in a redundant fashion. This doubles the capacity of the FDDI network to 200 Mbps. A dual ring has the capability to extend to a distance of 62 miles, which is a remarkable distance by any means.

American National Standards Institute committee X3–T9 developed FDDI. FDDI conforms to the OSI reference model and easily connects multi-protocol LANs.

ATM

Asynchronous Transfer Mode (ATM) is a high-speed, connection-oriented networking technology that is used in both LANs and WANs. ATM networks are much more expensive than other networks because of the equipment needed. ATM networks require special hardware and software techniques and use optical fibers for connections. Another important thing to remember about ATM networks is that they use fixed-size frames called *cells* to transmit data. Because cells are a fixed size, ATM hardware can transmit data quickly.

ATM networks use a connection-oriented service. Before a cell can be sent, the node wanting to transmit the data first must contact the switch to determine a destination. The originating node will inform the switch of the destination address where it wants to send data. The switch then contacts the destination to ensure that a path can be established. If the destination node rejects the request, or if it cannot be found, the request will fail.

If the connection between the nodes can be established, the switch will choose an identifier for that connection and notify the originator that the path is successful. The originator then will use the identifier when sending and receiving the cells. When it is finished using the connection, the originator will let the switch know that it is finished. The switch, in turn, disconnects the two nodes.

The ATM Adaptation Layer

The ATM adaptation layer (AAL) is the layer that is between ATM and the higher layer protocols that want to use the ATM service. The main purpose of AAL is to resolve any conflicts with a service that is being required by a user and the services that are available at the ATM layer. The AAL tracks user information in the ATM cells and also transports timing information. Simply put, AAL is a mechanism that is used for the segmentation and reassembly of packets. There are two defined sublayers within the AAL:

▼ **The convergence sublayer**—This layer will enter header and trailer information that contains user service data. The information contained in the header and trailer is data priority information and error-handling information.

▲ **The segmentation and reassembly sublayer**—This layer will divide the information contained in the convergence sublayer for placement into an ATM cell. It will add a header that contains information on how to reassemble the information at the destination.

ATM Adaptation Layer 1   AAL1 is used to transfer constant bit rate data, or a telecommunication service in which data transmission is at a constant rate, which is time dependent. AAL1 sends timing information with data that is being transmitted, which ensures that the timing information can be recovered. AAL1 also provides error recovery and logged notification when recovery is not successful.

ATM Adaptation Layer 2   AAL2 is used to transfer variable bit rate data, or a telecommunication service in which data transmission is at a variable rate, which is time dependent. AAL2 also sends timing information with the data that is being transmitted to ensure that source node timing information is known at the receiving node. AAL2 also provides error recovery and logged notification when recovery is not successful.

ATM Adaptation Layer 3   AAL3 is used to transfer variable bit rate data, which is not time dependent. AAL3 supports message mode services, which are transported in a single AAL interface data unit, and streaming mode services, which might require more than one AAL interface data unit. AAL3 is connection oriented.

ATM Adaptation Layer 4   AAL4 is used to transfer variable bit rate data, which is not time dependent. AAL4 operates in a connectionless mode. It supports the same services that are supported by AAL3, which is time-independent traffic in a connectionless mode.

ATM Adaptation Layer 5   AAL5 is used to transfer variable bit rate data, which is not time dependent. It is connection oriented, but does not have the error recovery supported in other layers. AAL5 is easy to implement and has greater speed than previous layers.

CABLING

There are many different considerations when designing a network. Speed, accuracy, and cost are just three of these considerations. The same considerations used in determining the hardware must be also used to determine how you will connect nodes to transport data. There are four types of commonly used cabling:

▼ Thick coaxial cable

■ Thin coaxial cable

■ Unshielded twisted pair (UTP)

▲ Fiber

Thick Coaxial Cable

Thick coaxial cabling is approximately 0.5 inch in diameter. Because it was the first type of cabling used with Ethernet, sometimes it is referred to as *standard Ethernet*. The copper core of thick coax enables it to carry a signal about 1,600 feet. Because of this, sometimes it is used as a backbone, connecting smaller networks that utilize thin coaxial cabling.

Thick coaxial cable is the original cabling used with Ethernet networks (see Figure 1-11). Every 8.2 feet has a black hash mark, which shows where a network node can be attached. Placing devices closer than this causes electrical reflections that can be seen as errors by other nodes on the network.

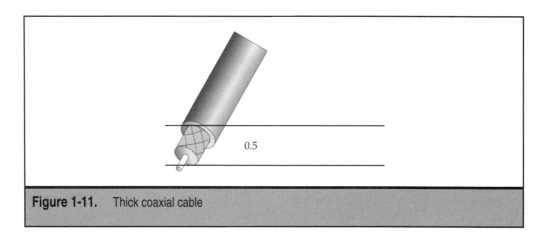

Figure 1-11.   Thick coaxial cable

A transmitter-receiver (transceiver) is used to connect the node to the coaxial cable. It is the device that will receive and send the data that is being passed to and from its node. The transceiver cable connects the Ethernet controller to the cable. It can be up to 164 feet long. The coaxial cable must be pierced to physically connect the transceiver to the coax.

Thin Coaxial Cable

Thin coaxial cable is about .25 inch in diameter. This allows it to be more flexible than thick coaxial cabling; therefore, it is easier to work with. Thin coaxial cables (see Figure 1-12) can carry a signal for approximately 607 feet before the signal starts to become weak.

Thin coaxial cable is very similar to thick coaxial cable, except you do not have to pierce the cable to physically connect the transceiver to the coax. Instead, the Ethernet controller connects to the external transceiver directly (see Figure 1-13).

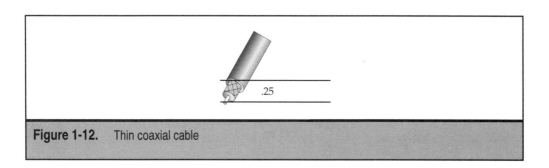

Figure 1-12.   Thin coaxial cable

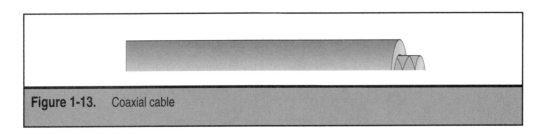

Figure 1-13. Coaxial cable

Unshielded Twisted Pair Cabling

Unshielded twisted pair (UTP) became the most popular of all the cabling when it was introduced in 1990 (see Figure 1-14). The maximum cable length is approximately 325 feet. The term twisted relates to the fact that there are two wires twisted together. Twisting the cabling improves the signaling strength. There are UTP specifications that define how many twists are allowed in each foot of cable.

Categories of UTP Cabling

There are five types, or categories, of UTP cabling used in data communications:

▼ **Category 1** refers to the traditional telephone cables and is not used with data transfer.

■ **Category 2** certifies for data transmission up to 4 Mbps. Category 2 consists of four twisted pairs.

■ **Category 3** certifies for data transmissions up to 10 Mbps and consists of four twisted pairs with three twists per foot.

■ **Category 4** certifies for data transmissions up to 20 Mbps and consists of four twisted pairs.

▲ **Category 5** certifies for data transmissions up to 100 Mbps and consists of four twisted pairs of copper wire.

Fiber Optic Cabling

In fiber optic cabling, optical fibers carry digital data signals in the form of modulated pulses of light. This is a very secure way to transfer data, as there is no way to "tap" the

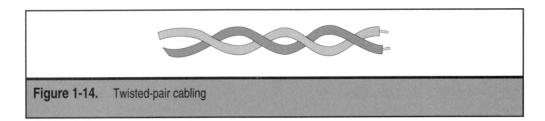

Figure 1-14. Twisted-pair cabling

cable to intercept data, as is possible with other forms of cabling. Fiber cabling is excellent for high-speed and high-capacity data transmission.

Fiber cabling consists of fibers that are thin cylinders of glass, known as the core, which are surrounded by a concentric layer of glass. Each strand of glass passes signals in one direction; therefore, a cable must consist of two strands in separate jackets. One strand will transmit while the other receives.

Cabling Speeds Within Cabling Types

Table 1-1 provides information about various Ethernet cable standards.

FRAMES AND CELLS

Frames and cells are units that are used to transport data in a switched environment. Although their functions are very similar, they are very different. A *frame* is used to transport data normally in an Ethernet or a token-ring network, whereas a *cell* is used primarily in an ATM environment. A cell often is referred to as a Protocol Data Unit (PDU) and is a 53-byte fixed size. Five bytes of the cell are used as the header, and 48 bytes are used as the body (where information that is being transmitted is located). The frame is not of fixed size. The 802.3 standard specifies that the frame is a minimum of 64 bytes and a maximum of 1,518 bytes.

Frame switches can be considered fast multi-port bridges. This is because frames are variable in size; therefore, much like bridges, frame switches know how to handle the variable length PDUs. A big difference is that bridges were developed with the purposes of connecting networks to each other, whereas the main purpose of a switch is to speed up traffic. A bridge uses software to make forwarding decisions, whereas a switch usually has silicon hardware to make forwarding decisions. A frame switch has multiple ports, each of which is a dedicated connection to an attached network device. Also, port speeds on many frame switches are adjustable.

10Base-2	10 Mbps	Coaxial cable
10Base-5	10 Mbps	Coaxial cable
10Base-T	10 Mbps	Twisted pair
100Base-T	100 Mbps	Twisted pair
100Base-TX	100 Mbps	Twisted pair
100Base-FX	100 Mbps	Fiber optic
1000Base-T	1 Gbps	Twisted pair

Table 1-1.   Ethernet Cabling Standards

Cell switching is more appropriate for networks that are sensitive to delays or have very stringent bandwidth needs. Cell switching is a connection-oriented technology; it guarantees a certain level of performance through your network. Cell switching is more expensive to install and maintain than is frame switching, and it is much more complex to administer.

TRANSMISSION CONTROL PROTOCOL (TCP)

The Transmission Control Protocol (TCP) is a connection-oriented protocol; this means that TCP requires that a connection be established before the transmission of data. This ensures that data originating on one node will be delivered without error to the destination node. TCP takes the data that is to be transmitted and fragments it into packets. The packets then are transmitted through the Internet layer to the destination node, which re-assembles the packets into data again.

The Internet layer of the TCP/IP reference model contains the Internet Protocol (IP). IP is the standard that is responsible for routing packets and addressing devices. It is responsible for sending IP datagrams throughout the network.

TCP is capable of performing a function known as *flow control*. Flow control allows the sending, or source, node to adjust the amount of data it is sending to ensure that it is not overwhelming the destination node with too much data at once. TCP is capable of sending a control signal from the destination node when its buffers become full, indicating that it cannot accept data at the moment. The source node, in turn, adjusts the data flow rate to a slower pace until it is notified that it can pick up the pace again.

TCP also is capable of performing a function known as *sequencing*. Sequencing is the capability of TCP to put the packets in the same order they were sent, thus alleviating the need to resend data. Packets do not always take the same route to a destination node. Quite often this means that packets will not be delivered in the same order they were sent.

TCP can be compared to a telephone conversation. When the source user dials the phone, they wait until they are sure that a connection is made and that they have the intended recipient on the phone before transmitting data, or beginning their conversation. There are three steps to a TCP transmission:

1. A connection is established.
2. Data is transmitted.
3. The connection is terminated.

User Datagram Protocol

The User Datagram Protocol (UDP) is a connectionless protocol, which means that data is sent and is assumed to be arriving intact. Connectionless does not require a connection to be established prior to data transmission. Because of this, it is much quicker than TCP, as it is not waiting for requests and acknowledgements. UDP is useful for applications that are not requiring flow control. It is useful for transmitting short request-reply applications that are needed quickly.

UDP takes a datagram and transmits it to the IP. Once it has done that, it no longer concerns itself with that datagram. It is not capable of confirming that the datagram is received and is not capable of recovering data that is not delivered. Much like TCP can be compared to a telephone call, UDP can be compared to sending a letter. The person sending the letter, the source, puts the letter in an envelope, addresses the envelope, and then puts it in the mailbox. At this point, he or she assumes that the letter will arrive at the destination.

SIGNALING

A signal is an electronic impulse that fluctuates. The variations of the fluctuations represent coded information. In other words, a signal is the data that is being transmitted throughout the network.

There are two techniques that can be used to transmit signals over cable: baseband transmission and broadband transmission.

Baseband Transmission

Every device on a baseband network has the ability to transfer data bi-directionally. Some devices can even transmit bi-directionally at the same time. Signals gradually become weaker as they travel and sometimes can become distorted and unrecognizable. For this reason, baseband systems might use a device known as a repeater to receive and retransmit data along the way.

Baseband transmission utilizes digital signaling over a single frequency. Signals flow in discrete pulses of light or electricity. With this form of transmission, the entire channel's capacity is used to transmit a single data signal. The total bandwidth of the cable is determined by the difference between the lowest and the highest frequencies that are being carried over that cable.

Broadband Transmission

Broadband transmissions use analog signaling and a wide range of frequencies. Because the signaling is analog, it is continuous and non-discrete. Signaling flows in both directions, and is in the form of electromagnetic or optical waves. Broadband transmission allows for multiple analog transmissions to be supported simultaneously on a single cable. Instead of a repeater, broadband systems use what is known as an amplifier to ensure the signals remain strong.

IP ADDRESSING

Every node on an IP network has a unique address, called an IP address. IP addresses are used very similarly to how addresses work for our homes. Many nodes having only one connection to the network have only one address. However, devices that have connections to multiple networks will have an individual address for each connection.

An IP address contains 32 bits. The IP address is divided into four equal sections, known as octets. Each octet is converted into a decimal number (from 0–255), and is separated by a dot. This is why the format of IP addressing also is referred to as dotted-decimal notation. The IP address is arranged into two individual parts. The first part is the network to which the node is connected to; and the second part is the host number, or node interface. Even though these parts are variable in length, they can never exceed 32 bits in length.

IP Address Classes

IP addressing is broken into four different classes for different network sizes. Figure 1-16 is a graphical depiction of these classes. Each address class is divided by a line that determines which part of the address is the network address, and which one belongs to the node interface. The classes are identified alphabetically.

An IP addresses class can be determined by three high-order bits. Class A addresses are used by networks that have more than 2^{16} (or 65.536) hosts. Class B addresses are used by networks that have between 2^8 (or 256) hosts and 2^{16} hosts. Class C addresses are used in networks that have less than 2^8 hosts. Class D addresses are reserved for multicast addresses, and Class E addresses are reserved for future use. The Class of IP address that meets your needs, as you can see, is dependent upon the size of your network (population wise).

Class A Address

Class A addresses contain just the first octet defining the network number and have the following characteristics:

▼ The first bit is always 0, leaving the remaining seven bits for the network number, and the other three octets to identify the node number.

■ There are a maximum of 126 networks that can be defined.

■ Addressing begins with a number between 1 and 126.

■ Each network is allowed up to 16, 777, 214 host nodes.

■ Node interfaces cannot contain all 0s or all 1s.

▲ Network addresses 0 and 127 are not used.

Class B Address

Class B addresses contain the first two octets defining the network number and have the following characteristics:

▼ The first two digits are always 1,0, leaving the remaining 14 bits for the network number, and the remaining two octets to identify the host node.

■ Addressing begins with a number between 128 and 191.

▲ Each network is allowed up to 65,534 host nodes.

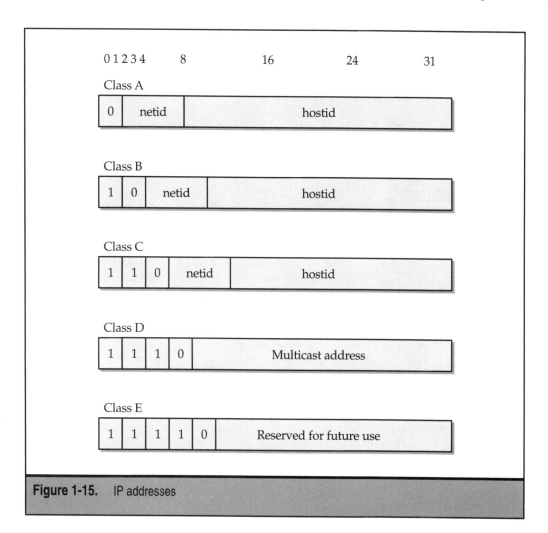

Figure 1-15. IP addresses

Class C Address

Class C addresses contain the first three octets defining the network number and have the following characteristics:

▼ The first three digits are always 1,1,0, leaving the remaining 21 bits for the network number; the remaining host node is identified by the last octet.

■ Addressing begins with a number between 192 and 223.

▲ Each network can have a maximum of 254 hosts.

Class D Address

Class D addresses are reserved for special purposes. They are used for multicasting, which is a special way of transferring data through the Internet. The first four bits of a Class D address are always 1,1,1,0.

Class E Address

Class E addresses are for experimental use. The first four bits of a Class E address are always 1,1,1,1.

Subnet Addressing

Many corporations are assigned only one IP network address from its service provider, but might have multiple LANs. To access the Internet from a LAN, each LAN must have a unique network address. This is why subnet addressing was developed. With subnet addressing, you can take a unique network address, and by slightly manipulating the network portion of it, you will give each LAN a variation of the same network address. This gives each LAN the individuality that it needs to perform.

MULTICASTS VERSUS BROADCASTS

Broadcasting and multicasting are very similar, in that the intention of both is to get an identical message out to multiple network nodes. The primary difference is that broadcasts send the messages to everyone, whereas multicasts allow nodes to determine if they are to participate or not.

A multicast is the transfer of information from a single sender, or source node, to multiple receivers on a network. This is used mainly when there is a need to update remote users from a home office, or to send out informative group newsletters and announcements. Multicast is only one of the Internet Protocol Version 6 (IPv6) packet types. A broadcast is a multicast packet type intended for and accepted by everyone and every node address that is in the network.

NETWORK STANDARDS

So, you might be asking yourself by now, "who sets up the standards and rules governing internetworking?" To answer this question, let's break networking standards into two categories: standards that are defined by industry, and standards that are defined by products.

Standards defined by industry are developed and defined by multiple vendors. These types of standards are monitored by organizations that are composed of individuals who have a related networking interest. In these standards bodies, you will find a vast array of individuals such as employees of networking companies, representatives of various colleges, members of users groups, and representatives from the U. S. Department of Defense.

Standards Organizations

American National Standards Institute (ANSI) is the organization responsible for developing and maintaining standards for multiple networking functions. These include codes, signaling schemes, and so forth. ANSI is responsible for ANSI/IEEE 802 and FDDI standards. ANSI is the primary standards body in the United States.

The Electronic Industries Association (EIA) sets the standards for electronic components. These include the RS232C and RS422 standards, which specify the characteristics of connections between devices on a network. Together with the Telecommunications Industry Association (TIA), they are responsible for EIA/TIA-449, which is a standard allowing higher-speed data exchange over synchronous lines; and the EIA/TIA-568, which provides specifications for UTP wiring and wire cabling for various networking systems and topologies.

The Internet Architecture Board (IAB) sets the standards for Internet activities in the United States. The IAB provides an oversight of the standards development for Internet protocols and procedures. They are responsible for domain name registration through the Internet Network Information Center (InterNIC).

The International Electrotechnical Commission (IEC) is responsible for developing and publishing the standards for all electronic and related technologies. Manufacturers of electronic equipment use the IEC's standards to ship equipment.

The Institute of Electrical and Electronics Engineers (IEEE) acts as the coordinating body for communications, electronic, electrical, and computing standards; such as IEEE802.3 and 802.5 standards. IEEE ensures that systems from multiple vendors are able to communicate with few limitations and adjustments. IEEE subcommittees have developed the standards for LAN configurations and Logical Link Control (LLC) for various data access methods, among others.

The Internet Engineering Task Force (IETF) is part of the IAB. The IETF consists of network professionals who provide technical insights and recommendations to the engineering and developments of Internet protocols and standards.

The Internet Research Task Force (IRTF) is an organization that works on problems associated with TCP/IP and the Internet.

The International Standards Organization (ISO) is a worldwide standards organization that is responsible for creating international standards in various areas, including communications. ISO is best known in networking for its Open Systems Interface (OSI) reference model.

Request for Comments (RFCs)

As we well know, there is no individual, vendor, organization, or society that owns the Internet. There are many organizations that create and maintain standards. There also is documentation of work on the Internet. Individuals and groups can submit proposals for new—or revisions to current—protocols and standards. These submissions are known are Requests for Comments (RFCs).

RFCs can be short or very detailed; they can be simple or complex; they can be standards or new ideas; and they can even be jokes. RFCs are edited by a member of the IAB, and are numbered sequentially in the order they are written. RFCs can be obtained from many different sources throughout the Internet. Ohio State University has an excellent listing of RFCs, which you can find at http://www.cis.ohio-state.edu/hypertext/ information/rfc.html.

Another good way to learn where to obtain them is to ask your network administrator.

CONCLUSION

We have covered the very basics of networking. The information presented in this chapter is enough to build a firm foundation for the rest of the information found in this book. You have just made the very important first steps toward understanding networking with Nortel Networks. You now know there is a lot that goes on when you click the print icon, send an e-mail, or point your Web browser to an Internet site. There is plenty of electronic chatter moving the future of not only our professional lives but also our personal lives. There is so much that goes into a network, and we are sure that as you move through the pages of this book, you will not only have a better understanding of the products in our networks, you will have a greater appreciation of it all.

CHAPTER 2

Introducing
Nortel Networks

It is hard to imagine that something most of us take for granted today was unheard of 15 years ago. Yet, most of us feel very empty without our e-mail (and overwhelmed at times when we have it); we don't know how we got along without the ability to look up that quick reference; order a book, movie, or even a pizza without leaving our chair. We can play games, listen to music, and even watch the news. All this is brought to us by what we now know as the Internet. In the last chapter, we covered the basics of networking. In this chapter, we go further in depth, exploring how Nortel Networks plays a huge part in it all.

AN OVERVIEW OF NORTEL NETWORKS—THE COMPANY

Not only is Nortel Networks a leader in the networking industry, it is a leader in telephony, data, wireless, and wire line solutions for the Internet. Nortel Networks has set its sights on creating a more powerful, faster, and more reliable Internet than ever before. It has offices and facilities in over eight countries, making it a very powerful global corporation.

As of the year 2000, Nortel Networks is a large company, employing over 70,000 employees worldwide. Within Nortel Networks, there are two major groups that define and develop networking communications devices to facilitate all networking needs. They are the Enterprise Solutions group and the Service Provider and Carrier group. This book focuses mainly on the Enterprise solutions, but we introduce the Carrier group as well.

The Enterprise Solutions Group

The Enterprise Solutions group provides IP-based data communications solutions and solutions that allow for electronic communications for all business needs. Nortel Networks can provide a cutting-edge mixture of LAN and WAN networking solutions as well as network management, security, and Virtual Private Networking (VPN) capabilities. Nortel Networks offers the following Enterprise Solutions networking products:

▼ AN Router product line

■ BN Router product line

■ Passport routing switch

■ Centillion ATM switches

■ Bay Stack product line

■ Optivity network and policy management

▲ Contivity Extranet switch product line

The Service Provider and Carrier Group

The Service Provider and Carrier Group provides the tools needed to create the high performance that today's business needs are demanding from the Internet. Because Nortel

Networks is a worldwide leader, it is able to offer experience and expertise in networking development for all types of networks worldwide. Nortel Networks is quickly providing customers the ability to define their own Internet and business networking needs.

Nortel Networks is providing access to Nortel Networks Unified Networks Solutions, which include the following:

▼   Optical Internet

■   Internet services

▲   Wireless Internet

Organizations worldwide are quickly forming cost-effective voice and data networks that are easy to manage and upgrade. Nortel Networks is giving customers the solutions they need to bridge the gap between wire line and wireless, between frame and cell, and between circuit and packet.

NETWORKING INFRASTRUCTURE

This book has been written for the purpose of discussing network *infrastructure*—the devices that make networks work. Although the devices mentioned in this book are developed by an industry leader, Nortel Networks, this book explains the basics of internetworking in such a way that both seasoned networking veterans as well as beginners can benefit from it.

With that said, let's start by introducing you to these devices:

▼   **Hubs**—Hubs normally are standard equipment in LANs and LAN segments. Most hubs actively regenerate and retransmit signals, much like a repeater does. Often hubs are called "multiport repeaters." Hubs that require power are called *active* hubs. There are other hubs that do not require power and do not regenerate the signal that is passing through it. Instead, they act as a connection point and are known as *passive* hubs.

■   **Repeaters**—Repeaters are placed throughout the network in various intervals for the purpose of boosting and amplifying analog signals. Repeaters also regenerate digital signals that are being transmitted. A repeater is very helpful in that it helps signals travel much farther on a cable that otherwise would be dropping information because of distance limitations and signal deterioration. With the advancements of technology, repeaters are not used nearly as much as they used to be.

■   **Bridges**—A bridge is a device that links two or more LAN segments together. A bridge monitors units of information (known as *packets*) that are passing through it and forwards only the packets that are destined for the other network.

■ **Switches**—Switches are simply multi-port bridges. They are message delivery devices that, using the best route available through a network, relay small units of information known as packets or *frames*. Switches transmit data at wire speed or slightly lower and enable simultaneous transmission of data to take place in the network.

■ **Routers**—A router is a networking device that forwards traffic between networks. Information is forwarded based on decisions that are made based on network layer information and routing table information. The router will determine which path is to be used to transmit network traffic. These decisions are based on routing protocols and algorithms that choose the best route. Routers transmit data between LANs and WANs. Without the router, there would be no Internet. Routers use the IP addresses discussed in the last chapter. A router must be capable of recognizing all network layer protocols that might be used to link networks.

■ **Remote Access Servers (RAS)**—As its name implies, remote access gives you the ability to connect to a central network from any location. A remote access server offers a way to easily manage these connections. A remote access server also provides a way to manage a network remotely in a cost-effective and an extremely efficient manner.

■ **Network Management Technology**—Network management is more than an individual watching to ensure things are working as they should be working. In networking, network management entails software applications that greatly enhance the capability to monitor and manage a network. Most of these applications provide a powerful set of tools that help ensure networks are performing and will continue to perform at the highest rates.

▲ **Network Security**—A lot of things have to be taken into consideration when you are implementing a network security policy. Not only are you ensuring that groups have access to what they need, you also have to ensure that some groups are not able to access things they do not need. You also have to be aware of the many hackers—some very malicious—who attempt to break into networks every day. Network security is configured and established not only within software applications, but also in hardware, protocols, and encryption services.

NETWORKING TERMS

It is important not only to understand the networking infrastructure; it is equally important to understand a few basic networking terms that are used in this chapter. This section is not intended to be a complete guide to networking terms, but only an introduction to terms that have not been introduced to you in this chapter. Please see Appendix A for more terms.

▼ **AppleTalk**—A networking protocol that allows for datagram transmission between Apple computer products and other computers.

■ **Basic Rate Interface (BRI)**—An Integrated Services Digital Network (ISDN) service. The BRI allows for two B channels and one D channel. The B channels allow for 64Kb/s bandwidth for data, and the D channel allows for 16 Kb/s for signaling and control.

■ **Border Gateway Protocol (BGP)**—A protocol that allows routers to forward destination availability information between BGP neighbors.

■ **Channel Service Unit (CSU)**—Connects between a LAN and WAN and acts like a buffer, ensuring that faulty equipment cannot affect one or the other.

■ **Digital Equipment Corporation Network (DECnet)**—A technology developed by Digital Equipment Corporation for WAN use that later was used in Ethernet LANs.

■ **Dynamic Random Access Memory (DRAM)**—Memory that stores electrical charges, which represent memory states. DRAM requires recharging, also known as refreshing.

■ **Digital Service Unit (DSU)**—A DSU connects DTEs to digital communications cables and ensures that data is formatted correctly before being transmitted.

■ **Data Terminal Equipment (DTE)**—A device or a node that is used to transmit or receive information (data).

■ **Exterior Gateway Protocol (EGP)**—A protocol that enables routers to forward destination availability information between EGP neighbors.

■ **Frame Relay**—A WAN protocol that was designed to perform high-speed frame (or packet) transmission.

■ **High-Level Data Link Control (HDLC)**—A data link protocol for full-duplex communication.

■ **Hot-swappable**—Having the capability to replace without disrupting normal operation and performance.

■ **Internet Protocol (IP)**—IP is the networking standard that is responsible for sending a datagram throughout a network. It is part of the TCP/IP suite of protocols.

■ **Internet Packet Exchange (IPX)**—IPX is the Novell protocol that provides for the delivery of datagram messages between a Novell NetWare server and a client.

- **LinkSafe**—A feature of the Passport product line that allows a redundant fiber path between two Gigabit Ethernet ports.

- **Open Shortest Path First (OSPF)**—A routing protocol that allows routers to exchange information based on the shortest path available.

- **Point-to-Point Protocol (PPP)**—A communication protocol that allows dial-up access to the Internet.

- **Primary Rate Interface (PRI)**—An Integrated Services Digital Network (ISDN) service. The PRI allows for 23 B channels and 1 D channel. These channels provide for a combined capacity of 1.54 Mb/s.

- **Redundancy**—Additional hardware, software, or links that provide for backup operation in case a primary hardware, software, or link component becomes inoperable.

- **Routing Information Protocol (RIP)**—A routing protocol used by both IP and IPX that allows information to be routed based on information provided in periodic updates.

- ▲ **Switched Multimegabit Data Service (SMDS)**—A service that is provided by the telephone company and allows LANs to connect to each other across WANs.

AN OVERVIEW OF NORTEL NETWORKS HARDWARE OFFERINGS

From small networks that connect users for the purpose of sharing files and resources to large WANs that interconnect multiple LAN segments and span hundreds of thousands of miles, Nortel Networks has a solution to fit multiple networking needs. From the Baystack hub to the more powerful 450 switches and Passport Routing switches, there are few networking issues Nortel Networks cannot resolve.

We begin this section by discussing some of the routing solutions Nortel Networks has to offer.

Nortel Networks Routers

A *router* is a powerful network device that forwards data based on routing table information and network layer information. The router is configured to determine how and to where data is forwarded. A router has to be capable of recognizing a networking protocol and forwarding information in accordance with the protocol. Nortel Networks has some very impressive routing devices, some of which we discuss in this book. The following few pages provide an overview of Nortel Networks routing hardware.

Access Node (AN) and Access Node Hub (ANH) Product Line

The AN Router family (see Figure 2-1) provides Ethernet and token-ring LAN interfaces and data service unit/channel service unit (DSU/CSU) adapter modules, providing support to the typical remote offices. The ANH is capable of supporting up to 12 10Base-T hub ports and one DSU/CSU module adapter as well as supporting up to two ISDN Basic Rate Interface (BRI) interfaces.

The design configurations of the AN/ANH family provide for serial connections to remote offices, which provides increased flexibility to the networks of today. The AN/ANH is capable of supporting dial backup, dial-on-demand, and bandwidth-on-demand functionalities, which decreases WAN operating costs, making this a very efficient and versatile router.

Because the AN/ANH can be integrated with other BayRS services, it supports all major LAN and WAN protocols. The AN/ANH can maintain high production packet forwarding rates over multiple protocols, no matter how many interfaces are being used. This is a configurable router that also is easy to monitor and manage. The AN and ANH support standards-based tools that allow for simple problem resolution and remote network monitoring.

The AN and ANH supports all major routing protocols. Because of this, it can easily operate in a multi-vendor environment. As mentioned previously, the AN/ANH allows for dial-on-demand, which allows for remote connectivity on an as-needed basis. The dial backup feature provides for redundancy in case a primary link goes down, and the bandwidth-on-demand feature allows for a pay-as-you-go lease with the telephone company, decreasing the remote connections cost.

The AN/ANH acts as both a router and a hub in one platform. This makes equipment and management less complicated. They also support data compression, which enables more information to travel farther and more quickly.

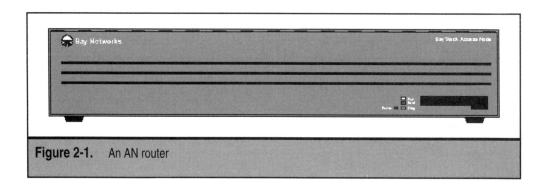

Figure 2-1.   An AN router

The Advanced Remote Node (ARN)

The ARN Router (see Figure 2-2) is developed with both functionality and the demands of corporate intranets in mind. By combining the functions of multiple devices, it simplifies the task of remote network management. The ARN offers 10/100Base-TX, 100 Base-FX, and token-ring interfaces, thus offering connectivity flexible enough to meet most LAN networking needs.

In addition to the LAN capabilities, the ARN offers two slots for modules that support a wide variety of WAN connectivity needs. This reduces the number of devices and amount of cabling needed for operation and facilitates remote network management. The ARN is an excellent choice for remote sites because of its versatility and functionality Table 2-1 outlines the networking functionality of the ARN router.

The Access Stack Node (ASN)

The ASN Router (see Figure 2-3) is a stackable router that offers cost-effective solutions for today's growing networks. It allows for almost transparent integration of multiple units connected and stacked as one router. A stack of four ASNs can support up to 48 network interfaces and has the capability to forward over 200,000 packets per second (pps).

The ASN supports all major networking protocols and WAN services. It supports 100Base-T, Ethernet, token-ring, FDDI, and all WAN interfaces. It supports the needs for remote network management by offering flexibility and modularity with performance and pricing that is ahead of industry norms. The ASN offers data compression on all WAN interfaces, which increases the speed of data, thus enhancing and encouraging WAN connectivity use.

The ASN supports "hot-swapping" by allowing the replacement of individual units within a stack without affecting the operation of the remaining stack members. It also allows for LAN interface and power supply redundancy, ensuring no loss in productivity should something go wrong. Alternate routing paths and dial-on-demand features add to the attractiveness of this switch because these features ensure network availability during peak traffic periods.

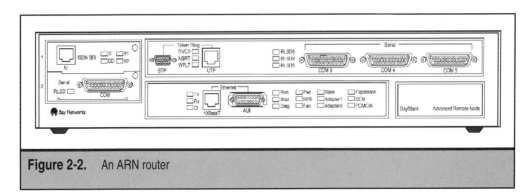

Figure 2-2. An ARN router

Network Protocols	IBM Integration	Bridging	Wide Area Networking
IP	Source route bridge	Transparent (Ethernet)	HDLC encapsulation
Novel IPX	LAN network manager agent	Translation bridge Ethernet/token-ring	PPP
AppleTalk Phase2	Data link switching for Ethernet and token-ring	Native mode LAN (NML)	Frame relay
DECnet Phase IV	Data link switching for SDLC		SMDS
Banyan VINES	Transparent sync pass-through		X.25
OSI	BSC pass-through		Dial backup
Xerox XNS		APPN bandwidth-on-demand, dial-on-demand	

Table 2-1. ARN Functionality

A four-stack ASN unit provides for the forwarding of over 200,000 pps. The ASN also provides for user-configured DRAM and cache options, allowing it to meet the high

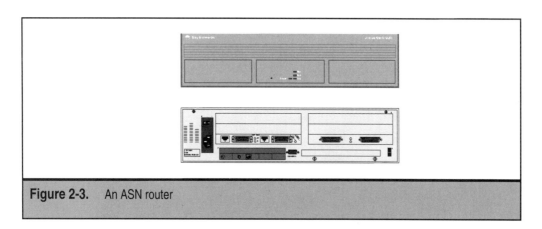

Figure 2-3. An ASN router

performance needs of even the most complicated of networks. Table 2-2 describes the networking functionality of the ASN router.

Backbone Node (BN) Products

Larger networks have a need for a device that is powerful enough to route information quickly and without errors, regardless of the topology or of the protocol of the information being sent. Important information is being routed over networks daily. Critical information most often is time sensitive in nature. There is a need for as many interfaces on the router as possible, with bandwidth that supports all the needs that users now have. Nortel Networks has stepped up to the plate to fulfill these requirements by offering the Backbone (BN). The Backbone node family (see Figure 2-4) consists of the Backbone Link Node (BLN) and the Backbone Concentrator Node (BCN).

A BN router can transmit double the amount of packets that its nearest competitor can. This is because the BN router allows multiple processors to function as a single logical router. The BN also features a multi-layered system software architecture and fault management capabilities that allow the BN to isolate problems before they affect information flow.

The BCN has the capability to provide forwarding of over 5 million pps. The BCN can support up to 104 WAN interfaces, 53 LAN interfaces, and 13 ATM or FDDI interfaces.

The BLN has the capability to support the forwarding of over 330,000 pps. The BLN can support up to 32 WAN interfaces, 16 LAN interfaces, and 4 ATM or FDDI interfaces.

Protocols	Bridging	Wide Area Networking
IP with RIP	Transparent (Ethernet and FDDI)	HDLC encapsulation
OSPF	Translation bridge	Point-to-Point Protocol (PPP)
EGP/BGP	Ethernet/token-ring	Frame relay
OSI	Ethernet-FDDI	SMDS
DECnet Phase IV	Token-ring/FDDI	X.25
Novell IPX with RIP, NLSP	Native mode LAN	ATM DXI
Banyan VINES		ISDN BRI
AppleTalk Phase 2		ISDN PRI

Table 2-2.   ASN Functionality

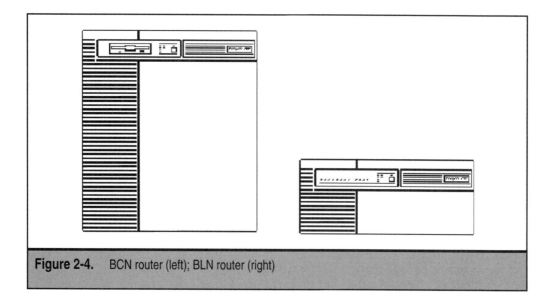

Figure 2-4.   BCN router (left); BLN router (right)

The BN router family supports the Bay Networks router services (BAYRS), and can greatly enhance interoperability between multiple protocol and multiple vendor networks. This is largely because the BN router family supports all major network and bridging protocols as well as wide area services.

The Nortel Networks BN product family supports the speed and agility demanded by even the most demanding networks that utilize Ethernet, Gigabit Ethernet, FDDI, and ATM. The ARE provides high performance in ATM-based architectures, supporting much more than 2,000 active virtual circuits and performs SONET routing between virtual LANs.

The BN routing family provides high bandwidth and availability, which is obtained by the use of a symmetric multiprocessor and hardware redundancy configuration options. Non-disruptive hardware hot-swap capabilities and dynamic software reconfiguration capabilities make this routing family very appealing. The BN also has the capability of supporting redundant links, modules, and power supplies.

Nortel Networks has a commitment to providing standards-based equipment. The BN product line is no exception to this commitment. The same link module and power supplies used in the BLN also are used in the BCN. This helps protect not only investments in equipment, but also in the individuals hired to maintain and configure that equipment.

Each processor module has the capability to perform operations for all networking protocols. Unlike many other routing systems, the BN family does not have a central CPU resource; rather it is a shared resource architecture. This means you are not left with only one or two CPUs to make all forwarding decisions, which not only can become a single point of failure; it also can greatly reduce your ability to enhance your network without the expense of upgrading your routing devices in the future.

The forwarding performance of the BLN and the BCN can increase as your network interfaces grow. Additionally, if a link module or a CPU fails, the stability of the network is maintained, as the remainder of the system will compensate for the loss. There is a direct connection between the CPU module and the link module, which further enhances and maximizes the overall performance of the router.

Nortel Networks BLN and BCN routers feature a multiprocessor architecture that achieves high availability as well as improved performance by distributing the processing power between all interface modules. This multiple processing architecture contains three elements:

▼ **Link modules**—Provide for the network interface connections that allow for LAN and WAN physical connections.

■ **Processor modules**—A FRE or ARE that is directly connected to the Link Module, forming an Intelligent Link Interface (ILI).

▲ **Processor interconnect**—Passes the information that is received on the link module to the processor module.

Table 2-3 contains reference information for the maximum number of link module interfaces that can be used within the BN router family. There is a column provided for both the BLN and the BCN routers. It is important to keep in mind that a FRE module is required for each link module installed.

The Passport 1000 and 8000 Series Routing Switch

Up until the last couple of years, routing and switching was considered a separate technology and remained separated throughout networks. The Passport routing switch, formerly known as the Accelar, brought an end to that separation by providing layer 3 routing capabilities in a switch chassis. The Passport routing switch can simultaneously perform IP and IPX routing and forward layer 2 traffic to different hosts on a VLAN (virtual LAN).

The Passport 1000 routing switch is capable of providing 10/100/1000 Mbps (megabits per second) switching and IP/IPX routing at wire speed on any port. The Passport 1000 routing switch can support low-latency and time-sensitive applications. It can implement features of layer 2 switching and layer 3 routing, and it also supports layer 4 control through filtering and prioritization. The Passport 8000 routing switch is capable of performing within a LAN and can perform as an edge switch in some of the larger LANs. The Passport 8000 is available with a 10-slot and a 6-slot chassis. It features a versatile chassis enabling unprecedented resiliency and reliability. Modules for the 8000 series can perform layer 2 switching, delivering over 50 Gbps (gigabits per second) of switching

LAN Interfaces (max. #)	BLN	BCN
Gigabit	4	13
(4) 10/100Base-T	16	52
100Base-T	8	26
Ethernet	16	52
Token-ring	16	52
FDDI	4	13
ATM	4	13
Serial Interfaces (max. #)		
Sync	32	104
Sync with Compression Coprocessor	32	104
HSSI	4	13
ISDN PRI/Multichannel T1:		
Dual	8	26
Quad	16	52

Table 2-3.   Backbone Node Interfaces

capacity. These modules can provide for connectivity to the network core over Fast Ethernet, Gigabit Ethernet, or ATM.

The Passport 1000 Series Routing Switch

Nortel Networks recognized the need for gigabit switching and router performance at the cost of traditional switch products. The Passport 1000 series routing switch offers the high performance of high-speed packet forwarding and also has the ability to transfer data with the control of IP and IPX routing. Because the Passport 1000 series routing switch can offer increased bandwidth combined with the intelligence to handle multicast and broadcast data traffic, it has set a new premise for the future of networking and establishes an industry-wide benchmark for things to come.

The Passport 1000 offers the support of 10 Mbps, 100 Mbps, and 1000 Mbps Ethernet technology, thus proving a smooth transition path for all three speeds. The Passport 1000 is capable of handling over 7 million pps and wire speed IPX and IP routing, and also provides wire speed access security.

The Passport 1000 allows you the freedom to introduce it into your existing networks without having to worry about major network reconfigurations. Regardless of your networking needs, there is a Passport that can fit into them. Within the Passport 1000 family are three designs: the Passport 1200 (see Figure 2-5), the Passport 1100, and the Passport 1150. This routing switch family offers standards-based interoperability with all Nortel Networks Ethernet and Fast Ethernet products.

Another benefit of the Passport 1000 series is that it provides for high performance with layer 2, 3, and 4 controls. It uses application-specific integrated circuit capabilities (ASIC), thus utilizing a new generation of control. Because it uses these ASICs for packet forwarding tasks, in lieu of a CPU it has the ability to use virtual LAN (VLAN) technology and has established priorities to run at high levels. ASIC technologies allow this routing switch the ability to filter at wire speed without hindering performance. Traffic also can be filtered using access lists, which help to determine whether a packet is to be dropped or forwarded based on its policy. These policy filters will allow you to deny access to certain groups and grant unlimited access to others.

The Passport 1000 series routing switch can easily be configured as a layer 2 switch, allowing for layer 3 to be implemented as needed. This makes it a very easy-to-implement networking device. The Passport 1000 can easily support over 24,000 addresses, and there are various modules that offer the freedom of configuration to suit each network's needs.

The Passport 1000 has multiple redundancy features that provide for a fail-safe environment. With the 1200, users have the opportunity to install a second silicone switch fabric (SSF), which allows the switch to continue operating in the event of a primary CPU

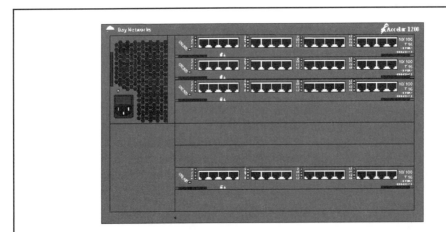

Figure 2-5. A Passport 1200 routing switch

failure. All of the 1000 series routing switches offer redundant power and optional fail-safe, which provide for cabling redundancy and gigabit switch-over on Gigabit Ethernet port modules.

The Passport 1100   The Passport 1100 supports Gigabit Ethernet, 100Base-FX, or 10/100 Mbps Ethernet ports. It includes 16 10/100 Mbps Ethernet ports and has two built-in expansion slots. It is capable of supporting redundant power and link-safe. All 1100 modules are hot-swappable.

The Passport 1150   The Passport 1150 Routing Switch is capable of supporting 10/100 Mbps Ethernet, 100Base-FX, and Gigabit Ethernet ports. The 1150 base unit has four Gigabit Ethernet ports and two additional expansion slots for Field Replaceable Units (FRU). The 1150 has the capability of a redundant power supply and link safe. All 1150 modules are hot-swappable.

The Passport 1200   The Passport 1200 Routing Switch has an 8-slot chassis. It can be configured with up to 12 Gigabit Ethernet ports, up to 96 10/100Base-TX Ethernet ports, 96 100Base-FX ports, or a combination of these three technologies. The 1200 can support redundant power, redundant gig links, and redundant switch fabric modules. All modules for the 1200 are hot-swappable. The following are some of the performance statistics available for the Passport 1100, Passport 1150, and Passport 1200.

▼ **Performance Throughput**
  - Model XLR1200 7.0 Gbps
  - Model XLR1100 4.5 Gbps
  - Model XLR1150 7.0 Gbps

- **Forwarding Rates**
  - Model XLR1200 7.0 million pps
  - Model XLR1100 6.5 million pps
  - Model XLR1150 7.0 million pps

- **Prioritized Output Buffering**
  - Model XLR1200 96 MB
  - Model XLR1100 32 MB
  - Model XLR1150 20 MB

- **Shared Memory Switch Fabric**
  - 2 MB (with prioritization)

- **IP Routing and Switching Speeds**
  - Wire speed for 10/100/1000 Mbps Ethernet ports

- **Routing Protocols**
  - RIP
  - RIP2
  - OSPF
  - IPX RIP
  - IPX SAP
  - IGMP
  - Distance Vector Multicast Routing Protocol (DVMRP)
- ▲ **Bridging and VLAN Protocols**
  - Up to 127 VLANs
  - 802.1Q trunking
  - 802.1d Spanning Tree group
  - IP multicast via IGMP snooping
  - IP multicast routing via DVRMP and IGMP

The Passport 8000 Series Routing Switch

Much like the Passport 1000 Routing Switch, the Passport 8000 (see Figure 2-6) series delivers high-performance layer 2 switching and layer 3 routing capabilities, at wire speed. The Passport 8000 supports routing technology, switch technology, and LAN connectivity; and provides 128 Gbps of switching capacity scalable to 256 Gbps.

The Passport 8000 enterprise switch is available in the 10-slot Passport 8010 chassis and the 6-slot 8006 chassis. The Passport is ideal for wiring closets and backbones that demand high bandwidth and availability. The Passport 8006 is designed for closets and backbones that have space concerns. The Passport 8100 modules are intended to be used in desktop switching environments, whereas the Passport 8600 modules are designed for large LAN backbones where performance is important.

In the Passport 8000 series chassis, up to three power supplies can be installed, all of which are hot-swappable. The chassis allows for temperature monitoring, automatically reporting overheating. The chassis supports redundant power and processor modules.

The Passport 8000 provides for complete security for the LAN by restricting the network access to authorized users. It supports hardware-based filtering for security classification based on information received on each packet. Performance information for the Passport 8000 is listed in Table 2-4.

Nortel Networks Switches

Switches are a very important part of any LAN. Switches are used primarily to connect to workgroups, wiring closets, and power PCs. High standards and high performance are only minimum requirements for the switching devices in the networks of today.

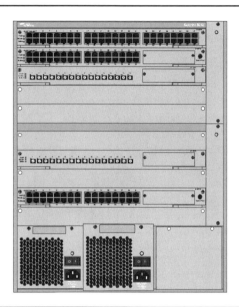

Figure 2-6.   A Passport 8000 series routing switch

Nortel Networks offers some very impressive switches that surpass switching industry requirements. The switches listed in the following are only a few of the switches Nortel has to offer.

Architecture	Passport 8100	Passport 8600
Switch capacity	50 Gbps (scalable)	128 Gbps (scalable)
Layer 2 switching	24 Mpps	96 Mpps
IP/IPX routing	N/A	96 Mbps
Gigabit Ethernet ports	64	64
100Base-FX ports	160	192
10/100 ports (copper)	384	384

Table 2-4.   Passport 8000 Performance Information

The Baystack 350

The Baystack 350 switch (see Figure 2-7) is an affordable, high-performance workgroup switch. It offers support for 10/100 autosending on all UTP ports, allowing transparent transfer to 100 Mbps connections where end stations have the capability to transfer information at the Fast Ethernet rate. Upon connecting, all ports auto sense half-duplex or full-duplex connections on any switch to switch configuration.

The Baystack 350-12T offers 12 10Base-T/100Base-TX ports, whereas the Baystack 350-24T offers 24 10Base-T/100Base-TX ports. Both models offer a Media Dependent Adapter (MDA) slot for all three speeds of Ethernet and therefore can support high bandwidth throughput throughout a LAN or LAN segment.

The Gigabit Ethernet MDA is available with link safe, which provides redundancy by providing two fiber connectors. When one of the connectors fails, the other connector picks up this connection, thus protecting network traffic integrity. The Baystack 350 offers 2.5 Gb per second switching, ASICs support, and MAC Layer frame forwarding. It can operate at a peak level of 3 million pps.

▼ **Performance Specifications (64-byte packets)**

- ■ Aggregate throughput 3 million pps
- ■ Switched 10 Mbps Port forwarding rate 14,880 pps
- ■ Switched 100 Mbps Port forwarding rate 148,810 pps
- ■ Switched 1000 Mbps Port forwarding rate 1,488,100 pps

■ **Network Protocol and Standards Compatibility**

- ■ IEEE 802.3 CSMA/CD
- ■ IEEE 802.3i 10Base-T
- ■ IEEE 802.3u 100Base-T
- ■ IEEE 802.1D MAC Bridges
- ■ IEEE 802.3z 1000Base-SX/LX

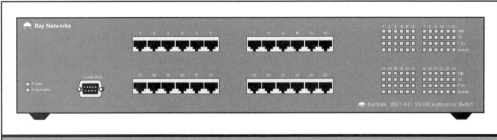

Figure 2-7. A Baystack 350

- **Gigabit Cabling Distance Specification**
    - 1000Base-SX on MMF (50 um)550 m
    - 1000Base-SX on MMF (62.5 um)260 m
    - 1000Base-LX on MMF (50 um)550 m
    - 1000Base-LX on MMF (62.5 um)550 m
    - 1000Base-LX on SMF (10 um)5 km
- **Gigabit and 100Base-FX Cabling Type**
    - 62.5/125 micron MMF
- **Gigabit and 100Base-FX Connector Type**
    - SC type connector
- ▲ **Memory**
    - Processor DRAM 2 MB
    - Flash Memory 1 MB

The Baystack 410 and 450

The Baystack 410 and 450 switches are stackable, offering flexibility and high-speed Ethernet switching. The Baystack 450 switches (see Figure 2-8) provide high-performance switching for wiring closets. They also provide flexibility for networks that are experiencing rapid changes and growth. The Baystack 410-24T provides 10Base-T networking solutions and can be included with a stack of Baystack 450s.

The Baystack 410 and 450 include many advanced features found in switches today (discussed in Chapter 4). The wire speed throughput offered by the Baystack 450 operates at a peak rate of 3 million pps. The maximum throughput offered by the Baystack 410 is 1 million pps.

A maximum of eight 450-12F switches can be stacked. This will offer up to 128 100Base-FX ports. The 450-12F also is stackable with the Baystack 410-24T, the 450-24T, and the 450-12T, providing for remarkable flexibility. The Baystack 410 and 450 switches are connected to each other with a Cascade cable. The unique thing with the Baystack 410 and 450 switches is that they offer redundant Cascade cabling. This ensures network integrity in the event of a node failure.

Baystack 410/450 features are as follows:

- ▼ **Performance**
    - Aggregate throughput (BayStack 450 Switches), 3 million pps
    - Aggregate Throughput (BayStack 410-24T Switch), 1 million pps
    - 10 Mbps Port forwarding rate, 14,880 pps
    - 100 Mbps Port forwarding rate, 148,810 pps
    - 1000 Mbps Port forwarding rate, 1,488,100 pps

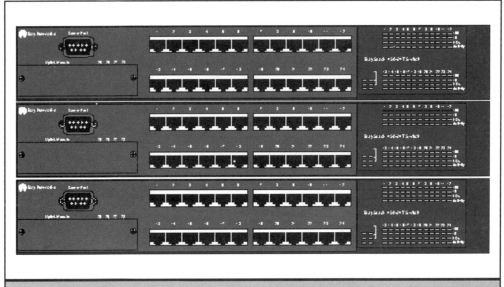

Figure 2-8. A stack of Baystack 450s

▲ **Network Protocol and Standards Compatibility**

■ IEEE 802.3 CSMA/CD

■ IEEE 802.3i 10Base-T

■ IEEE 802.3u 100Base-TX

■ IEEE 802.1D MAC Bridges

The Centillion 50, 100, and System 5000 BH LAN-ATM Switches

The Centillion switching family (see Figure 2-9) offers LAN Ethernet, token-ring, and ATM solutions to fulfill the needs of any corporate LAN. The Centillion switches increase the performance of any LAN by increasing connection bandwidth to networking devices that demand speed.

The Centillion switching product line offers LAN-ATM integration to Ethernet and token-ring LANs. Because the Centillion switch offers this integration, it allows for a simple migration between the three topologies. This is a very unique feature and a huge benefit as a networking solution.

The Centillion LAN-ATM switch allows for redundant power supplies and all modules are fully hot-swappable. All modules for the Centillion LAN-ATM switch contain buffer memory and ASIC technology. The Centillion is capable of providing load-sharing and fast recovery links that support most network switching needs.

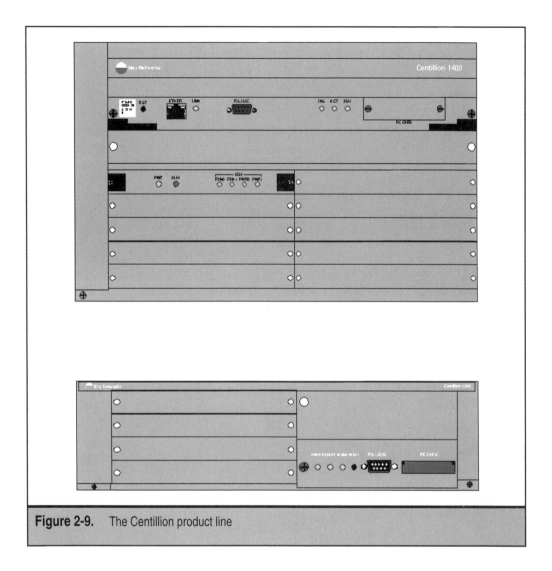

Figure 2-9.   The Centillion product line

MCP facilities enable LAN emulation, ATM virtual circuit signaling, and inter-switch topology services. The Centillion LAN-ATM switch fully complies with and supports ATM Forum standards, such as

▼   Private Network-to-Network Interface (PNNI)

■   LAN emulation

■   User to Network Interface (UNI)

▲   Switched Virtual Circuit (SVC) 3.0 and 3.1

The UNI SVC signaling ensures that the Centillion LAN-ATM switch is compatible with a multi-vendor ATM environment. PNNI enables ATM switches to determine the best path to use when establishing virtual connections. PNNI also communicates key Quality of Service (QOS) metrics, ensuring the path selection best suits the needs of the applications needs.

The Centillion 50   The Centillion 50 is designed for work groups and small network segments. The Centillion 50 chassis has slots for three switch modules. The switch modules also are interchangeable with the Centillion 100 switch.

The Centillion 100   The Centillion 100 is designed for medium-sized LANs and wiring closets. Its chassis can support up to six switch modules, which are interchangeable with the Centillion 50 switch platform. The Centillion 100 also is configured with two power supplies to increase availability of the switch.

The 5000BH   The System 5000 BH is an industry-leading, high-performance switching solution. Not only does the System 5000Bh offer the same switching capabilities of the Centillion 50 and 100. The system 5000 BH chassis provides remote access services, frame-based Ethernet and token-ring routing, ATM routing, ATM wide area services, and Multi-Protocol over ATM (MPOA) server facilities.

Features of Centillion LAN-ATM switches are as follows:

▼ **Aggregate Capacity**
- Centillion 50 6 Gbps
- Centillion 100 10 Gbps
- System 5005BH 10 Gbps
- System 5000BH/BHC 20 Gbps

■ **Redundant Power**
- Centillion 50 optional
- Centillion 100 standard
- System 5005BH standard
- System 5000BH/BHC standard

■ **Module Slots**
- Centillion 50 3 slots
- Centillion 100 6 slots
- System 5005BH 8 slots—6 for Centillion modules
- System 5000BH/BHC 14 slots—12 for Centillion modules
- All modules are hot-swappable

▲   **Standards Compliance**

■   CCITT 1.361 ATM layer specification

■   ATM Forum UNI 3.0 and 3.1

■   ATM Forum LAN emulation (LANE) v1.0

■   ATM Forum Private Network-to-Network Interface (PNNI)

■   ATM Forum Multi-Protocol Over ATM (MPOA)

■   ATM Forum Interim Interswitch Signaling Protocol (IISP)

AN OVERVIEW OF NORTEL NETWORKS SOFTWARE APPLICATIONS

All the hardware that Nortel Networks has to offer provides various software applications that allow easy access to the device for monitoring, maintenance, and configuration. The Site Manager application offers a graphical user interface (GUI) view of the Baystack router family. The Device Manager application package offers an excellent and easy-to-use GUI for the Passport 1000/8000. The GUI application used by the Centillion 50/100 and the 5000BH product families is the Speedview application package. In addition to the GUI application interfaces, each one of the hardware devices that we have mentioned has a non-GUI interface as well. Let's take each of the product families that we have discussed and introduce the software applications that are used to configure and maintain these devices.

Nortel Networks Router Software Applications

The Nortel Networks routers have the capability to be configured and maintained by Site Manager, Technician Interface (TI), and Bay Command Console (BCC). All three perform basically the same functions, although there are times where one application might be more appropriate to use than another; therefore, it is important to have a general understanding of each application. Chapter 6 discusses these applications in depth.

Site Manager: An Introduction

Site Manager is a straightforward GUI interface that allows users a simple-to-use application for configuring the Nortel Networks routers. Site manager can transfer files, download and save the router log, reset slots, reset or reboot the router itself, and perform many more functions.

Site Manager can be loaded to many different PC platforms, but does have minimum system requirements. It is important to review the release notes before loading Site Manager onto your PC to ensure that you meet all of the minimum requirements.

There are some router configuration requirements that must be met before you can use Site Manager. You must have a valid IP address assigned to the router, and an SNMP community name must be known. It also is very important that you use a compatible version of Site Manager. You can determine which version of Site Manager is to be used by the following methods:

If your router code is 14.00 (or previous), you must subtract 6 from that number to determine which version of Site Manager you must use. For example,

```
Router code 12.05 - 6 = 6.05
```

In this example, the router code version being used is 12.05. We subtract 6 from the 12.05 and discover that the minimum code version of Site Manager we have to use is 6.05.

If your router code version is 14.00 or higher, the minimum version of Site Manager that has to be used it the same version as the version of router code. For example,

```
Router code 14.00 = Site Manager version 14.00
```

In this example, the router code version is 14.00, so we know that because it is 14.00 or higher, the Site Manager version that we can use is 14.00.

If there are any doubts about what version of Site Manager to use, you can look at the release notes for the version of router code you need to match, and it will tell you what version of Site Manager to use.

The Technician Interface (TI)

The TI allows the user to connect to a router through a console port or through a telnet session and is a required application for the initial configuration of the router. Before Site Manager can be used, TI must be used to set up the initial IP address on an interface to allow the router to be accessed by Site Manager.

The TI has the capability to allow the user to use simple script commands to access the Management Information Base (MIB) and review network status. The TI also allows the user to use a complex instruction set known as MIB objects, attributes, and instances. There also are some useful command-line syntax commands that allow for monitoring and review.

The TI is a useful and a necessary application tool, but is complicated to use for configuration changes, which is why many prefer to use Site Manager. Many engineers prefer using the TI for implementing MIB changes, but often this can take years of experience.

The Bay Command Console (BCC)

The BCC is an addendum application for the TI. The BCC uses script files, which offer an easier way to use applications for router configuration. The BCC is not a GUI, but it is a configuration tool that is much simpler to use than what the TI has to offer. One of the big benefits of the BCC is that it offers users the ability to telnet, dial in, or connect to a console interface to have modification abilities that were not offered previously.

Nortel Networks Switch Software Applications

The Nortel Networks Passport routing switches have the capability to be configured and maintained by Device Manager, the GUI, or Command-Line Interface (CLI). Both perform basically the same functions, although there are times where one application might be more appropriate to use than another; therefore, it is important to have a general understanding of each application.

Device Manager

Device Manager is the primary method that is used for configuring the Passport routing switch. Device Manager is to Passport routing switches much what Site Manager is for the Nortel Networks routers. Device Manager uses SNMP to manage the Passport routing switch.

To use Device Manager, like Site Manager for routers, you must have an IP address established on an interface for connectivity purposes. Device Manager also offers additional flexibility in that you have the capability of monitoring multiple Passport devices and Baystack 450 switches within one running session of Device Manager.

As with any version of software, it is a good practice to verify release notes before installation to ensure your PC meets minimum operating requirements. It is also a good habit to get into to verify release notes of the routing switch code version you are using to ensure that you have the correct version of Device Manager.

The Command-Line Interface (CLI)

The CLI gives user the ability to connect to the Passport routing switch through a telnet session, dial-up, or the device's serial port. With the CLI, users have the ability to make all changes to the Passport routing switches that are available in Device Manager.

The CLI offers different levels of access:

▼ **Read Only**—Allows a user to connect and view settings and configurations, but will not allow the user to make any changes.

■ **Read/Write**—Allows a user to connect and view settings that are not related to security. In other words, changes to passwords cannot be made.

■ **Read/Write Layer 2**—Allows a user to connect and view settings and configurations, but will allow changes to only the layer 2 parameters.

■ **Read/Write Layer 3**—Allows a user to connect and view settings and configurations, but will allow changes to only layer 3 parameters.

▲ **Read/Write All**—Allows a user to connect and view settings and configurations as well as make any changes to the device.

Nortel Networks Centillion 50, 100, and 5000BH Software Applications

The Nortel Networks Centillion 50, 100, and 5000BH switches have the capability to be configured and maintained by Speedview, the GUI, or CLI. Both software applications perform separate functions and are not as closely related as other device application packages. That is why it is important to understand the basics of both packages and how they relate to the Centillion product line. We discuss these applications in depth in Chapter 4.

Speedview Versus CLI

Of all the GUI applications Nortel Networks has to offer, Speedview probably is the most important. This is because the Centillion 50/100 and 5000BH cannot be configured through the CLI. Speedview is much easier to use than some of the other GUI applications, because it comes with some very powerful utilities not yet offered with its counterparts, Site Manager and Device Manager.

The version of Speedview you can use is dependent on the version of code you are running. As a general rule, however, if the release number of the code matches the Speedview release number, it is compatible. As with the other devices, it is important to refer to the release notes for compatibility confirmation.

Speedview can be connected to the Centillion 50/100/5000BH through a serial connection or through the SNMP process. If you are using SNMP to connect, you will have to have a valid IP address configured on an interface.

The CLI for the Centillion 50/100/5000BH is used for monitoring and browsing but cannot perform configuration steps. It is basically for troubleshooting assistance.

CONCLUSION

In this chapter we discussed Nortel Networks hardware and the software that is used to configure, monitor, and maintain the hardware devices. We also took a brief look at Nortel Networks, a company that is making tremendous strides to improve the Internet and how we connect to it. The way the networking industry is growing is exciting; technology is evolving at a rate that is unsurpassed. Because of this growth, the need for upgrades and expansion remains in an ever-changing state.

The Nortel Networks enterprise products are the backbone of many corporate networks today. There are improvements being made daily to the hardware and software to keep up with the demands of network users. Many corporations are now exploring new technologies to support their core network needs, but it is safe to say that the enterprise products will be around and utilized for many years to come.

Looking ahead, Chapter 4 discusses the layer 2 nodes that were mentioned in this chapter; Chapter 5 discusses the layer 3 nodes. It is recommended that you refer back to this chapter as often as necessary for an overview of the Nortel enterprise products.

CHAPTER 3

Nortel Networks Certifications

Over the past few years the networking industry has experienced unparalleled growth. This growth has driven the need for more technical talent trained to design, install, manage, and troubleshoot the complex network infrastructures common in today's organizations. Unfortunately for many companies, finding enough knowledgeable and experienced staff members is almost impossible. In the current job market an engineer with 3-4 years of experience can choose from many job offerings. An individual with 3-4 years of experience and a few well-chosen industry certifications can write his or her own ticket!

It is a common practice for software and hardware vendors to provide multiple levels of certifications on their products. This serves three purposes. First, certification influences buying decisions. If a company is preparing to upgrade its network and the network manager is certified on a given product line and not on its competitor's products...well, you can see where that will lead. Second, certification programs are money makers. With books, online training, classroom training, self-study courses, and testing, vendors are cleaning up. That's not to say that administrating the certification program is not without costs, but if they were not making money, most companies would shut their programs down. Finally, certification ensures a certain level of competence in the engineering staff. Nothing makes a vendor look worse than products that do not perform as promised. However, most performance problems are not caused by bad hardware or software, but by incorrect configurations. A certified individual is less likely to misconfigure a product than a non-certified person.

So, why should you be interested in Nortel Networks certifications? First, Nortel is recognized as a major industry player, thus ensuring that well-paying jobs will be available. Second, compared to the number of Microsoft, Novell, or even Cisco certifications that have been awarded, Nortel has awarded very few. This keeps the value of the certification from becoming diluted. In the networking industry a person with a certification but little or no experience is referred to as a "paper professional"; for example, a paper MCSE (Microsoft Certified Systems Engineer), or paper CNE (Certified NetWare Engineer), or paper CCNA (Cisco Certified Network Associate). The fact that there are fewer study guides, so-called boot camps, and practice tests on the market to help one attain Nortel certification helps to maintain the overall integrity of the designation itself. You have to have experience with Nortel products to do well on Nortel certification tests. This book is a great place to get started. Third is recognition; it's always nice to have people recognize your brilliance! Take the test! Frame the certificate! Hang it on the wall in your office. Enjoy having your coworkers come to you with their really difficult questions...and being able to answer them. And finally: more money. Enough said.

CERTIFICATION OVERVIEW

Nortel offers one of the most unique certification programs in the industry. Most vendors support only one track toward certification; for example, test 1 = certification 1. Nortel has a totally different outlook. To attain Nortel certification two engineers might take totally different tests based upon their respective expertise; for example, test 1 = certification 1 and test 2 = certification 1. Both are certified professionals, but the tests they took were designed to gauge the knowledge of each individual in a specific technology or product line. This enables the professional to specialize rather than being forced to take tests based on products that he or she does not use.

Nortel offers certification at three different levels: specialist, expert, and architect. Within each of these levels are two tracks: support and design. Someone who installs, configures, and performs maintenance tasks on networking hardware will want to follow the support track; the one who is called upon to perform design functions will want to follow the design track.

SALES CERTIFICATIONS-NORTEL NETWORKS CERTIFIED ACCOUNT SPECIALIST (NNCAS)

Nortel Networks account executives (Nortel's sales force) and reseller salespeople are encouraged to obtain the Nortel Networks Certified Account Specialist (NNCAS) certification. This certification recognizes a fundamental level of knowledge of Nortel Networks products, solutions, and related technologies.

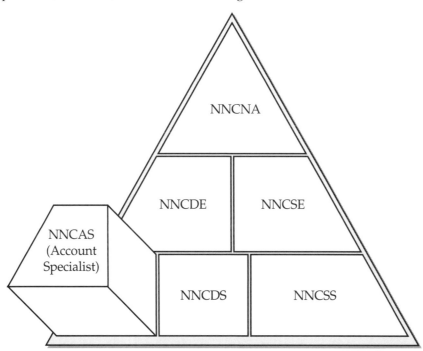

NNCAS Overview

The NNCAS Certification provides a guarantee to employers that their sales staff possesses a certain level of knowledge of the Nortel product line. To attain this certification, a candidate must pass three exams: two Sales, Technology, and Product (STP) exams and one

Unified Networks Sales Solution exam. Nortel provides study guides and case studies to prepare for the exams on its certification Web site at http://www12.nortelnetworks.com/training2/certification/nncas.html. The same information can be requested on CD-ROM free of charge by e-mailing Nortel Networks at nortel@tmgcorporation.com and mentioning Part# AY1124057C.

Most vendor certification exams require a visit to the nearest Sylvan-Prometric testing center (learn more about Sylvan on the Web at www.sylvan.net) and at least a $100 testing fee. The NNCAS does not require this. Nortel decided that to reach the widest possible pool of candidates and to make the certification as accessible as possible, they should make testing for the exams Web-based. Thus, anyone with an Internet connection and enough time to study can try for the NNCAS designation. The lack of a test center requirement might make you think this certification is easy to obtain; please do not let this fool you. The tests are demanding and require quite a bit of study to pass them.

The innovative manner in which Nortel has designed its certification program allows for specialization early on in the process. A salesperson can evaluate his or her target market and decide which of the many learning modules to download from the Nortel Networks Web site based on customer requirements.

Sales, Technology, and Product Exams

The following STP exams currently are available to fulfill the requirements of the NNCAS certification:

▼ LAN exam (required)

■ WAN exam

■ Voice exam

■ IP Telephony exam

▲ Network Management exam

Each exam has from one to four learning modules associated with it. Mastery of the information contained in the learning modules will lead to mastery of the appropriate test. Table 3-1 shows the exams and related learning modules.

NOTE: The STP LAN exam is required for the NNCAS certification because a basic understanding of LAN technologies is required of anyone in the networking industry.

The STP LAN exam covers basic layer 2 devices, hubs, and switches as well as higher-end switching products and Internet connectivity devices. The WAN STP exam challenges a candidate's basic knowledge of routers, VPN, and optical networking. Voice technologies such as Nortel's Norstar key system, Meridian PBX, and messaging products are the focus of the voice STP test. The IP Telephony exam covers Nortel's line of Windows NT–based phone switches. And finally, the Management STP exam tests an individual's knowledge of the Optivity network management platform as well as NetID

LAN (Small to Medium Business)	WAN	Voice	IP Telephony	Management
BayStack Hubs and Switches	Virtual Private Networks– Contivity	Norstar Meridian 1- CallPilot	Building an Internet Protocol (IP) Telephony Network	Optivity Enterprise Network Management
Campus Switching Products	Nortel Networks Routers	Symposium Messaging	Succession for Enterprise	NetID & Optivity Policy Services
Business Communications Manager (Enterprise Edge)	Passport Creating the Optical Internet		Succession Communications Server for Enterprise	
Internet Appliances (BayStack instant Internet, BayStack 910 WebCache)				
STP LAN exam	STP WAN exam	STP Voice exam	STP IP Telephony exam	STP Management exam

Table 3-1.   STP Modules and Exams

(a DHCP and DNS server) and Optivity policy services. If all this sounds daunting, please do not be discouraged; the bulk of this will be covered in detail in later chapters.

Unified Networks Solutions Exams

The seven exams available to fulfill the Unified Networks Solutions portion of the NNCAS designation are

- ▼ LAN Campus ATM Solutions
- ■ LAN Campus Ethernet Solutions
- ■ Small Business Solutions
- ■ WAN Enterprise Solutions
- ■ VPN Enterprise Solutions
- ■ IBM Enterprise Solutions
- ▲ INCA M10 Solutions

Most candidates will find the Unified Networks Solutions portion of the NNCAS to be the most difficult. This test requires critical thinking and an understanding of the best ways to position specific Nortel Networks products in a sales/design situation. This is not a standard test for which you might memorize facts, regurgitate them for the test, and then forget what you have learned a few days later. These tests require study and comprehension of the principles discussed, not memorization.

It has become common practice in the networking industry to sell networking gear not based upon products, but on solutions to problems. The difference is that in a product-based sale, a salesperson sells equipment based on the specifications of one or two different products. However, in a solution-oriented environment, all a customer's needs are taken into account and a design solution is crafted by a salesperson. By understanding the business need for a product, a salesperson is able to sell a customer a solution, not just a box with a lot of bells and whistles.

To assist individuals in promoting Nortel Networks solutions, the Unified Networks Sales Solutions modules were developed; each focuses on a specific customer environment. The information provided in each of the modules references common networking scenarios and offers solutions based on Nortel products. A case study that demonstrates the implementation of the concepts and solutions is included in each proposed solution.

NNCAS candidates must select and complete one of the following Unified Network Sales Solutions modules. Each of the modules is composed of seven or eight sub-modules. The following module descriptions were taken directly from the Nortel Networks Web site at http://www12.nortelnetworks.com/training2/certification/unssol.html.

LAN Campus ATM Solutions   The LAN Campus ATM course covers the development of LAN Campus ATM solutions for enterprises based on their critical requirements and applications. The course identifies customer requirements and positions the Nortel Networks ATM products that best fit those customer requirements. Finally, the course describes a number of case studies in which LAN Campus ATM enterprise solutions have been successfully implemented.

LAN Campus Ethernet Solutions   The LAN Campus Ethernet course covers the development of LAN Campus Ethernet network solutions based on a customer's critical requirements and applications. The course identifies customer requirements and positions Nortel Networks products that best fit those customer requirements. Finally, the course presents a case study in which a LAN Campus Ethernet solution is successfully implemented.

Small Business Solutions   This course is designed to assist Nortel Networks and business partners; sales, systems engineering, and product support personnel to sell and support Nortel's voice and data communications solutions in the small-to-medium business customer base. It provides an overview of Nortel's Small Business Solutions (SBS) strategy, solutions portfolios, typical customer requirements, and competing solutions. Topics include the BayStack IP infrastructure products (including VPN and Internet connectivity solutions), along with multi-access services and voice/data integration delivered by Business Communications Manager, and voice solutions delivered by Norstar.

VPN Enterprise Solutions   The VPN Solutions for Enterprises course provides information about the business drivers, technology enablers, and products that make Virtual Private Networks one of the major forces changing the way enterprise customers view and define networking. This course includes a brief history of the evolution of virtual private networks. In addition, it covers customer requirements, decision criteria, and product solutions in depth. This course also includes modules describing common VPN deployment models, VPN applications, and a comprehensive case study.

WAN Enterprise Solutions   In the WAN Solutions for Enterprises course, you will learn how to create a wide area solution for enterprise customers using Nortel Networks router products and based on the customer's critical business, applications, and network requirements. Topics such as current network environment and decision criteria enable you to understand the customer environment these products serve. A technical solution is presented, first introducing a generic solution, and then positioning Nortel Networks' products to best solve customer requirements. A case study is used to show the implementation and how business problems were solved using Nortel Networks' enterprise router products.

IBM Network Enterprise Solutions   The IBM Enterprise Network Solutions course is designed to provide sales, technical support, and system engineer personnel with the initial information necessary for the positioning and implementation of Nortel Networks SNA-based products in an IBM environment.

INCA M-10 Solutions   This Solutions course is designed for the Inca M10 Unified VoIP Specialist Certification. The Inca M10 Solutions course covers the development of network solutions based on a customer's critical needs and applications. The course identifies customer requirements and helps determine the best fit for the Nortel Networks Inca M10 product to meet those customer requirements. Finally, the course presents a case study in which an Inca M10 solution is successfully implemented.

   The solutions modules discussed earlier can be downloaded from the Nortel Networks Web site in multiple formats, including MS PowerPoint, Adobe Acrobat, and Real Networks Real Player. The download address is http://www12.nortelnetworks.com/training2/certification/unssol.html.

NNCAS Conclusion

Once you have studied the appropriate material and are comfortable with your knowledge level, by all means visit the Nortel Networks Web site and take the tests. When you pass the three tests to become a Nortel Networks Certified Account Specialist, Nortel will send you a personalized certificate suitable for framing as well as a very nice pen. Nortel Networks Certified Account Specialists also are authorized to use Nortel Logos on business cards and stationery. The NNCAS certification provides a wonderful introduction to the world of data networking as seen by Nortel.

SUPPORT CERTIFICATIONS

The Nortel Networks support certifications provide a candidate with a multitude of specialization options. With two levels of certification available within the support track, an engineer's level of competence can be accurately represented.

Nortel Networks Certified Support Specialist (NNCSS)

At the specialist level within the support track only one test is required. There are six exams to choose from, thus enabling a candidate to specialize early in the certification process. All of the exams at the specialist level are proctored electronic exams available at Sylvan Prometric testing centers worldwide. The cost to take a test is a reasonable $125, payable at registration time.

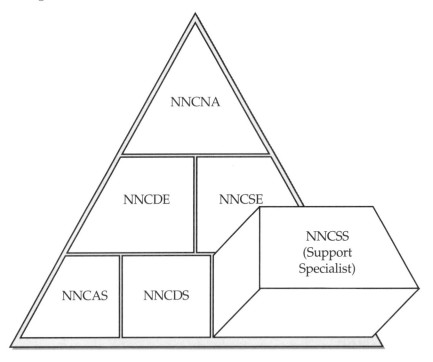

The exams currently offered are

▼ Hubs and Shared Media Core Technology

■ Routing Core Technology

■ Switching Core Technology

■ Multi-Service Access Core Technology

■ IP Telephony Core Technology

▲ Business Communications Manager (formerly Enterprise Edge) Core Technology

These technical exams are a mix of technology-oriented topics as well as some basic product installation and configuration questions.

Core Technology Exam Objectives

This book does not cover all the exam objectives for all the Core Technology tests; however, it gives you a good overview of the technology and products covered in the exams. Over the next few pages we cover the exam objectives, as stated on the Nortel Networks Web site, in detail. Use these objectives to gauge your understanding of the topics covered in the Core Technology exams. When you feel comfortable with the material, it's time to take the test. The following information was taken directly from the Nortel Networks Web site; updated information is available at http://www12.nortelnetworks.com/training2/certification/techexams.html#corexam.

Hubs and Shared Media Core Technology Exam

BayStack Ethernet Hubs

▼ Describe features, functions, and components of BayStack Ethernet hubs.

■ Identify management and configuration options for BayStack Ethernet hubs.

■ Describe functions of LED indicators on BayStack Ethernet hubs.

▲ Install and configure an Ethernet network using BayStack Ethernet hubs.

Intro to System 3000 Concentrators

▼ Describe the features, functions, and components of System 3000 concentrators.

■ Describe the various modules available for the System 3000 chassis.

▲ Describe System 3000 backplane options.

Intro to Fast Ethernet

▼ Identify Fast Ethernet-supported physical media.

■ Identify the repeater types and their operational characteristics.

▲ Identify the strategies involved in migrating from Ethernet to Fast Ethernet.

5000 Chassis

▼ Describe features, functions, and components of the System 5000 concentrator.

■ Describe functions of the LED indicators on the System 5000 concentrator.

■ Identify System 5000 backplane options.

■ List the various modules available for the System 5000 chassis.

■ Describe the functionality of the Supervisory Module of the 5000 chassis.

- Install and configure an Ethernet network using System 5000 concentrators.
- Install and configure a Fast Ethernet network using System 5000 concentrators.
- Install and configure a token-ring network using System 5000 concentrators.
- List the various modules available for the System 5000 chassis.
- Install and configure a Fast Ethernet network using System 5000 concentrators.
- ▲ Install and configure a token-ring network using System 5000 concentrators.

Ethernet Connectivity for Distributed 5000 Hubs

- ▼ Differentiate between cascaded and local Ethernet segments.
- Describe the features, functions, and components of the Distributed 5000 Ethernet hubs.
- ▲ Install and configure an Ethernet network using Distributed 5000 hubs.

Intro to Hub Connectivity

- ▼ Describe the role of a hub in the network.
- Explain the numbering scheme for various Bay network hubs.
- ▲ Describe the network fit for BayStack System 3000, Distributed 5000 and System 5000 hubs and concentrators.

Intro to Network Management

- ▼ Describe the basic functions of network management.
- Describe the capabilities of SNMP.
- Associate network management levels with the features they support.
- Describe the bootp/TFTP process.
- ▲ Configure NMM for basic operation. Identify various hardware management options.

5005 Chassis

- ▼ Describe features, functions, and components of the System 5005 concentrator.
- Describe functions of the LED indicators on the System 5005 concentrator.
- Differentiate System 5000 and System 5005 concentrator features, functions, and components.
- Describe features, functions, and components of the System 5005 concentrator.
- Describe functions of the LED indicators on the System 5005 concentrator.
- ▲ Differentiate System 5000 and System 5005 concentrator features, functions, and components.

Network Management Tools

▼ Identify the main tasks in each of the five areas of the OSI network management model. Describe how Optivity uses SNMP to provide network management functions.

■ Identify the tasks that can be performed with Optivity Campus Command Center and Optivity views, applications, and utilities.

▲ Identify the Optivity views and applications that are used to perform different network management tasks.

Ethernet Network Design

▼ Distinguish between collapsed backbone and distributed backbone.

■ Describe Ethernet network design guidelines.

▲ Compare and contrast characteristics of Ethernet physical media.

Ethernet Troubleshooting

▼ Define standard Ethernet troubleshooting procedures.

■ Describe common Ethernet errors.

▲ Identify, isolate, and correct common problems in an Ethernet network.

BayStack 50x Token-Ring Hub

▼ Describe features, functions, and components of BayStack 50x hubs.

■ Identify management and configuration options for BayStack 50x hubs.

■ Describe functions of LED indicators on BayStack 50x hubs.

■ Install and configure a token-ring network using BayStack 50x hubs.

■ Describe features, functions, and components of BayStack 50x hubs.

■ Identify management and configuration options for BayStack 50x hubs.

■ Describe functions of LED indicators on BayStack 50x hubs.

▲ Install and configure a token-ring network using BayStack 50x hubs.

Token-Ring Network Design

▼ Describe token-ring network design guidelines.

■ Explain how cable layout affects trunk topology.

■ Describe the use of distributed, sequential, and collapsed backbones.

▲ Design basic token-ring networks with BayStack 50x, System 3000, and System 5000 solutions. Describe token-ring network design guidelines.

Token-Ring Troubleshooting

▼ Define standard token-ring troubleshooting procedures.

■ Describe common token-ring errors.

■ Identify, isolate, and correct common problems in a token-ring network.

■ Define standard token-ring troubleshooting procedures.

▲ Describe common token-ring errors. Identify, isolate, and correct common problems in a token-ring network.

Router Core Technology Core Technology Exam

Router Hardware

▼ Differentiate among various Nortel Networks router models.

■ Differentiate among Bay Networks field replaceable units (such as link modules, net modules, expansion modules, and so forth).

■ Differentiate among the FRE, FRE-2, and ARE routing engines.

▲ Interpret various router status indicators. Differentiate between port-to-port and slot-to-slot data flow.

Router Software

▼ Differentiate among various image files for Nortel Networks routers.

■ Describe local boot processes on various Nortel Networks routers.

■ Identify the Nortel Networks router models and interface types that support EZ Install, Net Boot, and directed Net Boot. Describe how the image builder tool is used to modify a boot image.

■ Describe how the report generator tool can be used to document contents of a configuration file.

▲ Describe the major differences among EZ Install, Net Boot, and directed Net Boot.

Technician Interface

▼ Describe the different types of TI connections to the various types of Nortel Networks routers.

■ Describe various ways to log into and out of the Nortel Networks router.

■ Demonstrate ability to use TI scripts.

■ Demonstrate ability to use various operating commands to mange the router.

■ Use TI to view and save event logs.

▲ Use TI to perform system administration functions such as boot, run diagnostics, display software version, set passwords, and so forth.

Site Manager Basics

▼ Describe the purpose of using Site Manager.

■ Explain supported Site Manager configurations.

■ Describe the role of the IP stack in the configuration of Site Manager on the PC.

■ Define the router configuration functions: local, remote, and dynamic.

■ Describe the function of the Statistics Manager and how it can be used to verify proper operation of any circuit you configure.

■ Describe how the I Builder tool is used to modify a boot image.

▲ Describe how the Report Generator tool can be used to document contents of a configuration file.

IP Addressing

▼ Define the addressing standard used for IP communications.

■ Identify the appropriate subnet mask for a given IP addressing scheme.

▲ Define the appropriate IP network address to be assigned to each physical network in a given IP addressing scheme.

Source Route Bridging

▼ Explain the function of the Routing Information Field (RIF) of a source route frame.

■ Explain the route discovery process in a Nortel Networks router operating in a source route environment.

■ Explain how the token-ring end station parameters can be used on Nortel Networks routers operating as a Source Route Bridge.

■ Explain the basic principles of Source Route Bridging.

▲ Demonstrate ability to interpret Source Route Bridge parameters on a Nortel Networks router operating in a source route environment.

Transparent Spanning Tree Bridging

▼ Describe the operating principles of a transparent bridge.

■ Describe the difference between forwarding and flooding a frame.

■ Describe ways to ensure a loop-free bridge topology.

■ Define the global and interface parameters that manage transparent bridge operations on a Nortel Networks router operating as a transparent bridge.

■ Define the parameters that govern the operation of the spanning tree algorithm.

▲ Describe the operating principles of a translational bridge.

Management Information Base

▼ Describe the architecture of the Management Information Base (MIB).

▲ Identify the Technician Interface (TI) commands used to display and modify the Bay Networks MIB.

IP Services

▼ Define the primary and secondary functions of IP.

■ Describe what can be contained in the IP header and the functions of the various components.

■ Describe the purpose and function of commonly used IP services, such as ARP, RIP, static routes, circuitless IP, Proxy ARP, RARP, and so forth.

■ Explain the basic structure of an IP traffic filter template.

■ Differentiate among various types of IP traffic filters such as in-bound, out-bound, and so forth.

▲ Identify the predetermined criteria for IP traffic filters and their functions.

Router Management

▼ Describe the architecture of Simple Network Management Protocol (SNMP).

■ Configure a Nortel Networks router and Site Manager workstation for proper SNMP community name access.

■ Describe filter options within the Events Manager.

■ Configure a Nortel Networks router to send traps to any remote IP station.

▲ Understand features and functions of Events Manager, Router Files Manager, Statistics Manager, and Trap Monitor.

Switching Core Technology Exam

Networking Concepts

▼ Identify the differences between bridging and routing.

■ Match the various components of an 802.3 Ethernet frame with their respective functions.

■ Identify the correct definition of a collision domain.

■ Identify the correct definition of a broadcast domain.

■ Match the definitions that correspond to the first three layers of the OSI model.

■ Match the following terms with their definitions: repeater, bridge, router, and transceiver.

■ Identify the correct definition for CSMA/CD.

■ List the various speeds at which a standards-based implementation of Ethernet operates.

▲ Match the following terms with their definitions: twisted pair, fiber optics, and coax.

Bridging Concepts

▼ Identify the features and functions of the spanning tree protocol.

■ List the characteristics of a learning bridge.

■ Identify the flooding, forwarding, and learning process of transparent bridges.

■ Identify the characteristics of Transparent Bridging.

■ Identify the characteristics of Source Route Bridging

▲ Identify the function of a routing table on a network bridge.

Frame-Switching Concepts

▼ Match the definitions to the various types of VLANs.

■ Identify the function and application of the proposed 802.1Q specification.

■ List the steps for VLAN formation in both cell- and frame-switched environments.

■ Identify differences between cut-through, and store and forward switching.

▲ Identify the characteristics of frame- and cell-switching technologies.

Cell-Switching Concepts

▼ Identify the difference between a PVC and an SVC.

■ Match the LECS, LEC, LES, and BUS with their appropriate definitions.

■ Identify a PVP.

■ Match the terms PVC and PVP with their appropriate definitions.

■ Identify various types (AALs) and their uses.

■ Identify UNI and NNI interface differences.

■ List the functions of each LANE comp.

■ List how LANE services VCCs are established.

▲ Identify the function of ILMI.

BayStack 350 Switching

▼ Identify instances in which BayStack 350/350T-FHD would be used.

■ List the hardware features of the BayStack 350/350T-FHD switches.

■ List the software features of the BayStack 350/350T-FHD.

- Identify the configuration parameters and requirements of the BayStack 350/350T-FHD switches.

- List in order the steps required to implement VLANs on BayStack 350/350T-FHD switches.

- Identify the upgrade process for the BayStack 350/350T-FHD switches.

▲ List in order the steps to configure MultiLink trunking on a BayStack 350.

BayStack 303/304 Switches

▼ Identify instances in which BayStack 303/304 switches would be used.

- List the hardware features of the 303/304 switches.

- Identify the configuration parameters and requirements of the BayStack 303/04 switches.

▲ List the advanced features of the BayStack 303/304 switches.

BayStack 450 Switching

▼ Identify instances in which BayStack 450 switches would be used.

- List the hardware features of the BayStack 450 switches.

- List the software features of the 450 switches.

- Identify the configuration parameters and requirements for the BayStack 450 switches.

- List in order the steps required to implement VLANs on the BayStack 450 switches.

▲ Identify the upgrade process for the BayStack 450 switches.

Multi-Service Access Core Technology Exam
Telephony Basics

▼ Identify the characteristics of loop-start and loop-disconnect signaling, off-hook, and on-hook states.

- Describe the operation of loop-disconnect dialing.

- List and identify features of Dual-Tone Multi-Frequency.

- Compare the operational environments of analog/digital telephones.

▲ Compare and contrast the operations of two-wire and four-wire telephone sets.

PBX Overview

▼ List and identify the typical components of a PBX.

- Explain the call routing process of a PBX.

▲ Compare and contrast the voice interfaces on a typical PBX.

Voice Fundamentals

▼ Compare T1 and E1 characteristics.

■ Describe the analog-to-digital conversion process of speech.

■ Compare A-Law and U-Law.

■ Describe the T1 (DS1) interface as it pertains to AMI/B8ZS.

■ Compare the use of D4 and ESF framing techniques.

■ Explain CAS on E1 interfaces.

■ Explain CCS on E1.

■ Explain the need for PBX synchronization.

■ Explain G.721-, G.723-, and G.726-related data rates/speech quality.

■ Explain relationships among PCM, DPCM, and ADPCM.

■ Explain G.728, G.729, G.729a, CELP, LD-CELP, and CS-ACELP.

■ Describe negative implications of using compression with modems.

■ List factors that cause echo.

■ Identify the primary causes of delay in networks.

■ Identify the types of echo cancellation.

■ Describe each suppressor and echo canceller, and ITU standards.

■ List common PBX trunk signaling methods.

■ Describe A-bit signaling in CAS.

■ Explain the advantage of SS7.

■ Explain CCS versus CAS.

■ Compare and contrast enterprise transporting voice using TDM and VoFR.

■ Explain the end-to-end processing of information using TDM.

▲ Describe the basic Frame Relay protocol.

Voice Switching

▼ Describe the advantage of cell switching.

■ Describe the evolution of voice networks.

▲ Identify the benefits of voice switching.

Passport 4400 Basics

▼ Identify bandwidth-saving technologies utilized by the 4400.

■ Identify the voice/fax services offered by the 4400.

■ Identify the key voice components of the 4400.

- Identify the IP services of the 4400.
- Identify the video services supported by the 4400.
- Identify the WAN link services supported by the 4400.
- ▲ Identify the legacy data services supported by the 4400.

Passport 4400 Architecture and Operations

- ▼ Identify the hardware modules of the 4400.
- Define the dip switch, jumper settings, and LIM module settings.
- Define the number of ports and connections for each hardware module.
- Define the PANL, PVC, Port, and other characteristics.
- Define the relationship of physical ports to logical netlinks.
- Define the bridging and routing support within the 4400.
- Define the 4400 layers within the network link.
- Define the basis of the CLI architecture.
- Define the method of boot and application software download.
- Define what is meant by active/committed banks.
- Define IF indices.
- ▲ Define DNA addresses.

Passport 4400 Network Configuration

- ▼ Configure bridging and routing on the 4400.
- Configure the various DCE/DTE settings for central, regional, and branch units.
- Configure and manage virtual ports.
- Identify how third-party routers use IP and RFC 1490 to interface with the 4400.
- Identify characteristics of the GCM.
- ▲ List the various types of backup options within the 4400.

Passport 4400 Voice

- ▼ Define the utilization/characteristics of NAS/NAC.
- Identify configuration parameters for ingress/egress tables.
- Identify the utilization of ingress/egress manipulation strings.
- Interpret what the lights on the T1/E1 modules represent.
- Identify the configuration parameters for analog/digital voice.

- Define ABCD bit changes in a T1/E1 environment.
- Define call restrictions.
- ▲ Configure Hoot&Holler.

Passport 4400 LAN/WAN Functions

- ▼ Configure bridging, routing, IP, and IPX filtering on a 4400.
- Identify RFC 1490 interface characteristics and configuration parameters.
- Identify characteristics of TCP fields.
- Identify characteristics of IP fields.
- Configure RIP1, RIP1C, and RIPll.
- Define ARP spoofing/RIP delta functions.
- Define ISDN hardware components and framing services.
- Configure Frame Relay on a 4400.
- Configure HTDS/HDLC.
- Configure PPP.
- Define and configuration for CBR traffic.
- Identify troubleshooting CLI commands for WANs.
- ▲ Identify legacy protocols/configuration parameters.

Network Design

- ▼ Define the configuration parameters for the GCM.
- Define the use and interpretation of line bandwidth/SVC CIR and so forth.
- Define the user and configuration of transfer priorities.
- Define the use and configuration of CIR and BECN in a Passport 4400.
- ▲ Define traffic management parameters.

IP Telephony Core Technology Exam

Demonstrate and understand the following:

- ▼ PBX system and its components.
- Telecommunications fundamentals and signaling systems.
- Overview of satellite and paging systems.
- VoIP devices, protocols, and standards.
- ISDN concepts, architecture, and protocols.
- Packetized voice networking.

- How traffic can be sent over IP networks.
- Voice over ATM and frame relay.
- How to establish a call over the public switched telephone network (PSTN).
- Architecture of the Internet compared to PSTN.
- Challenges associated with VoIP.
- Benefits of using VoIP.
- Protocols and standards associated with VoIP (H, 323, SIP, and MGCP).
- Network and technology issues associated with VoIP.
- ▲ Quality of Service (QoS) issues.

Business Communications Manager Core Technology Exam
Hardware Configuration

- ▼ List the Media Bay Module types available on Enterprise Edge.
- Describe the terminal and line interfaces supported by each of the Media Bay modules.
- Describe the relationship between the DIP switch settings of the Media Bay Modules and the line and station numbering assigned by Enterprise Edge.
- Describe the environmental requirements for installing an Enterprise Edge System.
- Describe the power requirements for an Enterprise Edge installation.
- ▲ Describe the procedure for replacing a defective Media Bay Module.

Configuration Interfaces and Setup

- ▼ List the connection options for connecting to an Enterprise Edge for system configuration.
- Describe the procedure for connecting to an Enterprise Edge using an IP connection with the default IP address.
- Describe the procedure for configuring a new IP address and reconnecting to the Enterprise Edge.
- Describe the procedure for launching Unified Manager on the PC being used to configure Enterprise Edge.
- Describe the procedure for downloading the Java Applet for configuring the PC.
- Describe the procedure for downloading configuration client software to the configuring PC.
- ▲ Describe the procedure for selecting market profiles.

Key Code Administration

▼ Describe how to identify the system ID for the Enterprise Edge system.

■ Explain the term "key code" and the purpose of key codes.

■ List some important features that require key code activation.

■ Describe how to retrieve key codes for the Web-based KSR using the authorization codes and the system ID.

▲ Configure (activate) Enterprise Edge options using key codes.

Configuring Lines and Trunks

▼ List the line/trunk types.

■ Describe default line numbering and pre-assignments to specific line types.

■ Describe the basics of a T1 line and its capabilities.

■ Explain the term line pool and the use of line pools.

■ Explain the term "access codes."

■ Explain the term "direct inward dialing" and why these lines are used.

■ Explain the signaling that allows Enterprise Edge to route a DID call to a specific set.

■ Explain the term "target line" and the role it plays in relating a DID call to a particular set.

■ Configure lines.

■ Configure access codes.

■ Configure target lines.

▲ Describe a procedure for configuring a test phone to test lines.

Configuring System Features

▼ List system features that can be programmed.

▲ Configure system features.

Configuring Set/Terminal Features

▼ List key set features that can be programmed.

■ Describe the operation of some of the key set features.

■ Describe a procedure for programming a template set and using it to copy features to other sets.

■ Describe the prime set.

■ Describe line appearance options.

■ Configure sets/terminals, including individual set names.

▲ Configure the receptionist set.

Configuring Voicemail

▼ Describe the procedure for launching Voicemail Manager.

■ Configure general system configuration settings and passwords.

■ Describe the term "class of service" as it applies to voicemail.

■ Describe the procedure for establishing additional classes of service (beyond default classes of service).

■ Configure general delivery mailboxes.

■ Configure system administration mailboxes.

▲ Describe procedure for auto-building mailboxes.

Configuring Auto Attendant

▼ Configure (record) greetings.

■ Configure greeting tables.

■ Configure (input) a company directory.

▲ Configure CCR trees.

Backup and Restore

▼ Describe the procedure for downloading (backing up) a system configuration.

▲ Describe the procedure for uploading (restoring) a system configuration.

NNCSS-Not as Easy as It Looks

With only one test to take, the NNCSS would seem to be an easy certification to obtain. However, after reading through the exam objectives for the different tests, the reader will see that obtaining the NNCSS is anything but easy. That's not to say that the NNCSS by any means is impossible either; with a little hard work and perseverance you can succeed in passing one of these tests.

Nortel Networks Certified Support Expert (NNCSE)

The Support Specialist designation enables an engineer to specialize in one technology. The Support Expert certification requires a wider range of knowledge and expertise. To become an NNCSE, a candidate must already be a Certified Support Specialist and must pass an additional Core Technology exam as well as three Advanced Product exams. The NNCSE is a very difficult and time-consuming certification; however, the rewards in compensation, promotion, and recognition are well worth the investment.

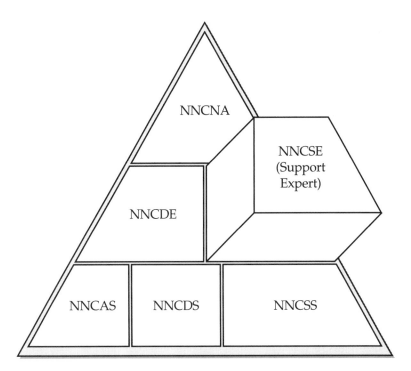

We have discussed the Core Technology exams in detail in the last section; in this section we will go over the Advanced Product exams and their objectives. Currently there are only four Advanced Product exams available:

▼ WAN/Advanced IP Configuration
■ Network Management with Optivity
■ Using the Accelar (Passport) 1000 V2.0
▲ Centillion Switching V4.0

Rather than cover the basics of a technology such as routing or switching, the Advanced Product exams cover a specific enterprise data product in great detail; for example, the Centillion ATM switch or the Optivity Network Management platform.

Advanced Product Exam Objectives

As was suggested earlier in reference to the Core Technology exams, use these objectives to gauge your readiness for the Advanced Product test. If you would like to reference this information online (to check for changes for example), visit http://www12. nortelnetworks.com/training2/certification/techexams.html#advprod and click the Advanced Product exam of your choice. The following exam objectives were taken directly from the Nortel Networks Web site.

WAN/Advanced IP Configuration Exam Objectives

WAN Overview

▼ Describe the HDLC frame format and channel operation.

■ Explain the implementation and operation of a multi-line circuit.

■ Describe the use and operation of BOFL packets by a Nortel Networks router.

■ List the HDLC-based WAN protocols.

▲ Identify the available log entries required to monitor the status of the WAN services.

Frame Relay

▼ Describe the components, topologies, and characteristics of a frame relay network.

■ Describe frame relay permanent virtual circuit (PVC) assignments.

■ Identify link management options and line status sequences.

■ Describe the Nortel Networks service record functions, implementations, and management.

■ Describe the different protocol and address resolution issues and options in a frame relay environment.

■ Explain frame relay network operation over a fully meshed network using service records containing multiple PVCs.

▲ Explain frame relay network operation over a non-fully meshed network using service records containing multiple PVCs or single PVC.

Protocol Prioritization and Traffic Filters

▼ Explain the function and operation of Nortel Networks protocol prioritization.

■ Identify the priority queuing and de-queuing algorithms used to prioritize traffic.

▲ Describe the use of protocol prioritization in the frame relay environment.

Point-to-Point Protocol

▼ Describe the components of PPP.

■ Explain the operation of the Link Control Protocol and the Network Control Protocol.

■ Identify the various phases of link operations for a PPP link.

■ Explain the purpose of Link Quality Monitoring (LQM).

▲ Describe the various types of LCP messages.

Data Compression

▼ Identify the type of data compression and the supported protocols used in a Nortel Networks implementation.

■ List the types of data compressed and the location of data within a packet.

■ Describe the use of history tables in data compression.

▲ List and describe the functionality of the different compression modes.

Dial Services

▼ Discuss the implementation of dial-on-demand, dial backup, and bandwidth-on-demand applications.

■ Describe the implementation of ISDN, raise DTR, V.25bis, and Hayes signaling applications.

■ Identify event log messages, which can be used to troubleshoot dial services.

▲ Identify Technician Interface (TI) commands used to monitor the status of dial service connections.

Routing Information Protocol (RIP)

▼ Explain the purpose and implementation of variable length subnet masks.

■ Describe the components and interactions of the IP routing software on a Nortel Networks router.

▲ Describe the differences between the RIP-1 and RIP-2 protocols.

OSPF Overview

▼ Define the major features of Open Shortest Path First (OSPF).

■ Describe the relationship between the link state database (LSDB), the shortest path first (SPF) tree, and the routing table.

■ Define the four types of networks supported by OSPF.

■ Examine the event log to verify the formation of an adjacency and identify causes for failures.

▲ Describe the process of forming an adjacency.

OSPF Areas

▼ Identify advantages and disadvantages of areas and summaries.

■ Describe the different types of routers in an OSPF environment.

■ Discuss the implementation of network summaries in an OSPF environment.

■ Identify the various types of link advertisements used by OSPF.

▲ Discuss the use and implementation of virtual links in OSPF.

OSPF External Routes

▼ Describe external routes in an OSPF environment.

■ Discuss the calculation and implementation of external routing metrics in an OSPF environment.

▲ Discuss the use of announce/accept policies in an OSPF environment.

Introduction to BGP-4

▼ Explain the differences between Interior Gateway Protocol (IGP) and Exterior Gateway Protocol (EGP).

■ Define the terms stub autonomous system (AS), transit AS, and multi-homed non-transit AS.

■ Describe the characteristics of the Border Gateway Protocol (BGP).

▲ Explain the difference between Exterior BGP (EBGP) connections and Internal BGP (IBGP) connections.

Network Management with Optivity Exam

Network Management Components

▼ Differentiate essential network management elements.

■ Summarize the OSI network management areas.

■ Categorize the OSI model for networking.

■ Differentiate SNMP Manager/Agent components.

■ Identify the Optivity Enterprise suite of applications.

■ Identify the hardware and software requirements for the Optivity Enterprise suite of applications.

■ Summarize Nortel Networks agent features.

▲ Identify Nortel Networks NNM and probe hardware.

Discovering the Network

▼ Describe the network topology processes for Nortel Networks devices.

▲ Describe the steps necessary for network discovery.

Documenting the Network

▼ Summarize Enterprise Command Center documentation functions.

■ Summarize Routerman documentation features.

■ Summarize NetAtlas documentation features.

■ Summarize NodalView documentation features.

■ Summarize Expanded View documentation features

▲ Summarize Agent Manager documentation features.

Baselining and Performance Management

▼ Define the measurement points of baselining a network.

■ Summarize performance statistics.

■ Summarizing Optivity performance tools.

■ Configuring Optivity performance tools.

▲ Summarize the four levels in which Optivity tools collect performance statistics.

Configuration Management

▼ Describe configuration switching.

■ Describe LANarchitect modes.

■ Demonstrate ability to use the LANarchitect application to balance traffic across System 5000 hub segments.

▲ Manage redundant links.

NetArchitect Overview

▼ Summarize the usage of the three NetArchitect applications.

■ Distinguish the File Manager device file system components.

■ Categorize the steps to retrieve device configurations.

■ Summarize the revision control database (RCD) stored configuration files.

▲ Describe device configurations.

Fault Management

▼ Describe components of the Optivity Fault Management system.

■ Categorize the levels of fault management tools.

▲ Utilize fault management tools at the enterprise, network, data link, and physical levels.

Optivity Processes and Command-Line Equivalents

▼ Summarize Optivity processes.

■ Summarize Optivity application command-line equivalents.

▲ Summarize Optivity configuration files.

Using the Accelar (Passport) 1000 V2.0 Exam
Accelar Overview

▼ List the technologies supported by the Accelar 1000 Routing Switch.

■ Describe the types of information available from the tracelog facility.

■ Describe the types of information available from the syslog facility.

■ List the features of the various Accelar Routing Switches (1100, 1150, 1200, and 1250).

■ Describe the various modules for the Accelar product line.

▲ Describe the correct placement for the Accelar family of products in the enterprise network.

Accelar System Configuration

▼ Configure an initial IP address on the Accelar Routing Switch.

■ Update the Accelar system image using TFTP.

▲ Configure an Accelar switch for TFTP boot using the runtime CLI.

Accelar Layer-2 Configuration

▼ Configure the Accelar Routing Switch to use spanning tree and spanning tree groups.

■ Configure a port-based VLAN.

■ Configure tagged ports on an Accelar Routing Switch.

■ Configure MLT on the Accelar Routing Switch.

■ Configure a policy-based VLAN.

■ Display the forwarding database for a particular VLAN.

■ Describe layer 2 frame processing and forwarding in an Accelar switch.

■ Explain the term "spanning tree groups."

■ Configure a MAC-based VLAN.

■ Configure IGMP on the Accelar Routing Switch.

■ Explain the term "management access policies."

■ Describe the characteristics of link safe.

■ Define the term "locked ports."

▲ Implement layer 2 login control on the Accelar Routing Switch.

Accelar Layer-3 Configuration

▼ Configure IP routing across VLANs.

■ Configure IP routing on a routing switch port.

■ Configure an OSPF Network with a single-area backbone.

■ Configure the Accelar to support both IP-RIP version 1 and IP-RIP version 2.

■ Configure an OSPF network with multiple areas.

■ Configure the Accelar Routing Switch to advertise networks learned through OSPF networks using RIP.

■ Describe layer 3 frame processing and forwarding in an Accelar switch.

■ Configure IPX routing on the Accelar Routing Switch.

■ Describe the possible reasons for implementing IP announce policies.

■ Configure DHCP on the Accelar Routing Switch.

■ Configure a static route on the Accelar Routing Switch.

■ Configure the Accelar Routing Switch to advertise networks learned through RIP networks using OSPF.

■ Display the IP Address Resolution Protocol table.

■ Configure IP announce policies on the Accelar Routing Switch.

■ Configure VRRP on the Accelar Routing Switch.

■ Configure OSPF Area Summaries.

■ Describe the operation of DVMRP.

■ Configure Bootp on the Accelar Routing Switch.

■ Configure UDP forwarding on the Accelar Routing Switch.

■ Describe IGMPv2.

▲ Describe IGMPv1.

Managing the Accelar Switch

▼ View statistics using CLI.

■ Use Device Manager to perform specified management tasks (such as software upgrades, port management, view statistics, flush FDB, reset switch, and so forth).

■ Display the chassis system parameters using Device Manager.

▲ Identify the correct procedure to access the Accelar Routing Switch with Web management.

Centillion Switching V4.0 Exam

Bridging, Switching, and VLAN Review

▼ Describe the flooding, forwarding, and learning processes of transparent bridges.

■ Explain the Spanning Tree Protocol to block looping.

■ Describe the RIF information process of Source Route Bridges.

■ Describe the basics of frame-switching and cell-switching technologies.

▲ Explain how frame- and cell-switching technologies create VLANs.

Centillion Switch Overview

▼ List and describe the general features of the Centillion switch.

■ Describe the C50, C100, and 5000BH chassis and placement of modules.

■ Describe the functions of the Master Control Processor and list the available modules.

■ Explain the hardware redundancy features of the Centillion switch.

■ Describe the features and role of SpeedView and the Command-Line Interface (CLI).

■ Explain bridge groups and the types of ports that compose a bridge group.

■ Describe virtual ports, list the Vport types, and compare and contrast the types.

■ Describe the features of the TokenSpeed, EtherSpeed, and ATMSpeed modules.

■ Describe the virtual token-ring feature.

■ Explain how source route RIF proxy works.

■ Give an overview of frame processing and forwarding within a Centillion switch.

▲ Explain the redundant MCP feature of the Centillion switch.

Command-Line Interface Applications

▼ Use the CLI in command mode to view switch parameters and statistics.

▲ Use the CLI in config mode to configure default and IP parameters.

SpeedView for Windows

▼ Install the SpeedView for Windows application on a PC with the proper system requirements.

■ Use a variety of methods to connect the management workstation to the Centillion switch and upload and download configurations.

■ Register multiple switches using Simple Network Management Protocol (SNMP).

■ View a switch, enable and disable ports, and reset the switch.

■ Download the proper system image file for both the Centillion 100 switch and the model 5000BH chassis.

■ Perform basic switch configurations using the system, network management, switching mode, and static station windows.

▲ Explain the function of TokenSpeed, EtherSpeed, and ATMSpeed module configuration parameters.

ATM Review

▼ Explain how the ATM model is used to pass cells from end system to end system.

■ Identify ATM address format fields.

▲ Differentiate between a user-to-network interface (UNI) and a network-to-network interface (NNI).

Centillion Mode and ATM Switching

▼ Differentiate a Centillion circuit saver network from a GIGArray network and explain how each network type processes frames.

■ Plan and configure a switch for both load balancing and redundancy.

■ Plan and assign PVPs and PVCs for Centillion LAN clients (CLCs) and pass-through connections using SpeedView for Windows.

■ Configure CLCs in circuit saver and turbo modes using SpeedView for Windows.

▲ Describe how VPort bridging operates through combining VPort types.

ATM Addressing and Signaling

▼ Assign logical ATM addresses to Centillion switches in a network.

■ Plan Interim Inter-Switch Protocol (IISP) link use in a network.

■ Configure logical IISP link groups.

■ Given an ATM network topology, select the appropriate signaling configuration.

■ Configure port signaling parameters for ATMSpeed modules.

▲ Plan and configure an ATM call routing table for IISP links.

LAN Emulation Review

▼ Define the purpose and use of LANE.

■ Describe the function of each component of LANE.

■ Explain how LANE moves information in the network.

▲ List and explain how the LANE Services VCCs are established.

Centillion-Based LAN Emulation Applications

▼ Configure the LAN Emulation Server and Broadcast and Unknown Server (LES/BUS) pairs.

■ Configure the LAN Emulation Configuration Server (LECS).

▲ Configure a LANE VPort (LEC) on a Centillion switch.

Redundant LANE Services

▼ Configure the Centillion network to use redundant LES/BUS pairs.

▲ Use the show Vport and show LES commands to identify the LES/BUS pair that an LEC is using.

PNNI Overview

▼ Describe the PNNI hierarchical model.

■ Describe the roles of PNNI nodes, peer group leaders, and border nodes.

■ Differentiate between inside links and outside links.

■ Explain how the Hello protocol is used on the Routing Control Channel.

■ Summarize how PNNI topology information is exchanged within and between peer groups.

- ■ Explain the relationship between level indicators, node identifiers, and peer group identifiers.
- ▲ Explain the use of source routing, crankback, and alternate path selection with call establishment.

Centillion PNNI Implementation

- ▼ List the PNNI functions that are supported on the Centillion 100 and 5000BH switches.
- ■ Identify scenarios in which Centillion switches can be deployed using PNNI.
- ▲ Configure PNNI on Centillion 100 and 5000BH switches.

Using SpeedView Filters

- ▼ Describe the NetBIOS filter and proxy features.
- ■ Describe the capabilities and applications of packet filtering.
- ▲ Explain the functions of packet filter parameters.

NNCSE Conclusion

The NNCSE is among the toughest certifications to earn in the industry. With the NNCSS as a prerequisite, an additional Core Technology, and three Advanced Product exams required for certification, the NNCSE does not come easily. However, with study and practice the certification is attainable.

DESIGN CERTIFICATIONS

Many network engineers start their careers in a support role either in equipment configuration or managing previously installed gear. After a few years of this kind of work, some prefer to move into a network design position. In many ways this is the more interesting of the two roles. The design professional must understand the specifications and potential of a given product or group of products to create an appropriate design. This calls for traditional "support" knowledge of the equipment. In addition, the design professional must understand the network as a whole and be aware of budgetary constraints. The best design is not always the one that gets packets from point A to point B the fastest. More often it is the design that meets customer requirements for speed, reliability, and supportability; and (hopefully) comes in under budget. The Nortel Networks Certified Design Specialist and Expert designations were developed with such people in mind.

Nortel Networks Certified Design Specialist (NNCDS)

The Design Specialist certification combines the knowledge of the Support Specialist with the wider product knowledge of the Account Specialist and adds considerable design elements.

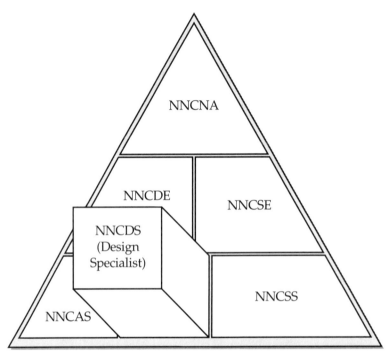

A NNCDS should be able to

▼ Identify and classify customer requirements.

■ Position Nortel Networks products in a competitive environment.

■ Design a network topology.

■ Develop bid responses to customer requirements.

▲ Possess industry knowledge.

To complete the NNCDS certification and prove that they have met the preceding criteria, a candidate must pass one Core Technology exam, two Sales Technology and Product exams, and two Unified Networks Design Solutions exams. The STP exams are the same ones offered for the Account Specialist designation. The Unified Networks Design Solutions exams mirror the Unified Networks Sales Solutions exams with an additional sub-module that addresses specific network design considerations. Current NNCASs should find the material very familiar and the design aspect an interesting addition.

As we have already covered the exam objectives for the STP and the Unified Networks Sales/Design Solutions exams as well as the Core Technology material, we will not go over them in detail again; instead a listing of the test options is given here.

Sales, Technology, and Product Exams

The following STP exams currently are available to fulfill the requirements of the NNCDS certification; two of these are required:

- ▼ LAN exam (required)
- ■ WAN exam
- ■ Voice exam
- ■ IP Telephony exam
- ▲ Network Management exam

Unified Networks Solutions Exams

Of the seven exams available to fulfill the Unified Networks Solutions portion of the NNCDS designation, two of the following tests must be completed.

- ▼ LAN Campus ATM Solutions
- ■ LAN Campus Ethernet Solutions
- ■ Small Business Solutions
- ■ WAN Enterprise Solutions
- ■ VPN Enterprise Solutions
- ■ IBM Enterprise Solutions
- ▲ INCA M10 Solutions

Core Technology Exams

Six exams are available that will meet the Core Technology requirement of the NNCDS; only one must be completed. They are as follows:

- ▼ Hubs and Shared Media Core Technology
- ■ Routing Core Technology
- ■ Switching Core Technology
- ■ Multi-Service Access Core Technology
- ■ IP Telephony Core Technology
- ▲ Business Communications Manager (formerly Enterprise Edge) Core Technology

The design specialist designation is a worthwhile certification goal. Many companies are looking for someone with not only a configuration and support background, but design experience as well. Network infrastructure projects often fail due to poor initial design; business leaders are recognizing this fact. To rectify the situation they are willing to pay more for someone who can keep the mistakes from occurring in the first place. The NNCDS is a great way to prove that you can provide a solution to such problems.

Nortel Networks Certified Design Expert (NNCDE)

Nortel Networks describes the NNCDE as a designation that "recognizes an advanced level of network design, planning, and optimization using Nortel Networks solutions." As the reader will see from the requirements listed in the following, the certification requires an advanced level of study as well. The NNCDE is targeted at senior-level network engineers, network designers and planners, and high-level consultants.

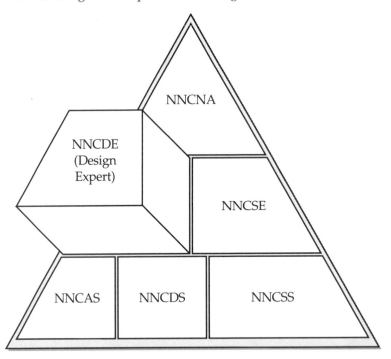

To successfully meet the requirements of the certification, you should be able to

▼ Manage multi-function evaluation teams and bid response.

■ Prioritize customer requirements.

■ Optimize the network based on end user applications or value-added services.

■ Apply advanced knowledge of Nortel Networks solutions.

- ■ Possess knowledge of industry direction.
- ▲ Possess an ability to design detailed network topologies.

To complete the NNCDE, the candidate must have already earned the NNCDS and must pass an additional Core Technology exam, an Advanced Product exam, and a Network Design exam. The process of preparing for the Network Design test is worthwhile even for someone who is not planning to take the exam. Principles of network design are good to know even for a networking "newbie." Understanding why we do something often leads to greater understanding of how to do it better. This is as true of networking as it is of any other skill in life. As we have already covered the exam objectives for the Core Technology and Advanced Product tests in previous sections, we will list only the available tests and go over the exam objectives for the Network Design test in detail.

Core Technology Exams

Six exams are available that will meet the core technology requirement of the NNCDS. One of the following is required in addition to NNCDS:

- ▼ Hubs and Shared Media Core Technology
- ■ Routing Core Technology
- ■ Switching Core Technology
- ■ Multi-Service Access Core Technology
- ■ IP Telephony Core Technology
- ▲ Business Communications Manager (formerly Enterprise Edge) Core Technology

Advanced Product Exams

There are four Advanced Product tests currently available. Of the following, one is required:

- ▼ WAN/advanced IP Configuration
- ■ Network Management with Optivity
- ■ Use of the Accelar (Passport) 1000 V2.0
- ▲ Centillion Switching V4.0

Network Design Exam Objectives (Required Exam)
Network Design Methodology

- ▼ Define the key terms and concepts of network design.
- ▲ Identify features of a good design methodology for use in network design.

Information Gathering

▼ Identify the statement of work content.

■ Identify the types of information required to perform a network design.

■ Identify the steps in the information gathering process required to perform a network design.

■ Identify network requirements from given customer business requirements.

▲ Identify the technology requirements as defined in the network requirements.

Network Architecture

▼ Define network architecture.

■ Identify the strategy or process used to develop network architecture.

■ List basic rules that can be used when defining the network architecture.

▲ Given a set of customer requirements and problem definition statements, draw a high-level network diagram.

Campus Technology

▼ Compare and contrast the functionality and major differences among the various campus technologies.

■ Identify how the campus technologies are used within the network design.

■ Compare how different campus technologies impact the network design goals.

■ Define the basic rules of campus technologies that apply to the network design.

■ Given a set of customer requirements, assemble Nortel Networks products to come up with a viable solution.

▲ Given a set of customer requirements, determine the campus technologies to be implemented in a viable network design.

WAN Technologies

▼ Identify the major differences among the key WAN technologies.

■ Define the basic network design rules that apply to the various WAN technologies.

■ Evaluate how the WAN technologies apply to meet the different network connectivity requirements and special workload requirements.

■ Explain how the key WAN technologies impact the network design goals.

▲ Given a set of customer requirements, assemble Nortel Networks products to come up with a viable solution.

Remote Network Access

▼ Compare and contrast the functionality and major differences between the different remote access technologies and security architectures.

■ Identify the special authentication and security requirements of remote access technologies.

■ Explain how key remote access technologies and security issues impact network design goals.

■ Implement correct routing protocols to allow for Internet access.

■ Define the basic rules that apply to the various remote access technologies and security implementations.

▲ Given a set of customer requirements, determine the firewall configuration to be implemented in a viable network design.

Routing Architecture

▼ Compare and contrast the functionality and major differences among the various routing protocols.

■ Explain the basic rules and how they are applied when developing the routing architecture.

▲ Discuss how network goals affect the routing architecture.

IP Addressing Architecture

▼ List the benefits of hierarchical addressing.

■ Identify techniques that provide for optimal manageability, summarization, and dynamic acquisition.

■ Explain the basic rules and how they are applied when defining the addressing plan.

■ Design a network layer addressing and naming model that meets given network design guidelines.

▲ Given a set of customer requirements, determine the routing architecture to be implemented in a viable network design.

Passport 4400

▼ Describe the features and benefits of multi-service networks.

■ Define network design goal considerations for multi-service networks.

▲ Discuss the interoperability between the Passport 4400 and 6400 products.

Network Design Conclusion

Network engineering is one of the hottest job markets in the computer industry and network design positions often are considered the pinnacle of an engineer's achievement. A design certification often is the clincher when it comes to getting a coveted network design job. The highest paid engineers usually have such titles as network design engineer, network planning engineer, or network architect.

NORTEL NETWORKS CERTIFIED NETWORK ARCHITECT (NNCNA)

The NNCNA is considered one of the most prestigious certifications in the industry. This is due mostly to the depth and breadth of experience and knowledge required to obtain the certification. Unlike other vendors' top certifications, the NNCNA requires the candidate to have advanced knowledge of the industry as a whole, not just vendor-specific product knowledge. Nortel describes the certification as follows: "This designation recognizes an advanced level of consulting, technical, and design expertise. To achieve this credential, candidates must pass a rigorous portfolio assessment, a highly regarded method for certifying advanced level practitioners that allows candidates to illustrate and document significant dimensions of their professional life." The addition of the portfolio assessment to the certification requirements adds a whole new dimension to the process. In the following pages you will see that the NNCNA is perhaps the most difficult yet meaningful designation available in the networking field.

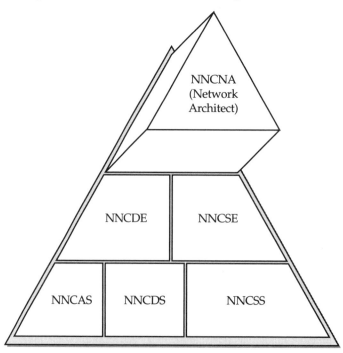

The successful candidate should be able to do the following (this information was taken from the Nortel Networks Web site at www.nortelnetworks.com):

▼   Interpret customer business drivers.

■   Influence customer decision making.

■   Influence network architecture and product direction.

■   Exhibit expert-level knowledge in multiple technological disciplines.

■   Integrate Nortel Networks solutions in a multi-vendor environment.

■   Demonstrate advanced knowledge of competitor products.

▲   Develop network evolution strategy.

Requirements

Completion of NNCNA portfolio assessment is a two-part process.

To achieve the Nortel Networks Certified Network Architect designation, a two-part portfolio assessment evaluation is utilized. The NNCNA portfolio assessment requires candidates to submit documentation supporting their high level of networking experience. This method of assessment allows the advanced level professional to illustrate and document significant dimensions of his or her professional life.

Becoming a Nortel Networks Certified Network Architect (NNCNA) is a two-part process: Candidates first must meet minimum education and experience requirements criteria through documentation of related work experience, industry-recognized certifications, and formal education.

Part 1 Application Highlights

1.   Candidates complete the part 1 portfolio application that requires documentation of education, training, and experience in network architecture.

2.   Candidates return, completed part 1 portfolio to Nortel Networks.

3.   Part 1 portfolio submissions are evaluated by the Nortel Networks architect program manager based on the program guidelines.

4.   Candidates are notified of the status of their portfolios. Candidates who pass part 1 are sent a part 2.

5.   In the portfolio application, candidates who fail to meet the strict criteria of part 1 are notified of deficiencies in the documentation of experience and education. They may resubmit part 1 within one calendar year for no additional fee. (These candidates can apply within the next grading cycle.)

Required Materials for Part 1

▼ Part 1 application.

■ Document 5 major network design projects, including description of project scope, your role in the planning, design, implementation, operations, and optimization of the project. (*An abbreviated description is acceptable if networking diagrams, RFPs, or documentation examples are provided.*)

■ Tally 500 points from the matrix regarding industry-recognized certifications.

■ Provide copies of score reports, certificates.

■ Provide a $1,000 application fee.

▲ Provide a current résumé, which must document five years of networking experience (two of which must be in network design) and formal education. Also provide a copy of your degree (if applicable; if not, skip this item).

Supplemental Achievement-Point System   In addition to the requirements previously stated, candidates must demonstrate supplementary experience and education. Evidence of a candidate's fulfillment of this requirement must be shown by accumulating at least 500 points from the following categories: experience, formal education, and industry certifications.

Experience	Points Awarded

50 Points for each additional year of networking experience beyond 5 years (Example: 5 years *additional* networking experience = 50 x 5 = 250)

DOCUMENTATION: Your experience should be documented on your résumé.

Formal Education	Points Awarded
None	0
Associate's degree or equivalent (2 years from a formal college or university)	25
British Higher National Certificate (HNC)	25
British Higher National Diploma (HND)	35
Bachelor's degree or equivalent (4 years from a formal college or university)	50
Master's Degree or equivalent (post-college degree from a formal college or university)	100
Doctorate, professional, terminal degree, or equivalent (post-college degree from a formal college or university)	150

> **NOTE:** Only the highest degree attained will count toward a candidate's total point structure. For example, an NNCNA candidate with a Master's degree will not receive additional credit for having attained a Bachelor's degree. Your education should be documented on your résumé and photocopies of degrees (if any) should be provided.

The following are industry certifications that currently are recognized by the NNCNA program. Although candidates might have achieved other certifications, only the following will count toward the required point system.

Nortel Networks	Industry Certifications	Points Awarded ✔
	NORTEL NETWORKS CERTIFICATIONS *A Minimum of 150 points required from Nortel Certifications* .	
	Nortel Networks Certified Account Specialist	25
	Nortel Networks Certified Support Specialist or Bay Networks Certified Specialist	50
	Nortel Networks Certified Design Specialist	50
	Nortel Networks Certified Support Expert or Bay Networks Certified Expert	150
	Nortel Networks Certified Magellan Engineer	150
	Nortel Networks Certified Design Expert	200

First Tier Networking Certifications

Cisco	Cisco Certified Network Associate	25
	Cisco Certified Design Associate	50
	Cisco Certified Network Professional	100
	Cisco Certified Design Professional	100
	Cisco Certified Internetwork Expert (CCIE)	150
Ascend	Ascend Certified Technical Expert	100

Nortel Networks	Industry Certifications	Points Awarded	✔
First Tier Networking Certifications			
3Com	3Wizard	50	
	Master of Network Science	100	
	Newbridge Wise Certification	100	
Xylan	Xylan Certified Switching Specialist (XCSS)	50	
	Xylan Certified Switching Expert (XCSE)	100	
Network General	Certified Network Expert (Network General [CNX])	100	
Second Tier Networking Certifications			
Microsoft	Microsoft Certified Professional (MCP)	25	
	Microsoft Certified System Engineer (MCSE)	75	
Novell	Certified Novell Administrator (CNA) or Certified NetWare Administrator	25	
	Certified Novell Engineer (CNE) or Certified NetWare Engineer	50	
	Master Certified Novell Engineer or Master Certified NetWare Engineer (Master CNE)	75	

NOTE: Only the highest certification attained within each category will count toward a candidate's total point structure. For example, an NNCNA candidate who is a Nortel Networks Certified Support expert will not receive additional credit for having attained Support Specialist Certification. The highest certification will prevail.

Part 2 Highlights

Upon successful completion of part 1, the NNCNA candidate must respond to a real-world, complex networking case study. Case studies are based on actual Nortel Networks customer scenarios

- ▼   Most case studies involve multi-vendor scenarios.
- ■   Candidate has six weeks to complete proposed solution.
- ■   Solution response must meet specific format requirements.
- ■   Estimated time for candidate to complete a response is 40 hours.

- Part 2 portfolio submissions are scored by a team of currently certified NNCNA consultants. Candidate responses are graded "blind"; judges do not know the identity of candidates. Nortel staff might contact candidates to set up a teleconference to elicit clarification of their solutions.

- Candidates are notified of their pass/fail status within 30 working days of the submission date.

- Candidates who pass are awarded the NNCNA credential. An official notification and NNCNA welcome kit will be sent to all new NNCNAs. The welcome kit includes

  - Nortel Networks Certified Network Architect confirmation letter

  - Nortel Networks Certified Network Architect computer bag/portfolio

  - Nortel Networks Certified Network Architect plaque

  - Nortel Networks Certified Network Architect crystal recognition piece

  - Nortel Networks Certified Network Architect logo sheet

- ▲ Candidates will have their NNCNA status updated in the CertManager Database within two weeks. (See http://www.galton.com/~nortel/.)

CONCLUSION

Although Nortel does not have the best-known certifications in the marketplace (a stronghold of Cisco), they certainly do have some strong contenders. To date, it has been Cisco's marketing muscle that has brought its certifications to the forefront of the industry; however, the content of the Nortel offerings soon will enable them to catch up. It is the hope of the authors that Nortel will catch on and start marketing the strength of its certifications to the rest of the industry, as Cisco has done. The wise networking professional will add the certifications now, so that as more hiring managers are looking for the designations on résumés, those who are Nortel certified will stand out.

CHAPTER 4

Switching Technologies

The last few chapters discuss networking basics, what Nortel is, and the value of Nortel Networks certifications. All that information provides a necessary foundation for the rest of this book. In this chapter we discuss the principles of layer 2 and layer 3 switching. We also cover quite a few design considerations and give the reader a good overview of some of the underlying network protocols.

THE NETWORK DOMAIN

Network domains are one of the most important ideas in computer networking. A good understanding of the domain concept is vital to the understanding of basic design principals. Depending on the technology being dealt with, the term "domain" could have many definitions. The three types of network domains we are concerned with now are collision, token, and broadcast. They are defined as follows:

▼ **Collision Domain** is any network segment in which collisions can occur either because the hosts share the same cable (as is the case with thicknet or thinnet) or hub (or group of hubs).

■ **Token Domain** is any group of hosts that share a token in a token sharing environment.

▲ **Broadcast Domain** is a group of hosts that will receive broadcast messages sent from any member of the group.

Collision Domains

Collision domains are found in Ethernet networks, by far the most common networking platform in use today. Chapter 1 introduced you to the CSMA/CD concept by which Ethernet is able to sense whether any data is being transmitted over the wire. Because not all hosts on the network receive data at the same time it is possible for two machines to start transmitting simultaneously (see Figure 4-1). When this happens, it is known as a *collision*. Both hosts are able to detect when this collision occurs, and each will wait a random amount of time before attempting to send again. This waiting and retransmitting can cause a very noticeable slowdown in the network. These collisions become more likely as hosts are added to the segment. The more hosts in a segment, the more collisions; the more collisions, the slower the network. Obviously it is important to keep collision domains as small as possible.

Token Domains

The shared medium in a token-ring network is known as a *token domain*. Using a token passing scheme, a token-ring network controls which host can transmit at any given time. A "token" is generated on the network, and this token is passed from host to host until it reaches a station that has information to transmit. Once the station has the token, it transmits as needed (see Figure 4-2). A host is allowed to transmit information only when it

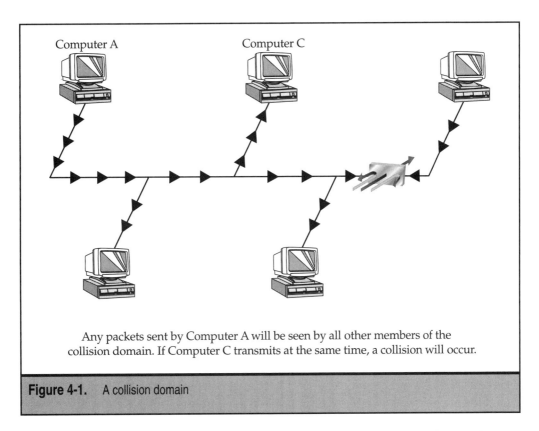

Any packets sent by Computer A will be seen by all other members of the collision domain. If Computer C transmits at the same time, a collision will occur.

Figure 4-1.   A collision domain

has the token. This eliminates collisions; however, the network still bogs down when too many hosts are connected as it takes longer for a host to receive the token as the network grows larger. For this and a number of other reasons token-ring is not commonly being installed in new networks today; therefore, we focus on Ethernet and its cousins Fast Ethernet and Gigabit Ethernet for the majority of this chapter.

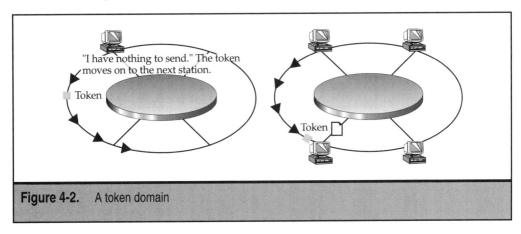

Figure 4-2.   A token domain

Broadcast Domains

The major differentiator between a broadcast domain and a collision domain is the type of traffic associated with each. A collision domain encompasses any and all traffic on the segment, whereas a broadcast domain includes only broadcast traffic (see Figure 4-3). The use of switches in the LAN greatly reduces the size of collision domains; however, the only way to make the broadcast domain smaller is to shrink the size of the network.

Broadcasts are the bane of today's newer switched networks because whereas switching allows for larger segments without collisions, the larger segments produce more broadcast traffic. Although broadcasts are necessary, not all hosts on the network need to receive all broadcasts from all other hosts. When a station receives a broadcast that it does not need, it drops the packet; therefore that message has wasted network bandwidth. Shrinking the size of the broadcast domain therefore is necessary for the sake of efficiency. The size and placement of a given broadcast domain can be manipulated by the use of virtual LANs or VLANs. VLANs allow a broadcast domain to be configured on a per-port or per-protocol basis (see Figure 4-4). This allows network managers to adjust the size and placement of broadcast domains as they see fit.

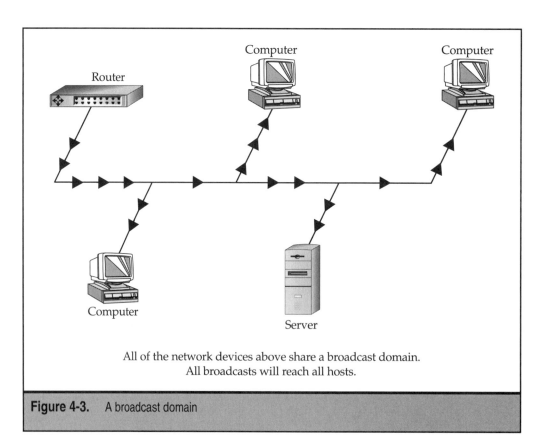

All of the network devices above share a broadcast domain.
All broadcasts will reach all hosts.

Figure 4-3.   A broadcast domain

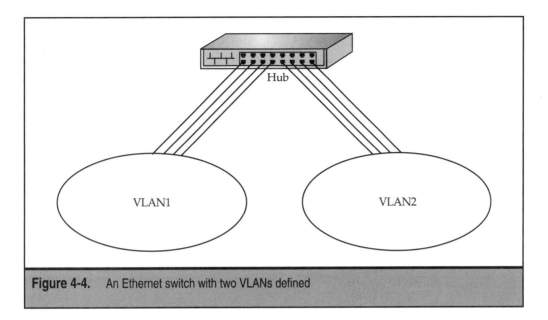

Figure 4-4. An Ethernet switch with two VLANs defined

The Need for Smaller Networks

As the number of users and bandwidth-intensive network applications grow, so too does the need for faster network response time. There are only two ways to increase the speed of the network. The first one is rather obvious: Increase the speed of the network media. For example, upgrade from Ethernet to Fast Ethernet, or from Fast Ethernet to Gigabit Ethernet. The second is less obvious, but often has more of an impact on performance: Segment the network. Smaller networks tend to bring user end stations closer to network resources and therefore increase response time. Smaller networks also reduce the number of collisions and broadcasts present on the wire at any given point.

Network managers are doing two things to speed up their networks: upgrading to newer technology and implementing VLANs. Fast or Gigabit Ethernet is an incredible upgrade from 10Mbps Ethernet, and VLANs work wonders when it comes to network segmentation.

HUBS AND SWITCHES: HOW THEY DIFFER

Switches and hubs both operate at layer 2 of the OSI reference model. Both generally use RJ-45 connectors (similar to phone connectors) and Ethernet cables to connect to hosts. The major difference between the two lies in how they forward traffic (see Figure 4-5). When a hub receives a packet on an interface, it immediately forwards it out all other interfaces. In contrast, when a switch receives a packet on an interface it looks into the packet for the destination MAC address and forwards the packet only to the interface that knows about the destination MAC address. This not only conserves bandwidth, but also virtually eliminates collisions.

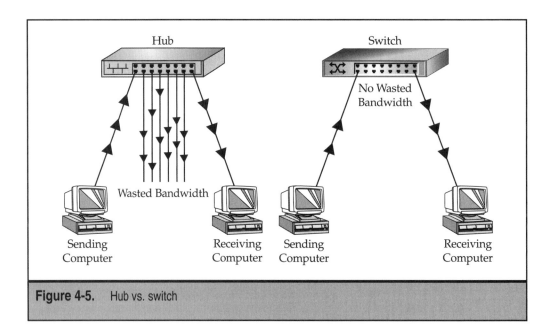

Figure 4-5.   Hub vs. switch

Design Issues

When it comes to layer 2 network design the choice of whether to use hubs or switches often is the first decision that must be made. Although switches generally are better for bandwidth-intensive applications, there are some situations in which they actually can forward data more slowly than hubs. Because a hub doesn't have to do any "thinking" about where to forward a packet (it simply floods information out all interfaces except the one it came in on), it is able to move data with less *latency*. (Latency is the period of time that a packet is held by a network device before it is forwarded.)

In a network with few hosts or little traffic, a hub often is a better solution than a switch; however, as more hosts are added and more traffic is placed on a hub-based network, response times will slow down. In a large network in which many layer 2 devices must be cascaded, a switch almost always outperforms a hub.

NOTE: Connecting two layer 2 devices together through a cross-over cable is known as *cascading*. A *cross-over cable* is similar to a regular network cable except the send and receive pairs have been reversed.

There are a few other things to consider when evaluating whether to use hubs or switches in the network:

▼ **Bandwidth** How much is needed? Are there many graphical applications that will run over the network? How many users will be active on this segment at any given time? Many bandwidth-intensive applications or a high number of users will require the use of switches for adequate network performance.

■ **Future growth** How fast will the network need to grow to support the requirements of the organization? If the organization is growing quickly, the investment in switching technology will save money in the long run.

▲ **Cost** Switches cost more than hubs. If the network does not require a large amount of available bandwidth and does not foresee much growth in the future, the choice is easy: Go with hubs. However, if the network is small but experiencing steady growth in both users and applications, the choice is more difficult.

The technically inclined often overlook price considerations. It's a wise network engineer who is able to make product recommendations based on not only a performance evaluation, but price versus performance criteria. For example, if a given switch outperforms the competition in all respects by 5%, is it the correct switch to buy? Not always. If the top performing switch costs 25% more than the nearest competitor, is the extra 5% performance boost worth what could cost an additional few hundred, or even a few thousand, dollars? It might be, but it depends upon the network and its associated applications.

It is important to work with the business leaders who make the final purchase decision when evaluating network hardware. An engineer must understand what is important to those in charge to properly satisfy their needs. Sometimes in our quest for the most efficiency (in essence, speed) we forget that we are here to support the users of the network. Most users really don't care if it takes them 15 seconds to transfer a file rather than 12.

The bottom line? Price often is the most important consideration when designing networks.

THE NORTEL FRAME SWITCHING PRODUCT LINE

This book is not an all-encompassing guide to every Nortel Networks product. If it were it would be four times its current length. With that in mind, we will cover only the most commonly installed Nortel switching products. The two product lines we will cover are

▼ BayStack Switching

▲ Passport 1000/8000 Series Layers 2–3 Switching

BayStack Switching

We will spend the bulk of our time in this section covering the BayStack 303-304 models, and the 350-450 10/100/1000 series. The BayStack name comes from the original company that developed the product line, Bay Networks. Nortel acquired Bay Networks in

1998 and changed the name of the combined companies to Nortel Networks. For the sake of simplicity we will refer to Nortel Networks as Nortel from time to time.

BayStack 303-304

The 303 and 304 series switches have been around longer than any of the other switches we cover in this chapter. They have proven to be very stable in their long life; they are also the lowest speed switches we will discuss.

BayStack 303 Specifications   The BayStack 303 contains the following specifications:

▼ 24 10Mbps 10Base-TX RJ-45 Ethernet ports

■ 1 10/100Mbps autonegotiating (An autonegotiating switch is able to sense and adjust its speed accordingly whether the device attached to a port is capable of 10 or 100Mbps speeds) 100Base-TX Ethernet port

■ One Media Dependent Adapter (MDA) supporting either a single autonegotiating 10/100Base-TX or 100Base-FX port

■ 1 DB-9 console port for console-based management

▲ 476,192 64-byte packets per second (pps) throughput

BayStack 304 Specifications   The following are the BayStack 304 specifications:

▼ 12 10Mbps 10Base-TX RJ-45 Ethernet ports

■ 1 10/100Mbps autonegotiating 100Base-TX Ethernet port

■ One MDA supporting either a single autonegotiating 10/100Base-TX or 100Base-FX port

▲ 1 DB-9 Console port for console-based management

The 10/100 autonegotiating switch port can be used to provide a high-bandwidth connection to a server in a small network or an uplink to a core switch in a larger network.

BayStack 303/304 Features   Both the BayStack 303 and 304 share the following feature set:

▼ A menu-driven user interface available through console connection or Telnet. The switch supports two simultaneous Telnet sessions.

■ A Web-based management interface available to Netscape 3.0 or higher and Microsoft Internet Explorer 4.0 or higher users.

■ Simple Network Management Protocol (SNMP) manageability. We cover SNMP in more detail in Chapter 8.

■ Up to eight port-based VLANs.

■ Multiple language support.

■ Support for the Optivity network management platform.

- Port mirroring, which allows traffic from one port to be "mirrored" or transmitted on another port for trouble-shooting purposes.

- Up to eight specific destination address filters.

▲ 387,206 64-byte pps throughput.

BayStack 303/304 Initial Configuration   To access the switch for initial configuration, an RS-232 cable with a female DB-9 connector will need to be attached to the console port on the switch and the serial port on the PC. The terminal emulation program (HyperTerminal on a Windows-based PC) will require the following settings:

▼ VT100 terminal

- 9600 baud

- No parity

- 8 bits

- 1 stop bit

- Windows terminal emulator = no

▲ Terminal preferences = function, arrow, and control keys active

After connecting the switch and PC through the console cable, power up the switch by plugging it into a power source. It is important to have your console cable connected before you turn the switch on so that you are able to watch the boot process. After connecting to the switch for the first time, a language will have to be selected (see Figure 4-6).

```
1 ---English
2 ---French/Francais
3 ---German/Deutsche
4 ---Japanese
5 ---Spanish/Espanol
6 ---Italian/Italiano
7 ---Chinese

Current Selection:

Please enter number for selection:
```

Figure 4-6.   BayStack 303/304 Language Selection screen

Simply select the number that corresponds to the desired language. Once this is done the main menu will be displayed (see Figure 4-7).

The BayStack 303/304 switch is designed to work "out of the box." That is, it can be placed into the network without configuration and will function as a member of a single VLAN. To fully realize the management potential of the switch, however, a few parameters must be set using the console connection; they are IP address, subnet mask, and gateway address. They can be set by entering the following commands from the main menu:

1. Select System Configuration from the main menu by typing 2.

2. Select Switch Network Configuration by typing 1 (see Figure 4-8).

3. Type 1 to refresh the screen and display the current IP address.

4. Enter the IP address you have chosen for the switch and press a key to continue.

5. Type 2 to refresh the screen and display the current subnet mask.

6. Enter the subnet mask appropriate to your network and press a key to continue.

7. Type 3 to refresh the screen and display the current gateway address.

8. Enter the gateway address for your network and press a key to continue.

```
*********************************************************************************
                    Bay Networks BayStack 303 Ethernet Switch

IP Address:         [127.0.0.2]
Mac Address:        [00:00:81:12:12:12]
Software Version:   [2.0]
System Up Time:     [0d:00h:01m:30s]
Switch Status:      [Switching]


*********************************************************************************

                                  Main Menu

1 -- System Information
2 -- System Configuration
3 -- Troubleshooting
4 -- Access Control
5 -- System Reset/Upgrade
6 -- Exit


Enter Command  ([ESC] -Previous Menu [Space] -Refresh Screen)
```

Figure 4-7.   BayStack 303 main menu

```
************************************************************************************
                    Bay Networks BayStack 303 Ethernet Switch

IP Address:           [127.0.0.2]
Mac Address:          [00:00:81:12:12:12]
Software Version:     [2.0]
System Up Time:       [0d:00h:01m:30s]
Switch Status:        [Switching]


************************************************************************************
                        Switch Network Configuration

1 -- IP Address
2 -- IP Subnet Mask Address
3 -- Default Gateway Address
4 -- Spanning Tree Protocol (enable/disable)



Enter Command  ([ESC] -Previous Menu [Space] -Refresh Screen)
```

Figure 4-8.   BayStack 303 IP configuration screen

Before disconnecting from the switch it is advisable to configure Telnet and/or Web access and passwords from the Access Control menu. The Access Control menu is accessed through selection 4 from the Main Menu.

The BayStack 350-450 10/100/1000 Switches

The BayStack 350 comes in two flavors. The first offers only port-based VLANs and will be covered first. The second is similar in almost all aspects to the BayStack 450 (the 350 cannot utilize a cascade cable) and is discussed in the 450 section, later in this chapter.

The Four Versions of the Traditional 350   The 350 comes in four different flavors, each differing in port number and/or type:

▼   The Model 350F-HD contains 24 autonegotiating 10/100Base-TX ports and 2 100Base-FX fiber ports.

■   The Model 350F contains 12 autonegotiating 10/100Base-TX ports and 2 100Base-FX fiber ports.

■   The model 350T-HD contains 24 autonegotiating 10/100Base-TX ports.

▲   The model 350T-HD contains 16 autonegotiating 10/100Base-TX ports.

BayStack 350 Features   The BayStack 350 boasts an impressive feature set. These features are listed here:

▼ 1.6 million 64-byte packets per second (pps) throughput.

■ Port mirroring, which allows traffic from one port to be "mirrored" or transmitted on another port for troubleshooting purposes.

■ Port-based VLANs allow the switch to be divided into two or more logical segments. For example, the switch basically becomes two 8-port switches instead of one 16-port switch.

■ RMON (Remote Monitoring), the four groups of which are shown in the following. RMON is covered in detail in Chapter 8.

■ Statistics

■ History

■ Alarms

■ Events

■ SNMP (Optivity) and Telnet management. Up to four simultaneous Telnet sessions can be active at one time. Passwords can be set for security purposes.

▲ MLT (MultiLink Trunking) enables multiple ports to be grouped together for greater bandwidth. For example, two 100Mbps ports could be put into an MLT group for a total of 200Mbps total throughput. This is very useful for connections from an edge switch back to the network core.

BayStack 350/450 10/100/1000   The BayStack 350/450 10/100/1000 series is a higher performance version of the basic BayStack 350. With almost double the throughput, the ability to stack up to eight units (450 only) together to form one logical switch, and greater flexibility when it comes to VLANs, the BayStack 350/450 10/100/1000 switches have become one of Nortel's top sellers.

BayStack 350/450 10/100/1000 Features   The BayStack 350/450 10/100/1000 switches contain the following features:

▼ Up to 3 million 64-byte packets per second (pps) throughput.

■ Full line speed switching using a 2.56 Gigabit-per-second switch fabric.

■ Fail-safe stacking (450 only) allows up to eight switches to be managed as one logical switch. Requires one cascade module per switch and appropriate cascade cables.

■ SNMP management, or Simple Network Management Protocol.

■ One MDA slot supporting multiple media types including Gigabit Ethernet. It is from this feature that the BayStack 350/450 10/100/1000 gets the "1000" in its name. The addition of the Gigabit module allows the BayStack series to scale to the size and speed requirements of today's growing networks.

- Multiple VLAN types, including VLAN Tagging (802.1Q), which allows two or more VLANs defined on one switch to communicate with the same VLANs on yet another switch using only one trunk connection.

  Protocol-based VLANs are automatically set up based upon the protocol that the host attached to a port is utilizing for network communication. This keeps IP and IPX traffic, for example, separate from each other on the network.

- IGMP Snooping enables a switch to define which ports will receive IGMP multicast streams. IGMP multicasts are sent out to an entire broadcast domain. By "snooping" into certain packets, the switch is aware of which ports have attached hosts that are interested in the multicast. Switches that are able to perform IGMP snooping are able to filter a significant amount of traffic before it reaches hosts that are uninterested in the transmission.

- MLT or MultiLink Trunking, supporting

  - Switch-to-switch trunks

  - Switch-to-server trunks

  - Port mirroring

    Port-based allows all traffic from one port to be "mirrored" or transmitted from another port for troubleshooting purposes.

    MAC address–based allows "conversations" between two MAC addresses to be transmitted from a port that neither MAC is connected to for troubleshooting purposes.

- RMON (Remote Monitoring) has four groups:

  - Statistics

  - History

  - Alarms

  - Events

- Traffic prioritization (802.1p) prioritizes traffic based on priority queuing as defined by the 802.1p specification.

BayStack 350/450 10/100/1000 Initial Configuration   The first steps for configuring the BayStack 350/450 10/100/1000 switch are identical to the instructions for configuring the BayStack 303/304. You will need the same console cable and terminal emulation settings. The BS (BayStack) 350/450 is similar to the BS 303/304 in that it also is designed to function out of the box (without configuration). If you want a very high-performance desktop or edge switch that functions in only one VLAN and is not managed, an out-of-the-box configuration will work fine. However, this kind of configuration does not make use of the features that the BS 350/450 family is known for. In this section we will cover a basic installation of the BayStack 450.

The first step in configuring the BS 350/450 is adding an IP address for management purposes:

1. Connect the console cable per the instructions given in the BS 303/304 section and then power up the switch. You will see a screen similar to Figure 4-9. Press CTRL+Y to access the main menu.

2. Press the I key on the keyboard or select IP Configuration from the menu (Figure 4-10).

3. Type the IP address you have chosen for the new switch in the In-Band Switch IP Address field and then press ENTER (see Figure 4-11).

4. Type the subnet mask for the switch in the In-Band Subnet Mask field and press ENTER.

5. Type the default gateway address for the segment the switch is on in the Default Gateway field and press ENTER.

The switch now has a management IP address and is ready for further configuration via Telnet or console cable. The menu-driven system of the BS 350/450 is easy to follow and understand, making additional configuration simple and efficient.

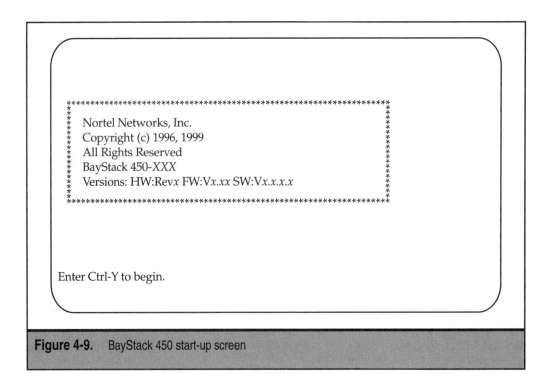

Figure 4-9. BayStack 450 start-up screen

```
                    BayStack 450-24T Main Menu


                    IP Configuration/Setup...
                    SNMP Configuration...
                    System Characteristics...
                    Switch Configuration...
                    Console/Comm Port Configuration...
                    Display Hardware Units...
                    Spanning Tree Configuration....
                    TELNET Configuration...
                    Software Download...
                    Configuration File...
                    Display Event Log...
                    Reset
                    Reset to Default Settings
                    Logout


   Use arrow keys to highlight option, press <Return> or <Enter> to select option.
```

Figure 4-10. BayStack 450 main menu

```
                        IP Configuration/Setup



             BootP Request Mode:  [ BootP Disabled        ]


                         Configurable      In Use        Last BootP
                         ----------       ----------     ----------
   In-Band Stack IP Address:   [ 0.0.0.0 ]                0.0.0.0
   In-Band Switch IP Address:  [ 0.0.0.0 ]                0.0.0.0
   In-Band Subnet Mask:        [ 0.0.0.0 ]    0.0.0.0     0.0.0.0

   Default Gateway:            [ 0.0.0.0 ]    0.0.0.0     0.0.0.0



   Use space bar to display choices, press <Return> or <Enter> to select choice.
   Press Ctrl-R to return to previous menu. Press Ctrl-C to return to Main Menu.
```

Figure 4-11. BayStack 450 IP configuration screen

Passport 1000/8000 Series Switching (Formerly Accelar)

We have talked in previous sections about the need to segment networks into ever smaller collision and broadcast domains. With high-speed switching we are able to create collision domains that consist of only one host. That solves half of the segmentation problem, but traditional switching does not address broadcast-related issues. The only way to reduce the size of a broadcast domain is to reduce the size of the network. VLANs were created to address this issue; however, when a packet needs to cross multiple VLANs to reach its destination, it must be routed. Routing is inherently slower than switching due to the fact that in order to make a routing decision the router must look further into the packet than a switch does. Remember: A switch makes decisions based on layer 2 (MAC address) information. On the other hand, a router forwards packets based on layer 3 data (an IP address, for example). Switches also are able to use hardware to come to forwarding decisions, whereas routing generally is performed in software—yet another reason switching is faster.

The bottleneck created in switched networks when traffic must pass through multiple VLANs (and therefore be routed) has been addressed by a newer technology called layer 3 switching. This new technology is aimed at creating switches that are layer 3 protocol-aware, but are able to avoid the slowdowns inherent to routing.

The Passport 1000 and 8000 series of layer 3 switches were developed to solve the problems associated with communication over multiple VLANs. In this section we will discuss the architecture of the Passport series as well as basic configuration.

The Passport 1000 Series Switches

The PP1000 series is available in many hardware configurations. The individual boxes look a bit different but are configured using the same command-line interface or Device Manager.

Device Manager is a windows-based program used to configure Passport switches. It provides a GUI (graphical user interface) for the switch that makes configuration very straightforward. The different Passport models are discussed here.

Passport 1200   The PP1200 is housed in an 8-slot chassis. Slots 5 and 6 are reserved for management modules called the Silicon Switch Fabric (SSF). Only one module is active at any given time; the other provides redundancy. The SSF is the "brain" of the switch housing the CPU, memory, and switching fabric. The SSF not only controls the actual switching fabric, but also the line cards that connect to other switches or directly to hosts. With two slots dedicated to switch management, only six are left for I/O modules. The modules available are outlined here:

XLR1216TX-B	16-port 10/100Base-TX
XLR1216TF-B	14-port 10/100Base-TX and 2 port 100Base-FX
XLR1216FX-B	16-port 10/100Base-FX
XLR1208FX-B	8-port 10Base-FX

XLR1208FL-B   8-port 10Base-FL

XLR1202SX-B   2-Port 1000Base-SX

XLR1202SR-B   2-Port 1000Base-SR with LinkSafe connection

After adding two SSFs the remaining six slots can be populated with any combination of the preceding modules. The PP1200 has a backplane capacity of 7 Gigabits per second and a packet forwarding rate of 7 million packets per second. The PP1200 comes with dual redundant power supplies. In the event that one power supply should fail, the other will take over supplying power to the switch. The power supplies are hot-swappable, so one power supply can be removed or replaced without powering down the whole unit. This switch was designed for the network core due to its relatively high port density and management redundancy.

Passport 1250

The PP1250 is a 4-slot chassis–based switch. One slot is devoted to the SSF leaving only three slots available for line cards. The PP1250 supports the same line cards as the PP1200 and is designed for areas of the network where high throughput is required but port density is less important. The PP1250 has a backplane capacity of 3.5 Gigabits per second and a packet-forwarding rate of 5 million packets per second.

Passport 1100

The PP1100 differs from the PP1200 and PP1250 in that it is not chassis based. However, it is semi-modular with a fixed configuration of 16 10/100Base-TX ports and two expansion slots. The modules available to populate the expansion slots are as follows:

XLR1108TX-B   8-port 10/100Base-TX

XLR1108FX-B   8-port 10/100Base-FX

XLR1104FX-B   4-port 100Base-FX

XLR1102XD-B   2-port Gigabit module (long haul)

XLR1102SX-B   2-port 1000Base-SX

XLR1102SR-B   2-port 1000Base-SR with LinkSafe connection

XLR1101SX-B   1-port 1000Base-SX

The PP1100 has a backplane capacity of 4.5 Gigabits per second and a packet forwarding rate of 6.5 million packets per second. The switch also has dual redundant power supplies that are not field replaceable.

Passport 1150

The PP1150 also is semi-modular with a fixed configuration of four 1000Base-SX ports and two expansion slots. The PP1150 supports the same modules as the PP1100. The PP1100 has a backplane capacity of 7 Gigabits per second and a packet-forwarding rate of 7 million packets per second. The switch also has dual redundant power supplies that are not field replaceable.

Passport 1050

The PP1050 has a fixed configuration of 12 10/100Base-TX ports and a single 1000Base-SX port. The PP1100 has a backplane capacity of 2.2 Gigabits per second and a packet for-warding rate of 3.3 million packets per second.

Passport 1051

The PP1051 adds LinkSafe redundancy to its gigabit port to differentiate itself from the PP1050. In all other respects, the PP1050 and 1051 are identical.

Passport 1000 Series Initial Configuration

In this section we will create a basic layer 2 configuration for a PP1000 series switch. Due to the similarities between the PP1000 and PP8000 configuration tools, we will save layer 3 examples for the Passport 8600 section.

Logging On to the System   To access the switch for initial configuration, an RS-232 cable with a female DB-9 connector will need to be attached to the console port on the switch and the se-rial port on the PC. The terminal emulation program will require the following settings:

▼   VT100 Terminal

■   9600 baud

■   No parity

■   Eight bits

▲   One stop bit

Once the configuration terminal is ready, simply power up the switch. You will see output similar to this:

```
*******************************
 * Bay Networks,Inc.           *
 * Copyright (c) 1996-1998      *
 * All Rights Reserved          *
 * Passport 1100                *
 * Software Release 1.x.x       *
 *******************************
```

```
Login: rw

Password: **

Passport-1200#
```

At the login prompt enter **rw**; type the same thing for the password. Both the 1000 and 8600 series Passport switches support five layers of security; they are listed in Table 4-1.

Configuration   Configuring the Passport as a layer 2 switch consists of the following steps:

1. Confirm that all ports are in the default VLAN.
2. Assign an IP address to the default VLAN.
3. Specify a default gateway address or default route.

Access Level	Description	Default Login	Default Password
Read-only	Allows viewing configuration and status information.	ro	ro
Layer 2 (read-write)	Allows viewing and changing configuration and status information for layer 2 functions.	l2	l2
Layer 3 (read-write)	Allows viewing and changing configuration and status information for layer 2 and layer 3 functions.	l3	l3
Read-write	Allows viewing and changing configuration and status information across the switch.	rw	rw
Read-write-all	Allows all the rights of read-write access and the ability to change passwords.	rwa	rwa

Table 4-1.   Passport 1200 Access Levels

4. To configure the Passport as a layer 2 switch, confirm that all ports are in the default VLAN using the command:

```
Passport-1200#  show vlan info
```

5. The display will show the VlanId (1) and list the port members.

6. To assign an IP address to the default VLAN, enter

```
Accelar-1200# config vlan 1 ip create <ipaddr/mask>
```

Where 1 is the VLAN ID of the default VLAN and <ipaddr/mask> is the IP address/subnet mask you are assigning it. For example,

```
Accelar-1200# config vlan 1 ip create 10.10.10.1/24
```

7. Specify a default gateway address/default route.

When configuring IP on most layer 2 switches, you need to specify the IP address of the device and the IP address of the default gateway. Because the Passport switch is a routing switch, adding a default route is equivalent to specifying a default gateway in a layer 2–only switch.

Use the following command to specify the default route:

```
config ip static-route create <ipaddr/mask> next-hop <value> cost <value>
```

For example,

```
Passport-1200#  config ip static-route create 0.0.0.0/0 next-hop 10.10.10.1 cost 1
```

Where 0.0.0.0 is the default route and 10.10.10.1 is the IP address of the next hop router.

8. Disable routing with the command:

```
Passport-1200#
config ip forwarding disable
```

9. To save the configuration, enter

```
Passport-1200#  save
```

The Passport now has an IP address and is ready to be managed by the CLI (Command Line Interface) or Device Manager. A copy of Device Manager on CD-ROM should be included with any Passport purchase.

The Passport 8000 Series

The Passport 8000 series switches are Nortel's flagship switching product. With a backplane capacity of 50 gigabits per second on the PP8100 and maximum 256 gigabits per second on the PP8600, the Passport 8000 series is far and away the highest performing switch in the marketplace today. The PP8000 series consists of two switches designed for different functions within the network. The Passport 8600 functions as a layer 2 or 3 switch and is positioned for network core applications, whereas the Passport 8100 functions only as a layer 2 switch and is designed for edge switching. User workstations and printers are considered to be "edge" devices and as such would be connected to the PP8100.

In this next section we cover the features of the different chassis and I/O modules available for the PP8000 series. We also discuss switch configuration and design considerations.

Common Features

The PP8100 and PP8600 share many common features. This reduces cost by allowing network managers to keep fewer spare parts on hand. We cover the features that the two platforms have in common first and then move on to individual switch specifications.

Passport Chassis

Both the PP8100 and PP8600 are chassis-based switches. There are two chassis form factors available: the Passport 8010 and Passport 8006. (The Passport 8003 will be available soon.) The PP8010 provides ten slots, whereas the PP8006 provides only six. The Passport 8000 series chassis supports redundant power supplies. Both AC and DC power supplies are available, and they can be combined in the same chassis. A Passport 8010 chassis with more than six installed modules requires a minimum of two power supplies for a non-redundant configuration. A redundant configuration for such a chassis requires three power supplies. A Passport 8006 requires only two power supplies for redundancy. In a chassis with a non-redundant power supply configuration, if one power supply fails, the system loses power and network connectivity.

Management Interfaces

Both the PP8100 and PP8600 can be managed through the same CLI as of software version 2.0. Device Manager also is available for both platforms.

The Passport 8100

The PP 8100 is designed for situations in which high port density as well as high-speed connections to the network core are needed. The Passport 8100 modules include a switch management module and input/output (I/O) modules. For CPU system redundancy two management modules may be installed. The I/O modules support different types of Ethernet interfaces with different speeds, port counts, and media types. The following Passport 8100 modules are available:

▼ **PP 8190SM**—Management module for the chassis

■ **PP 8132TX**—32-port 10/100Base-TX I/O module, with an MDA slot for optional Media Dependant Adaptors

■ **PP 8148TX**—48-port 10/100Base-TX I/O module

▲ **PP 8108GBIC**—1000Mbps Ethernet I/O module with eight bays for installing gigabit interface converters (GBICs)

Slots 5 and 6 in the PP8010 chassis are reserved for PP 8190SMs; therefore, only eight slots are available for I/O modules. Any of the modules can be removed and replaced while the system is running. This ensures maximum uptime in a high availability environment.

Passport 8190SM   The Passport 8190SM Switch Management Module provides central-ized management capabilities for the Passport 8010 and 8006 chassis. Image, configura-tion, and log files are maintained on the flash memory (onboard and PCMCIA) of this module. The PP 8190SM also provides out-of-band management using the Ethernet port on the module.

Redundancy is achieved by placing a Passport 8190SM module into slots 5 and 6 of the chassis. When running normally, the second module is in standby mode. If the pri-mary PP 8190SM fails, the secondary module will initialize and the switch will continue to function. When the secondary PP 8190SM module completes initialization, it resets the switch. The PP 8190SM in slot 5 is the default primary management module; the module in slot six is in standby mode. Physical features on the front panel of the Passport 8190SM module include a management port, a DCE/DTE switch for the console port, a console port, a modem port, a reset button, a PCMCIA card slot, and status LEDs.

Passport 8132TX   The PP 8132TX module is a single-slot I/O module for the Passport 8010 or Passport 8006 chassis. The module contains 32 10/100Base-TX autosensing switched ports. An expansion slot allows you to install an MDA to provide additional port types. Additional port types that can be installed include 10/100Base-T, 100Base-FX, and Gigabit Ethernet ports. If a Passport 8190SM is not present, this module will provide switch man-agement using 1.0 or 1.1 code.

Passport 8148TX   The PP 8148TX module is a single-slot I/O module for the Passport 8010 or Passport 8006 chassis. The module contains 48 10/100Base-TX autosensing switched ports.

Passport 8108GBIC   The Passport 8108GBIC I/O module provides eight slots for install-ing any of four types of gigabit interface converters. These fiber ports allow server attach-ments, or inter-switch links to be made. Only four GBICs are currently available:

▼   1000Base-SX

■   1000Base-LX

■   1000Base-XD

▲   1000Base-ZX

Initial Configuration   The PP8100 will function as a layer 2 switch immediately after com-pleting its boot cycle. Without a management IP address and default gateway, however, it will not be accessible for further configuration.

The configuration of the PP8100 is very similar to the PP1000 series configuration. Be-cause of a few minor differences, instructions for a sample layer 2 configuration have been included here. Note that the PP8100 has one less security option at login; this is be-cause the PP8100 does not have layer 3 functionality.

The Boot Process   When you turn on the power supplies, the switch begins its automatic boot process. The switch first tries to boot from the PCMCIA card, then from the internal flash memory, and finally over the network. If a terminal is connected to the console port, you can watch the system messages as the switch goes through its boot sequence. This boot order can be modified using the boot monitor command-line interface. While the Passport 8190SM module is booting, the I/O modules boot using their local image files, which check to see if a Passport 8190SM is installed in the chassis. When the PP 8190SM module finishes its boot process, the I/O modules send a load request. The PP 8190SM then sends the most current version of the switch code to the I/O modules. The I/O modules then reboot using the newly loaded image. The entire process can take up to one minute.

Logging On to the System   In order to access the switch for initial configuration a cable and connector will be needed to match the Passport switch male's DTE connector (DB-9), with the DCE/DTE switch on the chassis set to DTE. The terminal emulation program will require the following settings:

▼   9,600 baud

■   No parity

■   Eight bits

■   One stop bit

▲   No flow control

Once the configuration terminal is ready, simply power up the switch. You will see output similar to this:

```
Login: rw
Password: **
Passport-8010#
```

At the login prompt enter **rw** and type the same thing for the password. The 8000 series Passport switch supports four layers of security; they are listed in Table 4-2.

Access Level	Description	Default Login	Default Password
Read-only	Allows viewing configuration and status information.	ro	ro
Layer 2 (read/write)	Allows viewing and changing configuration and status information for layer 2 functions.	l2	l2

Table 4-2.   Passport 8100 Access Levels

Access Level	Description	Default Login	Default Password
Read/write	Allows viewing and changing configuration and status information across the switch.	rw	rw
Read/write-all	Allows all the rights of read/write access and the ability to change passwords.	rwa	rwa

Table 4-2. Passport 8100 Access Levels *(continued)*

Configuration   Configuring the Passport switch as a layer 2 switch consists of the following steps:

1. Confirm that all ports are in the default VLAN.
2. Assign an IP address to the default VLAN.
3. Specify a default gateway address or default route.
4. Confirm that all ports are in the default VLAN using this command:

   ```
   Passport-8010# show vlan info ports
   ```

   The display will show the VlanId (1) and list the port members.
5. To assign an IP address for management, use this command:

   ```
   Passport-8010# config bootconfig net mgmt ip <ipaddr/mask>
   ```

   where <ipaddr/mask> is the IP address/subnet mask that is being assigned (for example, 10.10.10.1/24).
6. Specify a default gateway address/default route.

   When configuring IP on most layer 2 switches, you need to specify the IP address of the device and the IP address of the default gateway.

   Use the following run-time CLI command to specify the default route:

   ```
   Passport-8010# config bootconfig net mgmt route net 0.0.0.0 <ipaddr>
   ```

   In each of these commands, ipaddr specifies the IP address of the default gateway.

7. To save the configuration, enter

```
Passport-8010# save config
```

The PP8100 is now ready be configured further using the command line or Device Manager. See the Nortel Networks PDF titled "Reference for the Passport 8000 Series Command Line Interface Switching Operations" for more advanced configuration instructions. The PDF is available from the Nortel Networks Web site (http://support.baynetworks.com/library/tpubs/pdf/Passport/207308B.pdf).

Instructions for configuring the Passport 8100 using Device Manager are available at http://support.baynetworks.com/library/tpubs/pdf/Passport/207414B.pdf.

The Passport 8600

The PP 8600 is designed for high-speed network core switching. One switch fabric module is required for each Passport 8600 switch; for CPU system redundancy and double switch fabric capacity, two switch fabric modules can be installed. The I/O modules support different types of Ethernet interfaces with different speeds, port counts, and media types. The following Passport 8600 modules are available:

▼ PP 8690SM—Switching fabric module for the chassis

■ PP 8648TX—48-port 10/100Base-TX I/O module

■ PP 86124TX—24-port 100Base-FX I/O module

■ PP 8608GBIC—1000Mbps Ethernet I/O module with eight bays for gigabit interface converters (GBICs)

▲ PP 8608SX—8-Port 1000Base-SX Ethernet I/O module

Like the PP8100, slots 5 and 6 in the PP8010 chassis are reserved for the PP 8690SF; therefore, only eight slots are available for I/O modules. All modules in the Passport 8600 are hot-swappable. The ability to change out failed modules without resetting the equipment has become a requirement in today's data centers because of the sheer volume of data being transmitted and the high cost of downtime.

Passport 8690SF   The Passport 8690SF Switch Fabric Module is the heart of the Passport 8600 switch. Unlike the PP8100, the Passport 8600 will not function without at least one management module. The Passport 8690SF module contains the core switching fabric, a CPU subsystem, and a real-time clock. The core switching fabric is used to switch all traffic through the Passport 8600 modules. The CPU subsystem manages the switching fabric and the other I/O modules. Redundancy is achieved by placing a Passport 8690SF module into slots 5 and 6 of the chassis. When running normally, the second module is in standby mode. If the active CPU fails, the standby CPU assumes the management functions for the switch within one second. The module then must relearn all routing and VLAN information for the switch. Both the primary and secondary switch fabrics are used for passing traffic; only the CPU functions are in standby mode in the secondary switch. The PP 8690SM in slot 5 is the default primary management module; the module in slot six is in standby mode.

Physical features on the front panel of the Passport 8190SM module include an Ethernet management port, a DCE/DTE switch for the console port, a console port, a modem port, a reset button, a PCMCIA card slot, and status LEDs.

Passport 8648TX   The PP 8648TX module is a single-slot I/O module for the Passport 8010 or Passport 8006 chassis. The module contains 48 10/100Base-TX autosensing switched ports.

Passport 8624FX   The PP8624FX module is a single-slot I/O module for the Passport 8010 or Passport 8006 chassis. The module contains 24 100Base-FX ports for long-distance connections to edge switches or remote servers.

Passport 8608SX   The PP8624FX module is a single-slot I/O module for the Passport 8010 or Passport 8006 chassis. The module contains 8 100Base-SX ports providing functionality similar to the PP 8624FX using different fiber connectors.

Passport 8608GBIC   The Passport 8108GBIC I/O module provides eight slots for installing any of four types of gigabit interface converters. These fiber ports allow server attachments, or inter-switch links to be made. The ability to mix and match fiber connector types allows for easy integration into existing networks without having to run new fiber. Only four GBICs are currently available:

▼   1000Base-SX

■   1000Base-LX

■   1000Base-XD

▲   1000Base-ZX

Basic Configuration   The PP8600 is one of the most robust and flexible layer 3 switches ever made. As such, the configuration options are almost endless. Thus far, we have not covered the basics of how routing works; therefore, we will create only a simple layer 3 configuration as this time.

The sample configuration procedures in this section will allow you to set up the Passport 8600 switch as a

▼   Layer 2–only switch.

▲   Layer 3 switch with a port-based VLAN and a brouter port using RIP (Routing Information Protocol). A *brouter* is a device that functions as both a switch (bridge) and a router.

The Boot Process   The boot process for the PP8600 is almost identical to that of the Passport 8100, the only difference being that the I/O modules do not boot to an internal image first. When you turn on the power supplies, the switch begins its automatic boot process. The switch first tries to boot from the PCMCIA card, then from the internal flash memory, and finally over the network. If a terminal is connected to the console port, you can watch the system messages as the switch goes through its boot sequence. This boot order can be modified using the boot monitor command-line interface.

Layer 2 Configuration Example   The Passport 8600 Series modules provide layer 2 switching as soon as they are installed. The default configuration includes a single VLAN with a VLAN ID of 1 that contains all the ports in the switch. An IP address and default gateway are all that is needed for management of the switch.

Logging On to the System   In order to access the switch for initial configuration, a cable and connector will be needed to match the Passport switch male DTE connector (DB-9) with the DCE/DTE switch on the chassis set to DTE. The terminal emulation program will require the following settings:

▼   9,600 baud

■   No parity

■   Eight bits

■   One stop bit

▲   No flow control

Once the configuration terminal is ready, simply power up the switch. You will see output similar to the following:

```
Login: rw
Password: **
Passport-8600#
```

At the login prompt enter **rw** and type the same thing for the password. The 8600 series Passport switch supports five layers of security; they are listed in Table 4-3.

Access Level	Description	Default Login	Default Password
Read-only	Allows viewing configuration and status information.	ro	ro
Layer 2 (read/write)	Allows viewing and changing configuration and status information for layer 2 functions.	l2	l2
Layer 3 (read/write)	Allows viewing and changing configuration and status information for layer 2 and layer 3 functions.	l3	l3

Table 4-3.   Passport 8600 Access Levels

Access Level	Description	Default Login	Default Password
Read/write	Allows viewing and changing configuration and status information across the switch.	rw	rw
Read/write-all	Allows all the rights of read/write access and the ability to change passwords.	rwa	rwa

Table 4-3.   Passport 8600 Access Levels *(continued)*

Layer 2 Configuration Example   The Passport 8600 Series modules provide layer 2 switching as soon as they are installed. The default configuration includes a single VLAN with a VLAN ID of 1 that contains all the ports in the switch. An IP address and default gateway is all that is needed for management of the switch. Configuring the Passport as a layer 2–only switch consists of the following steps:

1. Confirm that all ports are in the default VLAN.
2. Assign an IP address to the default VLAN.
3. Specify a default gateway address or default route.
4. To configure the Passport as a layer 2 switch, confirm that all ports are in the default VLAN using this command:

   ```
   Passport-8600#  show vlan info
   ```

   The display will show the VlanId (1) and list the port members.
5. To assign an IP address to the default VLAN, enter

   ```
   Passport-8600#  config vlan 1 ip create <ipaddr/mask>
   ```

   Where 1 is the VLAN ID of the default VLAN and <ipaddr/mask> is the IP address/subnet mask you are assigning it (for example, 10.10.10.1/24).
6. Specify a default gateway address/default route.

   When configuring IP on most layer 2 switches, you need to specify the IP address of the device and the IP address of the default gateway. Because the Passport switch is a routing switch, adding a default route is equivalent to specifying a default gateway in a layer 2–only switch. Use the following command to specify the default route:

```
config ip static-route create <ipaddr/mask> next-hop
<value> cost <value>
```

or

```
config ip static-route create default next-hop <value>
cost <value>
```

For example,

```
Passport-8600# config ip static-route create 0.0.0.0/0
next-hop 10.10.10.1 cost 1
```

or

```
Passport-8600# config ip static-route create default
next-hop 10.10.10.1 cost 1
```

Where 0.0.0.0 is the default route and 10.0.0.1 is the IP address of the next hop router.

7. Disable routing with this command:

    ```
    Passport-8600# config ip forwarding disable
    ```

8. To save the configuration, enter

    ```
    Passport-8600#  save config
    ```

Layer 3 Configuration Example   This sample configuration will create two VLANs on the switch. VLAN 1 will consist of all ports on the switch except port 1/24, which will be included in VLAN 3000. RIP will be run on both VLANs. Any traffic bound for an alternate VLAN will need to be routed. A logical view of this configuration is shown in Figure 4-12.

To configure the switch as a layer 3 (routing) device with a single, port-based VLAN and a brouter port, follow these steps:

1. Add IP addressing information to VLAN 1.

2. Create an IP address on a VLAN using the following command:

    ```
    config vlan <vid> ip create <ipaddr/mask>
    ```

    Where <vid> is a unique VLAN identifier (numbered 1–4095) and <ipaddr/mask> is the IP address and mask.

    Enter the following command exactly:

    ```
    Passport-8600# config vlan 1 ip create 10.10.10.1/24
    ```

3. Add IP addressing information to port 1/24.

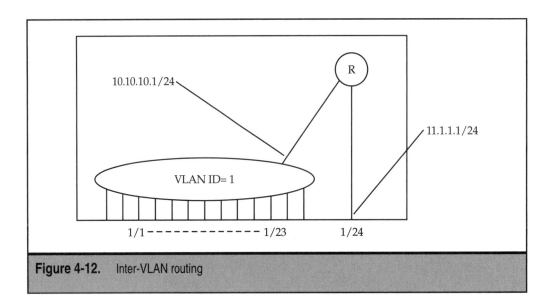

Figure 4-12. Inter-VLAN routing

4. Create a brouter port by assigning an IP address to a port using this command:

   ```
   config ethernet <port> ip create <address/mask> <vid>
   ```

   Where <port> is a physical interface in the form {<slot/port>}, <ipaddr/mask> is the IP address, <vid> and is the VLAN ID.

5. Enter the following command exactly:

   ```
   Passport-8600# config ethernet 1/24 ip create 11.1.1.1/24 3000
   ```

6. Enable RIP routing globally using the command:

   ```
   Passport-8600# config ip rip enable
   ```

7. Configure RIP parameters for each interface.

8. To enable or disable the RIP protocol on a VLAN interface, use the following command:

   ```
   config vlan <vid> ip rip <enable|disable>
   ```

9. To enable or disable the RIP protocol on an Ethernet interface, use the following command:

   ```
   config ethernet <ports> ip rip <enable|disable>
   ```

10. Enter the following command exactly for VLAN 1:

    ```
    Passport-8600# config vlan 1 ip rip enable
    ```

11. Enter the following command exactly for Ethernet 1/24:

```
Passport-8600# config ethernet 1/24 ip rip enable
```

The PP8600 is now ready to be configured further using command line or Device Manager. See the Nortel Networks PDF titled "Reference for the Passport 8000 Series Command Line Interface Switching Operations" for more advanced configuration instructions. The PDF is available from the Nortel Networks Web site at http://support.baynetworks.com/library/tpubs/pdf/Passport/207308B.pdf.

Instructions for configuring the Passport 8000 series using Device Manager are available at http://support.baynetworks.com/library/tpubs/pdf/Passport/207414B.pdf.

CONCLUSION

Nortel Networks has developed a powerful line of switching products that are revolutionizing enterprise networks around the world. With the advent of layer 3 switching technologies, network speed and resiliency have increased exponentially. Nortel's Passport 8000 series switches have been designed from the beginning to support the upcoming 10 Gigabit Ethernet specification. Network managers should feel comfortable basing their infrastructures on such a platform.

CHAPTER 5

Nortel Networks Routers

In Chapter 2 we discussed the Nortel Networks enterprise products, including the router family. In this chapter we discuss the Nortel Networks routers in more detail, such as connectivity options, practical application, and functionality. Because the Nortel Networks routers can be configured to perform bridging (and because bridging is contained in the NNCSS Router Certification exam objectives), we also discuss bridging in this chapter. The Nortel Networks routing family delivers the highest possible performance and reliability in enterprise networking. These routers can meet the demands of even the most demanding networks. Nortel Networks routers can support a large variety of WAN protocols (discussed in Chapter 7) and multiple environments. In this chapter, we discuss the role of a router and different ways to utilize a router. We also discuss the Nortel Networks router family and the various ways of connecting to the Nortel Networks routers for configuration purposes.

ROUTER OVERVIEW

Routers operate at layer 3 of the OSI reference model. A router is a networking device that routes data between networks. See Figure 5-1 for an example of two different LANs connected to each other by two routers. A router determines where to forward its data based on network layer information and routing tables. Routers determine what paths network traffic will follow. These decisions are made by gaining information about the network; utilizing algorithms to choose the best route; and by following rules, or protocols, to route information and communicate with LAN segments. A router has to be capable of recognizing different network layer protocols and should be capable of routing many different protocols. Put simply, the router will take information that is provided in a packet and route the packet from one LAN to another. Routers are capable of communicating with each other to help them determine the best route to take from LAN to LAN.

The Function of a Router

The Nortel Networks routing family connects networks locally and around the world. Because these routers are capable of interpreting many different communications protocols, there is a multitude of configuration options available to the administrator. You can consider a bridge an intelligent repeater; a router then can be considered an intelligent bridge. Routers operate at layer 3 of the OSI reference model, which means they are able to translate information from layer 1, layer 2, or layer 3 to layer 1, 2, or 3. Routers are capable of connecting like and unlike network types. Routers are actual devices or a node within a network. They are configured with and maintain their own network addresses. The other nodes within the network will forward information to the router, which analyzes the data and then forwards it to the appropriate destination. Routers are capable of finding the shortest path to send information to a destination and can make dynamic changes to adjust to bandwidth requirements and network traffic.

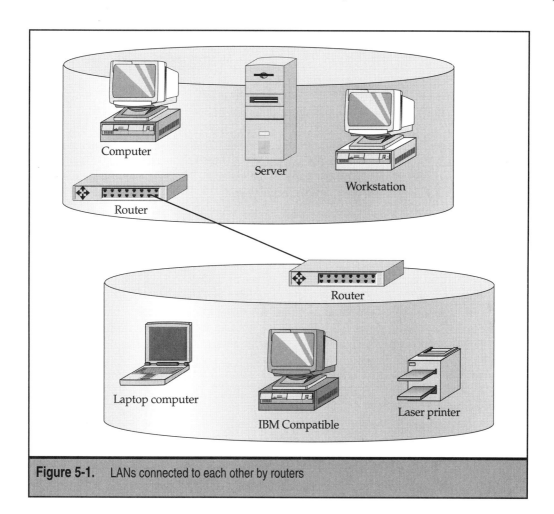

Figure 5-1.   LANs connected to each other by routers

Router Interface Modules (Types)

Because Nortel Networks routers are required to support the demands of many different networks, there are a lot of different interface types that are available. All interfaces types allow for and support dynamic configurations.

LAN interfaces include the following:

▼   **Ethernet/IEEE 802.3**—The ANSI IEEE (pronounced "an-see" "eye-triple E") standard 802.3 includes the rules for configuring Ethernet LANs, determining what physical media types can be used, and how the network should interact. The Ethernet/IEEE 802.3 interface includes an RJ45 connector and a 15-pin AUI connector. Cabling is available to attach these connectors to a variety of other Ethernet media. The following is an example of an Ethernet 100Base-T module for the BN router family.

■ **Fiber Distributed Data Interface (FDDI)**—The ANSI IEEE specification developed for high-performance fiber-optic ringed networks that operate at 100 Mb/s. The FDDI interface includes an RJ11 connector and two media interface connectors. Cabling is available for both Multi-Mode Fiber (MMF) and Single-Mode Fiber (SMF), both of which are 100 Mb/s. The following is an FDDI link module for the BN router family.

▲ **Token-ring/IEEE802.5**—The ANSI IEEE Standard 802.5 is the IEEE standard for token-ring networks and includes the same rules for token-ring as IEEE 802.3 does for Ethernet. The IEEE 802.5 token-ring interface supports shielded twisted-pair cabling. This is an example of a token-ring link module for the BN routing family.

WAN interfaces include the following:

▼ **High-Speed Serial Interface (HSSI)**—HSSI offers the performance of a LAN over a WAN. It is capable of operating at speeds up to 52 Mb/s. As its name suggests, this interface is used to connect the router to a high-speed link such as a T3 line or a fiber transmission system known as Optical Carrier-3 (OC3). The type of interface is serial, and the connection is made through a DSU/CSU.

NOTE: OC-3 can transmit data at a rate of 155 Mb/s.

■ **Integrated Services Digital Network Basic Rate Interface (ISDN BRI)**—ISDN is based on a set of communications standards set up for the digital transmission of data, voice, and video over WANs. BRI is one of the two services offered by ISDN. The ISDN BRI interface connects the router directly to an ISDN BRI line.

■ **ISDN Primary Rate Interface (ISDN PRI)**—ISDN PRI is the other of the two services offered by ISDN. This type of interface connects the router directly to an ISDN PRI line.

■ **Multichannel E1 (MCE1)**—E1 is the European communications interface that transmits data at a rate of 2.048 Mb/s. MCE1 is an interface that allows multiple connections to be transmitted over a leased point-to-point link. This interface connects the router directly to an E1 line.

■ **Multichannel T1 (MCT1)**—T1 is the North American equivalent of E1, operating at a rate of 1.544 Mb/s. MCT1 is an interface that allows multiple connections to be transmitted over a leased point-to-point link. This interface connects directly to a T1 line. The following illustration shows an example of a BN router MCT1 link module.

▲ **Synchronous (sync)**—Synchronous signals are locked in to a specific clocking frequency. The sync interface is used to connect the router to a T1, an E1, or a lower speed line. The connection is made through a terminal adapter, a DSU/CSU, a modem, or an ISDN line. Here you can see examples of quad-sync and sync link modules.

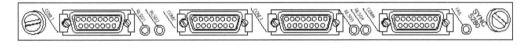

Bridging

A bridge is a device that has the capability to monitor and forward frames to a destination network based on the destination MAC address of the frame. Bridges connect and forward data between LANs. Operating at the data link layer of the OSI reference model, a bridge connects two or more LANs to each other and forwards information only if it is destined to one of its connecting LANs. Nortel Networks supports multiple bridging algorithms, including source route bridging, translational bridging, transparent learning bridging, and source route transparent bridging. The spanning tree algorithm has been included in this section and is supported for both source route and transparent learning bridging.

The four kinds of bridging are

▼ Source route

■ Transparent

■ Translational

▲ Source route transparent

The Spanning Tree Algorithm

The spanning tree algorithm was developed to ensure that a loop-free topology is maintained in networks in which a parallel bridge exists. If spanning trees were not utilized in these networks, it is probable that a bridge would accept and forward frames indefinitely. Figure 5-2 is a simple example of an indefinite loop.

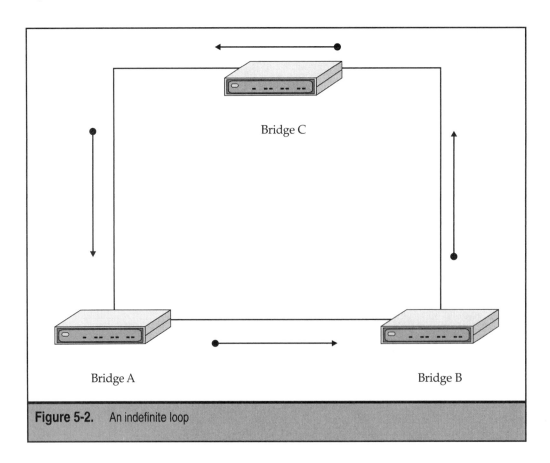

Bridge C

Bridge A

Bridge B

Figure 5-2.   An indefinite loop

The spanning tree algorithm is able to produce a logical "tree" in a network, regardless of how the bridges are arranged. It ensures that there is a single path from one endpoint to another. Spanning tree also has a high degree of fault tolerance in that it provides the network the capability to reconfigure paths when there is a bridge or link failure.

There are several values that must be determined when configuring spanning tree in a network:

▼ A multicast address for all bridges within the network (this is automatically determined by the bridge software)

■ A cost (assigned value) for each port

■ A network identifier for each bridge

■ An identifier for each port

▲ An established priority for each port

Once these values are assigned, the bridges begin forwarding a frame known as a Bridge Protocol Data Unit (BPDU). The BPDU's purpose is to develop a single topology that contains no loops. BPDUs are transmitted from bridge to bridge quickly, so it does not take long for the bridges to determine what paths to use.

During the spanning tree development process, the bridges will elect a root bridge, which will be the bridge that has the lowest priority value. If two or more bridges have the same value, the bridge with the lowest MAC address will be chosen as the root bridge. The bridges then will determine path costs, which is the cost of the path to the root bridge from each of the other bridge's ports. Each LAN then will be assigned with a designated bridge, and each bridge will assign a root port. All other ports will be placed in a "blocking" state. If spanning tree reconfigures, some of the blocking ports will become active. These active ports are considered to be in a forwarding state.

Source Route Bridging (SRB)

IBM developed Source Route Bridging (SRB) as a way to bridge token-ring network traffic between all LANs (see Figure 5-3). Token-ring networks use SRB. SRB connects token-rings and provides software needed to transfer a frame from one ring to another. SRB gets its name because it is assumed that the source node will determine all frame forwarding routes. In SRB, the source node determines the path that a frame will use to reach its destination. The source node also is capable of performing route discovery, which enables it to learn all available paths that connect it to various destinations. Because an SRB bridge does not contain any forwarding tables, all decisions to forward are based on data contained in the frame that is being forwarded.

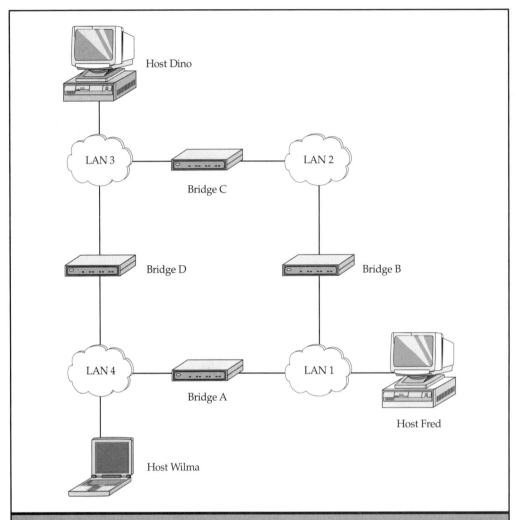

Figure 5-3. Source route bridging involves connecting LANs and bridges

Transparent Bridging

Digital Equipment Corporation (DEC) originally developed transparent bridges in the early 1980s. Transparent bridges are used to transport frames in Ethernet networks. Often, transparent bridges are known as learning bridges because they learn the topology of the networks by analyzing the source MAC address of incoming frames and then build a table that is used to determine a host's accessibility. The transparent bridge then drops or forwards the frames based on information contained in the acquired forwarding tables. Because it uses the spanning tree algorithm, it can ensure a loop-free topology (see Figure 5-4).

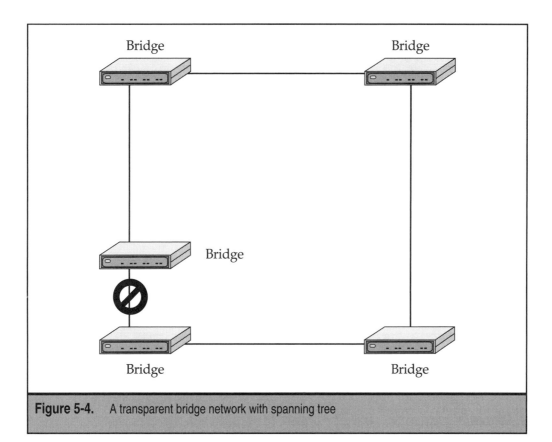

Figure 5-4. A transparent bridge network with spanning tree

Translational Bridging

Translational bridging allows dissimilar LANs to be bridged together. For instance, you can bridge Ethernet to token-ring, or Ethernet to FDDI. Bridging networks that are different requires the bridge to reverse the bit order because the MAC address representation is different on Ethernet, token-ring, and FDDI. Ethernet transmits the lowest order bit first, whereas token-ring and FDDI transmit the highest order bit first.

Translational bridging of Ethernet to token-ring (or vice versa) is allowed with only non-routable protocols. This is because the MAC addresses are carried in the data portion of a frame. It is simple to convert addresses that are contained in the header, but conversion of MAC addresses that are contained in the data portion can be difficult, if not impossible. Translation bridging between Ethernet and FDDI allows the following protocols:

▼ IP

■ OSI

■ DECnet

▲ Non-routable protocols

Source Route Transparent Bridging

Source Route Transparent (SRT) bridging combines transparent bridging algorithm and SRB algorithm by using a Routing Information Indicator (RII) bit to distinguish frames that are using one or the other algorithm. The RII can be either a 0 or a 1. If the RII is a 1, a Routing Information Field (RIF) is present in the frame, and the bridge then will employ the SRB algorithm. If the RII is a 0, an RIF is not present in the frame, and the bridge then will employ the transparent bridging algorithm.

The IEEE 802.5 Routing Information Field (RIF)

The IEEE 802.5 MAC field containing the Routing Information Field (RIF) is structured as shown in Figure 5-5.

As shown in the example, the RIF is divided into two main fields: the routing control field and the routing identifier field. The routing control field is further divided into four fields: the type field, the length field, the D bit, and the largest frame. There is an additional frame, but it is not used. The routing identifier field is further divided into two fields: the ring number field and the bridge number field.

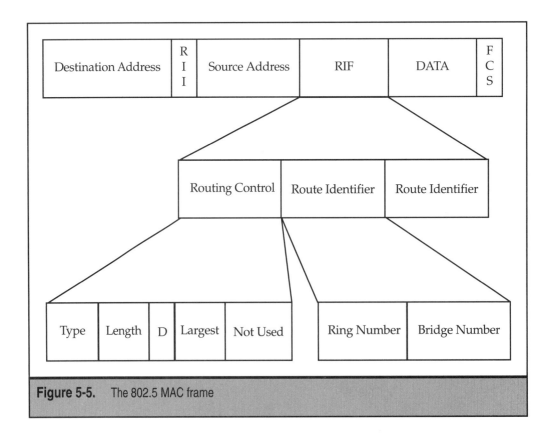

Figure 5-5.   The 802.5 MAC frame

▼ **The Routing Control Fields**

■ **Type**—Identifies which type of routing control is being used.

■ **Specifically routed**—Where the source node has supplied the route.

■ **All paths**—Route is discovered as the frame is transmitted through the network.

■ **Spanning tree explorer**—Only spanning tree bridges will forward the frame, adding bridge and ring information as they forward the frame.

■ **Length**—Identifies the total length of the RIF.

■ **D bit**—Identifies and controls the direction the frame is traveling.

■ **Largest frame**—Identifies the largest frame size that can be handled.

▲ **The Routing Identifier Fields**

■ **Ring number**—An assigned value that identifies the ring.

■ **Bridge number**—An assigned value that identifies the bridge. This value should follow the value of the attached ring unless it is parallel with another bridge connecting two rings.

TYPES OF ROUTERS AND WHEN TO USE THEM

Just like there are many different network types, there are many different router types. Each type of router supports different needs. This is mainly because every network has different needs and it would less cost effective to produce only one router to encompass every possible need that a network might have. There are three main routing scenarios that we will introduce briefly:

▼ Local routing

■ Remote routing

▲ Backbone routing

Local Routing

When you hear the term "local routing" it probably refers to a router that is within a LAN and is forwarding information between nodes within that LAN (see Figure 5-6). Because hubs and switches are cheaper and very reliable, local routers are not that common. Again, all this is determined by the needs of the network. If speed and bandwidth within the network are a concern, a router in the local environment is a very good option.

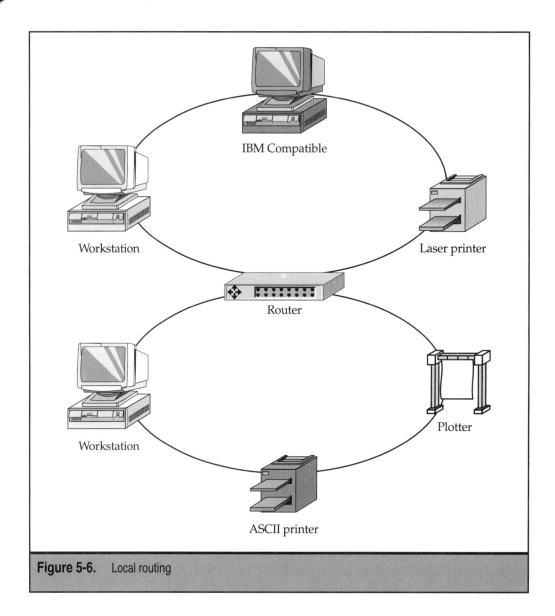

Figure 5-6.   Local routing

Remote Routing

Many corporations have a requirement for network connectivity for remote offices. There are many different scenarios that can be covered here and many different configurations to meet those needs. Suffice it to say that a remote router does not have the demands that some of the higher-end routers do, but they do need to be reliable when they are needed. Figure 5-7 depicts a remote routing environment.

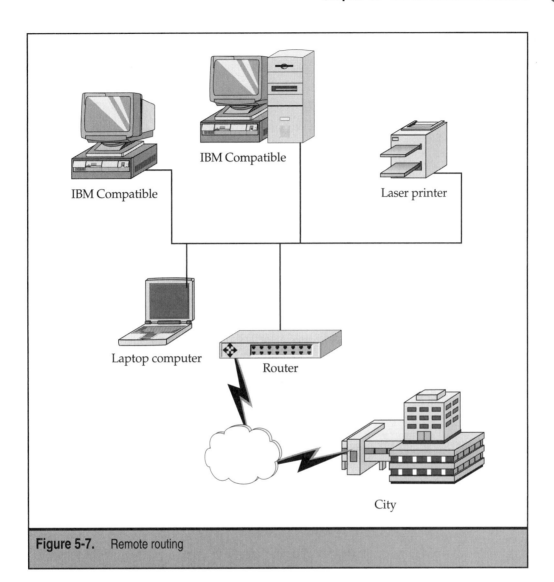

Figure 5-7. Remote routing

Backbone Routing

Backbone routers need to be powerful. They need to be capable of handling a lot of traffic very quickly. Backbone routers (see Figure 5-8), as the name implies, are the backbones of the network. They are located through the network core and often are the main focal point between LANs or are the interface between a LAN and a WAN. The routers that operate at the core level should be considered mission critical, for if they are incapable of handling the demanding tasks that are expected of them, the entire network will be incapable of operating. Configurations for the backbone are network dependent.

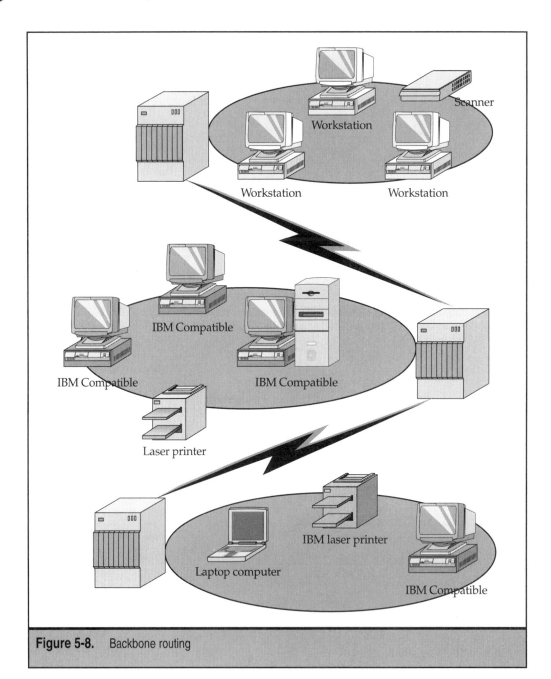

Figure 5-8. Backbone routing

ROUTING IP

The primary function of Internet Protocol (IP) routing is to take data from a higher-layer protocol, create a datagram, and forward that datagram to destination nodes within the network. IP also is responsible for fragmenting the datagram and reassembling it when it arrives at the destination.

Basic IP Routing Overview

IP is part of the TCP/IP protocol suite and is defined in RFC 791. IP is the standard that is used to send the basic unit of networking data known as the IP datagram, and it provides a connectionless system of delivery.

IP uses a 32-bit layer 3 addressing scheme. This address scheme is formatted in dotted-decimal notation. Dotted-decimal notation is a 32-bit integer that contains four 8-bit numbers that are written in base 10. The dotted portion of dotted-decimal is the fact that each of these 8-bit (or octet) sections is separated by a period (dot). The layer 3 addressing scheme, or IP addressing scheme, is used to set paths throughout an IP network. Table 5-1 shows several examples of dotted-decimal notation and how it is converted from the binary notation.

32-bit Binary Notation	Dotted-Decimal Notation
10000000 10000000 10000000 00000001	128.128.128.1
00001010 00000011 00000010 00000000	10.3.2.0
10000001 11000000 00000000 00000000	129.192.0.0
10000011 00000101 00110000 00000000	131.5.48.0
11111111 11111111 11111111 11111111	255.255.255.255
00000000 00000000 00000000 00000000	0.0.0.0
00000001 00000011 00000111 00001111	1.3.7.15

Table 5-1.   Dotted-Decimal Notation Conversion Example

IP also allows for packet fragmentation in case a received packet is too big to be transferred on a network in a single packet. IP also utilizes what is known as Time To Live (TTL), which eliminates the possibility that a packet will get caught in a loop if it is unable to locate its destination.

Format of an IP Datagram

Figure 5-9 is a visual representation of the format of an IP datagram. An IP datagram is the packet format that is defined by IP. A packet is a block of data that carries all necessary information to deliver the packet to its destination. The information that is contained in the IP datagram allows it to be transmitted throughout the network independently from any other packet. The following information is contained within the IP datagram:

▼ **Time to live**—TTL is a counter that will specify the number of hops that an IP datagram will take before the datagram is discarded. This alleviates the possibility of a datagram getting caught in an indefinite loop. A hop is a term that defines a packet passing through a router or a bridge.

■ **Source address**—The 32-bit address of the sending node.

■ **Destination address**—The 32-bit address of the receiving node.

■ **Version**—The version field is a 4-bit field that identifies the IP version of the protocol that was used to generate the datagram. This is important as it ensures that all nodes are interpreting the datagram correctly. If a datagram is received by a node that is using a different version, the node will reject the datagram.

■ **Header length**—A 4-bit field that identifies the length of the header.

■ **Type of service**—Specifies how the datagram should be handled. The value that is indicated in this field will indicate priorities, delays, minimum cost, and so forth.

■ **Total length**—Identifies, in octets, the total size of the datagram. The maximum size of any datagram is 65, 535 octets.

▲ **Datagram identifier**—This is an ID that is assigned to the datagram. This is useful when the message that needs to be sent exceeds the 65, 535 limit of a datagram and has to be fragmented into more than one datagram.

Address Resolution Protocol (ARP) Overview

The Address Resolution Protocol (ARP) is the Internet protocol that binds MAC addresses with an IP address for a given node. This is necessary because the higher-level IP software is dependent on the data link layer for data delivery. Nodes will use ARP when they have determined that the destination node is within a network that is directly attached to its own. The source node is capable of accomplishing this by comparing the network portion of the IP address with the network portion of the destination node's IP address.

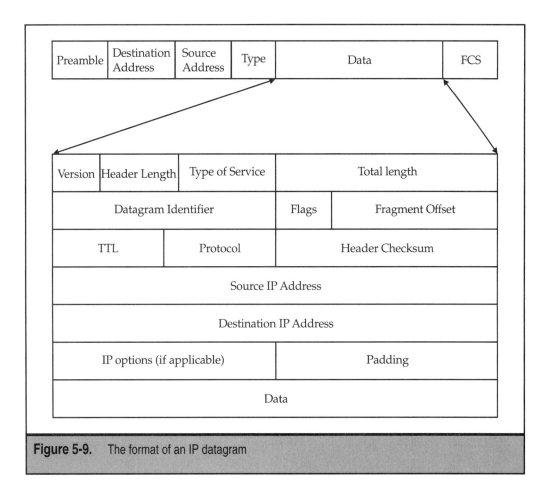

Figure 5-9.   The format of an IP datagram

The ARP message is transmitted across a network in the data portion of a frame. The following information is contained within the ARP message (see Figure 5-10):

▼ **Hardware**—Contains the interface type that it is looking for. This will be identified by a specific value. The hardware types and their values are as follows:

   ■ **Frame Relay**—15

   ■ **Ethernet**—1

   ■ . **Serial**—20

   ■ **Switched Multimegabit Data Service (SMDS)** —14

   ■ **High-Level Data Link Control (HDLC)** —17

■ **Protocol**—An assigned value that identifies the type of upper-layer protocol address that is being supplied by the source node. IP addresses are given an assigned value of 0800.

■ **Hardware length and protocol length**—This item will identify the length of the MAC address and the length of the protocol address.

■ **Operation**—Identifies whether the information contained is an ARP request or an ARP response. An ARP request will be identified with a 1; an ARP response is identified with a 2.

■ **Sender hardware address**—Identifies the MAC address of the source node.

■ **Sender Internet address**—Identifies the IP address of the source node

■ **Target hardware address**—Identifies the MAC address of the destination node.

▲ **Target Internet address**—Identifies the IP address of the destination node.

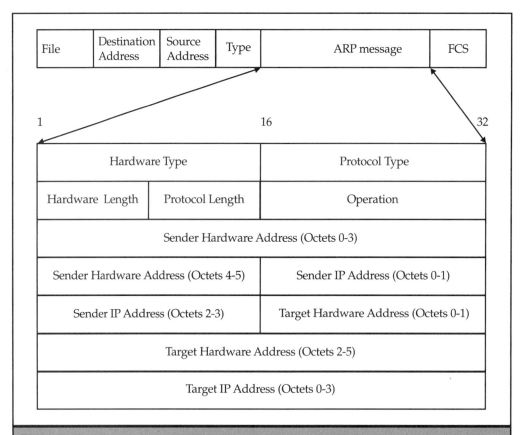

Figure 5-10.   The format of an ARP message

For a source node to connect to the destination node, the IP address of the destination node must be known. When using ARP it is assumed that all possible source nodes know the IP address of all potential destination nodes. Many TCP networks will maintain a LAN IP to MAC translation table on the host node. This is called the ARP table and is simply a section of RAM that contains the address translation mapping information.

Once a source node has determined the IP address of the destination node, the source node will look at its ARP table to determine the MAC address of that destination node. If the destination's information is contained in the ARP table of the source node, no ARP request is sent. In this case, IP is capable of binding the IP and MAC addresses and sending the IP datagram to the data link for transmission to the network and ultimately the destination node.

If the destination MAC address is not found in the ARP table of the source node, the source node will send an ARP request packet, addressed to the network in a broadcast mode. Remember that a broadcast goes to all stations on the network. The destination MAC address for a broadcast will be all Fs (FF-FF-FF-FF-FF-FF). Because this is a broadcast, all stations will receive the packet, but only the station with the IP address from which the source node has requested a response will respond.

The node that contains the IP address from which the source node was requesting a response then will send an ARP response packet to the original source node. The ARP response is not broadcasted; rather it is addressed to the MAC address of the node that had originally sent the ARP request. Once the originator receives a reply to its request, it will update its ARP table and then attach the MAC address to the packet it wants sent, and will transmit it to the network for delivery to the destination node.

Routing Information Protocol

The Routing Information Protocol (RIP) was developed to enable network numbers and the paths associated with the networks to be learned and well known on an Internet. RIP provides a method of distributing network numbers to facilitate routing. Because routing allows any node to distribute information to any other node, it is necessary for the nodes to know each other's network numbers, and to know whom to contact if a network number is not known.

Non-local routing of datagrams is performed using routers. Routers are able to forward and receive information transmitted on a network by reading and updating an internal database table that will list network numbers and the paths that are associated with those networks. RIP allows this information to be dynamically maintained.

Implementation of RIP first appeared in the late 1960s when it was employed by ARPAnet. It was devised by the Xerox Corporation, and is used by the Xerox Network System (a protocol that allows network nodes to use the files of other network nodes as if they are their own). RIP was adopted as an Internet standard in 1988, but was not intended to be the primary routing algorithm for routing IP. RIP began to be widely accepted as the norm, especially after it was embedded in the Berkeley UNIX operating system.

It is important to remember that most end user workstations do not invoke the RIP protocol. Most workstations connect to a router through a default gateway and do not track network addressing or path information. Also keep in mind an RIP packet will never leave its own LAN. Routers that are using the RIP protocol will receive an RIP packet, update their tables if necessary, and then discard the update packet. The routers then will determine other LAN routing information by adding a cost to the just-received tables count. Once the information has been added to this information, the routers will broadcast their tables to attached nodes.

The RIP packets contain header and data fields that are needed by destination nodes to determine the purpose of the RIP packet. A graphical example of the format of an RIP packet is shown in Figure 5-11. Descriptions for the fields in the RIP packet are listed here.

▼ **Version**—Identifies the version of RIP that is being used by the packet. Currently, there are two versions of RIP.

■ **Family of net (value)** —Identifies the protocol that owns the packet.

■ **IP address**—Identifies the IP address of the destination network. The node that is requesting the packet will fill this field in.

▲ **Distance to network**—Indicates the distance (by cost) from the receiving node to the sending network. The receiving node will add a cost of 1 to this field before forwarding it to the attached nodes.

The command field identifies the reason for the packet; a number that corresponds with an associated command identifies this reason. The following is a list of the commands and their corresponding numbers:

▼ The value of 1 identifies a request for routing table information.

■ The value of 2 identifies a response.

Command	Version	Not Used	Family of Net X	Not Used	IP Address of Net X	Not Used	Not Used	Distance to Net X

Figure 5-11.   The format of an RIP message

- The value of 3 identifies that trace mode is on. This function is obsolete.
- The value of 4 identifies that trace mode is off. This function is obsolete.
- ▲ The value of 5 is used by Sun Microsystems and is reserved by it for internal use.

Default Routes

Default routes are a concept used by TCP/IP networks and are not a feature that is used by other network protocols. Default routes are very similar to static routes and are maintained on the router and the user's end station.

Because the end stations do not support RIP, they have to be connected to the router by a default gateway or default route. The end station will determine if an IP address is local or not and will forward the information that is destined to a non-local destination to the router through the default route. The end station then relinquishes the information to the router and trusts that the router will use the information it has learned to forward the data to the correct destination's path.

A router can also be assigned a default route, which can be identified in the routing table as 0.0.0.0. This is intended for a packet that is received and is destined for a network that is not in the routing table of the router that has received the packet. The router will forward that information to the router it has identified as its default, hoping that the default router will have the routing information to forward the packet to its destination. This process continues until the packet either finds a router that can send it to the destination or it is received by the last router, which is unable to forward it because of a lack of routing information; thus sending a control message back to the originator.

Routing Table

A routing table is a table that is part of the router. It contains the destination address, next-hop address, and other route metrics for every route that is known by the router that the table belongs to. There are three major events that cause the router to update its routing table:

- ▼ If a table is received and it contains a hop count to a network that is lower than the hop count that is currently logged in its table, it will replace its entry with the information that was received.
- If a table was received and it contains a network that currently is not part of its routing table, it will add the new entry.
- ▲ If a packet is forwarded to another network and is passed through a specified router and the next-hop count to a network destination is changed, the router will change the entry it has in its routing table.

A routing table contains three elements: the network number, the hops to the next network, and the next router in the path to that particular network. An example of a routing table is shown in Figure 5-12. Routing table fields can vary depending on the update mechanism that is being used. As we mentioned previously, RIP is the most commonly used update mechanism.

A routing table that is used by the RIP protocol will contain the following values:

▼ **Network number**—The network identification number of the specified network.

■ **Next router to deliver to**—Identifies the router that the packet should be delivered to if the network that the packet is destined for is not directly available. This also is known as the next-hop address.

■ **Hops**—Identifies the metric count of how many routers the packet has to pass through before it reaches its destination. 1 identifies the route as a local route.

■ **Learned from**—It is quite possible that there are many algorithms used in a particular router. Because of this, the learned from field will identify how a route was learned (such as RIP, BGP, OSPF, and so forth).

■ **Time left to delete**—Identifies the amount of time left before a route is deleted from the routing table.

▲ **Port**—Identifies the physical port on the router that the routing table information was received from.

[1:1]$ sho ip routes

Destination	Mask	Proto	Age	Cost	NextHop Addr
0.0.0.0	0.0.0.0	RIP	66	2	110.10.0.5
110.10.0.0	255.255.255.0	RIP	11	11	110.10.0.7
110.20.0.0	255.255.255.0	Local	1250	0	110.20.0.1

3 routes in table

Figure 5-12. A routing table

Subnetting

In Chapter 1 we discuss the classes in IP addressing. Using classes, an IP address can be assigned based on the number of nodes that are part, or potentially part, of a network. Remember that Class A addresses allow quite a few hosts but very few networks. Class B addresses allow more networks and fewer hosts than Class A networks. Class C networks allow a lot of networks and fewer hosts.

The problem with using classes is that you have a choice of many hosts or many networks. Because of this, more Class B and Class C addresses were being requested and assigned than were Class A addresses, but they also were not being fully utilized. The full potential of the Class B and C addresses was not realized by many of these the addresses were assigned to. It would be similar to flying on a fully booked 100-passenger airplane that allows only 27 people on board each trip (which for those who frequently fly might not be a bad thing).

Subnetting allows networks to be more efficient in using the IP address classes. It is efficient for corporation as well as Internet routing. Subnetting enables you to rearrange and reassign some of the host portions of the IP address to the network portions of the IP address.

As corporate networks grew and more network numbers were being assigned and many sites began implementing routing on their LANs, they had to assign multiple network numbers to accomplish this. This was very beneficial, but many problems began to arise. The biggest problem was that routing tables were filling up quickly.

Many corporations began subnetting their networks to prevent these problems, but this became a concern as there were no defined standards for this practice. The standard that defines subnetting IP address is RFC 950. A network mask that covers the network portion of the IP address is known as the *natural mask* (no subnetting involved). A network mask that uses the subnetting practices defined in RFC 950 is called a *subnet mask*.

NORTEL NETWORKS ROUTING FAMILY PRODUCT OVERVIEW

The Nortel Networks routing family is broken down into two basic groups: the *access product* and *backbone node* families. The access product routers include the Access Stack Node (ASN), the Access Remote Node (ARN), and the Access Node (AN) or Access Node

Hub (ANH). The backbone node routers include the Backbone Link node (BLN), the Backbone Link Node version 2 (BLN-2), and the Backbone Concentrator Node (BCN).

Access Product Routing Family

The Nortel Networks access products are in a different class from the backbone node routing family, because they do not have a backplane and therefore do not utilize the PPX bus architecture that the BN routing family does. The access product routing family performs all processing on the motherboard. We introduce the ASN, AN/ANH, and ARN routers in this next section.

ASN

The Access Stack Node (ASN) is a stackable router that will allow up to four ASN routers in a single stack. This is a huge benefit because it allows for growth within local, remote, and backbone routing scenarios. A stack that contains the maximum of four ASNs can support up to 48 interfaces. The ASN can operate as a remote router, but also can perform as a backbone router when a maximum of four is utilized.

AN/ANH

The Nortel Networks Access Node (AN) and Access Node Hub (ANH) are part of the Baystack product family. The AN is an excellent, cost-effective choice for local and remote routing needs. The AN is a fixed configuration that contains a single Ethernet, token-ring, or one of each. It also has two sync interfaces. The ANH is an integrated hub that comes in two different models. The ANH-8 contains 8 Ethernet ports, and the ANH-12 contains 12 Ethernet ports.

Access Remote Node

The Access Remote Node (ARN) is an excellent choice for a remote office or within a small LAN. The ARN base unit allows for a single LAN connection that can be either Ethernet or token-ring and two WAN connections. The ARN can be upgraded to allow for a maximum of five WAN and two LAN ports.

Backbone Node Family

Nortel Networks backbone node (BN) products are fully redundant systems that are capable of supporting a maximum of 13 FDDI ports or 104 LAN/WAN ports. The BN products can perform outstandingly well in a backbone network. The BN products are fault resilient, configured with symmetric multiprocessors, redundant power supplies, redundant processor interconnect, and the redundant software storage capabilities.

The BN products contain a minimum of one System Resource Module (SRM) providing data path interconnect arbitration. An option is available to add an additional SRM, doubling your router bandwidth availability. A Parallel Packet Express (PPX) processor interconnect allows processing at up to 1 Gb/s. A redundant PPX is available, which ensures reliability for system availability. Each network link module used in the BN routers is controlled by the Fast Routing Engine (FRE, FRE-2, FRE-2/60) processor module, which uses a Motorola 68040 central processor, which operates at up to 60MHz and contains up to 64 Mb of RAM. We discuss the differences in the three types of FRE cards shortly, but because they perform the same functions, we refer to them as simply the FRE module for the purposes of this chapter. System software and configuration files are stored on a flash Electronic Erasable Programmable Read-Only Memory (EEPROM) module, or *flash card*. Each FRE module has an available slot for a flash card. This allows for multiple redundancies for system software and configurations.

BLN/BLN-2

The BLN and BLN-2 can be configured with a single FRE card/link module combination. This combination is known as the Intelligent Link Interface (ILI). The BLN and BLN-2 have five slots in the chassis (see Figures 5-13 and 5-14). Slot number 1 is reserved for the SRM; the remaining four slots offer a variety of ILI connection configurations. It is important to note that each link module requires a processor module to operate.

The BLN and BLN-2 offer a total of five slots in the front of the chassis and five slots in the back of the chassis. The link module (modules that contain the network interface ports) are contained in the back of the chassis. The FREs are contained in the front. The SRM in slot 1 of the rear is referred to as the System Resource Module-Link (SRM-L), and the SRM in the front, which is optional, is referred to as the System Resource Module-Front (SRM-F). The SRM-L contains a 25-pin D-connector that allows a terminal or modem connection to the router for Technician Interface (TI) access. TI is the command-line interface (CLI) that is used for diagnostic and maintenance operations.

BCN

The BCN is a powerful router (see Figures 5-15 and 5-16 for front and rear views). It contains 13 slots that will allow a total of 104 LAN/WAN interfaces or up to 13 FDDI links. It is a rack-mounted base unit that can have up to four load sharing redundant power supplies. The power supplies, as well as the link modules, all are hot-swappable (meaning they can be exchanged without having to shut down the router).

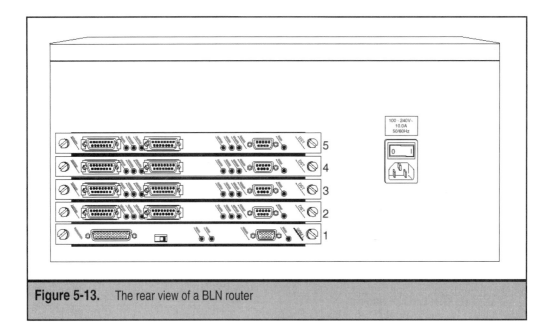

Figure 5-13.   The rear view of a BLN router

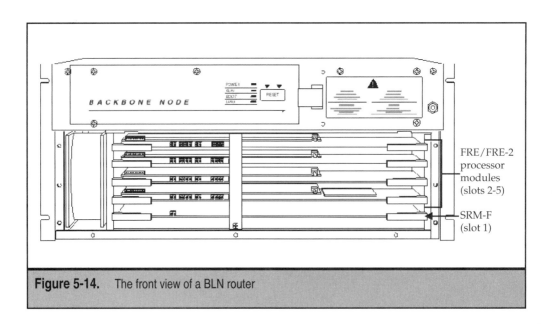

Figure 5-14.   The front view of a BLN router

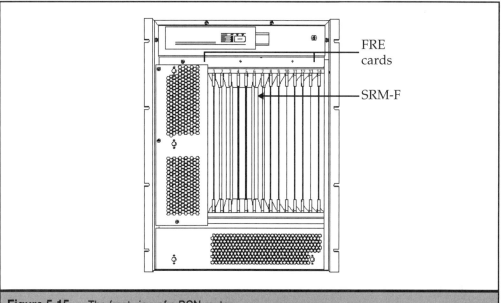

FRE
cards

SRM-F

Figure 5-15.   The front view of a BCN router

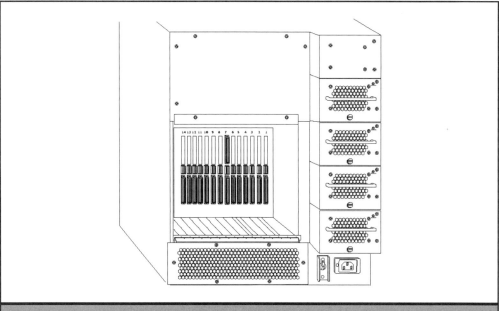

Figure 5-16.   The rear view of a BCN router

The System Resource Module   The BCN uses a System Resource Module (SRM) that provides arbitration of the Parallel Packet Express rails. The PPX rails also are known as the backplane. You are required to use one SRM on the link side of your BCN. This SRM is known as the SRM-L. If you want to double the PPX utilization, an additional SRM can be added to the FRE card side of the BCN. This SRM is known as the SRM-F. The SRM-L is located in slot 7 on the link side, and the SRM-F is in slot 7 on the FRE side.

The Parallel Packet Express   The Parallel Packet Express (PPX) provides a fast transport medium for the transfer of data packets from one processor to another. It contains four rails that make up the midplane interconnection between the FRE side and the link module side of the BCN. Each of the four rails contains eight data lines and multiple signaling lines. Data is transported one octet at a time over the PPX. The PPX uses a random path selection to maintain load balancing (or sharing the workload between rails).

ROUTER SYSTEM SOFTWARE AND FILES

Nortel Networks uses some very important system software and files that are vital to the routers' performance. The operating system used by the Nortel Networks routing family is the Gate Access Management Entity (GAME). The routers also require an image file and a configuration file that can be manipulated and determine the router configuration.

Each router requires a boot image file and a configuration file. These are stored on a flash card, or might be part of the device on some earlier product versions. The following lists all files that should be located on the flash card (boot media); the boot up files are discussed in detail immediately following.

The image file for the type of router that is being used:

▼ **an.exe**—For the AN/ANH router

■ **asn.exe**—For the ASN router

■ **bn.exe**—For the BN router family

▲ **arn.exe**—For the ARN router

The boot PROM upgrade file for the type of router that is being used:

▼ **asnboot.exe**—Used to upgrade the boot PROM on an ASN router

■ **freboot.exe**—Used to upgrade the boot PROM on a FRE card (part of the BN family)

■ **arnboot.exe**—Used to upgrade the boot PROM on an ARN router

▲ **anboot.exe**—Used to upgrade the boot PROM on an AN/ANH router

The diagnostic PROM upgrade file for the type of router that is being used:

▼ **asndiag.exe**—Used to upgrade the diagnostic PROM of the ASN router

■ **frediag.exe**—Used to upgrade the diagnostic PROM on a FRE card

■   **arndiag.exe**—Used to upgrade the diagnostic PROM on an ARN router

▲   **andiag.exe**—Used to upgrade the diagnostic PROM on an AN/ANH router

config—The config file (short for configuration) is the default configuration file for the router. It contains all necessary information that pertains to the router. This file is loaded during the boot process.

debug.al—The debug.al file is a file that contains aliases, or predefined commands, that are created to invoke TI commands.

install.bat—install.bat is a batch, or script, file that is necessary to load an initial IP address onto the router. The IP address must be loaded to allow management of the router through Site Manager software. This file is used on all routers except the ARN and is discussed in detail in Chapter 6.

install_arn.bat—Similar to the install.bat, but used for the initial configuration of an IP address on the ARN.

There is an initial config file on the flash card that can be used as a backup in case something has happened with the config file. Keep in mind that these files are basic and do not contain the information that has been configured on your router. It is always a good idea to back up your config to an alternate location (other than your local boot medium). The initial config files are as follows:

▼   **ti_asn.cfg**—Specific to the ASN

■   **ti_arn.cfg**—Specific to the ARN

▲   **ti.cfg**—Used by all other routers

Table 5-2 contains information about the different file types and which ones are used with the various routers.

File Types	Files	AN/ANH	BLN/BCN	ARN	ASN
Image	an.exe	X			
	arn.exe			X	
	asn.exe				X
	bn.exe		X		
Common	config	X	X	X	X
	debug.al	X	X	X	X
	install.bat	X	X		X
	inst_arn.bat			X	

Table 5-2.   System Files

File Types	Files	AN/ANH	BLN/BCN	ARN	ASN
	ti.cfg	X	X		
	ti_arn.cfg			X	
	ti_asn.cfg				X
Boot PROMs	arnboot.exe			X	
	asnboot.exe				X
	freeboot.exe		X		
	anboot.exe	X			
Diag PROMs	arndiag.exe			X	
	asndiag.exe				X
	frediag.exe		X		
	andiag.exe	X			

Table 5-2. System Files (*continued*)

Gate Access Management Entity

Gate Access Management Entity (GAME) is the operating system used by the Nortel Networks Routing product family. All Nortel Networks routers use the GAME operating system, which is part of the boot image described next.

Boot Image Files

The executable image file that contains the runtime image as well as the GAME operating system is called the boot image file. The boot image files have different names, depending on the routing family they are used on:

▼ **an.exe**—The boot image file for the AN and ANH routers

■ **arn.exe**—The boot image file for the ARN routers

■ **asn.exe**—The boot image file for the ASN routers

▲ **bn.exe**—The boot image file for the BLN, BLN-2, and BCN routers

As you can see, it is easy to determine the router image that is to be used with which router.

The Nortel Networks Router Boot Process

Remember in Chapter 1 when we discussed the boot process (POST) of a personal computer? Much like the personal computer, the Nortel Networks routers perform a similar test when they are booting up. The type of router that is being booted determines the boot process that is used.

The BN Boot Process   The BN router family will perform a diagnostics test first (similar to the POST diagnostic testing done by a PC). Once that is done, they will request system software over the PPX rails. If the router is able to locate and load the image file, the router will request the config file, also over the PPX rails. After the config file is located, it is loaded. Once the system software and the configuration files are located and loaded, the router is ready to transmit data.

The ASN Boot Process   The ASN router family will perform a diagnostics test first. Once that is done, the router will request system software over the Stack Packet Exchange (SPEX) modules. If the router is capable of locating and loading the image file, the router will request the config file, also over the SPEX modules. After the config file is located, it is loaded. Once the system software and the configuration files are located and loaded, the router is ready to transmit data.

NOTE: The ASN also can use the boot processes used by the AN and ANH routers when it is used as a remote router.

The AN and ANH Boot Process   The AN and ANH were designed to be used at remote sites. Because of this, the AN and ANH employ a variety of methods for obtaining and booting the system software and configuration files. The methods used by an AN and ANH router for boot-up and the circumstances in which each are used are as follows:

▼   **EZ Install**—If the router uses EZ Install, the AN and ANH will perform a diagnostics test first. Once the diagnostic test is done, the router will send a BootP request for an IP address to the remote router. The remote router will provide an IP address to the requesting router, which in turn will request the location of the system software and configuration file. If the files cannot be located, the router then will load the system software and configuration files from its flash card.

■   **NetBoot**—If the router uses NetBoot, the router will perform diagnostics testing first. Once the diagnostics testing is complete, the router will send a BootP request to a predetermined BootP server, which will send the router directions to the TFTP server. The TFTP server will be used to load the system software and configuration files from a location that is provided to the router from the BootP server.

▲ **Directed NetBoot**—If the router uses directed NetBoot, the router will perform diagnostics testing first. Once the diagnostics testing is complete, the router will attempt to TFTP the system's software and configuration files from a predefined location.

UPGRADING

To keep up with changes that are being introduced to networks daily, it becomes necessary to upgrade the enterprise hardware from time to time. This holds true for the Nortel Networks routing family and the software tools used to configure the routers.

Router Upgrade Overview

Software releases occur occasionally for functionality upgrades and bug fixes as well as major software upgrades that encompass new features, function improvements, and bug fixes. Often there also are architectural changes and enhancements that have been introduced since the last major release.

With every code upgrade, there also is an upgraded software configuration package that is introduced. This section focuses on the router software and Programmable Read Only Memory (PROMs). Site Manager, the configuration software, is discussed in detail in Chapter 7.

Upgrading the Nortel Networks router is a relatively simple process, but it is important to ensure that all versions of hardware and software are compatible with each other before you begin. Keep in mind that each new major release of code probably contains new functionalities and enhancements, which mean additions to the previous versions of code, and ultimately that means memory and storage requirements may have changed.

Make sure there is enough free contiguous space on the flash card to hold the new image file. You also must determine whether you need to upgrade the PROMs on the hardware. Some code will support only specific hardware PROM versions, and it is necessary to upgrade the PROMs when upgrading code.

Each time a version of code is released, there is supporting documentation known as the release notes. The release notes will identify all the compatibility information for the code and provide useful information about upgrading code.

Upgrading Boot PROMs

After you have determined what PROM versions are compatible with the version of code you are upgrading to, you need to verify what PROMs are currently being used. This can be done through Site Manager and the TI through MIB commands, which are discussed in Chapter 6.

To upgrade the PROM, it is necessary to "burn" the existing PROM with the new PROM image. This is performed by transferring the software to the flash card through TFTP and opening a TI session (discussed in Chapter 6). The prompt you will see is similar to this:

Network Blueprints

Table of Contents

The OSI Model

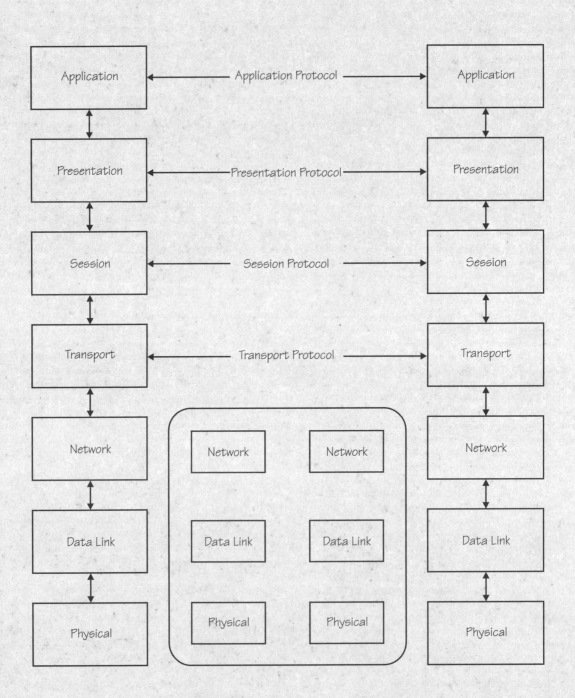

Nortel LAN

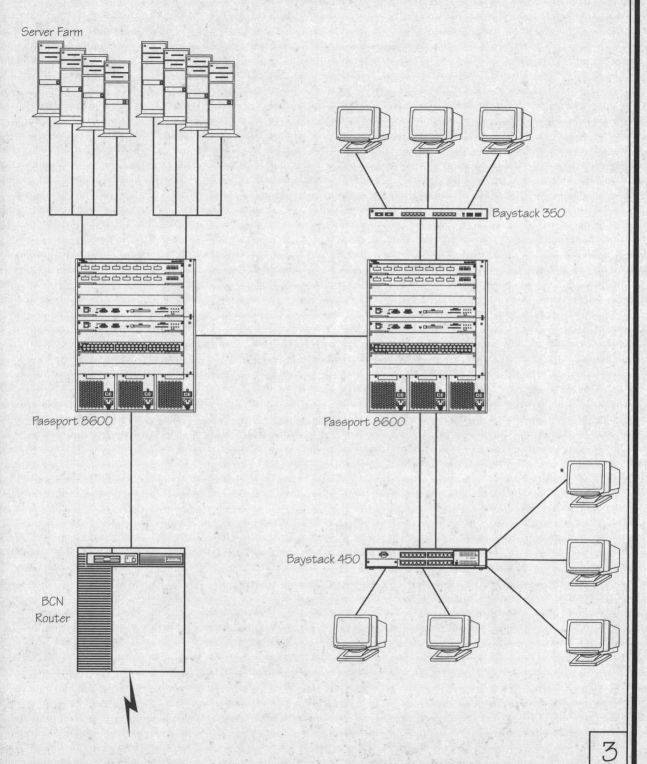

Server Farm

Baystack 350

Passport 8600

Passport 8600

BCN Router

Baystack 450

3

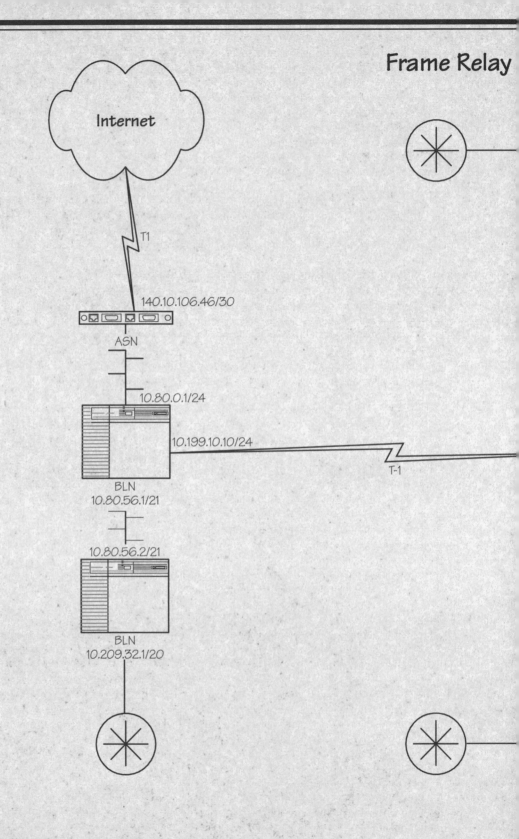

Internet

T1

140.10.106.46/30

ASN

10.80.0.1/24

10.199.10.10/24

T-1

BLN

10.80.56.1/21

10.80.56.2/21

BLN

10.209.32.1/20

WAN

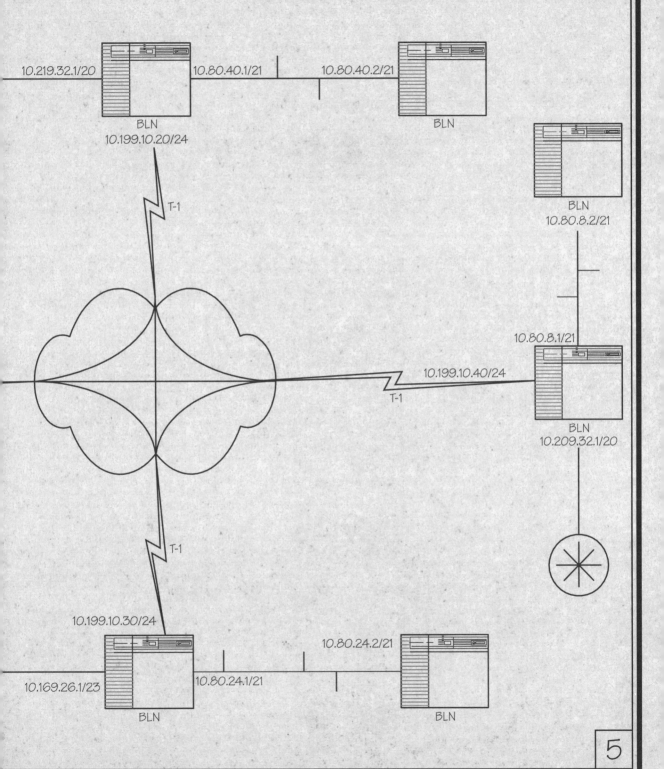

10.219.32.1/20

10.80.40.1/21

10.80.40.2/21

BLN

BLN

10.199.10.20/24

BLN
10.80.8.2/21

T-1

10.80.8.1/21

10.199.10.40/24

T-1

BLN
10.209.32.1/20

T-1

10.199.10.30/24

10.80.24.2/21

10.169.26.1/23

10.80.24.1/21

BLN

BLN

Physical Redundancy

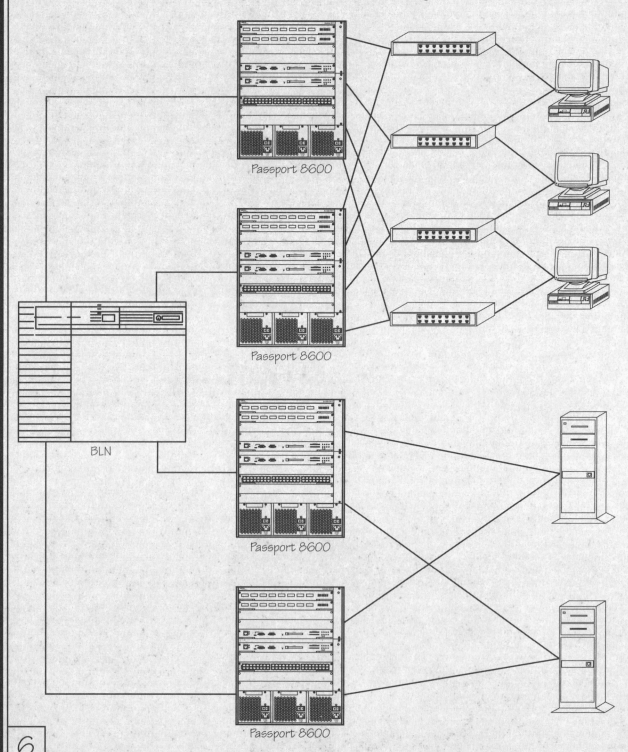

Passport 8600

Passport 8600

BLN

Passport 8600

Passport 8600

6

A Passport Layer 3 Switched Network

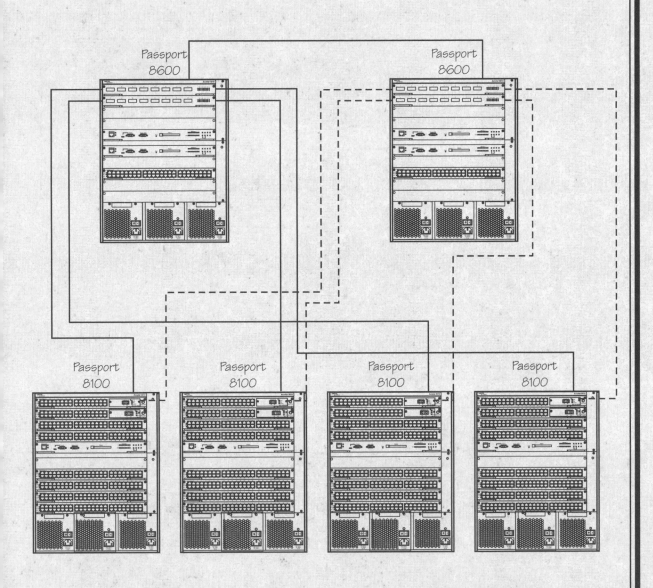

Passport 8600

Passport 8600

Passport 8100

Passport 8100

Passport 8100

Passport 8100

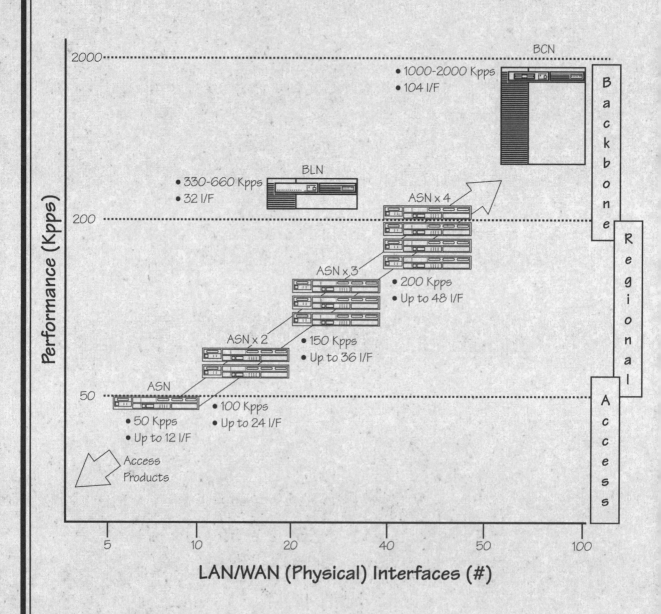

Nortel Networks Router Performance Chart

Performance (Kpps) — vertical axis: 50, 200, 2000

LAN/WAN (Physical) Interfaces (#) — horizontal axis: 5, 10, 20, 40, 50, 100

BCN
- 1000-2000 Kpps
- 104 I/F

BLN
- 330-660 Kpps
- 32 I/F

ASN x 4

ASN x 3
- 200 Kpps
- Up to 48 I/F

ASN x 2
- 150 Kpps
- Up to 36 I/F

ASN
- 100 Kpps
- Up to 24 I/F

- 50 Kpps
- Up to 12 I/F

Access Products

Backbone

Regional

Access

```
[1:]$
```

At the command prompt, you will enter the following command:

```
[1:1]$prom -w [volume-number:source-file] [ID of slot to be upgraded]
```

This command erases the current PROM on slot 3 and burns the PROM with the new software. This command can upgrade the boot PROMs as well as the diagnostic PROMs. Following is an actual procedure for upgrading boot and diagnostic PROMs that many engineers have used and now follow every time it is necessary to upgrade these PROMs. For our purposes, we will assume that the flash card containing the upgrade software is on slot 1. Also note that [slot ID] identifies the slot number where the PROM that is being upgraded is located.

Procedures for Upgrade of ARE Boot PROM   To upgrade the boot and diagnostic code in a ARE Router PROM, enter the following command to update the boot code in PROM:

```
prom -w 1: areboot.ppc [slot ID]
```

Enter the following command to verify the new boot code:

```
prom -v 1: areboot.ppc [slot ID]
```

The TI will display information similar to the following:

```
prom: slot 1 completed successfully
```

Enter the following command to update the diagnostic code in PROM:

```
prom -w 1 : arediag.ppc [slot ID]
```

Enter the following command to verify the new diagnostic code:

```
Prom -v 1: arediag.ppc [slot ID]
```

To upgrade the boot and diagnostic code in a FRE PROM, update the boot PROM by entering

```
prom -w 1 : [Boot_PROM_source_file] [slot_ID]
```

NOTE: Once you enter the prom command, it must run to completion. The CTRL+C (abort) command is disabled for the duration of the PROM command execution to allow it to run to completion. Updating takes from 2–10 minutes per PROM. Verifying takes up to 2 minutes per PROM.

Update the diagnostic PROM by entering

```
prom -w 1:[Diag_PROM_source_file] [slot_ID]
```

Verify the PROM upgrade by entering the following command:

```
prom -v 1:[Diag_PROM_source_file] [slot_ID]
```

For example, for a boot PROM, enter

```
prom -v 1: [freboot.exe | asnboot.exe | anboot.exe |arnboot.exe]
[slot_ID]
```

For a diagnostics PROM, enter

```
prom -v 1 [frediag.exe | asndiag.exe | andiag.exe |
arndiag.exe][slot_ID]
```

The system verifies that the PROM image on a designated flash volume (that is, the image file used as a source for upgrading the PROM) matches the image actually stored in the boot or diagnostics PROM, on a designated slot. When you use the -v option, the console displays one of the following messages after the verification terminates:

```
prom: slot 1 completed successfully
prom: PROM data does not match file data on slot 1
```

If the operation succeeds, the new images stored in the boot and diagnostic PROMs run when you reboot the router. If the operation fails, the console displays a message describing the cause of the failure. Once you have burned the PROMs and verified that they are now upgraded, you are ready to upgrade the system software.

Upgrading System Software

Nortel Networks router software is released onto CD-ROM for distribution. Nortel Networks also maintains a customer service site where authorized individuals can download software upgrades.

Router code is simply a series of executable files. These files can be manipulated for customization to allow you to load only those functions that are actually needed for your network's purposes.

Most likely, you will want to transfer your image file to the flash card in the router. To do this, you probably will want to make a backup copy of your current running configuration file and the current image file that you are running. If you do not have a backup flash card to use, you should rename the files that you are currently using and keep them on your flash card.

You most likely will want to use TFTP to transfer your image file to the flash card for the upgrade. This can be done through Site Manager or Technician Interface (TI), which are discussed in detail in Chapter 6.

The current configuration file will need to be saved along with the new code. This also can be performed in either Site Manger or TI. To verify the executable files prior to the upgrade, you can use the readexe command in TI. Command syntax is discussed in Chapter 6.

Once you have the new image file ready on the flash card and the config saved, you can reboot the router by either shutting it off and turning it on, or using the boot command. This process will bring the router back up and it will boot with the new code version.

Once the router has come up, there are a series of checks that should be performed to verify that router is functioning properly. These checks are nothing more that commands to determine that all loaded processes return and all configured circuits return in an active state.

CONCLUSION

In this chapter we discussed the functionality of the Nortel Networks router and the files that are needed for operation, as well as what the purpose of each file. We also discussed some of the networking protocols that were used to log network address information.

The upgrading information that was provided in this chapter is something you will probably want to use as your network needs grow. Although this chapter is not an in-depth configuration instructional guide, it is an introduction to the functionality of the Nortel Networks routing family.

As there are many different business types with many different needs, Nortel Networks has a router that can accomplish those needs. The redundancy offerings as well as the configuration capabilities make these routers very desirable in today's business world.

CHAPTER 6

Accessing the Nortel Networks Router

In the last chapter, you were introduced to the Nortel Networks routing family. We have discussed some of the many functions these routers can perform. Although they are capable of transmitting millions of bits per second, they need instructions to get them started. In this chapter, we discuss the various ways to connect to the Nortel Networks AN and BN routing families. We also discuss the software used to configure the router and will provide examples of the most frequently used commands. Another very important part of the Nortel Networks routers is the Management Information Base (MIB) and the event log, both of which are discussed in detail in this book. It is important for the reader to keep in mind that this is a beginner's guide and in no way should be considered an in-depth instruction book on configuring the Nortel Networks AN and BN routers. We have provided enough information to get you started and to help you understand what functions are available through the various interfaces and commands.

CONNECTING TO THE NORTEL NETWORKS ROUTER

Each of the Nortel Networks routers discussed in Chapter 5 have various ways to connect for router management and configuration purposes. The option you choose really depends on your physical location and the physical location of the router. A connection option also is dependent on what management tools you want to use. We start out this section discussing the various connectivity methods.

Out-of-Band Connection

Out-of-band describes a channel of communication that does not reside within the network facilities, or in-band facilities. Out-of-band access generally is achieved through a modem attached to a router's console port (remote out-of-band), or through a laptop or PC that is attached to a router's console port through a cable that is connected to the serial interface on the PC or laptop.

The serial ports, or console ports, reside in different areas of the router depending on the type of router that you are configuring:

▼   The BLN, BLN-2, and BCN routers all contain the console port on the SRM-L. The console connection on the SRM-L is a 25-pin connector.

■   The AN, ANH-12, ASN, and ARN all have their connections on the rear panel of the chassis. This connection is a 9-pin connector.

▲   The ANH-8 has a console connection on the front panel of the chassis. Like the other AN routers, this connection is a 9-pin interface.

Local Out-of-Band Connection

The local out-of-band connection is achieved by the connection of an RS232 cable to the appropriate console port on the Nortel Networks router. The other end of the cable must be connected to the serial port on a VT-100–compliant device, such as a PC, ASCII terminal, or a laptop. The console parameters must be set to the following:

Bits per second	9,600 baud
Data bits	8 data bits
Parity	None
Stop bits	1
Flow control	Hardware

On a PC or laptop that is using Windows 95, these parameters are set from a HyperTerminal session. This is accessed from the menu bar by clicking Start | Programs | Accessories | HyperTerminal. Figure 6-1 is an example of the HyperTerminal port settings.

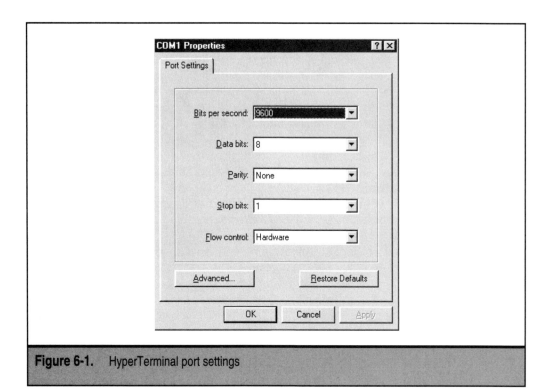

Figure 6-1.   HyperTerminal port settings

Remote Out-of-Band Connection

The remote out-of-band connection is achieved by the connection of an RS232 cable to the appropriate console port on the Nortel Networks router. The other end of the cable is attached to a modem. The console parameters must be set to the following:

Bits per second	9,600 baud
Data bits	8 data bits
Parity	None
Stop bits	1
Flow control	Hardware

The console port also must be configured for modem operation, and the modem parameter on the router must be changed from the default (disabled) to enabled. Once the configuration parameters are set correctly, connection is made by dialing from the user's interface through a modem to a modem attached to the router. When the connection is made, a login screen will appear and the connection is complete.

Telecommunications Network (Telnet) Protocol

Telecommunications Network (Telnet) Protocol is an Internet standard that is defined in RFC 854. Telnet provides an in-band connection to the Nortel Networks routers. In-band connection means that the signals are transmitted within the network.

Telnet is a protocol that provides for remote terminal connection and allows a user of a particular host to access and log into a remote host. Telnet allows a user to connect to a host that it is not directly attached to and interact with the host as if the user were connected directly to the host.

Telnet can be used once TCP and IP are configured on the Nortel Networks router. Telnet allows you to configure the router as a Telnet client or a Telnet server.

When configuring the router as a Telnet server, you are allowed access to the router from another workstation that is acting as, or configured as, a Telnet client. When you obtain access to a router that is configured as a Telnet server, you are performing what is known as *inbound Telnet*.

When configuring the router as a Telnet client, you are allowed to establish an outgoing, or outbound, Telnet session with a remote host. This allows you to obtain easy access to a remote router that is configured as a Telnet server from a router that is configured as a Telnet client. When you obtain Telnet access to a router from a router that is configured as a Telnet client you are performing what is known as *outbound Telnet*.

Inbound Telnet

A device that is capable of invoking the Telnet session and connecting to a remote device is known as the *Telnet client*. The remote device is considered the *Telnet server*. If the connection is established, the Telnet server is performing an inbound Telnet session. An example of this is shown in Figure 6-2. A user attempts to connect to a remote router by issuing a Telnet command followed by the IP address of the router that the user wants to connect to. If a connection can be established, a login screen is shown and the user can log in and make the appropriate changes to the router.

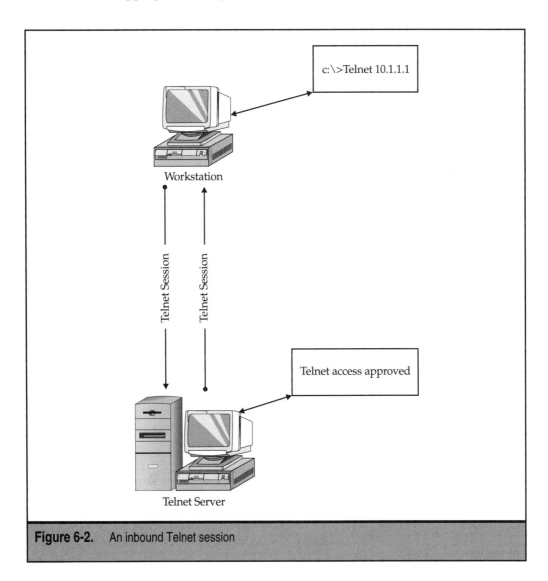

Figure 6-2. An inbound Telnet session

Outbound Telnet

An outbound Telnet session is made if a local out-of-band connection is made to a local router. A Telnet session is invoked from the local router to a remote router. If a connection is established, the local router is performing an outbound Telnet session. An example of this is shown in Figure 6-3. A user attempts to connect to the remote router through a local out-of-band connection to a local router by issuing a Telnet command followed by the IP address of the remote router. If a connection is made, a login screen appears and the user can log in and make the appropriate changes to the remote router.

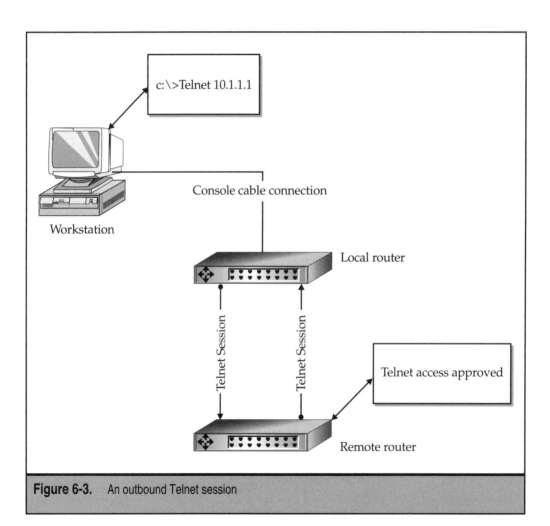

Figure 6-3. An outbound Telnet session

CONFIGURING AND MANAGING THE NORTEL NETWORKS ROUTERS

Once you have obtained a connection to the router, you will want to view, add, change, or delete values that have been established for the configuration of the router. All configurable values for the Nortel Networks router are maintained in the Management Information Base (MIB). The MIB is a database that describes objects as they pertain to your router. The MIB is accessed by the Simple Network Management Protocol (SNMP), described in detail in Chapter 7. The MIB contains names that identify objects that can be managed in the network. Also contained in the MIB is information about the objects. The MIB allows the manipulation and configuration of the router and also provides a way to obtain statistics about the network that have been obtained by the router.

There are three ways of accessing the MIB: the Technician Interface (TI), Bay Command Console (BCC), and Site Manager. Site Manager provides a graphical interface to the router, whereas both TI and BCC are command-line interfaces.

The Technician Interface (TI)

The TI is the only way to interact with a router until an Ethernet link is established between the workstation and the router. BCC is run on TI and therefore needs TI so it can operate. TI is a simple command-line interface and can operate under the following connections:

▼ Local out-of-band connection

■ Remote out-of-band connection

▲ Telnet session

TI is used to install and maintain the configuration of the router. It also can be used to monitor the router's operation, manage the router, configure (add, change, or delete) the router, and diagnose and perform troubleshooting of the router.

TI software is loaded automatically when the router is booted. It resides in the router's operating system kernel and does not have to be loaded separately as other software does. In a system that contains multiple slots, TI automatically is loaded in the first slot that boots and loads an operating system; however, it can be run on any slot that contains a processor module. This allows for TI redundancy throughout the routing platform.

NOTE: The ASN can operate with up to four routers in a stack. In the ASN, the TI can be run on each router separately so if you were to connect a console cable to each ASN, you actually can have four TI sessions running at the same time.

Logging In to a TI Session

Once you have connected to a Nortel Networks router, you will receive a login screen (see Figure 6-4).

Bay Networks, Inc. and its Licensors.
Copyright 1992, 1993, 1994, 1995, 1996, 1997. All rights
reserved.

Login:

Figure 6-4. A TI login screen

There are two access levels: user and manager. For security purposes, each level of access offers certain functions.

▼ **Manager access (read/write access)**—Allows the user to connect and make any changes that are available to the TI.

▲ **User access (read-only access)**—Allows the user to connect and only browse the TI.

NOTE: As the name implies, read/write access allows a user to access and make all changes that are available. This holds true for any of the Nortel Networks products. Read-only access allows users to access and review settings, but not to make any changes.

Manager access is gained by typing **Manager** at the login prompt:

Login: Manager

User access is gained by typing **User** at the login prompt:

Login: User

NOTE: It is important to remember that TI commands are case sensitive and if typed in the wrong case will return an error.

Once you have accessed the TI through either one of the access methods, you will receive a prompt:

[x:y] $

x identifies the slot number from which the TI process is now running. In the ASN, x identifies which router in the stack is running your TI session; so if you are running your TI command on ASN 3 of a stack, x will be 3.

y identifies the port number that you are currently connected to. This number will always be one (1) except for the ASN. On the ASN, y identifies the number of the router in the stack that you are connected to; so if you are connected to the second ASN of a stack, y will be 2.

To log out of a TI session, use the logout command:

```
[x:y]$  logout
```

If you have logged out correctly, you will receive either a login screen or notification that you have logged out of your TI session. The type of confirmation you receive depends on whether you are connected through a Telnet session or an out-of-band connection.

A Telnet session logout verification message:

```
[x:y]$  logout

TI session logged out.

**Goodbye.**
```

An out-of-band logout verification screen:

```
[x:y]$  logout

Bay Networks, Inc. and its Licensors.

Copyright 1992, 1993, 1994, 1995, 1996, 1997, 1998. All rights reserved

Login:
```

Categorization of TI Commands

The commands that are offered for the TI interface can be broken into different categories, depending on the function they perform. These categories are

▼ **TI script commands**—Script commands, or scripts, are developed to allow the user access to certain functions that are performed through the MIB interface (which is discussed in upcoming pages of this chapter).

■ **TI operating commands**—Commands that are available through the command-line interface, allowing simple checks and verification of the systems settings and performance. This can be broken down into two categories: the operating commands (which allow the user to view settings) and the management commands (which allow the user to make changes to the file structure). There are so many commands that are available to a user that we discuss only the basic commands in this section.

▲ **TI MIB access commands**—Commands that will access the Management Information Base and will allow the user to make additions, changes, and deletions of an MIB value through MIB lists, sets, and gets.

NOTE: When there is a release of software code, it is important to remember that a major release will contain new features and quite often new scripts and command files. Therefore, it is important to ensure that any functions that are needed for your network are realized and made part of the image file you will be upgrading to.

TI Script Commands   TI scripts are files that are loaded onto a flash card for use. Scripts contain MIB commands that allow a command to be entered without having to poll the individual's MIB object in the MIB. Scripts allow you to display information about running processes (protocols, circuits, lines, services, and so forth) and will allow you to enable or disable certain processes. Scripts will provide a simple network troubleshooting tool and will allow remote connection for support services. It is important to note that when new code is introduced to your router, the scripts often are different from the scripts that were used for your previous code. Therefore, it is important to ensure that you are using the scripts that are provided for the version of router code you are using.

Scripts normally are stored on a second flash card, depending on the number of scripts that need to be accessed. The following commands will enable you to determine which scripts are available and will access these scripts:

▼ **show**—Displays certain information about the system. This command is very useful when you are troubleshooting problems.

■ **monitor**—Displays certain information about the system and will refresh periodically. This command is very useful when you are troubleshooting problems.

■ **enable**—Allows the user to enable certain features.

■ **disable**—Allows the user to disable certain features.

▲ **menu**—Provides an interface to all of the available scripts that are local to the router. This command will output all available script items and a user interface to choose which items you want to access and receive information from.

install.bat   A very important script command is the install.bat. This script file is used to configure the initial IP interface on the router. This IP address allows the user to connect to the router using Site Manager. Before running install.bat, you must know the following information:

▼ The slot and port numbers where the IP address is to be configured

■ The IP address and subnet mask that you will be adding on the interface

■ The IP routing type and SNMP community details

▲ Trivial File Transfer Protocol (TFTP) default volume number and whether you want to enable FTP and Telnet

Once this information is gathered, you can run install.bat from the command-line interface (CLI) prompt. For instance (assume that the file install.bat is loaded on the flash card in volume 1):

```
[x:y]$  run 1:install
```

After this command has been entered, the router will ask you for the information you have requested. After the router has gathered the required information, the router displays a summary listing of the configuration settings and then prompts you to save the configuration file. Because the install.bat process is making dynamic changes to the router, it is not necessary to reboot the router when you are finished. If you make a mistake during the install.bat process, you can reboot the router with the ti.cfg file and re-run the install.bat script file. The following is an example of the install.bat process:

```
[1:1]$ install

  More Mode: OFF

  Lines per screen: 24


------------------------------------------------------------------

                #    #  ##  ###  ##### #### #
                ##  # # # # #   #    #    #
                # # # #  # ###    #    ### #
                #  ## #  # # #   #    #    #
                #   # ## # #   #    #### ####

                #   # #### ##### #    #  ## ###  #  #  ###
                ##  # #     #    #     # # # # ## # # # #

                # # # ###    #    #  # # # # ### ##   ###
                #  ## #     #    # # # # # # # # # #     #
                #   # ####    #    #  # ## # # # # ###

                 ###   #  # ### ## #  #     ### ##### #    ### #####
                 #    # # # # #  #  # #     #     #  # # # # #   #
                 #    # # # # #  ##   ### ###    # #  # ### #   #
                 # # # # # # #  # #       #    # ##### # #   #
                  ###  #### ### ## # #     ###    # # # # # #   #
                      #

Release: 14.00  Date/Time: Mon Dec  6 22:08:33 GMT 1999  File/
Ver: install.bat(/main/58)
```

```
                    Copyright 1993-1999
-----------------------------------------------------------------------


                         Introduction
                         ------------


This part of the Quick-Start procedure configures the initial IP
network interface on the router.  You perform this procedure so that
the router can communicate with the network management station.

Each step of this procedure is further described in the Quick-Start Guide.
As you perform the procedure, refer to the Quick-Start Guide for
additional helpful information and examples.

When you are finished with this procedure, the router will be able to
communicate with the network management station over the IP network. You
are then ready to install the network management software, as described in
in the Quick-Start Guide.

Each procedure step requires you to do one of the following things:
        1. Enter a number that corresponds to a selection.
        2. Enter 'y' for Yes;  'n' for No; 'q' for Quit.
        3. Enter a word or phrase referred to as a "text string."
        4. Enter <Return> to accept default displayed in [].

You must press the <Return> key after entering one of the above responses.

Press <Return> to Continue, q<Return> to Quit:


-----------------------------------------------------------------------


              Preliminary Information You Need to Know
              ----------------------------------------


Before you begin this procedure, you should gather the network
information listed below:

You Need to Know This Information:              For Example:
---------------------------------              ------------
Type of Net Module connecting the router's     DENM
IP network interface to the Site Manager.

Slot number where the Net Module resides.      2

Module number where the Net Module resides.    1

Communication type and connector number        Ethernet 10bT1
```

```
IP address of initial IP network interface        192.32.10.189

Subnet mask of initial IP network interface       255.255.255.0

IP address of Site Manager workstation            192.32.10.200

Do you wish to continue? (y/n)[y]: y


-----------------------------------------------------------------------

Step 1.  Specify the slot number where the Net Module resides.

                        Slot Menu for Net Module
                        ------------------------

   Slot    Module    Net Module             Processor Module
   ----    ------    ----------             ----------------
     1        1      DENM                    ASN
     1        2      SE100NM                 ASN
     1        3      Empty                   ASN
     1        4      DSNM                    ASN

Slot 1 selected.
Enter the module number [1]:



-----------------------------------------------------------------------
Step 2. Specify the Net Module and network interface information for
        the initial IP connection to the Site Manager.

Net Module: DENM

Driver Type: Ethernet


Connector Menu
--------------
1. 10bT1 or AUI1
2. 10bT2 or AUI2

Enter connector number [1]: 1


Recommended Circuit Name: E111

Enter circuit name [E111]: E11


-----------------------------------------------------------------------
```

Step 3.   Specify the IP configuration information for the network
          interface.

```
                     IP Configuration Menu
                     --------------------

 IP address format:              ###.###.###.###

 IP subnetwork mask format:  ###.###.###.###
                      Example: 255.255.255.0



Enter IP address in dotted decimal notation: 193.20.214.2


Enter IP subnetwork mask in dotted decimal notation: 255.255.255.0


Is the router connected to the same local area network as
the Site Manager workstation? (y/n)[n]: n


------------------------------------------------------------------------

                  SNMP Community Management Menu
                  ------------------------------

Setting up SNMP community management is optional.

It allows you to limit control of this router to a single
Site Manager workstation at a given IP address.  The default
is to allow any Site Manager from any workstation to manage
and to configure the router.

Note: You can later configure this using Site Manager.

Do you wish to set SNMP community management? (y/n)[n]: y

Enter IP address of Site Manager workstation: 193.20.214.1


Enter SNMP management community name [public]: public


-----------------------------------------------------------------
Step 4.   Select TFTP default volume.

                     TFTP Default Volume Menu
                     -----------------------
```

```
Do you want to enable TFTP? (y/n) [y]: y



 NVFS File System:

VOL    STATE      TOTAL SIZE    FREE SPACE    CONTIG FREE SPACE
----------------------------------------------------------------
 1:    FORMATTED   8388608       522118          521580

Enter volume number [1]: 1



TFTP default volume is 1:

------------------------------------------------------------------------
Step 5.  Select FTP default volume.

                                   FTP Menu
                                   --------

Do you want to enable FTP? (y/n) [n]: y



 NVFS File System:

VOL    STATE      TOTAL SIZE    FREE SPACE    CONTIG FREE SPACE
----------------------------------------------------------------
 1:    FORMATTED   8388608       522118          521580

Enter volume number [1]: 1



FTP default volume is 1:

------------------------------------------------------------------------
Step 6.  Enable TELNET

                   Enable the Technician Interface via TELNET
                   -----------------------------------------

Do you want to enable TI TELNET? (y/n) [n]: y



TI TELNET enabled.

------------------------------------------------------------------------
```

```
Step 7.  Enable HTTP

                      Enable the HTTP (Web) Server
                      ----------------------------

Do you want to enable the HTTP (Web) server? (y/n)[n]: n




------------------------------------------------------------------------

                          Configuration Summary
                          ---------------------


Net Module:            DENM
Module Number:         1
Connector:             1
Slot:                  1
Circuit Name:          E111
IP address:            193.20.214.2
IP subnetwork mask:    255.255.255.0
TFTP Default Volume:   1:
FTP Default Volume:    1:
TI TELNET:             Yes
Site Manager's IP:     193.20.214.1
SNMP Community name:   public
HTTP Server:           No

NOTE: The Connector value in the above Configuration Summary
is the Connector number as seen on the ASN Net Module Bracket.
Note, however, that within the event log and the MIB browsing
utilities such as Site Manager's Quick Get and the Technician
Interface's debug scripts, connectors are numbered by a
combination of their Connector number and Module number. The
interface you have selected will henceforth be referred to
as Connector 11.
------------------------------------------------------------------------


Press [RETURN] to continue:




------------------------------------------------------------------------
Step 8. Specify a name for the configuration file.

                       Save configuration to a file.
                       -----------------------------


The Quick-Start configuration of the router is now complete and active.
```

```
Do you wish to save this configuration to a file? (y/n)[y]: y

Default file name is startup.cfg on the current volume.

NOTE: Do *NOT* name this file 'config'. Later, you may wish to rename
      this file 'config' after you perform a named boot and verify its
      operation.

Enter file name [startup.cfg]: nnbg.cfg

----------------------------------------------------------------------
Step 9.  Test this initial IP interface configuration.

                            TEST IP Interface
                            -----------------

IP Interface 193.20.214.2 is alive


IP Interface test stopped by user.

The router installation procedure has completed but is untested.
----------------------------------------------------------------------

Exiting...
```

TI Operating Commands   The TI operating commands allow you to perform operations such as rebooting the router, checking directory information, getting command syntax assistance, and more.

> **NOTE:**   In TI, a slot number will be referred to as a volume number. For instance, slot 2 is equal to volume 2; more specifically, the flash card in slot 2 is volume 2.

boot—The boot command will reboot the router. If used without any parameters, or with a minus (–), it will boot the default image and config file. If you want to specify a different image file or configuration file, you will have to specify the directory that the files are in and the file names.
   The command

```
[x:y]$  boot
```

will boot the router with the image file and config file in the default volume.
   The command

```
[x:y]$  boot 3:bn.exe 1:newconfig.cfg
```

will boot with the image file bn.exe from slot 3 and will boot with the configuration file 'newconfig.cfg' from slot 1.

The command

```
[x:y]$  boot - 3:newest.cfg
```

will boot the image file from the current volume and the file 'newest.cfg' from volume 3.

NOTE: In the preceding example, a minus sign is used to command the router to use the default image file.

cd—Will change from one volume to another.

The command

```
[x:y]$  cd 4:
```

will switch from the current volume to volume 4.

dir—The directory command will list all of the files that are contained on the flash card of the current volume (slot) that TI is running from. To list the files on another volume, you will enter the dir command, followed by the volume number that contains the flash card from which you are asking for a listing.

The command

```
[x:y]$  dir
```

will list all of the files on the current volume (see Figure 6-5).

The command

```
[x:y]$  dir 3:
```

will list all the files that are contained on the flash card that is in slot 3.

help—One of the most often used TI commands is the help command. The help command will provide a list of the TI operating commands that are available to the user and will provide usage information and command definitions.

The command

```
[x:y]$  help
```

will provide a complete list of TI operating commands and the syntax requirements. The help command is shown here:

```
[x:y]$ help
!         [<repeat count>]
alias     [<name> [["]<alias_value>["]]]
arrayenv  [-a] <variable name> "<string1>" ["<string2>" ...]
atmarp    table [<options>] <IP address>
```

```
[1:1] $ dir

Volume in drive 1: is
Directory of 1:


File Name            Size      Date      Day      Time
------------------------------------------------------
awsphx2.cfg         237096    07/11/2000   Tues.   16:18:12
nsm8up5.cfg          16136    07/11/2000   Tues.   16:17:17
asn.exe            6889628    07/12/2000   Wed.    13:41:25
asnboot.exe         246392    07/12/2000   Wed.    13:43:20
asndiag.exe         225884    07/12/2000   Wed.    13:43:27
config                 504    07/12/2000   Wed.    13:43:40
debug.al             12319    07/12/2000   Wed.    13:43:43
install.bat         237335    07/12/2000   Wed.    13:43:45
ti_asn.cfg             504    07/12/2000   Wed.    13:43:51


  8388608 bytes - Total size
   522470 bytes - Available free space
   522470 bytes - Contiguous free space
```

Figure 6-5.   The dir command

```
bcc
bconfig   <image | config> <local | network> [<IP address> <pathname>]
bconfig   -d <image | config>
boot      [<vol>:<image_name>|- <vol>:<config_name>|-]
cd        [<vol>:][<directory>]
clear     <sub_commands> <flags>
clearlog  [<slot ID>]
commit
compact   <volume>:
copy      <vol>:<filename1> <vol>:<filename2>
cutenv    -s -d<delimiter> [-f<list>|-c<list>] <variable> "<text string>"
date      [<mm/dd/yy>] [<hh:mm:ss>] [<+|-><hh:mm>]
delete    <vol>:<filename>
diags     [<slot ID>]
dinfo
dir       <vol:>
disable   <entity> <option>
echo      [["]<string>["]]
```

```
enable    <entity> <option>
enumenv   <start #> [+<incr.> <variable name> [<variable name> ...]
exec      [-load|-unload] <command name>
export    {<variable name> ...}
firewall  <sub_command>
format    <volume>:
fwputkey  [<key_string> <ip_address>] | [clearkey]
get       {<obj_name>|<obj_id>}.{<attr_name>|<attr_id>|*}[.{<inst_id>|*}]
getcfg
getenv    [<variable name>]
gosub     :<label name>:
goto      :<label name>:
help      [-all|<command>]
history   [n]
if        "<string1>" [<=>|<!=>] "<string2>" [then]; command(s) ;
ifconfig [-s] [-d|-enable|-disable] <xcvr>|[-r4|-r16] <mau>
          [<IP addr> <mask> [<Next Hop>]]
ifconfig [-s] [-fr [-annexd|-lmi|-annexa]] | [-int_clk] | [-d|-enable|
          -disable] <com> [<IP addr> <mask> [<Next Hop>]]
instenv   <variable prefix> <mib-object name> [<mib-instance-pattern>]
ip        <sub_command> <flags>
ip6       <sub_command> [<options>]
ipsec     <sub_command> [<options>]
isdb <sub_command> [-s<slot>] [-c<connector>] [-p<port>] [<vol>:<filename>]
kexit
kget   <sub_command>
kpassword
kseed
ksession
kset   <sub_command> [<flags>]
ktranslate <old_npk>
let       <var. name> = <expression>
list      [[<instances> [<obj_name>]]]
loadmap   [<slot list> | all] [<filepath>]
log       [<vol>:<logfile>] [-d<date>] [-t<time>] [-e"<entity>"]
[-f<severity>]
          [-s<slot ID>] [-p[<rate>]] [-c<code #>]
log       [-x|-i] [-e"<entity>"] [-f<severity>] [-s<slot ID>]
log       -z [-s<slot ID>]
logout
mibget    [-n] [-p <pattern>] <object> <attribute var. array> <inst. id>
          <value var. array> <next_inst var.>
more      [on | off] [# of lines per screen]
mrinfo    [-r retry_count] [-t timeout_count] multicast_router
mtrace    [-M] [-O] [-U] [-s] [-w wait] [-m max_hops] [-q nqueries]
              [-g gateway] [ -e extrahops ] [-S statint] [-t ttl]
              [-r resp_dest] [-i if_addr] source [receiver] [group]
octetfmt  <variable name> <format option> <MIB object>
```

```
on          ERROR :<label name>:
osi <subcommand> [<options>]
osidata    -s <SLOT> -t <lsp_l1 | lsp_L2 | path_L1 | path_L2 |
                        adj_L1 | adj_L2 | adj_ES> -i <ID>
partition create|delete [<vol>:]
password   [<login-id>]
pause      <seconds>
permit     [ -file    [<vol>:]<filename> ] |
           [   <command>    [<attribute>] ] |
           [   <mib object> ]
ping       <-IP| -IPV6| -IPX|-OSI|-VINES|-AT|-APPN> <hostname|address>
           [-t<timeout>] [-r<repeat count>] [-s<size>] [-p] [-a<address>]
           [-m<mode_name>] [-iifindex] [-v] [-n]
pktdump    <linenumber> [-s<start>] [-c<count>]
printf     <format string>  <p1> <p2> ... <pN>
prom       [-v|-w] <vol>:<ROM Update File> <slot ID> [<slot ID> ...]
readexe    <vol>:<filename>
record     open [-fileonly] [-pause]  <vol>:<filename>
           record pause [on|off]
           record close
reset      [<slot ID>]
restart    [<slot ID>]
return      :<label name>:
revoke     <command> [<attribute>]
rsvp       <sub_command>
run        <vol>:<filename> [<p1> [... <p9>]]
save       {config|aliases|perm} <vol>:<filename>
save       log [<vol>:<logfile>] [-d<date>] [-t<time>] [-e"<entity>"]
               [-f<severity>] [-s<slot ID>]
securelogin
set        {<obj_name>|<obj_id>}.{<attr_name>|<attr_id>}.<inst_id> <value>
setenv     <variable name> "<text string>"
show       <entity> <option>
snmpserver view [view-name] [oid-tree] [included | excluded | list |
delete]
           community [community-name] view [view-name] [RO | RW | list | delete]

source     {aliases|env|perm} <vol>:<filename>
sprintf    <variable name> <format string>  <p1> <p2> ... <pN>
stamp
stop       <slot ID>
string     load|unload
system
tarp   <sub_command> <flags>
telnet     [-d] [-e escape_char] [hostname|address [port]]
tftp       {get|put} <name|address> <vol>:<file_spec> [<vol>:<file_spec>]
```

```
type      [-x] <vol>:<filename>
unalias   {<alias name>|*}
unmount   <volume>:
unsetenv  [<variable name> ...| [-l] [-g] *]
verbose   [on | off]
xmodem    rb|sb [ylwpn] filename...
wfsnmpkey <key_string> [encryption_alg_id]
wfsnmpmode <proprietary(3) | trivial(1)>
wfsnmpseed <community> <manager> [-|<val1>] [-|<val2>] [-|<val3>]
           [-|<val4>] [-|<val5>]
```

The command

```
[x:y] $  help help
```

will provide a list of all TI operating commands in a tabled format (see Figure 6-6).

```
[x:y] $ help help

Usage:
help     [-all|<command>]

Privilege: Secure Shell & Manager & Operator & User

The Help command can be entered stand-alone to get general command syntax
or it can include one of the following command names for more detailed
information. The command help -all will display the help information
for all of the commands listed below.

alias     arrayenv   atmarp    bcc        bconfig   boot
cd        clearlog   commit    compact    copy      cutenv
date      delete     diags     dinfo      dir       disable
echo      enable     enumenv   exec       export    firewall
format    fwputkey   get       getcfg     getenv    gosub
goto      help       history   if         ifconfig  instenv
ip        ip6        isdb      kexit      kget      kpassword
kseed     ksession   kset      ktranslate let       list
loadmap   log        logout    mibget     more      mrinfo
```

Figure 6-6. The help help command

The command

```
[x:y]$  help <command>
```

will provide help text for the given command (see Figure 6-7 in which we ask for help on the *run* command).

```
[x:y] $ help run

Usage:
run     <vol>:<filename> [<p1> [... <p9>]]

Privilege: Manager & Operator & User


The Run command is used to read and execute the T1 commands in a
T1 script file. To locate script errors, use the "verbose on"
command first and then the run command. Now each line from the file
is displayed before it is executed allowing the line with the error
to be located. The -s flag can be used in combination with the on error
command to silently run a script file. If the script file is not present,
the run -s command returns silently allowing the on error handler to process
the error. The env. variable, RUN_SILENT, if defined, is the same as run -s.

  Syntax:

      run <vol>:<filename> [<p1> [<p2> [...<p9>]]]

      where <p1>...<p9> are optional input parameters to
      the script file. They may be referenced within the
      script file as follows:
          <p1> -> $1
          <p2> -> $2
          ...
          <p9> -> $9

      The special variable "$#" contains the number
      of parameters entered on the command line. It is set
      to zero if none are entered.
```

Figure 6-7.   An example of the help command used for assistance with a specific command

!—The repeat command will issue the last command that was entered. For example, you have entered the following command:

```
[x:y]$  help
```

As you have already learned, this will display a list of TI commands and associated syntax. Now for our purposes let's say you have already issued the help command. If you want to reuse the help command right away, you can re-type **help**, or can type the repeat command to have your command entered again. For instance,

```
[x:y]$  !
```

NOTE: It is assumed that this example is a little far-fetched. It would be just as simple to re-enter the command, or better yet, to enter the command "more on" before you re-enter this command. The ! command is useful with troubleshooting and using MIBs. Some MIB commands contain multiple characters, and if a MIB command needs to be entered multiple times, the ! command is a tremendous time saver.

history—You can use the history command to recall a list of the most recent commands that have been entered in the TI during the current session. By default, this number will be the last 20 commands, but that number can be changed to list up to the last 40 commands. The history command also can be used to recall a specific command from the list.

The command

```
[x:y]$  history
```

will provide a list of the most recently entered commands (up to the last 20 by default). See Figure 6-8 for an example of this.

The command

```
[x:y]$  history 3
```

will run the command that is listed as item 3 from the history command output. See Figure 6-9 for an example of the history command.

more—Is another widely used command. Very often (especially when viewing event logs) the command you enter will contain many pages of information. The default setting for TI is to display 24 lines of text and then pause to give the user an opportunity to review the output. The more command will allow the user an opportunity to turn this on or off. Examples of the more command are shown in Figure 6-10.

```
[x:y] $ history
    1 help
    2 more off
    3 help
    4 help help
    5 help dinfo
    6 help run
    7 help ping
    8 dir
    9 dir 1:
    10 dir2:
    11 help dinfo
    12 help
```

Figure 6-8. The history command

The command

```
[x:y]$   more off
```

will turn off the page pausing and will display output through completion.

NOTE: If you need to stop the output of a command before it reaches the end, you can stop it by pressing CTRL-C.

The command

```
[x:y}   more on
```

will restore the paging capabilities to default system settings.

```
[x:y] $ history 3
help
!      [<repeat count>]
alias      [<name> [["]<alias_value>["]]]
arrayenv [-a] <variable name> "<string1>"["<string2>"...]
atmarp    table [<options>] <IP address>
bcc
bconfig    <image | config> <local | network> [<IP address> <pathname>]
bconfig  -d <image | config>
boot    [<vol>:<image_name>|- <vol>:<config_name>|-]
cd    [<vol>:][<directory>]
clear    <sub_commands> <flags>
clearlog    [<slot ID>]
commit
compact    <volume>:
copy    <vol>:<filename1><vol>:<filename2>
cutenv    -s -d<delimiter> [-f<list> | -c<list>] <variable> "<text string>"
date    [<mm/dd/yy>] [<hh:mm:ss>] [<+|-><hh:mm>]
delete    <vol>:<filename>
diags    [<slot ID>]
dinfo
dir    <vol:>
disable    <entity> <option>
echo    [["]<string>["]]
enable    <entity> <option>
enumenv    <start#> [+<incr.> <variable name> [<variable name> ...]
```

Figure 6-9. The history command for a specific line number

NOTE: If you want to change the output before pausing from 24 to another number, this is accomplished by entering the number of lines after you have entered the more on command. The default is 24 lines per page, which is the maximum that can be shown on the screen.

clearlog—Will purge the event log. It is a good idea to save the current log before running this command. This command will erase all historical event information.

commit—Will ensure that any changes made through the MIBs are invoked and saved.

compact—Will regain available space that currently is unusable. For instance, the dinfo command returns the amount of available free space and contiguous free space in units of bytes. The compact command will purge deleted information from the flash card and will regain the difference between contiguous free space and available free space.

```
              [x:y] $ more off
                More Mode: OFF
                Lines per screen: 24

              [x:y] $ more on
                More Mode: ON
                Lines per screen: 24

              [x:y] $ more on 15
                More Mode: ON
                Lines per screen: 15
```

Figure 6-10.   The more command

date—Will display the current date and time and will allow you to change the current date and time.

delete—The delete command will delete a file from a specified flash card. It is very important to ensure that you specify the correct file name and volume number when using the delete command. TI does not verify actions, and you can easily lose vital information during this process.

The command

```
[x:y]$  delete 2:oldconfig.cfg
```

will delete the file 'oldconfig.cfg' from volume 2.

NOTE: Flash card space that contains deleted information cannot be used until the *compact* command has been used.

dinfo—The dinfo command will list all volumes (slots) that contain a flash card, the total size of the flash card, how much free space is available, and how much free space can be used (contiguous free space). Figure 6-11 shows an example of the dinfo command usage.

```
[x:y] $  dinfo

VOL       STATE        TOTAL SIZE       FREE SPACE        CONTIG FREE SPACE
- - - - - - - - - - - - - - - - - - - - - - - - - - - - - - - - - - - - - - - - -
2:        FORMATTED    16777216         9065013           9065013
```

Figure 6-11.   The dinfo command

format—The format command will erase everything from a flash card.

log—The log command will display the event log. There are multiple variables that can be specified, depending on the information you are trying to obtain.

password—This command allows you to change the manager and user passwords. Figure 6-12 shows the syntax and output from the password command.

NOTE: In the example, it is assumed you are in the manager mode.

```
[x:y] $ password
Changing password for Manager
Old password:
New Password:
Retype new password:
Manager password change.

[x:y] $ password User
Changing password for User
Old password:
New Password:
Retype new password:
User password change.
```

Figure 6-12.   Examples of the password command

ping—The ping command allows you to test the reachability of another node on the network. The following lists the protocols that the Nortel Network router supports for the ping command:

▼ IP

■ IPX

■ OSI

■ VINES

■ AppleTalk (AT)

▲ APPN

There are quite a few parameters that also can be added to the syntax of the ping command to specify certain conditions in which to invoke the ping command. These parameters are as follows:

▼ **-a**—Allows you the option of placing a source address that you want specified in the source address field of the Internet Control Message Protocol (ICMP) echo request packet.

■ **-p**—When this parameter is specified, the ping will generate a report that will provide hop information to the destination address that was specified in the ping.

■ **-r**—Specifies the number of ping messages to send. The default value is 3.

■ **-s**—Specifies the amount of data (in bytes) to send with each ping request. The default value is 16 bytes and is the size of the ping if no value is specified.

■ **-t**—Specifies the number of seconds in which the ping will time out.

▲ **-v**—Provides statistical information about the ICMP echo request packet.

The command

```
[x:y]$  ping 195.34.131.14
```

will send a ping request packet to the IP destination address 195.34.131.14.

NOTE: If you want to specify any parameter to the ping request, it will need to follow the IP address. Multiple parameters can be specified, but they need to have a space in between each parameter. The correct syntax for these parameters is a minus sign (-) followed by the parameter and, if applicable, a value.

prom—Programmable Read Only Memory. This command will allow you to read the current version of hardware proms that are loaded on a particular slot. This command will allow you to upgrade and verify prom upgrades. See Chapter 5 for an example of a prom upgrade.

save—Allows the config file to be saved. Also allows you to save an event log and allows aliases to be saved.

The command

```
[x:y]$  save config 1:config
```

will save the current running config to the flash card in volume 1 as a file named config.

stamp—The stamp command is used to list the image file that is being used and the date the file was loaded onto the router. Figure 6-13 is an example of the stamp command and its output.

TI Management Information Base Commands   There are a few commands that are accessed through the TI that allow you to access the Management Information Base (MIB). We discuss MIB in the next section of this chapter. For now we shall introduce these commands: list, list instances, get, set, and commit.

The Management Information Base

The Management Information Base is a database that contains MIB objects (commonly referred to as MIBs). These MIB objects can be accessed by the Simple Network Management Protocol (SNMP) and manipulated through the different user interfaces. The database contains information such as the name of the MIB object, setting, options, and so forth. The MIB database enables the user to configure a router and obtain statistics about the network that the router has obtained. The structure and concept of the MIB actually is quite simple, yet many people find this the hardest thing to master when learning about routers and other network devices.

The MIB is a very important part of your network. Understanding the MIB is one of the most important things that must be accomplished. The MIB is necessary when troubleshooting a router or diagnosing network problems. The MIB objects are accessed for network management and configuration purposes. They are identified by a sequence of numbers that are provided through a global naming tree.

[x:y] $ stamp

Image: rev/14.00/1D
Created: Thu Apr 20 20:34:00 EDT 2000

Figure 6-13.   The stamp command

The way that MIB objects are organized is defined by the Internet Engineering Task Force (IETF). The IETF has established a standard MIB object structure for vendors to use when defining the MIB objects for their products. This set structure is the global naming tree that was referred to in the preceding paragraph. The Object Identifier (OID) string is a series of numbers that defines the path to the MIB object. The OID string is lengthy, and each transition through the global naming tree is defined with a dot.

For instance, using a global naming tree enables you to assign a non-negative integer to an object; let's say the Alamo in San Antonio, Texas. For our OID, we will define the location of this object. The integers for this example are assigned as follows:

```
14 = San Antonio
88 = Texas
00 = is in
12 = The Alamo
```

Therefore, the OID string for our object "The Alamo is in San Antonio, Texas" is

```
12.00.14.88.
```

This illustrates the concept of how the OID string works; now we will take a look at the OID string and the MIB global naming tree, or MIB tree.

The Object Identifier (OID) String and the MIB Tree

The Object Identifier (OID) string defines a numeric path to a MIB object. It is a standard that is established by the IETF. The following values are standard values and are used by all vendors:

```
1 = ISO
3 = ORG
6 = DOD
1 = Internet
4 = Private
1 = Enterprises
```

Therefore, the OID that we have learned thus far is as follows:

```
1.3.6.1.4.1or ISO.ORG.DOD.Internet.Private.Enterprises
```

The remaining values of the OID string are private values and are vendor specific. The next value of the OID string for Nortel Networks products is always 18, which is reserved for Wellfleet.

NOTE: Bay Networks acquired Wellfleet; Nortel Networks acquired Bay Networks. The Wellfleet OID is still used by all Nortel Networks routers.

Therefore, the OID string that is used for all objects within the Nortel Networks routers will be

`1.3.6.1.4.1.18 (iso.org.dod.internet.private.enterprises.Wellfleet)`

The remainder of the OID will be specific to the object on the Nortel Networks router that you are accessing. Figure 6-14 shows how the OID is used in the MIB tree.

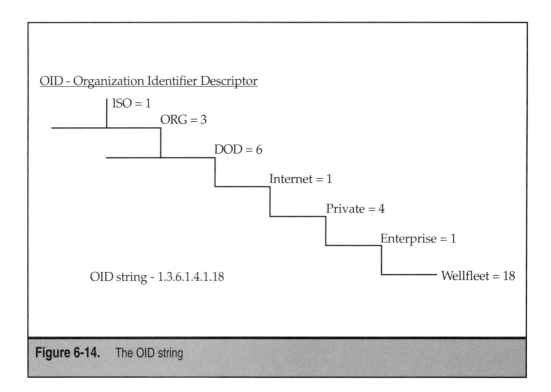

Figure 6-14.   The OID string

MIB Overview

In the preceding section, we discussed the OID string and the MIB tree. Now let's take a look at the structure of the MIB objects. A MIB object has four parts:

▼ **Object**—Stored data that serves a purpose. Each object is a collection of MIB objects.

■ **Attribute**—A variable parameter.

■ **Instance**—A manifestation of an attribute.

▲ **Value**—The data that is contained in a location of the MIB that is a combined sum of an instance of an attribute and the object the attribute is associated with.

The MIBs follow a set structure that remains consistent regardless of which MIB is being accessed. The MIB structure is as follows:

```
object.attribute.instance = value
```

For MIBs within the Nortel Networks router, there are a few things that remain the same. All objects that will be manipulated in a Nortel Networks router will begin with "wf" (for Wellfleet). Every object has several unique attributes that are associated with and can be assigned to the object; an instance is an identifier of the object and the attribute that has been chosen.

Hardware information or system information that is configured only one time on a router and is non-changing will always have a single instance identifier. This identifier will always be a value equal to zero. There are other instances that can be used to identify all attributes associated with a particular IP interface address, circuit number, or slot number.

MIB variables can be accessed directly through BCC or TI. MIB variables also can be accessed indirectly through Site Manager. MIB changes that are performed in TI will not be verified for errors. Therefore, it is advisable to do changes through Site Manager as often as possible. Additionally, it is very important to pay attention to spelling and case usage when performing MIB changes through the TI. MIB strings are case sensitive.

MIB Commands   There are five MIB access commands that are used in TI (the short form of each of these commands is listed in the parenthesis):

▼ **list (l)**—The list command will allow you to view object names and any associated identifiers to that object. The identifiers will be identified with an assigned numeric value.

■ **list –instances (l –i)**—The list –instances command will allow you to view the instances that are configured on a particular object.

- **get (g)**—The get command will allow you to view the value of an attribute.
- **set (s)**—The set command will allow you to change the value of an attribute.
- ▲ **commit (c)**—The commit command will change the value of an attribute in memory (see Figure 6-15).

NOTE: If the set command is used to change the value of an attribute but the commit command was not used, the command will not take effect.

When an MIB change is made through TI, the value is changed dynamically and cannot be reversed after the commit command has been used. You must be very careful when using TI to make MIB changes. If a value to a global protocol is changed, it will reset the whole router. Therefore, it is advisable to make such changes at such a time when there are fewer users accessing the router (late night or on a weekend).

Determining and Defining MIBs   Many MIB objects can be identified by the name of the MIB, so very often you can determine which MIB you will want by its name. Here is a list of common MIBs:

- ▼ wfHwEntry
- wfIpBase
- wfTcp
- wfIpIntfCfgEntry
- wfIpInterfaceEntry
- wfTelnet
- wfCircuitNameEntry
- wfIpNetToMediaEntry
- wfSnmpCommEntry
- wfSnmpMgrEntry
- wfTokenRingEntry
- wfCSMACDEntry
- ▲ wfProtocols

[1:N01FX I]$**s wfIpIntfCfgEntry.2.172.31.8.1.46 2;commit**

Figure 6-15.   Using commit

There also is a very useful tool that can assist you in defining MIBs contained within Site Manager. When Site Manager is installed on your PC, it is, by default, placed into the wf directory on your hard drive. Contained in the wf directory is a sub-directory called MIBS. You can open any of the files contained in the MIBS directory through any text editor program (such as Microsoft Word, Notepad, or Wordpad).

Most of the filenames in the MIBS directory will identify the MIB object types contained within the file. In the file is a very detailed description of each MIB object, attribute, and instance value. Also, usage syntax examples are provided.

The Analogy of the MIB   Using the MIBs for troubleshooting and configuration is a very helpful tool. There is nothing that cannot be done on the router that is not accessed through the MIBs. Learning to use the MIBs can be one of the hardest things to learn. This section has taken MIB changes to a very elementary level to help explain it better.

For the sake of simplicity we will discuss something we are all very familiar with: the automobile. We need to identify the automobile, the type of automobile, and the color. A list of attributes is provided, and the instance will be the type of car.

```
Object = wfCar
Attributes:
  wfColor=green
  wfModel=accord
  wfYear=2000
Instance = Honda
```

Now remember that the MIB structure is as follows:

```
Object.attribute.instance = value
```

Therefore, using the list that we have provided, let's put our examples into the correct MIB structure (the appropriate OID string examples are listed under each MIB string):

```
WfCar.wfColor.Honda = Green
1.3.6.1.4.1.18.2.3.4
WfCar.wfModel.Honda = Accord
1.3.6.1.4.1.18.2.5.4
WfCar.wfYear.Honda = 2000
1.3.6.1.4.1.18.2.67.4
```

NOTE: The OID strings and the MIBs in this example are intended to give you an easy-to-understand example of an MIB that might be used with a Nortel Networks router object. Take particular notice of the OID string. Do you recognize any part of it? Assume the value of 2 for car, 3 for color, 4 for Honda, 5 for Accord, and 67 for year.

You probably are asking yourself how exactly we would use the MIB command to make any sense out of this. Keep in mind that when using an MIB value, we also can use the OID for that value instead. Following are examples of MIB command usage:

NOTE: When using the TI MIB commands, you can use the whole command, or just the first letter of the command name; for example l or list, s or set, and so forth.

You want to list the object wfCar:

```
[x:y]$  l wfCar*
wfCar=1.3.6.1.4.1.18.2
```

You want to list all objects that contain wfC:

```
 [x:y]$  l wfC*
      wfCar=1.3.1.4.1.18.2
wfCart=1.3.6.1.4.1.18.9}
wfCarage=1.3.6.1.4.1.18.12
```

You want to list all attributes for wfCar:

```
[x:y]$  l wfCar
    wfColor=1
   wfModel=2
wfModel=3
```

You want to list all instances of wfCar:

```
[x:y]$  l -i wfCar
instances=Honda
VW
Chevrolet
```

To get all the attributes for an instance:

```
[x:y]$g wfCar.*.Honda
wfCar.wfColor=Green
wfCar.wfModel=Accord
wfCar.wfYear=2000
```

To get one attribute for all instances:

```
[x:y]g wfCar.1.*
wfCar.wfColor.Honda=Green
wfCar.wfColor.VW=Red
wfCar.wfColor.Chevrolet=Yellow
```

To get one attribute for one object:

```
[x:y] g wfCar.wfModel.Honda
wfCar.wfModel.Honda=Accord
```

To use the OID as a get:

```
[x:y] g 1.3.6.1.4.1.18.2.2
wfCar.wfModel.1 = Honda
```

To set an attribute for an instance:

```
[x:y] s wfCar.wfColor.Honda "Yellow"
wfCar.wfColor.Honda=Yellow
 [x:y] $  commit
```

Site Manager

Site Manager is an SNMP software application that provides a graphical user interface (GUI), which allows easy configuration of the Nortel Networks AN and BN router families.

Site Manager not only allows a user to configure a router; it also allows the user the ability to perform certain network management functions. Site Manager can connect to, configure, and perform these network management functions to any Nortel Networks router that it can gain IP access to. Site Manager can be loaded and run on a number of PC platforms, including

▼ **MS-DOS–based 486 PCs and higher**—Requires a Winsock-compliant IP stack

■ **Windows 95, 98, NT, and 2000**—Requires a Winsock-compliant IP stack

■ **Sun Workstations**—Runs on a UDP/IP stack that is part of the operating system

■ **HP 9000 Workstations**—Runs on a UDP/IP stack that is part of the operating system

▲ **RS 6000 Workstations**—Runs on a UDP/IP stack that is part of the operating system

NOTE: Winsock is an application programming interface that allows application developers to program applications in a manner in which multiple vendors can conform to and utilize the program. Because Site Manager is Winsock compliant, it can be used with any platform that contains a Winsock-compliant protocol stack.

To connect to the router with Site Manager, the workstation that is running Site Manager must have TCP/IP running. There are several different methods of connecting a Site Manager workstation to a Nortel Networks router:

▼ Direct connection between the workstation and the router's IP network interface.

■ Point-to-point protocol can be used where the Site Manager obtains access to the router by dialing a terminal server that supports IP.

■ Any Site Manager workstation that is running IP can connect through the IP network to the router.

▲ A remote PC can connect to a Site Manger workstation through a modem connection.

As mentioned previously, Site Manger is the preferred Nortel Networks router configuration application. Before you can use Site Manger, an IP interface must be configured on the router. Remember that running the install.bat script file through the TI, which was described earlier in this chapter, will provide you with the vehicle in which to add your management IP interface onto your router.

Connecting to the Router with Site Manager

Once an IP address has been configured on the router and Site Manager is loaded onto your workstation, you can connect to the router with Site Manger. Site Manager will open with a router connection options window (see Figure 6-16). The IP address 192.32.6.4 (which is a Nortel Networks default IP address) will show up in the IP address portion of this dialog box.

Replace the default IP address with the IP address of your router IP interface in the IP section of the router connection options window (see Figure 6-17). The next thing you want to enter is the SNMP community that you configured on the interface. The community string will default to 'public.'

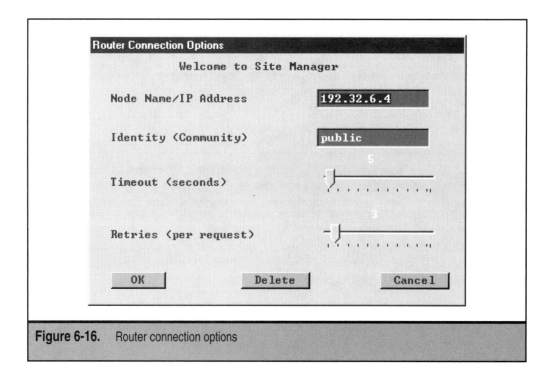

Figure 6-16. Router connection options

Router Connection Options

Welcome to Site Manager

Node Name/IP Address   193.21.214.2|

Identity (Community)   public

Figure 6-17.   Replacing the IP address on the router connection window

NOTE: For security reasons, the community string can be and is usually changed when the router is implemented in a production environment.

Once you have entered the correct information in the router command options window, click OK. When you have clicked OK, a connection will be established; you then will see the system information window (see Figure 6-18). The system information screen will contain the following information:

▼ **System Name/IP Address**—This is the IP address of the management interface that you have configured on your router.

■ **SNMP ID (Community)**—This is the community ID that was configured on your router.

■ **System Name**—This is a name that you have assigned to your router. This is useful when you have a network with thousands of routers to maintain. Most system names are the names of buildings, floors, or some ID that identifies the physical location of the router; however, it can be configured to be anything you want.

■ **Contact**—Usually the name and phone number of the individual responsible for the network operations.

■ **Location**—Usually the physical location of the router.

■ **Description**—Identifies the version of code that is installed on the router and the install date and time.

■ **MIB Version**—Identifies the version of MIB code that is loaded.

■ **Model**—Identifies the type of router that you are viewing.

■ **Power Supply 1–4**—Identifies the number of power supplies that are installed in the router, and the operating status of each.

■ **Redundant Power Supply**—Identifies the number of backup power supplies.

■ **Fan**—Identifies whether the router has a fan installed and whether operating status is applicable.

▲ **Temperature**—Identifies environmental status of the route.

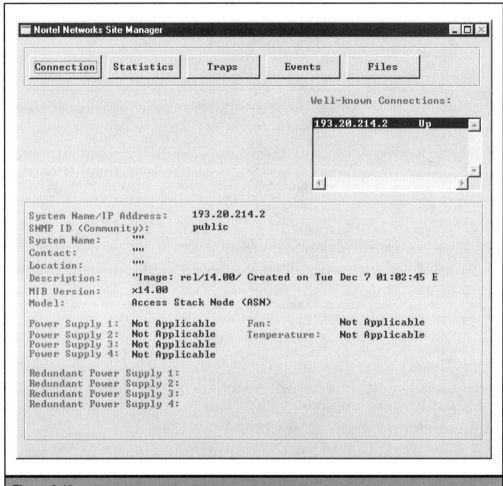

Figure 6-18. System information window

Site Manager Menu Options and Commands

In this section we discuss the various menu options and the associated functions these options provide. As stated previously, Site Manager is more than just a configuration tool; it is a management tool to assist in monitoring the router and network information gathered by the router. Keep in mind there is a lot of functionality that will not be covered in depth in this book, but an explanation of the frequently used functions will be discussed.

Refer back to the system information screen. We have already discussed the information that is contained in the bottom portion of this window, so now let's discuss the options that are available on the menu bar:

▼ **File**—Provides the option to exit Site Manager

■ **View**—Provides the option to refresh the current display

■ **Options**—Provides options for viewing the connections screen

■ **Tools**—Provides options and tools for network management, maintenance, and troubleshooting

▲ **Administration**—Provides administrative commands such as rebooting the router, resetting a slot, clearing the event log, pinging a device, and so forth

Site Manager Tools

Most of the menu bar items that were discussed in the last section are items that are self-explanatory, with the exception of the items that are listed under the Tools menu. The Tools menu contains various network management tools that can be very helpful in gathering statistics for troubleshooting and network performance purposes. These options are discussed in depth in another book published by Osborne/McGraw-Hill, *Nortel Networks: The Complete Reference* (ISBN 0-07-212027-4).

Available to you under the Tools menu is the Configuration Manager; this is the most often used tool in Site Manager. In the following you will find detailed information on this option. It is important to understand this option and the different selections that are available to you.

Configuration Manager   You are given a lot of benefits when configuring the router through Site Manager. Not only is it an easy-to-understand GUI interface; it also gives you the capabilities of configuring a router dynamically, remotely, and locally from a file folder. You can select the various file configuration options from the Tools menu in Site Manager, and then select the Configuration Manager. Listed under the Configuration Manager are the four options that you have to choose from when configuring the configuration file on the router (see Figure 6-19). The four modes that are provided to you as methods of configuring the router through Site Manager are

▼ **"Local File" mode**—This option allows the user to build and maintain router configuration files on their PC hard drives. To make changes to the router configuration file, the configuration file must be transferred to the local hard drive. Once a configuration file that has been manipulated is in local mode, the file must be transferred back to the router and saved. For the changes to be implemented on the router, the router must be rebooted with the new configuration file.

■ **"Remote File" mode**—This option is similar to the local mode except that instead of copying the file to your hard drive as you would in local file mode, Site Manager automatically will copy the configuration file from and to the router through TFTP. In other words, if you connect to the router and select the dynamic file mode option, Site Manager will TFTP the configuration file from the router to your hard drive and will TFTP the file back to the router when you have made your changes. Just like local file mode, the router must be rebooted before the changes go into effect.

■ **"Dynamic" mode**—This option will make changes to the router dynamically. The changes are not saved, however, until you save them to the configuration file on the flash card. If a mistake is made, you can recover using your original configuration file by rebooting the router. Once changes are made and saved, the new configuration remains as that configuration until other changes are made.

▲ **"Cache" mode**—This option is a combination of dynamic mode and remote file mode and is useful when Site Manager's router response time is slow. Cache mode will copy the running configuration on the router to the hard drive on the Site Manager workstation. Whenever a change is made to the configuration file in cache mode, the changes are recorded on the router and on the local file. Changes must be saved to the flash card to remain permanent to the router's configuration.

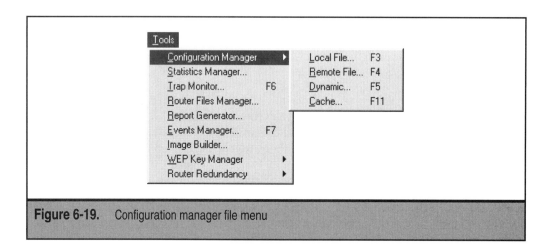

Figure 6-19.   Configuration manager file menu

Bay Command Console

The Bay Command Console is a command-line network management application. It is not automatically present when the router is booted; in fact, it must be run from the TI, similar to the method that the script files are run. The command that is used to get BCC running is

```
[x:y]$  bcc
```

BCC provides a lot of the functionality of the TI, but is inherently different. BCC also is similar to Site Manager in that it is more user friendly than TI. BCC also provides access to the MIB instances for quick troubleshooting and configuration checks. There are two modes that BCC can be run in:

▼ The BCC configuration mode

▲ The BCC initial mode

The BCC is supported in all Nortel Networks router platforms. It will run on ARE modules as well as FRE modules. To run BCC, each module must have a minimum of 8 MB RAM and 3 MB of free local memory.

TIP: 16 MB of RAM is recommended.

The BCC contains a configuration hierarchy similar to the directory file system that is used by DOS for a PC platform. BCC contains the parent object, with the child object defined under the parent in a tree structure. Each object that is contained in the BCC configuration system is assigned a root level that branches off to child levels, which branch off into further child levels, with the previous child level becoming the parent of the next child level. See Figure 6-20 for an example of this.

The BCC Initial Mode

The BCC contains two modes. The initial mode is the mode you will automatically be entered into when you initialize BCC (see Figure 6-21). This initial mode provides you with access to all of the commands you would use in TI. You will be able to identify whether you are in the initial mode by the prompt:

```
bcc>
```

The initial mode will allow you to monitor network statistics and view configuration settings. It also will allow you access to the configuration mode to make changes to the configuration of the router.

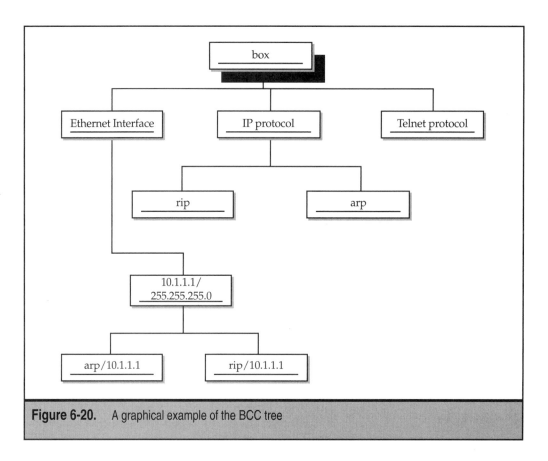

Figure 6-20. A graphical example of the BCC tree

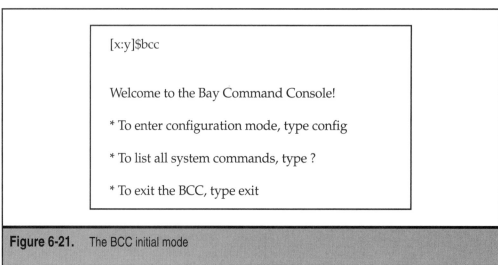

Figure 6-21. The BCC initial mode

The BCC Configuration Mode

The BCC configuration mode is used to configure the router. Typing the command 'config' after you have started your BCC session accesses the configuration mode of BCC. Once you have entered into configuration mode successfully, you will be given a 'box' prompt.

NOTE: When you access BCC while you are logged into the TI as Manager, you are automatically given read/write access. If you want to access BCC config mode as read-only, you can do this by specifying read-only when you type config.

For example,

```
config -read-only
```

If your prompt ends with a #, you are in read/write mode. If the prompt ends with a >, you are in read-only mode.

For instance,

box#—Identifies that you are in read/write mode

box>—Identifies that you are in read-only mode

The help command in BCC is a question mark (?) and will allow you to access online help from the box prompt. Figure 6-22 is an example of the help command used in the BCC configuration mode.

BCC Commands

The commands that are used in the BCC initial mode are similar to the commands that are used in TI. Figure 6-23 has a list of these commands, known as the system commands. The commands that are used in the BCC configuration mode are different from any other commands we have discussed thus far, and are what we will be focusing on.

Take a look at Figure 6-22. Notice that the command listing in the previous example is broken down into three separate sections:

▼ **Sub-Contexts**—Sub-contexts are the child contexts (directories) of the context you currently are in. For example, in the figure, access is a sub-context of the context box (where we are currently in).

■ **Parameters in Current Context**—These are the command parameters that can be used in the current context. Contact would be a parameter that would allow you to view and manipulate contact information.

▲ **System Commands**—System commands are the commands that are available in either mode of BCC. Many of these sub-commands are listed and defined in the next section.

```
box# ?

Sub-Contexts:
    access                hssi                      rmon
    atm                   http                      sdlc
    backup pool           ip                        serial
    board                 ipx                       snmp
    bridge                isdn-in-phone-list        srb
    console               isdn-switch               syslog
    demand-pool           llc2                      telnet
    dlsw                  mce1                      tftp
    dns                   mct1                      token-ring
    ethernet              nhrp                      tunnels
    fddi                  ntp                       virtual
    ftp                   radius                    wcp

Parameters in Current Context:
    build-date            description               system-name
    build-version         help-file-name            type
    console-slot-mask     location                  uptime
    contact               mib-counters
System Commands:
    ?                     exit                      pktdump
    back                  format                    prom
    bccExit               getcfg                    pwc
    bconfig               help                      readexe
    boot                  help-file-version         record
    cd                    history                   reset
    check                 ifconfig                  restart
    clear                 info                      rm
    clearlog              loadmap                   save
    commit                log                       securelogin
    compact               logout                    show
    config                lso                       snmpserver
    cp                    mbulk                     stamp
    cwc                   mdump                     stop
    date                  mget                      system
    delete                mlist                     telnet
    diags                 mnext                     tftp
    dinfo                 more                      type
    dir                   mset                      unmount
    disable               partition                 xmodem
```

Figure 6-22. The help command

```
bcc> ?
System Commands:

    ?                    exit                 pktdump
    back                 format               prom
    bccExit              getcfg               pwc
    bconfig              help                 readexe
    boot                 help-file-version    record
    cd                   history              reset
    check                ifconfig             restart
    clear                info                 rm
    clearlog             loadmap              save
    commit               log                  securelogin
    compact              logout               show
    config               lso                  snmpserver
    cp                   mbulk                stamp
    cwc                  mdump                stop
    date                 mget                 system
    delete               mlist                telnet
    diags                mnext                tftp
    dinfo                more                 type
    dir                  mset                 unmount
    disable              partition            xmodem
    display              password
    enable               ping
```

Figure 6-23.   BCC system commands

Command Listing   In this section we have listed the more popular BCC commands for easy reference:

▼ **back**—The back command can be used anywhere within your command session to return you to the root (box# or bcc>).

■ **bconfig**—This command is used to set up the boot configuration of the router.

■ **boot**—Used to boot the router. Like TI, this command can be used to boot to a specific image and config, or to defaults.

■ **clear**—The clear command is used to clear specified items. For example, to clear the routing table, you would used the following syntax:

```
bcc>clear ip route
```

- **clearlog**—Used to clear information in the event log.
- **config**—The config command is used to go from intial BCC mode to the BCC configuration mode.
- **cp**—The copy command. This command is used to copy the contents of a file to another file.
- **cwc**—The change working context command. This command is used to change your current context to another context.
- **exit**—The exit command is used to leave BCC.
- **help**—The help command is used to display information about a command or all commands. A question mark also can be used for help information.
- **info**—This command is used in configuration mode and is used to display system information.
- **lso**—This command is used in configuration mode and is used to list objects.
- **mbulk**—Used to give the MIB get for a specified MIB string.
- **mdump**—This command will provide a dump of every MIB set that is used in running configuration.
- **partition**—The partition command will allow the flash volume to be divided into multiple logical volumes.
- **pop**—Used to go back to the parent context. For example, if you are in the access sub-context of box, and you want to return to box, you can enter the pop command.
- **pwc**—The print working context command. This command will display the context structure, to assist in determining your current position in relation to the root.
- **rm**—Used to remove a file from a flash card.
- ▲ **tic**—Allows the use of a TI command from BCC. This command is used together with the TI command you would like to access.

CONCLUSION

In this chapter we have discussed the various ways to connect to and configure the Nortel Networks routers. We also discussed the various software packages that you can use for configuring and managing your routers. The commands that are provided within this chapter are the more widely used commands, but are not available. Make sure you understand your help tools and learn to use the MIBs, as they can be the best resource to use when troubleshooting.

CHAPTER 7

Routing Protocols

In Chapters 4 and 5 we discuss the networking devices that connect LANs to other LANs and eventually to WANs. We also discuss the purpose of these devices and the various networks that rely on them to transmit and receive data. In a perfect world, nothing would ever occur to disrupt the transport of network data; in actuality, there are endless fluctuations in data communications traffic patterns.

A network is subject to many changes. As the network grows, other devices need to be added to the network, changing its topology and the pathways that it knows to transport traffic. Traffic fluctuations can cause network devices to become inaccessible, which means the network must adjust the traffic direction to compensate for the outage this causes without end users being affected by the change. A loose cable also can cause a network to adjust its traffic patterns.

To ensure that network traffic remains reliable when the network itself has had a few changes, rules, known as protocols, must be defined for the network. Protocols also are important in that they provide all multiple data types, vendors, network topologies, and so forth a vehicle by which to communicate and reliably send and receive data between LANs.

INTRODUCTION TO NETWORK PROTOCOLS

A protocol is a standard procedure that regulates data flow between networks. A routing protocol is a standard procedure that regulates the flow of data between routers. We have learned that routing tables exist in routers for the purpose of determining how to get packets from one node to another. We also have learned that these tables are updated by sharing information between routers. These routers are using routing protocols to update this information.

In this chapter, we briefly introduce some of the protocols that are supported on the Nortel Networks routers. We will discuss the history behind these protocols and how they relate to the networks we use today. Because of the multiple variations of configuration possibilities, the configuration methods and variables are not discussed in this chapter.

AppleTalk Phase II

The AppleTalk protocol was established for the benefit of Macintosh computers and was developed with the following key goals in mind:

▼ Simplicity

■ Peer-to-peer between like network nodes

■ Open architecture

■ Seamless, or transparent, between different network nodes and protocol types

▲ Plug-and-play

All that is required for AppleTalk to run is the Local Talk hardware and a wire to connect it. Combined with Local Talk, AppleTalk allows you to build a network operating system for file and print sharing accompanied by an easy-to-use naming scheme.

In 1983, Apple was about to introduce its personal computer line and wanted to incorporate a networking protocol that was innovative, yet could adhere to other standards where possible. In this process, AppleTalk was born.

The AppleTalk protocol is responsible for configuring, enabling, and disabling the AppleTalk control modules at the end point nodes on a point-to-point link. The AppleTalk protocol uses the same method of packet exchange as the link control protocol (LCP), which is discussed later in this chapter. AppleTalk packets must wait until a PPP connection is established before it transmits data. If data is transmitted before the connection is established, the information will be discarded.

AppleTalk phase 2, which was introduced in 1989, defines the concept of non-extended and extended networks. Non-extended networks support a small number of devices and require only a single network number to be managed effectively. Extended networks support hundreds of nodes and require multiple network numbers for effective management.

Because of the growing popularity of the TCP/IP protocol and because TCP/IP works well with the Macintosh platform, the AppleTalk protocol is not being implemented as often as it used to be, although existing AppleTalk networks have no reason to change from AppleTalk.

Digital Equipment Corporation Network (DECnet) Phase IV

The Digital Equipment Corporation network (DECnet) was develop by Digital Equipment Corporation and was implemented onto LANs before many of today's LAN protocols were introduced. There have been several implementations of DECnet; however, we will discuss only DECnet phase IV, as it is the protocol supported by the Nortel Networks routers.

DECnet phase I was this first implementation of the DECnet protocol. It was introduced in 1975, and it ran on DEC's PDP-11 computers. The operating system it ran under was the RSX operating system. DECnet phase I allowed for node-to-node communication over a LAN. It was a simple but very powerful protocol for its time, providing many of the capabilities that modern protocols do over the Internet.

DECnet phase II was developed in 1978 and introduced many new features. It allowed for the addition of the TOPS-20 and the DMS operating systems. It also introduced a few advanced file transfer and file management capabilities and could support 32 nodes on a single DECnet network segment.

DECnet phase III was released in 1980 and was capable of supporting 256 network nodes. Remote login capabilities also were introduced in the DECnet phase III release. This also was the first phase of DECnet that supported IBM's systems network architecture (SNA).

DECnet phase IV was released in 1982 and is the phase most commonly found and supported in today's networks. DECnet phase IV introduced support for Ethernet and further increased the number of network nodes that could be supported. Additionally, the phase IV release provided support for X.25 packet-switched networks. It is important to mention that DEC did not provide support for TCP/IP in phase IV until the 1990s, so Ethernet TCP/IP functions were provided through the DEC Ultrix operating system.

NOTE: The Ultrix operating system actually was the Berkeley UNIX operating system that was set up to run on VAX computers.

A DECnet network is divided into areas. There are two types of routers within a DECnet network: level 1 routers, which keep track of the data flow within an area, and level 2 routers, which route traffic from one area to another. There can be a maximum of 63 areas in a DECnet phase IV network. There are two general node types in a DECnet area: end nodes, which are stations that do not have the ability to route, and a full function node that does provide the ability to route.

DECnet uses hierarchical routing, which is different from the routing standards used in most networks today. In a DECnet network, a source node will transmit information to a destination node through a path that is measured by the number of hops for the network. DECnet routing is not based on distance-vector (described later in this chapter), because DECnet calculates its route based on a cost factor that is different from the cost factor used in distance-vector.

DECnet phase IV uses two different message types: data messages and control messages. Data messages contain the information that is transferred between two end points. Control data is the overhead, or the messages that establish and maintain the data link session.

Novell Internet Packet Exchange (IPX)

Novell Internet Packet Exchange (IPX) is the Novell NetWare protocol that provides datagram delivery of messages. IPX provides for the communication between a network node and a Novell NetWare server. IPX supports a lot of applications and supports network addressing and routing.

IPX was built specifically to run over Ethernet, unlike other protocols that were developed and then later adapted to run over Ethernet. IPX also is capable of supporting multiple network architectures and can transparently exchange data between different LAN types.

Data that needs to be transmitted over a LAN must be formatted for transmission onto the LAN. Data that is submitted to IPX for transfer is encapsulated into a datagram. Once a datagram has been developed, the data-link layer will attach a header to the datagram; it then is called a packet. The IPX packet then can be transmitted to the destination node.

The IPX packet contains the following entities:

▼ **Checksum**—Ensures that the number of bits that are transmitted are equal to the number of bits actually received by the destination node.

■ **Packet length**—Indicates the total length of the IPX packet.

■ **Transport control**—Counts the number of hops that are encountered between the source and the destination node. If this number reaches 16, the packet is discarded.

■ **Packet type**—Indicates the type of data that is contained in the data field.

■ **Destination network**—Contains the 32-bit address of the network that the destination node belongs to.

■ **Destination node**—Contains the actual MAC address of the destination node.

■ **Destination socket**—Contains an indicator of the process to be assigned on the destination node.

■ **Source network**—Contains the 32-bit network address of the network that the source node belongs to.

■ **Source node**—Contains the MAC address of the source node.

▲ **Source socket**—Contains the socket number of the process that was assigned to the packet.

IPX uses routers to forward packets to different networks. Novell implements a routing function in its operating system that is known as an internal router and performs routing while it also is performing other functions. Another type of router that is used is called the external router, which is a node that contains multiple interfaces for the purpose of routing data. The external router has no other processes running at the time it is routing.

Nortel Networks routers also participate in a Novell network. The Nortel Networks routers can provide IPX routing as well as services advertisement protocol (SAP) functions. SAP is an IPX protocol that enables Novell servers to announce their services to routers and other servers throughout the network.

IPX uses a RIP algorithm to provide routing information updates throughout the IPX network. In a multiple protocol router, it is important to implement RIP for each of the protocols that are implemented. IPX RIP enables a workstation to determine the quickest route to a network by broadcasting a router request packet, which is answered by the router that is supporting IPX RIP or by the routing software on the Novell file server. RIP also allows routers to exchange network reachability information, respond to RIP requests, and notify other routers when a route changes. The routing information protocol is discussed later in this chapter.

Transmission Control Protocol/Internet Protocol (TCP/IP)

TCP/IP was an outgrowth of the Defense Data Network (DDN). Today the DDN refers to the protocols that are used by the Department of Defense or contain Department of Defense information.

TCP/IP is one of the fastest-growing WAN protocols. This is largely because of the huge popularity of the Internet, which uses a combination of the transmission control protocol and either the Internet protocol or point-to-point, which enables different applications to communicate.

In TCP/IP, information is transmitted across a WAN with an IP header, which usually is followed by a TCP header. This packet of information then can be transmitted over a large variety of link control mechanisms and network structures. The TCP header and its information also can be encapsulated into a PPP frame and then transmitted across a serial line, which can be either a dial-up or dedicated connection.

Before it was known as TCP/IP, the protocol was known as the network control protocol and was designed to run on multiple host nodes in various remote locations through a packet-switching network known as the Advanced Research Project Agency Network (ARPAnet). The Internet as we know it today was built parallel to the ARPAnet; ARPAnet was taken down in 1993.

TCP/IP contains many different application protocols that are required for the basic operation of TCP/IP. Remember that TCP/IP is a protocol suite and contains a family of protocols that work together to provide access to Internet data communication. TCP/IP includes the following Internet protocols, which are supported by the Nortel Networks routers:

▼ Border gateway protocol (BGP)

■ Exterior gateway protocol (EGP)

■ Open shortest path first (OSPF)

■ Routing information protocol (RIP)

▲ Routing information protocol version 2 (RIP-2)

It also is important to briefly discuss the suite of applications that were developed specifically for TCP/IP:

▼ Telnet protocol (Telnet)

■ File transfer protocol (FTP)

■ Trivial file transfer protocol (TFTP)

■ Simple mail transfer protocol (SMTP)

■ Domain name service (DNS)

■ Simple network management protocol (SNMP)

■ Boot protocol (BootP)

▲ Dynamic host configuration protocol (DHCP)

Internet Protocol (IP)

The Internet Protocol (IP) was designed to allow packet-switched communication between networks, forming an Internet. IP transmits datagrams to and from network nodes. IP is a connectionless delivery protocol that provides best-effort services. For IP networks to communicate, a router must be used to interconnect the networks.

There are two main types of routing protocols used in IP networks. The first of these routing protocols is known as the interior gateway protocol (IGP). IGP describes any protocol that is used to distribute routing information within a network. Two IGPs are supported by the Nortel Networks routers: RIP and OSPF.

The second routing protocol used in an IP network is the exterior gateway protocol. The EGP protocol is used to describe the processes involved in the exchange of information about the reachability of routers in different autonomous systems. To accomplish this, routers will establish an EGP neighbor relationship to allow the periodic exchange of reachability information. The EGP used within IP and supported by the Nortel Networks routers is the border gateway protocol.

The Border Gateway Protocol (BGP)   BGP is a protocol contained within the IP suite that is designed to move information between autonomous systems. The information that is shared pertains to the reachability of other BGP systems within the autonomous systems.

A BGP update will contain such information as the network number it belongs to, a list of the other autonomous systems that it has information about, path attributes between the systems, and routing information that it has gathered.

BGP was developed as an enhancement to the original EGP. The most popular versions of BGP in use today are BGP-3 (1991) and BGP-4 (1994). The two major enhancements that were introduced when BGP-3 came out were loop detection and reliable transport:

▼   **Loop detection**—Every BGP routing update will contain network reachability information and a list of autonomous systems it has learned. As the BGP updates are sent, the path of autonomous systems is updated and the local autonomous system number is assigned. Because the BGP routing update contains this information, the BGP nodes are able to compare this information and detect and eliminate possible loops.

▲   **Reliable transport**—BGP uses TCP to transport information between other BGP routers. Reliable updates are provided, with only keep-alive messages and network change information being exchanged.

BGP-4 contains the same enhancements that BGP-3 had introduced plus one other major enhancement known as classless interdomain routing (CIDR) support. Instead of using IP address network classes for network summarization, BGP-4 network updates contain an IP address and a prefix. This change reduces the amount of network information a router must maintain in its routing tables. This is a benefit for routers that have to maintain full Internet routes.

The Routing Information Protocol (RIP) As we discussed previously in this book, routers perform dynamic updating. Dynamic updating is the process routers use to provide network information updates. Prior to dynamic updates, many vendors provided and supported manual updates for routing table updates. This means that someone would have to enter network reachability information into routing tables manually.

As the Internet grew it became apparent that it would be too cumbersome to manually update routing tables. RIP was developed to provide routers with automatic routing updates. RFC 1058, written in 1988, is the standard that defines the RIP protocol.

RIP is based on a logic algorithm known as the distance-vector protocol. Distance-vector is a method to send information from router to router based on information contained in the routing table. The parameters that are obtained from the table are the vector, which is the network number of the network you are obtaining information from; and the distance, which is the cost (number of hops) it takes to get to that network.

Distance-vector updates are broadcast from routers to neighboring (locally connected) routers. The updates will contain the information as the source router learns it. The information will contain the vector and the distance between the source router and the network number of the final network. The distance between the router and the final network often is referred to as a *metric*.

RIP updates provide routers with information about the length of the shortest path from each of the neighboring routers to any known destination. RIP provides two types of updates: RIP requests and RIP responses. There also are two modes of RIP: passive mode and active mode. In passive mode, RIP will listen for RIP updates but will not broadcast any information it receives. In active mode, RIP will both listen to and broadcast RIP update information.

There are a few disadvantages to the RIP protocol. Because of the popularity and rapid growth of TCP/IP, RIP was developed without considering the massive amounts of routing table update information that are a part of many routers. Another disadvantage of RIP is that it broadcasts packets that will pass up to the upper-layer protocols on all stations in the network whether they support RIP or not. This disadvantage will become even more cumbersome when a router is using AppleTalk or IPX (RIP and SAP) as well as RIP. This would mean that that router will be sending an AppleTalk broadcast every 10 seconds, an RIP broadcast every 30 seconds, and an IPX (RIP and SAP) every 60 seconds.

RIP was developed to handle routing updates for smaller networks. It limits the amount of hops between a source network and a destination network to 15. If a hop count of 16 hops is logged, it means that the network is unreachable. There also are problems associated with convergence in RIP networks. Because RIP updates occur every 30 seconds, it is possible that an update from one station might be received before an earlier update is transmitted from another station. Because of these issues, there have been some rules added to the RIP algorithm:

▼ **Hold-down timer**—Defines the amount of time a route can remain in a routing table before it is marked as an unreachable route. Once the hold-down timer has expired, any routes that have not been updated will be aged out of the routing table.

- ■ **Poison reverse**—Defines how an RIP interface will advertise its learned routes.

- ■ **Split horizon**—A rule stating that a router will not broadcast a learned route through the interface that the route was learned on.

- ▲ **Triggered updates**—Triggers an RIP update if reachability changes are noticed on a given route. A triggered update will provide updates only on a route that has changed.

The Routing Information Protocol, Version 2 (RIP2)   Because of the many limitations that were discovered in the original RIP, RIP2 was developed. RFC 1723, written in 1994, is the standard that contains information about RIP2. RIP2 is fully backward compatible and contains all of the functionality of RIP. In addition to including everything that was contained in RIP and addressing the limitations of RIP, RIP2 also contains some additional features. Four of the additional features that were introduced in RIP2 are as follows:

- ▼ **Password authentication**—RIP2 allows for a RIP2 router to accept and process both unauthenticated and authenticated messages from an RIP or RIP2 router if it is configured to do so. If an RIP2 router is not configured to accept authentication, it will process only the unauthenticated messages it receives from a router that is running RIP or RIP2.

- ■ **Compatibility with RIP**—Ensures that an RIP2 router is able to communicate with an RIP or RIP2 router.

- ■ **Multicast support**—Unlike RIP, which uses broadcasting for message distribution, RIP2 supports multicasting for its packets and its datagram header.

- ▲ **Subnet masking**—RIP2 has established rules to understand and support subnet masking information contained in an IP datagram.

Open Shortest Path First (OSPF)   The OSPF protocol uses an algorithm known as the link state routing protocol. Unlike the distance-vector routing protocol, which provides periodic updates, the link state routing protocol updates only when a topology change has occurred.

OSPF is composed of a large network topology that normally is separated into multiple network segments. OSPF will provide routing table updates that contain route information based on actual metrics instead of hop count metrics. As we have already mentioned, OSPF uses the link state algorithm for routing table updates and will update only when needed or will send a multicast update every 30 minutes. OSPF also supports subnetting and is able to link subnet masks with an associated network IP address.

OSPF supports equal paths and therefore is desirable in networks that perform load balancing. OSPF converges quickly, is capable of authenticating route changes, and will provide direct support for multicasting.

OSPF routers pass information to other OSPF routers in the form of a link state advertisement. A link state advertisement will describe the portion of the OSPF routing domain that it is associated with. Each link state advertisement is flooded throughout the

OSPF routing domain. This will ensure that all OSPF routers in the routing domain will have the same information; therefore it can be certain that this information is reliable. There are seven different types of link state advertisements:

▼ **Type 1 (router links advertisement)**—This type of advertisement contains information about a neighbor router's links. Each router within the OSPF domain will generate a type 1 advertisement and will flood it within an area.

■ **Type 2 (network links advertisement)**—This type of advertisement contains information about all of the routers within a multiple access network. Only a designated area router will generate a type 2 advertisement and will flood it within the area.

■ **Type 3 (summary links advertisement)**—This type of advertisement contains information about reachable links in networks that are within other areas of the OSPF domain. An area border router will generate a type 3 advertisement and will flood it into an area.

■ **Type 4 (autonomous system boundary router summary advertisement)**—This type of advertisement obtains information about the cost from the router that is generating the advertisement to another autonomous system boundary router. An autonomous system boundary router will generate this type of advertisement and will flood it into an area.

■ **Type 5 (autonomous system external link advertisement)**—This type of advertisement contains information about the external network that is reachable by the router providing the advertisement. An autonomous system router will generate the type 5 advertisement, and it will be flooded to all areas with the exception of stub areas.

■ **Type 6 (multicast group membership advertisement)**—This type of advertisement contains multicast group information.

▲ **Type 7 (multicast OSPF advertisement)**—This type of advertisement contains information about the membership of OSPF multicast membership.

OSPF uses a metric that is based on line speed to determine route costing within the OSPF routing domain. When a link state advertisement is transferred between routers, the router will assign individual link cost information to the advertisement. The metric associated with that advertisement then is compared to other link state advertisements received. If multiple path information to a destination is found, the route with the lowest cost is entered into the routing table.

The hello protocol is the most basic exchange between routers. Simply put, in OSPF the hello protocol enables OSPF routers to discover each other and to build relationships. During the hello process, a designated router and a backup designated router is selected within a single area. After the hello protocol process has established a designated router and a backup designated router, routers on a LAN segment will begin to form adjacencies.

Adjacencies will allow two routers to exchange routing information with one another through link state advertisements.

As an adjacency is formed, the adjacent router's databases will synchronize. Once synchronized, the link state advertisement information will be transmitted to neighboring routers and compared with the link state advertisement information it currently maintains in its database. When completed, the newly formed link state advertisement list is transmitted to neighboring routers using a link state request packet. Each router will receive the request packet and will send a link state response packet. Once all link state requests are sent and a link state response is received, the routers will be considered fully adjacent.

An OSPF area is a group of networks and routers that are associated with those particular groups of networks. Each area will maintain its own copy of the link state database, which will enable the area to build in information that relates to its own topological database. There might be one area within an OSPF domain or multiple areas in a larger domain.

Each area will be identified with an area ID. The area ID is a 32-bit number that is formatted in the same manner as an IP network address. It is important to remember that even though an OSPF area ID and an IP address look similar, they are not the same. An OSPF area ID simply identifies an area and performs no other function.

Each area contains at least one router, and that router also is assigned a router ID. The router ID typically is assigned an ID number that matches one of the IP addresses on one of the router's interfaces.

The areas within an OSPF routing domain are connected to the network backbone through an area border router (ABR). An ABR is responsible for connecting the area to the network and summarizing area topology information to send to the backbone to be propagated to other OSPF areas. The ABR also will collect information from other areas and propagate this information to its area. An ABR is always part of two areas: the OSPF area and the backbone area.

Stub areas were created to reduce the amount of entries from external routes in the routing table. If an area has only one entry and exit point that is used for external network traffic, that area can be configured as a stub area. A stub area blocks the import of autonomous system external link advertisements, thus reducing the number of entries in the stub area's database.

TCP/IP Applications

Because IP provides connectionless delivery of TCP data, TCP provides certain application programs access to the network using a connection-oriented transport layer service. The TCP/IP applications that are supported by the Nortel Networks routers and services are discussed in this section.

The user datagram protocol (UDP) is an OSI layer 4 protocol and provides access to the network for application programs. UDP is an unreliable connectionless protocol. It allows the transfer of data between two endpoints before a session has been established. It is used for applications that do not require TCP services.

Bootstrap Protocol (BOOTP)   The BootP protocol is a standard that allows a client node to access startup information from a server. The RFCs that contain the rules for the BootP protocol are RFC 951 and, most recently, RFC 1542.

BootP has been used for many years. In earlier years, it was mainly used to provide startup information to workstations that did not contain a disk drive. BootP would enable these stations to get their boot-up information and configuration information from a remote server. To do this, these stations had a bootstrap protocol that was written on the PROM. The information contained in the PROM would be the workstation's IP address and subnet mask and the instructions for locating the remote server and booting up from the server.

BootP is a UDP/IP-based application that operates in two modes: the request mode and the reply mode. In the request mode, BootP sends a request to a remote server that contains the IP address and the MAC address of the node that is in need of boot-up information. In the reply mode, BootP provides a response from the server, providing the requested information.

Domain Name Service (DNS)   The DNS is a standardized name service that enables users to establish Internet connections to network nodes using recognizable names instead of network IP addresses that can be difficult to remember. There are many functions of DNS, but its main function is to map IP addresses into humanly usable names. Much like there are many functions of DNS; there are many RFCs that contain information about the uses of DNS. The two RFCs that contain the majority of the information of DNS are RFC 1034 and RFC 1035; both were written in 1987.

Consider for a moment how popular the Internet is. Now, consider how many hosts there are on the Internet. Consider how popular Internet mail services are and how many e-mail addresses there must be out there. Most of us have at least one. Now think how popular the Internet and the mail services would be if you had to memorize a series of numbers instead of simply typing in a name. If not for DNS services, the Internet would not be nearly as popular as it has become.

Dynamic Host Configuration Protocol (DHCP)   DHCP is a protocol that is used in networks that support multiple protocols. DHCP allows for the management of IP parameters on a network. DHCP is a superset of BootP, as it provides IP extended functions as well as the management of IP addresses.

Remember that because of the rapid growth of the Internet, IP addresses are in short supply. It is because of this that DHCP has become very popular. DHCP requires restrictions on the assignment of IP addresses and is capable of handing out IP addresses based on statistics. Because of this, you might have many users without overtaxing the IP addresses.

DHCP provides a way to transport configuration information from a server to remote nodes on a TCP/IP network. Once a node has received the configuration information, it is able to communicate with other nodes within the network.

DHCP was designed to use some of the features that are contained in BootP. This enables DHCP to communicate with BootP clients. DHCP allows remote nodes to connect to a DHCP server, obtain an IP address, and then return the address when the node is done with its session. This functionality is described in RFC 2132, written in 1997.

DHCP performs two main functions: It contains a database that stores network parameters for requesting nodes and allocates IP addresses. There are three methods of IP address allocation:

▼ **Automatic**—Automatic allocation means that a permanent IP address is assigned to a specific node.

■ **Dynamic**—Dynamic allocation means that an IP address is assigned to a node for a specific amount of time.

▲ **Manual**—Manual allocation means that an IP address has been reconfigured for a node and the server relays that information when the node logs in.

File Transfer Protocol (FTP)   FTP enables a node to access and transfer files to and from another node. FTP is one of the most popular file access protocols used by TCP/IP. The rules for FTP are included in RFC 959 (1985). FTP operates at layers 5, 6, and 7 of the OSI reference model.

FTP uses TCP as its transport protocol and is a method of reliably transferring files in a LAN and over a WAN. FTP gives the user complete control over the file transfer. In networking, many connections made between two endpoints are made with one node acting as the destination and one node as the source; therefore, there is a source port and a destination port. The FTP protocol uses two ports, which are always ports 20 and 21. For FTP to work, a node that wants to connect to another node must connect to both ports on that node.

Port 20 is the port that the end station will connect to initially. It is known as the control port. Once a connection is established, data can be transferred out of port 21, the data port. Commands are sent over the control port, and the actual file transfer will occur over the data port. There are a lot of commands that are contained within FTP; but only a few that normally are used:

▼ **bye**—Used to end a session

■ **cd**—Changes the directory on a remote node

■ **close**—Used to close a connection to another node

■ **dir**—Used to get a directory listing on a remote node

■ **get**—Used to get a file from a remote node

■ **hash**—Used to place a hash mark to show the file transfer progress on the monitor

■ **mget**—Used to get multiple files from a remote node

■ **mput**—Used to place multiple files onto a remote node

■ **open**—Used to open a connection to another node

▲ **put**—Used to place a file on a remote node

Simple Mail Transfer Protocol (SMTP)   SMTP is an electronic mail system that is used on the entire Internet. SMTP was developed specifically to act as the electronic post office for addressing mail to every user on every node on every network (both LAN and WAN). Combined with post office protocol (POP), which allows individual users to collect their electronic mail from a single server, SMTP allows users to connect to a network and obtain mail from a central mail depository.

RFC 821, RFC 822, and RFC 974 contain information about using the SMTP protocol. Earlier we discussed the DNS protocol and how big a part it played in the naming conventions for electronic mail. SMTP and POP are the actual protocols that make electronic mail possible. Mail can be sent and received with just SMTP, but POP and DNS make is much easier and much more efficient.

SMTP is a relatively simple protocol (hence the name "simple"). A user will create a mail message on a node and then will transfer the message to the SMTP application, which then stores the message. A mail server will periodically check to see if any mail needs to be delivered and will attempt to deliver any messages it might find. If the server is unable to deliver the mail the first time, it will continue to try to send the message; if after several attempts it is unsuccessful in sending the message, the server will delete it.

Telnet Protocol   The Telnet protocol is the standard defined for the remote out-of-band connection of two nodes. It is defined in RFC 854. It allows a user to connect to a remote node and interact with that node as if it were sitting at a keyboard that is directly attached to the remote node.

The Telnet protocol uses TCP as its transport protocol. It enables users to log onto any node in a TCP/IP network. Telnet can connect to a node using the services of the domain name server or by connecting to the remote node using its IP address.

Trivial File Transfer Protocol (TFTP)   The last of the application protocols we will discuss is the trivial file transfer protocol. TFTP is a file access protocol that is a simplified version of FTP. The biggest differences between TFTP and FTP is that TFTP does not allow transmission of multiple files with one command, it does not provide for password protection, and it does not provide directory capabilities.

TFTP is primarily used to upload boot files over a network; it is a very simple protocol to use. It also is often used in situations in which file storage space is limited, as TFTP is a much smaller file than FTP. TFTP does not use a reliable delivery service and therefore utilizes UDP instead of TCP/IP. It will transmit a control packet, which is the first packet sent. All subsequent packets are the data packets. The maximum packet size in TFTP is 512 bytes, so when a data packet is received that is less than 512 bytes, it signifies the end of the transfer.

Xerox Network System (XNS)

The Xerox network system (XNS) is a protocol that allows nodes to use the files and peripherals of other nodes on the network as if those files and peripherals were its own.

XNS was the first commercially implemented Ethernet protocol used to connect nodes within a LAN.

Because XNS specifications were so loosely written, vendors began making adjustments to the protocol to meet some vendor proprietary specifications. In the early 1980s, multiple vendors began to implement the XNS protocol until most network architectures were based on the XNS protocol.

A lot of problems arose because many vendors made proprietary changes to the protocol, and this forced companies to use a specific vendor's products in their networks. A major problem with this is that some vendors did not offer some network devices; therefore, if the company's network required a network device not offered by the vendor that supported their network, they would be forced into some very drastic changes or would not be allowed to meet their network's needs.

XNS segments protocols into five separate levels. Each of the XNS levels can be translated into layers of the OSI model. The XNS levels and the individual protocols that compose the XNS level structure are as follows:

▼ **Level 0**—Can be translated as the equivalent of layer 1 and layer 2 of the OSI reference model. The protocols that are members of this layer are the tools used to transport data within the network. These are

- X.25
- Ethernet
- Leased lines
- Other media types

- **Level 1**—Can be translated as the equivalent of layer 3 of the OSI reference model. This level describes the method of transmitting data. IDP is the protocol used at this level.

- **Level 2**—Can be translated as the equivalent of layer 4 of the OSI reference model. Contained within this level are basic communication primitives, such as

  - **Echo protocol**—Allows for network path reachability testing.
  - **Error protocol**—Provides a method of notifying nodes of transmission errors.
  - **Sequence packet protocol (SPP)**—Allows for the reliable transmission of data between network nodes.
  - **Packet exchange protocol (PEP)**—A response and request protocol similar to the function that UDP provides within the TCP/IP arena.
  - **RIP**—Provides a method of updating routing tables.

- **Level 3**—Can be translated as the equivalent of layers 5, 6, and 7 of the OSI reference model. Contained within level 3 are the connection protocols, defining the data structure and communication processing standards. Services within this level include

  - Printing services
  - Filing services
  - Date and time services
  - Naming services (clearinghouse)
  - Remote call services (courier services)

- **Level 4**—Can be translated as the equivalent of level 7 and covers the application protocols used within the XNS protocol.

Unlike TCP/IP, which assigns an individual network ID number to all individual network devices, XNS assigns a network number to a network segment and all workstations on that segment will use the same network number. Because of this, groups of workstations are identified by and share the same network number.

The most popular implementation of XNS is Novell NetWare's IPX protocol. IPX patterns itself after the IDP found in XNS level 1, and the SPP found in XNS level 2.

HIGH-LEVEL DATA LINK CONTROL (HDLC)

HDLC is a bit-oriented physical data link protocol that was developed by the International Standards Organization (ISO) for use with full-duplex data communications. There are many WAN protocols that are part of the HDLC protocol family. In this section, we will discuss the HDLC protocol family members that are supported on the Nortel Networks routers.

There are three main types of nodes that can use HDLC for data communications. They are

- **Primary node**—In charge of the data link operations. It is responsible for moving command frames to the secondary nodes and monitoring the secondary nodes for a response. The primary node also is capable of maintaining sessions with multiple secondary nodes at the same time.

- **Secondary node**—Responsible for generating an acknowledgement response frame to the primary node to verify the receipt of a command frame sent from the primary node. The secondary node is not capable of maintaining more than one session at a time.

- **Combined node**—Can receive and transmit both command and response frames to and from other stations. It maintains a peer-to-peer relationship with other combined nodes.

The HDLC Frame Format

HDLC is an architecture standard that is used by many vendors as a foundation for their proprietary point-to-point encapsulation protocol. There are many variations of HDLC including connection-oriented, connectionless, and connectionless with acknowledgement. Even though these variations exist, the HDLC frame format remains similar. The HDLC frame consists of six fields:

▼ **Flag field**—Composed of the first and last fields. The flag field identifies the beginning and the end of the frame. The value in this field is always the same value as hex 7E. The end of one frame can be the beginning field of the next frame. If there is data within other fields within the frame, HDLC will insert a zero into the data stream after five consecutive 1 bits. This prevents the frame from reflecting erroneous information.

■ **Address field**—Identifies the primary node that is transmitting the frame and the secondary node that is receiving the frame. The size of this field is dependent on the protocol.

■ **Control field**—Usually is 1 byte, but can be multiples of 1 byte if needed. This field contains the commands, responses, and sequence numbers that maintain the data flow between nodes.

■ **Information field**—Variable in length and contains the data that is being transmitted between nodes.

▲ **Frame check sequence (FCS) field**—Contains the information that is used to detect transmission errors between two data link nodes. The FCS is a 16- or 32-bit field and is generated by the cyclic redundancy check (CRC). The CRC is a method that is used to monitor and detect packet integrity.

NOTE: Most of the HDLC WAN protocols use the HDLC Frame Format.

Frame Relay

Frame relay is a high-speed WAN protocol that is used to transport data between LAN nodes that require high throughput for short periods of time. Frame relay was developed based on concepts and standards of ISDN.

ISDN is an international telecommunications network that is based on communication standards for the transmission of video, voice, and data over WANs. As we discussed in previous chapters, ISDN provides both basic rate interface (BRI) and primary rate interface (PRI) services.

Frame relay uses very little error detection and therefore is dependent upon high-level protocols for assistance with error control. Frame relay uses the concept of virtual circuits. There are two types of virtual circuits: the permanent virtual circuit (PVC), which is a dedicated connection between nodes normally used for a singular purpose; and the switched virtual circuit (SVC), which is an on-demand access link between two nodes.

Frame relay protocol services usually are provided by a public telephone company (known as the *telco*). The telco owns and maintains the frame relay network. There are occasions in which a company might have the need to and will build and maintain its own frame relay network

The frame relay standards are developed and maintained by the following standards bodies:

▼ American National Standards Institute (ANSI)

■ Frame Relay Forum (FRF)

▲ International Telecommunications Union (ITU)

The standards bodies develop the specifications used by the frame relay protocol. The specifications include the ways in which a router, also known as the data terminal equipment (DTE), will connect to a switch, also known as the data communications equipment (DCE). Other specifications decided on by the standards bodies are the process for encapsulating multiprotocol frames, ensuring the use of an HDLC frame format, management of the link between the DTE and the DCE, and the use of virtual circuits to establish endpoint communications over the public lines.

Permanent Virtual Circuits (PVC)

PVC is assigned by the telco in a frame relay network. To establish a connection between a source node and a destination node within the network, a Data Link Connection Identifier (DLCI) is assigned. The DLCI is known only locally between the DTE and the DCE. As the frame is transported through the frame relay network, the DLCI will change depending on the locally assigned DLCI between the DTE and the DCE on the destination link.

Once a DLCI is assigned to a destination of a network, that DLCI remains for that network portion. Therefore, each of the source nodes will know the destination node DLCIs and will know how to reach those destinations. This is known as global addressing. Global addressing is beneficial because it assists in troubleshooting network problems; all nodes are recognized by a specific DLCI.

It would not be cost effective for a telco to give unlimited bandwidth to any PVC that is established; therefore, a committed information rate (CIR) is assigned. The CIR is the maximum guaranteed bandwidth over a PVC. When purchasing frame relay services from a telco, the user will determine the amount of bandwidth he or she will need to transmit data. The user and the telco then negotiate a CIR, and the CIR is assigned based on this amount. Based on data traffic volume, anything above the CIR at any particular time for a user is potentially dropped.

An SVC uses many of the concepts of a PVC, but is a pay-as-you-go scenario. You only pay for the time you actually are using the frame relay services.

Nortel Networks Standard Protocol

The Nortel Networks standard protocol is a proprietary standard and can be used to connect a Nortel Network routers on a dedicated point-to-point line only to another Nortel Networks router. It is the default option when configuring a Nortel Networks router with Site Manager. The Nortel Networks standard protocol is designed to support multiple protocols, but will not work with other vendor routers.

Use of the Nortel Networks standard protocol is beneficial in that it can be used with virtually all revisions of router software that are supported by the Nortel Networks routers. The Nortel Networks standard protocol is easy to configure and troubleshoot. It also can support multiline configurations to increase the bandwidth of a link. Additionally, the Nortel Networks standard protocol uses the HDLC frame format, thus allowing multiple protocols to be routed over a single interface.

The Nortel Networks standard protocol uses a breath of life (BOFL) packet to test the integrity of the lines. A BOFL is a polling message that is sent over Ethernet or FDDI interfaces to all of the nodes on a LAN or over a WAN when there is a local router that is connected through a PPP link to a remote router. The main purpose of BOFL exchanges is to establish connectivity when an interface is idle.

The BOFL, by default, is transmitted every five seconds from every router that is using the Nortel Networks standard protocol, whether the line is up or down. A BOFL will remain on the local link and will not be bridged or routed across the network. Once a BOFL has been successfully received, the BOFL timer is reset. The BOFL does contain a timeout period that will determine an interface to be in a down state when a BOFL has been sent five times unsuccessfully (without being received by the router on the opposite end of the link).

NOTE: The number of attempts before determining a line is down is configurable through the router MIBs or within Site Manager. It is very important to ensure that both ends of a link are configured with the same BOFL timeout period.

The BOFL parameter is automatically enabled whenever a link is assigned the Nortel Networks standard protocol. The BOFL parameter is automatically disabled when a link is configured for frame relay, SMDS, X.25, or PPP.

NOTE: PPP with dial backup services will use the BOFL packets.

Point-to-Point Protocol (PPP)

The point-to-point protocol (PPP) is a dial-up communication protocol that provides dial-up services for network connection. It is a protocol that provides standards for a direct connection between nodes. PPP became a standard because HDLC did not prevent alteration. Because of this multiple vendors were creating a propriety implementation of HDLC (Nortel Networks used the Nortel Networks standard protocol). Eventually, this meant there were no clean (universal) direct dial-up connection protocols.

There are two sub-protocols that are contained within PPP. These are the link control protocol (LCP) and the network control protocol (NCP). LCP supports connection authentication such as password authentication protocol (PAP) and challenge handshake authentication protocol (CHAP), both of which are discussed in the following. LCP also uses link integrity verification, known as link quality monitoring (LQM).

LCP will establish and open a connection, configure, and then terminate the line. Once LCP has ensured that a connection is made, it will operate in the background until the processes are complete, and then will terminate the line. LCP is required for NCP to run. NCP manages the protocol communication between the connected nodes. The protocol communication is determined, established, monitored, and terminated by NCP.

Both LCP and NCP initialize PPP. There are five phases involved in establishing a PPP circuit:

▼ **Dead phase**—This is the phase that a PPP circuit begins in and ends in. The dead phase is used to determine whether or not a circuit is physically ready to transport data.

■ **Establish phase**—This is the phase that generates LCP. A configure request and acknowledgment is sent between the end points, ensuring a connection is established.

■ **Authenticate phase**—This is the phase that authenticates the endpoints using either PAP or CHAP. On a dedicated PPP line, this phase is optional, but is a required phase if the PPP line uses dial services.

■ **PAP**—A method of authentication that requires a caller to provide a password to obtain link establishment.

■ **CHAP**—A method of authentication that requires the endpoints to use a message and a response to establish a link. Sharing a "secret" does this. The first node will send a challenge message to the second node and a response with the secret will be the reply. The first node then takes the reply and verifies it to the reply that is expected. If the reply matches the secret on the first node, a connection can be established.

■ **Network phase**—This is the phase that uses the NCP to activate the appropriate supported network protocol that will be used to transmit data. Once the protocol has been established, the PPP circuit will transmit the data.

▲ **Terminate phase**—This is the phase that terminates the PPP connection. It can be caused by password authentication failure, a physical problem with the PPP connection, or PPP circuit quality issues; it can even be taken down administratively for diagnostic purposes. During this phase, the LCP will notify the NCP that the circuit is terminating, and then will send termination packets to end the circuit.

Switched Multimegabit Data Service (SMDS)

Switched multimegabit data service (SMDS) is a connectionless WAN service that provides high-speed connections for LANs through the public network. It is based on cell relay technology, which is a form of packet transmission that uses a 53-byte cell to transmit data. Cell relay is used in broadband integrated services digital network (B-ISDN) networks and often is referred to as ATM.

SMDS uses a digital services unit/channel services unit (CSU/DSU), which is discussed in Chapter 2. The SMDS DSU/CSU data that is contained in a frame and segments the data into fixed 53-byte cells. The cells are transmitted across the SMDS network; once received at the destination, the SMDS DSU/CSU reassembles the data back into frames.

SMDS is similar to frame relay because it is a protocol that is used to interconnect LANs. It usually is used to connect metropolitan areas and is not usually associated with long-distance networking. The link layer portion of SMDS appends address information to the front of user data and transmits the frame. SMDS is good to transmit a large portion of data over short distances.

X.25

The X.25 protocol was developed by telcos and is administered by the International Telecommunications Union-Telecommunications sector. X.25 is a global protocol that sets standard rules for OSI layers 1, 2, and 3. X.25 transports LAN traffic over public domain networks (PDN). A PDN is a packet-switched WAN that is controlled by the government. X.25 is so widely used because it allows multiple device types to communicate across networks at a low cost.

X.25 originally was developed to transport data over unreliable analog lines. X.25 accurately transmits this data and ensures error recovery by maintaining a buffer on both the source node and the destination nodes. The buffer will store information for retransmission purposes. The end nodes will ensure information is received error free.

X.25 is connection oriented when operating at layer 3; this is done by establishing a call before the transmission of data. Once a connection is established from one end point to another end point, data will be transmitted.

The International Telecommunications Union (ITU) defines the following layered services for the X.25 standards:

▼ **Physical layer**—X.25 layer 1, the physical layer, describes the physical connection and signaling that is to be used on the physical channel.

■ **Frame layer**—X.25 layer 2, the frame layer, ensures the error-free transmission of layer 3 data packets between the DTE and the DCE.

▲ **Packet layer**—X.25 layer 3, the packet layer, creates the X.25 packet. It also ensures that logical channels, or virtual circuits, are established and maintained between the DTE and the DCE. The X.25 packet layer is connection oriented, and it enforces packet sequencing.

X.25 will receive information that is to be transmitted and will create an X.25 packet by adding the appropriate header and trailer information. There can be a number of different sessions between different devices over a single link, as X.25 places each channel's information on a different logical channel. The packet then is placed into an HDLC frame and is transmitted over the link.

AN OVERVIEW OF THE SIMPLE NETWORK MANAGEMENT PROTOCOL (SNMP)

The SNMP is part of the TCP/IP protocol suite and is defined in RFC 1157. SNMP uses a common software application to manage LAN and WAN equipment. SNMP breaks network management into five categories:

▼ **Network account management**—Obtains network service information and information about which groups and individuals are using which services.

■ **Network configuration management**—Performs such tasks as daily monitoring of the physical and logical state of the network, tracks information on the hardware that is included within the network, tracks information on the software within the network, and registers applications and services on the network.

■ **Network fault management**—Monitors equipment proactively for problems, finds and corrects damaged equipment, and troubleshoots and tracks down network problems.

■ **Network performance**—Ensures that the network operates optimally by monitoring traffic on the network.

▲ **Network security**—Provides access control, data encryption, authorization, and security management.

An SNMP network will contain an SNMP manager, which is a software application that queries agents for information needed to monitor the network. SNMP agents are the interfaces between the SNMP manager and the MIB, which is used to control data flow. Agents normally transmit information only as it is requested; however, an agent will send an SNMP trap when a certain condition is met.

SNMP traps can be anything from a change in network or node status to an authentication failure. The network administrator who helps to proactively monitor the network also often defines traps.

SNMP uses command and protocol data units (PDUs) to send management information and to receive management information. There are five types of PDUs:

▼ **GetRequest**—Used to request a list of attribute values for managed objects

■ **GetNextRequest**—Used to traverse a table of objects

■ **GetResponse**—Returns attribute values for the GetRequest PDU

■ **SetRequest**—Used to change a selected object attribute value

▲ **Trap**—Used to report an error condition or network status change

SNMP provides what is known as a community string, which is a simple method of authentication for client and server access. The community string must match a client to a server, or access will not be allowed and a session will not be established. The community string is embedded in an SNMP packet, and if it does not match, the receiving station will discard the packet.

CONCLUSION

In this chapter we discussed the multiple standards protocols that are used by the Nortel Networks routers. To ensure that network traffic remains reliable when the network itself has had a few changes, standards, known as protocols, are defined for the network. Protocols also are important in that they provide all multiple data types, vendors, network topologies, and so forth—a vehicle by which to communicate and reliably send and receive data between LANs.

It is important to note that while most protocols are a standard, some can be manipulated to meet various vendor needs, and therefore may not be accepted by other vendors. As today's networks advance, advancements are also being made in the protocol types that are being used.

CHAPTER 8

Network Management
Overview

In the late 1970s, computer networks had grown from a simple layout of small, separate networks with no connection to each other into larger, interconnected networks. These larger networks became known as "internets." As these networks grew it became more and more difficult to manage (monitor and maintain) them, and soon it became evident that a network management protocol was needed.

The first protocol used was the Simple Network Management Protocol (SNMP). SNMP was designed in the mid-1980s to provide management capabilities among different vendors' products. It was commonly considered to be a "quick-fix" solution to network management issues as other, more robust protocols were being designed. However, after a few years no better choice became available and SNMP became the network management protocol of choice.

The way SNMP works is quite simple: It exchanges network information through messages, known as Protocol Data Units (or PDUs). A PDU can be seen as an object that contains variables that have both titles and values. SNMP employs five PDU data types to monitor a network: The first two read network device data; the second two set network device data; and the last, the trap, is used for monitoring network events (for example, network device startups and shutdowns).

Therefore, if a user wants to see whether a device is attached to the network, he or she can use SNMP to send out a read PDU to that network device. If the device is attached to the network, the management station will receive the PDU, its value being "the device is attached." If the device is shut down, it will send out a packet to the management station to inform it of the shutdown. In this case a trap PDU would be utilized.

THE ADVANTAGES OF SNMP

The greatest advantage to using SNMP is that its design is simple and therefore easy to implement on a large network, as it neither takes a long time to set up nor places much stress on the network. Also, its simple design makes it easy for a user to create variables to be monitored. In a lower-level perspective each variable consists of the following information:

- ▼ Variable title
- ■ Data type (for example, integer or string)
- ■ Whether the variable is read-only or read/write
- ▲ The value of the variable

The result of this simplicity is a network management protocol that is easy to implement and adds little load to the existing network.

Another advantage of SNMP is that it is in wide use today. This popularity came about when no other network management protocols appeared to replace the "quick-fix" implementation of SNMP. The result of this is that almost all vendors of network hardware (hubs, switches, routers, and so forth) design their products to support the SNMP standard, making it very easy to implement.

NORTEL'S SOLUTION TO NETWORK MANAGEMENT—OPTIVITY

The Optivity suite of network management products provides tight integration into networks designed using Nortel Networks hardware. In addition to basic SNMP management, the Optivity suite provides tools to configure not only Nortel hardware but competitors' products as well. In this chapter we will cover the three main applications that make up the Optivity suite of enterprise network management products: Optivity Network Management System, Optivity Network Configuration System, and Optivity NetID.

Optivity Network Management System (NMS)

The Optivity Network Management System (NMS) is designed to streamline management of networks based on Nortel products. Optivity NMS is based on a client/server architecture that allows users to access any Optivity Network Management System server in the network from one client installation. This approach provides access to important management tools from any workstation with a Web browser. Key NMS features include the following:

▼ Support for the following operating systems:

- Sun Solaris, HP-UX, and IBM AIX (server and client)

- Microsoft Windows NT 4.0, Windows 2000 (server and client)

- Windows 95/98 (client only)

- Optivity NMS complements third-party platforms such as HP OpenView or Tivoli TME 10 NetView, but does not require them.

- Java-based applications provide a consistent look and feel across UNIX, Windows, and Web interfaces.

- Access Control secures applications from unauthorized use and provides a customizable approach to user access.

- Component applications support DNS naming, which allows network devices to be managed by name instead of by IP address.

- Multiple device statistics can be sorted into one OmniView window for easy performance monitoring and comparison.

▲ Topology support for Nortel Networks StackProbes and WEB PocketProbes enable administrators to pinpoint probe deployment and access RMON, RMON2, and SMON data.

Application Overview

The Optivity NMS is made up of these 11 integrated tools:

▼ InfoCenter

■ OmniView

■ Path Trace

■ Fault Summary

■ Expanded View

■ BaySecure LAN Access

■ ATM CallView

■ Access Control

■ Monitor Level

■ Database Administration Tool

▲ Autotopology Manager

A brief description of each tool follows.

InfoCenter InfoCenter (see Figure 8-1) provides a centralized location for network administrators to visualize their network resources and launch local or Web-based applications. InfoCenter also provides a central launch point for other element managers such as Device Manager, Site Manager, and SpeedView. Using a folder-based interface, administrators can group their devices into logical groups by type, location, criticality, fault status, or any other appropriate attributes.

InfoCenter provides useful navigation tools that enable network administrators to move between physical topology and logical views with a single mouse click. InfoCenter views include

▼ **Internet**—Displays layer 3 network elements and interconnecting links such as broadcast domains, routing between broadcast domains, and routers connecting subnets to WANs.

■ **Data Link**—Displays layer 2 network elements and interconnecting links such as collision domains, bridging or switching between collision domains, and the logical segments of all switches.

■ **Physical**—Displays layer 1 connections between hubs, switches, and routers.

■ **Database**—Displays all objects regardless of OSI layer.

■ **Switch Community**—Displays any VLANs that contain the currently viewed objects.

■ **VLAN**—Displays the members of the current VLAN.

▲ **End Node**—Displays end nodes connected to the current devices.

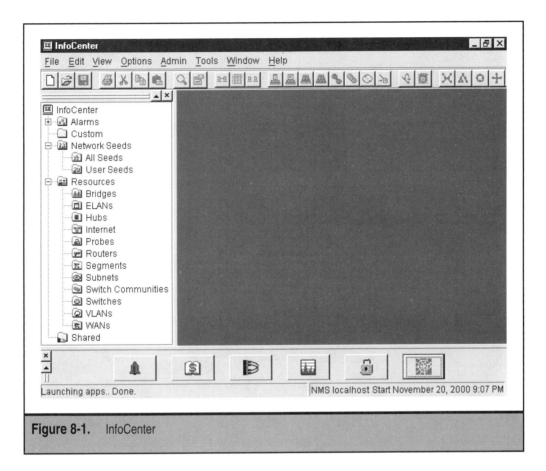

Figure 8-1.   InfoCenter

Network managers can use these tools to move from an Internet view of IP subnets to a physical view of all devices within the subnet and how they are connected. From there, users can quickly determine which VLANs the LAN devices are assigned to within the subnet. This allows administrators to change views from Internet to end node, logical to physical, all within the same application.

Fault status is instantly displayed in all views within InfoCenter. In addition, the folders themselves reflect the fault status of the devices within them, allowing an administrator to spot potential problems at a glance. The following applications can be accessed from within InfoCenter.

OmniView   The OmniView application (see Figure 8-2) provides complete statistics-gathering services that extend from the segment level down to individual nodes. A tree-structured interface simplifies navigation, enabling managers to move quickly through available data.

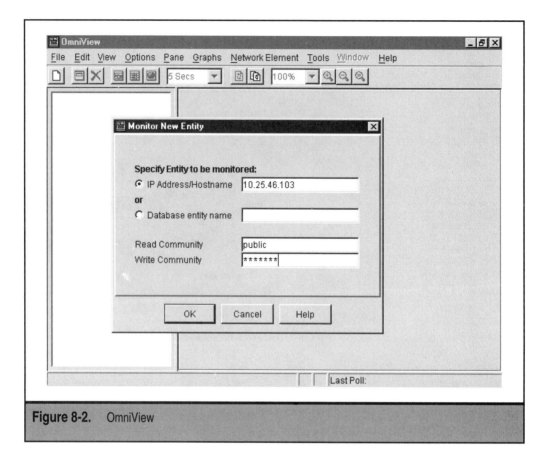

Figure 8-2. OmniView

Information gathered in OmniView can be displayed in either tabular or graphical format. Tabular output is grouped by "panes" of information, which contain objects often used by network managers. Graphing is accomplished by selecting a group of data points from the pane and choosing pie chart, line graph, or bar graph output.

OmniView also simplifies the process of moving between network concepts, from subnets down to ports on a device or from the port level to VLAN or subnet level; this provides an easy launching of the appropriate software to gather intelligent data reports. OmniView is capable of displaying data from VLANs and ELANs as well as protocol-based data from routers and RMON statistics from management agents and network probes.

OmniView users can create customized panes to query selected data. Using a browser-like interface, any supported MIB object can be selected as an attribute of the pane. In addition, simple mathematical formulas can be performed against multiple MIB objects, allowing a user to set up MIB equations for statistics such as utilization or bandwidth computation. Customized panes can be created based on any recognized MIB.

Almost all Nortel Networks equipment is supported as soon as the Optivity Integration Toolkit integrates their MIBs.

Fault Summary Optivity Network Management Systems provide a fault engine that links into topology to provide fault correlation. These faults then are summarized in a window that actually offers solutions to the displayed faults. Fault Summary (see Figure 8-3) allows only those faults that have been cleared, aged, or unmonitored to be deleted. It also includes a comment field for the manager to record notes on specific faults and support for automatic notification by e-mail or pager as soon as specified traps are received.

Path Trace Path Trace (see Figure 8-4) helps network managers visualize and troubleshoot a path between two end nodes. It also can be used to focus on a potentially faulty device attached to a single end node; thus Path Trace can help diagnose issues with

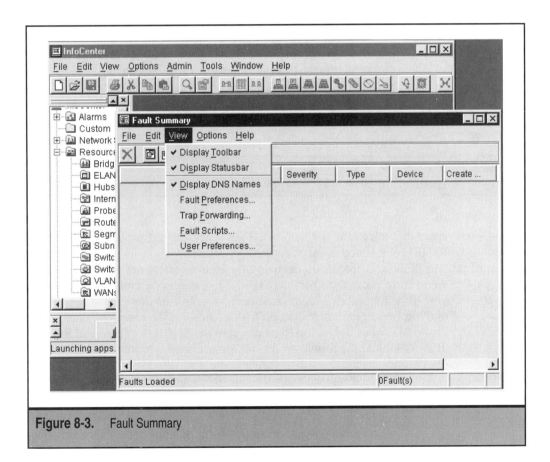

Figure 8-3. Fault Summary

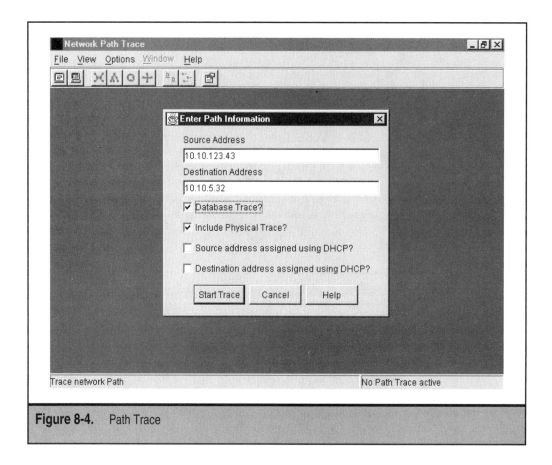

Figure 8-4. Path Trace

clients, servers, or other devices in the network. Path Trace also shows fault status of objects by the standard colors used in InfoCenter.

Path Trace simplifies the process of localizing the source of network problems. By using Path Trace and InfoCenter together, managers can establish a monitoring baseline (how the network functions under ideal conditions) for link or device characteristics. Data is saved into InfoCenter folders for later retrieval and comparison. InfoCenter's tool set then can be used to further define the issue down to the data link or physical level, or to expand the trace to look at the topology around the problem.

Expanded View   The workhorse of network management, Expanded View, presents a graphical view of a given network device, enabling managers to monitor, configure, and retrieve statistics from the device. Most of an administrator's time will be spent here until the NMS is fully configured.

BaySecure LAN Access   BaySecure LAN Access provides an easy-to-use graphical interface launched within Expanded View for configuring BaySecure intelligent hubs and switches. It protects networks from unauthorized access and included eavesdrop protection, Intrusion Control, and Autolearn or Adaptive Address Learning. The application enables managers to decide what actions are taken when a safeguard is challenged.

ATM CallView   Another application that is accessed from InfoCenter, ATM CallView provides specialized services for Centillion LAN-ATM switches. ATM calls, services, and virtual circuits are displayed in tabular or graphical view; the application also provides the ability to see variations in CallCount or CallView from one poll to the next.

Access Control   Access Control (see Figure 8-5) enables network managers to limit access to applications and application functions on a per-user, per-name basis. Access Control

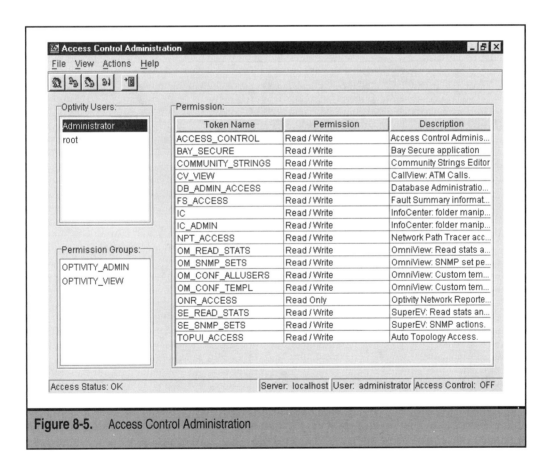

Figure 8-5.   Access Control Administration

can be set on a per-application basis, with users restricted from accessing sensitive applications, or granted read-write or read-only access. Administrators also can create a customized group of access permissions, thus allowing quick assignment of access privileges to a specific user.

Monitor Level   Monitoring levels becomes much more granular as managers gain full control over how they want to manage their networks. Accessible as a pop-up menu from InfoCenter, the Monitor Level graphical interface delivers control over fault correlation, Internet Control Message Protocol (ICMP) polling, trap registration, and topology on subnet, segment, device, or router interface.

Database Administration Tool   The Database Administration tool (see Figure 8-6) provides administrators with a quick method of backing up and restoring Optivity Network Management System databases. It also displays basic information on the data structures shared among different databases.

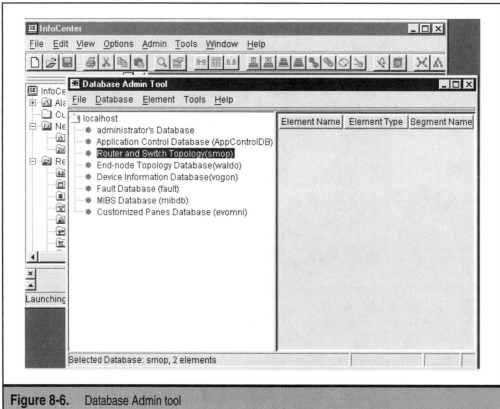

Figure 8-6.   Database Admin tool

Autotopology Manager   Autotopology Manager (see Figure 8-7) provides automatic discovery of all devices on the network, and then creates a topological map displaying the devices it has discovered. The Optivity NMS Autotopology Manager displays detailed status of the discovery as it occurs.

Optivity Integration Toolkit (OIT)

Networks are constantly changing; it seems new end stations and servers are added almost daily. The same is true of network hardware. Equipment vendors such as Nortel and Cisco release new products constantly. As hardware changes, so too must Optivity, just to keep up. Rather than release a new version of Optivity NMS to support a new piece of networking gear, Nortel created the Optivity Integration Toolkit (OIT). The OIT extends Optivity NMS (and a few other members of the Optivity family) by providing plug-ins to provide updated support for new devices and/or agents. The OIT also can be used to manually create launching points for other applications from within InfoCenter. Recently, Nortel committed to developing the OIT files necessary for immediate management

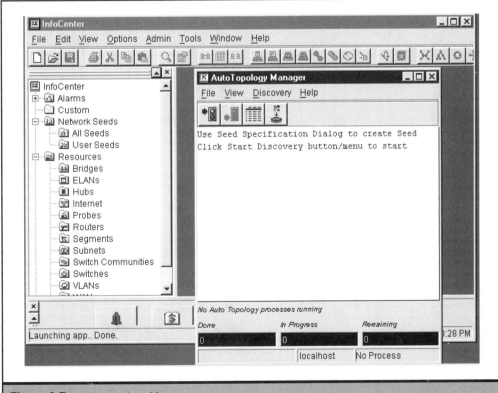

Figure 8-7.   Autotopology Manager

of all products as soon as they are released. Before this announcement it took up to three months before Optivity could fully manage new hardware due to the time it took for the OIT update to be released.

System Requirements

The traditional recommendation from Nortel was to run Optivity NMS on a UNIX platform as often as possible; however, with the speed available on Intel platforms today that school of thought is changing. The system requirements for supported platforms are listed in here.

System Requirements for Sun SPARC

▼ Sun SPARCstation 20 or UltraSPARC

■ 128 MB RAM minimum (256 MB recommended)

■ 600 MB free disk space

■ Color monitor

■ CD drive

■ 1.44 MB 3.5-inch floppy disk drive (recommended)

■ Sun Solaris 2.7 or 2.8

■ HP-UX 11.0

■ AIX 4.2,4.3.3

■ HP Network Node Manager 5.0 or 6.0 for Sun Solaris

▲ Tivoli TME 10 5.1.3 and 6 for Sun Solaris

System Requirements for Windows NT 4.0 or Windows 2000

▼ Intel-compatible 300 MHz Pentium II-type processor

■ 96 MB RAM minimum (128 MB recommended)

■ 600 MB free disk space

■ Color monitor

■ CD drive

■ 1.44 MB 3.5-inch floppy disk drive (recommended)

■ Microsoft Windows NT 4.0.0 SP 6a+ Resource Kit or Windows 2000+ Resource Kit

■ Tivoli TME 10 NetView 5.1.3 and 6 for Windows NT

▲ HP Network Node Manager 5.0 or 6.0 for Windows NT

Client Requirements for Windows NT and Windows 2000

▼ Intel-compatible 300 MHz Pentium II-type processor

■ 96 MB RAM minimum (128 MB recommended)

■ 600 MB free disk space

■ Color monitor

■ CD drive

▲ 1.44 MB 3.5-inch floppy disk drive (recommended)

Client Requirements for Windows 95/98

▼ Intel-compatible 233 MHz Pentium II-type processor

■ 64 MB RAM minimum (96 MB recommended)

■ 300 MB free disk space

■ Color monitor

■ CD drive

▲ 1.44 MB 3.5-inch floppy disk drive (recommended)

Installation Instructions for Optivity NMS on a Windows Platform

In the following few pages we discuss how to install the Optivity NMS on a Windows platform.

1. Log in to Windows with Administrator privileges and ensure that all programs are closed.

2. Insert the Optivity NMS 9.1 for Windows NT or Windows 2000 Client and Server Software CD or the Optivity NMS 9.1 for Windows NT, Windows 98, and Windows 2000 Client Only Software CD into your system's CD-ROM drive.

3. Start the Optivity NMS 9.1 Setup program. From the Windows Start menu choose Run. The Run dialog box opens. Browse to where your CD-ROM drive is located and select Setup.exe. Click Open and then click OK.

4. Select the Optivity NMS components you want.

5. Complete the Optivity NMS 9.1 Install program, accepting the default selections unless you want to customize your installation.

Ensure That All Optivity NMS Services Are Running

1. Open a Windows command prompt, and at the command line, enter:

```
optstatus -fe
```

2. If a service is not running

- From the Start menu choose Settings | Control Panel | Services. The Services dialog box opens.

- Select the Optivity service that is not running. All Optivity NMS 9.1 services begin with Opt.

- Click Start.

3. Enter your Optivity NMS software license key (provided by your Optivity sales agent).

Start Optivity NMS 9.1

1. From the Windows Start menu, choose Programs | Optivity | InfoCenter. The Connect to Optivity Server dialog box opens.

2. Type a valid user name, password, and the server hostname or IP address to which you want to connect. The Optivity InfoCenter window opens.

Start the Community Strings Editor and Add All Nondefault Device Community Strings   Perform this process only if you have devices on your network with nondefault community strings and are not integrating Optivity NMS 9.1 with a third-party network management system such as HP OpenView Network Node Manager.

1. From the InfoCenter menu bar, choose Admin | Community Strings. The Community Strings Editor window opens.

2. Type the community strings parameters in the text boxes and click Add. Repeat this step until you have added each nondefault community string.

3. Click Save.

Start AutoTopology Manager and Discover Your Network Resources

1. From the InfoCenter menu bar, choose Admin | AutoTopology Manager. The AutoTopology Manager window opens.

2. From the AutoTopology Manager menu bar, choose Discovery | Enter Seed Specification. The Seed Information dialog box opens.

3. Create a discovery seed. Type the following:

   - The discovery seed name

   - IP address of the router from which to start the topology discovery process

   - IP address of the start range of the network in which you want resources discovered

   - IP address of the end range of the network in which you want resources discovered

4. Click Apply.

5. Start the discovery. Click the Discovery toolbar button or from the menu bar, choose Discovery | Start Discovery.

6. In the InfoCenter contents pane, open your resource folders and ensure that you can view your discovered network resources.

   For more information about AutoTopology, refer to the online Help system or Using Optivity NMS 9.1 Applications (located on the Optivity NMS 9.1 Documentation CD).

Installation Instructions for Optivity NMS on a UNIX Platform

In the following few pages we discuss how to install the Optivity NMS on a UNIX platform.

1. Log in to your Optivity 9.1 UNIX station (server) as root.

2. Insert the Optivity NMS 9.1 for Solaris, Optivity NMS 9.1 for HP-UX, or Optivity NMS 9.1 for AIX software CD into your system's CD-ROM drive. The Optivity NMS 9.1 software CD mounts automatically on local Solaris stations.

3. To mount the CD-ROM drive on an HP-UX or AIX station:

   ■ Open a command terminal window and mount the CD-ROM drive. Change to the CD-ROM directory.

   ■ For Solaris, enter

   ```
   cd /cdrom/cdrom0
   ```

   ■ For HP-UX and AIX, enter **cd /<mount-point>**, where /<mount-point> is the name you have assigned to the mount point on your system

4. To start the Optivity NMS 9.1 Setup program from your Optivity NMS 9.1 UNIX server, enter

   ```
   ./install.
   ```

5. Select the Optivity NMS components that you want to install and complete the Optivity NMS 7.1 Installation program.

Set Your User Runtime Environment

1. As an Optivity NMS user, open a command terminal window and at the command line enter

   ```
   /opt/lnms/bin/LNMS_ENABLE
   ```

2. Using a text editor, add the appropriate following line to your shell file:

   ■ For the C shell, add the following to the *.chrsc* file: source **/usr/lnms/bin/opt_cshrc**

   ■ For the Korn shell, add the following to the *.kshrc* file: **./user/lnms/bin/opt_kshrc**

- For the Bourne shell, add the following to the *.profile* file:
  ./usr/lnms/bin/opt_kshrc

3. To update your environment, log out of your system, and then log in again and enter one of the following, as appropriate:

   - For the C shell: **source ~/.cshrc**
   - For the Korn shell: **. ~/.kshrc**
   - For the Bourne shell: **. ~/.profile**

Ensure That All Optivity NMS Daemons Are Running

1. At the command line, enter

   ```
   optstatus -fe
   ```

2. If the daemons are not running, enter the following to restart all the Optivity daemons:

   ```
   /opt/lnms/bin/optivity_apps start
   ```

3. Enter your Optivity NMS software license key provided by your Optivity sales agent.

Integrate Optivity NMS 9.1 with a Third-Party Network Management System   You can run Optivity NMS 9.1 as a standalone network management system or integrate it with supported third-party network management platforms such as HP OpenView Network Node Manager. Refer to *Installing and Administering Optivity Network Management System 9.1 for UNIX and Windows*, Chapter 2, located on the Optivity 9.1 documentation CD-ROM.

Start Optivity NMS 9.1

1. Open a command terminal window and at the command line, enter

   ```
   infocenter
   ```

2. In the Connect to Optivity Server dialog box, type a valid user name, password, and the server hostname or IP address to which you want to connect. The Optivity NMS InfoCenter window opens.

Start the Community Strings Editor and Add All Nondefault Device Community Strings   Perform this process only if you have devices on your network with nondefault community strings and are not integrating Optivity NMS 9.1 with a third-party network management system, such as HP OpenView Network Node Manager.

1. From the InfoCenter menu bar, choose Admin | Community Strings. The Community Strings Editor window opens.

2. Type the community strings parameters in the text boxes and click Add. Repeat this step until you have added each nondefault community string; then click Save.

Start AutoTopology Manager and Discover Your Network Resources

1. From the InfoCenter menu bar, choose Admin | AutoTopology Manager. The AutoTopology Manager window opens.

2. From the AutoTopology Manager menu bar, choose Discovery | Enter Seed Specification. The Seed Information dialog box opens.

3. Create a discovery seed. Type the following:

   ■ Discovery seed name

   ■ IP address of the router from which to start the topology discovery process

   ■ IP address of the start and end range of the network within which you want discovery to occur

4. Click Apply

5. Start discovery. From the menu bar, choose Discovery | Start Discovery. For more information about AutoTopology, see the online help system or refer to "Using Optivity NMS 9.1 Applications" (located on the Optivity NMS 9.1 Documentation CD).

6. In the InfoCenter Contents pane, open your resource folders and ensure that you can view your discovered network resources.

Optivity Network Control System (NCS)

As networks become larger and more complex, a better system of network management is needed. Managing a large routed network using only Site Manager can become overwhelming quickly as a single change on 50 routers could take hours to complete. The Optivity NCS allows network managers to make changes to multiple pieces of equipment simultaneously, thus greatly deceasing the time it takes to make network changes.

Optivity Network Configuration System is a client/server solution, with the server providing a central repository for all configuration information. Clients can either connect to the server using a standard Internet browser through the Java-enabled NETconfigurator application or use the standalone client application to view or modify configuration settings. Administrators can create accounts authorizing certain users to perform configuration tasks, thus providing security on the network. This and the client/server design enables multiple users to manage the network together.

Security   To control environments where multiple users are cooperatively managing network configurations, Optivity Network Configuration System provides a central security system to control user access. The multi-level access system permits or restricts access to specific databases based on user names or passwords. An audit log also tracks all configuration changes. This is an important feature in larger, dynamic networks where multiple network managers are frequently altering network configurations.

Image and Configuration Updates and Changes   Optivity NCS also provides a means to automatically distribute new configuration and image files through the Trivial File Transport Protocol (TFTP). By automating these tasks, the effort required to make configuration changes or perform software upgrades is greatly reduced. Automatic distribution of configuration updates can be scheduled for each device; if an update fails, the equipment is automatically restored to its former state, thus preventing major traffic disruptions. Network managers can be notified by e-mail of successful or unsuccessful updates.

Reporting   Reports can be easily generated on a selection of attributes within the database. The device's serial number, configuration file, and MIB information are included in these attributes.

NETconfigurator

NETconfigurator is capable of configuring multi-vendor/multi-service networks at the system level (rather than as individual devices). Network administrators can easily deploy configurations across multiple routers or switches utilizing a drag-and-drop graphical user interface (GUI). NETconfigurator can be run on either UNIX or Windows because of its underlying Java technology. It also provides a UNIX-like scripting interface for those who prefer a Command-Line Interface (CLI). The CLI provides functionality identical to that of the GUI.

   A few of the more prominent NETconfigurator features are discussed next.

VLAN Support   The Optivity NCS can be used to organize and configure VLANs across the BayStack 450 and Passport 1000 series switches. VLANs are defined as folders that are logical entries containing shortcuts to switch stacks or chassis and to the ports contained in them. This enables administrators to drill down into port-, policy-, subnet-, or MAC address–based VLANs.

Compare Feature   The compare feature provides an easy-to-read, side-by-side comparison of device configurations. An administrator can choose to compare the saved (on the server) configurations of two devices or a saved configuration with a live device. This provides simplified troubleshooting and an easy way to detect unwanted changes.

E-mail Notification   The NETconfigurator server contains a Simple Mail Transport Protocol (SMTP) client that allows a manager to set up automatic e-mail notification of events. A manager must simply specify the events he want to be notified of, a mail server to use, and e-mail recipients for automatic notification to take place.

OIT   The Optivity NCS also uses the OIT to support updated and new equipment.

Hardware and Software Supported by NETconfigurator

The following network devices can be configured using the NETconfigurator application.

BayRS

▼ BayRS 12.20, 13.00, 13.01, 13.10, 13.20, and 14.0

▲ All Bay Command Console (BCC) commands are supported

Nortel Networks Routers

▼ AN, ARN, ASN, BCN, BLN, and system 5000 routers

Cisco Routers

▼ 100x, 16xx, 25xx, 36xx, 4xxx, 7xxx, and 12xxx series routers supporting IOS (Cisco's routing software) versions 10.3 through 11.3

Passport 1000 Series Switches

▼ Passport 1050, 1051, 1100, 1150, 1200, and 1250 switches

■ VLAN and MLT drag-and-drop configuration

■ Configuration of port-based, protocol-sensitive, subnet-, and MAC-based VLANs

■ Configuration of speed, duplex, and administrative status at the port level

■ Port-level VLAN parameters

■ Port-level Spanning Tree parameters

■ IP configuration at both the port and VLAN levels

■ RIP configuration at both the port and VLAN levels

■ DHCP relay configuration at both the port and VLAN levels

■ Static route configuration

■ VRRP configuration at both the port and VLAN levels

■ SNMP configuration

▲ System-level Spanning Tree configuration

BayStack Switch Family

▼ BayStack 350-12T, 350-24T, 450-12T, 450-24T, 450-12F, 410-24T, and 460 switches

■ Stacked configuration of BayStack 450 switches

■ Agent versions 1.3.0, 1.3.1, and 2.0

- VLAN and MLT drag-and-drop configuration
- Port-based and protocol-sensitive VLAN configuration
- Speed and duplex configuration at the port level
- Port-level VLAN parameters
- Port-level Spanning Tree parameters
- System-level Spanning Tree configuration
- IP configuration
- SNMP configuration
- ▲ Image Upgrade Wizard

Hardware and Software Supported by NETarchitect

The following network devices can be configured using the NETarchitect application.

Centillion 100/5000 BH Modules

- ▼ Centillion Agent 4.0
- 5328HD EtherSpeed Switch Module
- 5455 16-port EtherSpeed 100Base-TX Segment Switch
- 5720 ATM MDA MCP Switch Module
- 5005BH Chassis
- Centillion 100 16-port EtherSpeed 100Base-TX Segment Switch
- Centillion 100 ATMSpeed/155 MDA Switch Module
- Centillion 100 ATMSpeed/155 MDA MCP Switch Module
- Centillion 100 4-port ATMSpeed/155 Multimode Fiber (MMF) Switch Module
- Centillion 100 ATMSpeed/155S Single-mode Fiber (SMF) Switch Module
- ▲ Centillion 100 ATMSpeed/155 UTP-5 ATM MDA

Technical Specification—File Management Support

- ▼ **Passport**—100, 1050, 11xx, 12xx, 86xx
- **Routers**—AN, ARN, ASN, BN, S5000
- **BayStack**—100, 150, 200, 250, 301, 302, 303, 350, 410, 450, 460, 28K
- **Centillion**—C20, C50, C100, S500BH, S5005BH
- **System 2000**—810M, 2310, 271x, 281x, 291x
- **System 3000**—331x, 332x, 3356, 3394, 341x, 351x, 352x, 391x
- **System 5000/D5000**—531x, 541x, 551x, 561x, 5660, 591x, 58K

- **Nautica Series**—Clam, Marlin (200, 250, 4000)
- **RMON Probes**—StackProbes
- **HPRM**—Passport Blade
- **Versalar**—5399, 8000, 15000
- **Passport**—44xx
- ▲ **Cisco Routers**

System Requirements for Optivity NCS

The Optivity Network Control System will run on multiple UNIX platforms as well as on Windows NT. This section covers the hardware and software required for a successful Optivity NCS installation.

Server Requirements for Windows NT 4.0 Service Pack 5

- ▼ Intel-compatible 300 MHz Pentium II-type processor
- ▲ Tivoli NetView 5.x, HP OpenView 5.x, 6.x, Optivity Campus/HP OpenView Workgroup Node Manager (none required)

Server Requirements for Solaris 2.5.1, 2.6, 2.7 (Solaris 7)

- ▼ SPARC/UltraSPARC
- ▲ HP OpenView 4.1.x, 5.0.x, 6.x, SDM 2.3 (none required)

Server Requirements for HP-UX 10.20, 11.00

- ▼ HP 700/800 series
- ▲ HP OpenView 4.1.x, 5.0.x, 6.x (none required)

Server Requirements for AIX 4.2, 4.3, 4.3.2

- ▼ RS/6000; PowerPC
- ▲ Tivoli NetView 4.1, 5.0, 5.1 (none required)

Server Requirements for RedHat Linux 5.2

- ▼ Intel-compatible 300 MHz Pentium II-type processor or SPARC/UltraSPARC

Client Requirements for Windows 95/98

- ▼ Intel-compatible 300 MHz Pentium II-type processor
- ▲ Optivity Campus/HP OpenView Workgroup Node Manager (none required)

To install the NETconfigurator for Windows (see Figure 8-8), server, and standalone client software, follow these steps:

1. Log in to a Windows 95, Windows 98, or Windows NT system.

2. Close any Windows programs that are running.

3. Insert the NETconfigurator CD into the CD-ROM drive.

4. From the Windows Start menu choose Run.

5. In the Run window, type the following command:

   ```
   <drive>:\Install\win32\ncs.exe
   ```

   A window opens informing you that the installation program is being prepared. After several seconds, the Optivity NETconfigurator splash window opens. Next, the InstallAnywhere Wizard starts, and the NETconfigurator installation program's Introduction dialog box opens.

6. Click Next. The Software License Agreement dialog box opens.

Figure 8-8. NETconfigurator Installation screen

7. Read the license agreement and do one of the following:

   ■ If you agree with the terms of the license, click Yes, and then click Next. The Important Information window opens.

   ■ If you do not agree with the terms, click No to exit the installation program.

8. Read the information in the Important Information dialog box and click Next. The Choose Install Folder dialog box opens.

9. Specify a location for the NETconfigurator files. You can install the NETconfigurator files in any directory on a local disk. The default directory is C:\Program Files\Optivity\NCS\NETconfigurator. If you are using NETconfigurator with a third-party Web server instead of the integrated Web server, you must create a link or an alias to the installation directory. (The details of how you link a file system directory to a Web directory depend on the Web server.) For example, you can install the NETconfigurator files in the default directory C:\Program Files\Optivity\NCS\NETconfigurator and then create a Web directory called NETconfigurator and map that directory to C:\Program Files\Optivity\NCS\NETconfigurator.

10. Click Next. The Choose Shortcut Location dialog box opens.

11. Specify the folder where you want to copy the NETconfigurator program icons. By default, the installation program copies the program icons into a folder called NETconfigurator 2.2.

12. Click Install. The installation program copies the files from the CD, and after a few moments, the Install Complete dialog box opens.

13. Click Done. This completes the installation process. Now you can verify the installation.

To install the NETconfigurator for UNIX, server, and standalone client software, follow these steps:

1. Open a command window.

2. Log in as root by typing the following command: su

3. At the password prompt, type your root password.

4. Navigate to the NETconfigurator installation files. For example, if the installation CD is mounted on the drive /cdrom, type the following command:

```
cd /cdrom/Install/<platform>
```

where platform is one of the following:

   ■ aix

   ■ hpux/10.20

- hpux/11.0
- solaris

5. Type the following command:

```
sh ncs.bin
```

6. A window opens informing you that the installation program is being prepared. After several seconds, the Optivity NETconfigurator splash window opens. Next, the InstallAnywhere Wizard starts, and the NETconfigurator installation program's Introduction dialog box opens.

7. Click Next. The Software License Agreement dialog box opens.

8. Read the license agreement, and then do one of the following:

   - If you agree with the terms of the license, click Yes, and then click Next. The Important Information dialog box opens.

   - If you do not agree with the terms, click No to exit the installation program.

9. Read the information in the Important Information dialog box, and then click Next. The Choose Install Folder dialog box opens.

10. Specify a location for the NETconfigurator files. You can install the NETconfigurator files in any directory on a local disk. The default directory is /opt/optivity/ncs/NETconfigurator. If you are using NETconfigurator with a third-party Web server instead of the integrated Web server, you must create a soft link to the NETconfigurator installation directory. For example, create a NETconfigurator directory in the Web server directory structure and link that directory to the NETconfigurator installation directory.

11. Click Install. The installation program copies the files from the CD and after a few moments, the Install Complete dialog box opens.

12. Click Done. This completes the installation process. Now you can verify the installation.

Starting the NETarchitect Installation Program

The NETarchitect software ships on CD-ROMs that are included in your Optivity NCS 2.2 package. To start the NETarchitect 2.2 installation, use the following steps. Figure 8-9 provides an example of this process:

1. Log in as root user.

2. Mount the NETarchitect CD-ROM for your operating system platform. There is one NETarchitect CD-ROM for each supported platform.

3. Ensure the following:

   - The X Window environment DISPLAY variable is set for root.

   - Network connections and external peripherals are fully operational.

   - The CD-ROM drive or remote file location is mounted.

4. Shut down all other software applications running on the system, including an existing version of NETarchitect.

5. In a command window, change to the location of the NETarchitect installation files. To determine the directory path, list the contents of the mounted software CD-ROM. For example, cd /cdrom/cdrom0/netarchitect2_2.

6. Enter the following command:

   ```
   ./install
   ```

   The Optivity NCS Installation window opens. The right pane of the window displays all installation queries. The left pane illustrates several of the Nortel Networks switch and router products that you can manage with NETarchitect. A status line below the left pane displays messages throughout the installation process.

7. Click Next. The installation program searches for the existing NETarchitect software. The installation program provides several options to customize your installation of Optivity NETarchitect 2.2.

Installation Options

Installation Directory. Confirm or change the parent directory for the Optivity NETarchitect home directory, */bn*a. Your directory selection must contain sufficient disk

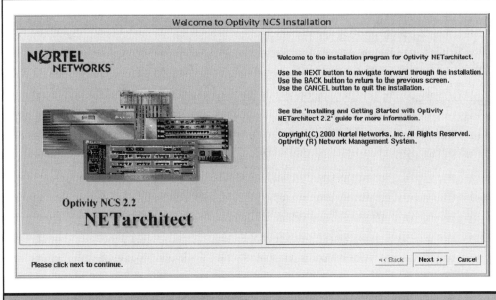

Figure 8-9.   NETarchitect Installation screen

space for the NETarchitect software. Current disk size requirements can be found in the documentation included with the software.

Make your selection in one of the following ways:

▼ To select the default installation directory, keep */usr/bn*a.

■ Enter the name of a different location for the *bna* directory.

▲ Click Browse to navigate to another location for *bna*.

NETarchitect creates a symbolic link called */usr/bna* to any alternative location you specify.

Database Directory. Confirm or change the database directory. The default directory, net_db, is below the NETarchitect home directory. Your directory selection must contain sufficient disk space for your network device data.

Make your selection in one of the following ways:

▼ To use the default database directory, do nothing.

■ Enter the name of a different directory.

▲ Click Browse to navigate to another location.

Domain Name. Confirm or change the *domain* name. A domain is a collection of NETarchitect database files that contain the NETarchitect configuration database and file archive for a collection of managed devices. You can manage any number of separate domains with a single NETarchitect 2.2 installation. For installations using a single domain, the name for the default domain is not significant. However, if you will use NETarchitect to manage more than one domain, enter a meaningful name for the initial domain database.

Client/Server. A default NETarchitect installation includes both client and server software. Installations with one or more local domain database require the client/server software. To install the server software, keep the default selection Client/Server. A client-only workstation has no domain database; it views or modifies domains on client/server workstations. To install the client software only, select Client Only, and then specify the hostname or IP address of an installed NETarchitect server that the client will access when starting NETarchitect. The server must be accessible on the network; the installation program verifies connectivity.

To advance from one option to the next, click Next in the Optivity NCS Installation window. After you complete all configuration options, the right pane of the installation window displays a confirmation message that lists your selections.

After you verify your installation options, complete the installation:

1. Click Install. The right pane echoes program output. There are no further prompts. The installation is complete when you see this message:

```
Optivity NETarchitect 2.2 Installation completed on: <date>
Installation of OPTBNA was successful.
```

2. When the installation completes successfully, the Save Log and Exit buttons in the right pane are enabled. NETarchitect automatically saves the log as /usr/bna/install.log, but you can save another copy to any directory.

3. Click Exit. The Optivity NETarchitect 2.2 installation process is now complete.

Optivity NetID

As business-critical applications are deployed over IP networks, the reliability of corporate intranets, extranets, and electronic commerce infrastructures has become a key consideration for network managers. Problems in IP addressing and DNS and DHCP management are a possible source of downtime in mission-critical IP networks. Optivity NetID streamlines configuration and management tasks to guard against these costly errors. Optivity NetID provides powerful, scalable, fault-tolerant IP addressing services, as well as DNS and DHCP management services to maximize efficiency in the enterprise IP environment.

Many organizations have developed a workaround approach to IP address management, such as a database applications developed in-house. These applications have limited functionality, are not standardized, and their operation often is dependent on a single employee. However, Optivity NetID is a full-featured, scalable product that can be managed by multiple administrators with differing levels of access. By integrating complex IP addressing tasks with DNS and DHCP management, the efficiency of management personnel can be greatly enhanced. Optivity NetID dramatically decreases the amount of time network managers have to spend on IP addressing and DNS and DHCP management. This approach also decreases the time spent on resolving problems that result from mistakes in the management of IP services.

Figure 8-10 illustrates a typical Optivity NetID architecture, indicating the relationships between the Optivity NetID servers, server managers, and databases.

Database

IP addressing information is stored in the Optivity NetID database (from Oracle or Sybase). Multiple users can access this information from the Optivity NetID Management Console.

Management Console

The NetID Management Console provides an easy-to-understand platform for IP address management and the Management of DNS and DHCP servers. The Java-based interface allows managers to access the central database from any standard Web browser. Views can be customized so administrators view networking information according to the fields he or she wants displayed. For example, DHCP configuration can be viewed either by server or subnet.

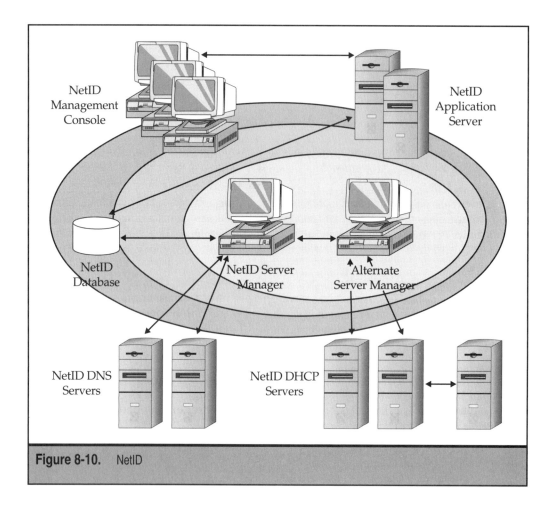

Figure 8-10.   NetID

Application Server

The Optivity NetID Application Server generates management consoles through which network administrators can look at and change the information stored in the database. The Application Server is responsible for saving network, subnet, host, DNS, and zone options specified by the administrator to the database. It also provides managers with updated network, DNS, and DHCP information.

Server Manager

The NetID Server Manager is the tie-in between the DNS and DHCP Servers and the central database. It provides the servers with their initial configuration and sends incremental configuration changes to servers across the network. The Server Manager also commits DNS and DHCP information to the database.

DNS Server

The Optivity NetID DNS Server is linked to the database by the Server Manager, and supports standards-based DDNS updates and DNS reconfiguration (changing server policy and zone structure). The NetID DNS Server is based on BIND 8.2.2 (BIND is the name of the DNS server found on most UNIX platforms; it is the *de facto* DNS standard) and is designed to interoperate with other BIND-compliant DNS Servers.

DHCP Server

The NetID DHCP Server is a BootP/DHCP server that is configured from the Management Console. The DHCP server automatically assigns IP addresses and names to specified hosts.

NetID's approach delivers built-in fault tolerance at every level, enabling administrators to solve network problems before a major outage can occur. Optivity NetID supports database replication to ensure the availability of IP address information. Multiple Server Managers also can be configured to maintain an open connection to the database.

Each NetID component continues to function independently if a database or WAN outage occurs. DNS and DHCP Servers operate using their local configurations and then automatically update the database as soon as connectivity is restored. Additionally, the DNS and DHCP servers generate alarms and warnings that are sent to the management console for administrators to act upon. In the event of a single server outage, a backup system is provided by DHCP redundancy and an additional DNS Server allows isolated outages to go almost unnoticed by end users.

The possibility of DHCP Server outages has kept many organizations from using DHCP services on their networks. Through DHCP redundancy, NetID virtually guarantees (with proper implementation) high availability of DHCP services. With a primary and a backup DHCP Server maintaining the same address ranges, DHCP clients are able to maintain an IP address even if the primary server goes down. Primary and secondary DHCP servers communicate using a server-to-server protocol. If the primary server fails to communicate with its backup server, the backup will automatically begin serving the primary's addresses.

CONCLUSION

As Enterprise Network resources have grown in size and scope, the need to quickly and efficiently manage those resources has gained strategic importance. Without adequate network management it is impossible to stay abreast of network problems. This leads to a reactive rather than a proactive stance on network design and planning issues. When staff has enough time to plan their work rather than spend their time "putting out fires," they not only get more done, their quality of work improves.

CHAPTER 9

Wireless Networking

In today's increasingly complex world, network connectivity is more important than ever. Notebook computers, Personal Digital Assistants (PDAs), and a host of other mobile computing tools are necessary components of the business marketplace. Although these tools offer the workforce unprecedented flexibility and freedom, they also highlight the limitations of current wired networks. These limitations will increase as mobile technology continues to advance. Organizations bound to wired networks might find their productivity and efficiency progressively reduced. For this reason, a robust and scalable wireless LAN solution is imperative.

WIRELESS LAN OVERVIEW

Until recently, wireless data networking had been composed of niche products that did not conform to any kind of standard. However, wireless LANs are reaching a new level of acceptability with mainstream organizations due to vendor adoption of the IEEE 802.11 standards. In the next few sections we will discuss the IEEE 802.11 standards both old and new. Understanding of this material will give us enough of a foundation to consider the merits of Nortel's wireless data offerings.

The Original Wireless Ethernet Standard

Wireless Ethernet standards are the responsibility of the IEEE 802.11 committee. The original 802.11 standard delivered shared bandwidth in the 1-2 Mbps range. With current technology advances, the new standard is able to support throughput of up to 11 Mbps. Similar in speed to wired Ethernet, the IEEE 802.11 standard defines the function of the Physical and Media Access Control (MAC) layers of the Ethernet frame. It uses the 83.5 MHz wide, 2.4 GHz Industry, Science, and Medical (ISM) band for transmission. This band is available for unlicensed operation worldwide, allowing products manufactured in one country to be used anywhere around the globe.

Physical Layer

The 802.11 specification supports two physical layer modes of operation: Direct Sequence and Frequency Hopping. A third mode, Diffuse Infrared, is quite cost effective but has very limited reach and therefore is not discussed.

In Direct Sequence (DS) operation the original data stream is multiplied by a spreading factor or "chipping code." This mode can supply 2 or 11 Mbps throughput to a particular user, dependent on the coding method used. Simultaneous transmissions are possible, but they have to be in a substantially non-overlapping spectrum and even then only a few concurrent streams are supported.

In contrast, Frequency Hopping (FH) mode utilizes one of 78 different 1-MHz channels for short intervals (around 100 ms or so), and then "hops" to another frequency decided on by a predefined algorithm. FH provides greater scalability because it allows for many simultaneous transmissions. Because the frequency changes 10 times per second, interference from other sources is low. Unfortunately, FH can support only 1 Mbps throughput to any given user. Both techniques are relatively immune to inappropriate data capture by a malicious user.

MAC Layer

The MAC layer specifies rules of access to provide contention arbitration regardless of which physical layer mode might be used. Like the traditional wired Ethernet standard (IEEE 802.3), wireless Ethernet (IEEE 802.11) uses Carrier Sense Multiple Access (CSMA). However, IEEE 802.3 uses it a bit differently, rather than collision detection (CSMA/CD) it uses collision avoidance (CSMA/CA).

Instead of detecting collisions on the Ethernet LAN and waiting a random amount of time before resending, it utilizes a request to send/clear to send (RTS/CTS) handshake to virtually eliminate the possibility of collision. The length of the data burst also is included in this RTS/CTS communication. Collision avoidance is used instead of collision detection because other transmitters might be too far away and therefore undetectable. This approach makes the 802.11 standard more bandwidth efficient than traditional 802.3 networks and therefore provides more relative throughput than its maximum 11 Mbps would seem to. The additional bandwidth efficiency is due to the lack of collisions on the network. Fewer collisions means fewer retransmissions, which allows packets to reach their destinations in a more timely manner.

Current Wireless Ethernet Standards

Whereas the original wireless LAN standards provided for bandwidth in the 1–2 Mbps range, the new IEEE 802.11a and IEEE 802.11b standards promise much higher sustained throughput. These new standards deliver maximum bandwidth ranging from 11 to 24 Mbps.

IEEE 802.11a

The IEEE 802.11a specification is based on a variant of Frequency Division Multiplexing (FDM) and can accomplish data modulation, which provides immunity to multipath echoes that are common in the indoor and mobile environments. All implementations are required to support 6, 12, and 24 Mbps throughput and can reach 54 Mbps in some implementations. The multi-rate capability of the MAC protocol guarantees that all devices communicate at the optimal data rate.

IEEE 802.11a is specified for use at 5 GHz. Unfortunately, this band is open only to unlicensed devices in the United States. Another problem with 802.11a is its low penetration power. This specification has limited success in transmitting through walls, doors, and other obstructions.

IEEE 802.11b

This version of the IEEE 802.11 specification uses the 2.4 GHz band and achieves 11 Mbps rates (with slower fallback options available) through a coding process derived from

Direct Sequence technology. FHSS is not supported due to certain FCC restrictions. The networking industry has focused on the 802.11b standard as the expected market leader.

Other Features of IEEE 802.11

Two other features of IEEE 802.11 are worth mentioning here: ad-hoc mode and low latency mode. Ad-hoc mode (see Figure 9-1) allows two wireless devices to communicate directly with each other without needing to go through a base station (Access Point). This is a useful feature for communicating wirelessly on an as-needed basis, even without a wireless LAN infrastructure. This holds a few advantages over infrared links that often are used for this purpose. Wireless technology provides greater range and is omni- directional in nature (meaning devices do not need to be directly aligned).

Low latency mode provides virtual class of service support to wireless LANs and creates wireless telephony opportunities (because voice traffic can be assigned a higher priority than data).

NORTEL'S WIRELESS LAN SOLUTION

Nortel's Wireless LAN (WLAN) product offerings provide all the advantages of a wired LAN without the limitations of wires. Laptop users can easily access network applications and resources such as e-mail, intranets, printers, and the Internet. Remote workers can quickly and simply create ad-hoc networks between two or more PCs for file and print sharing and workgroup collaboration. Desktop users working in temporary locations such as tradeshow halls or in hard-to-wire areas can still access the network without distance restrictions or the need for expensive cabling (see Figure 9-2).

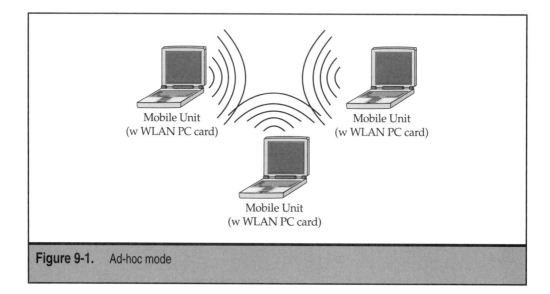

Figure 9-1.   Ad-hoc mode

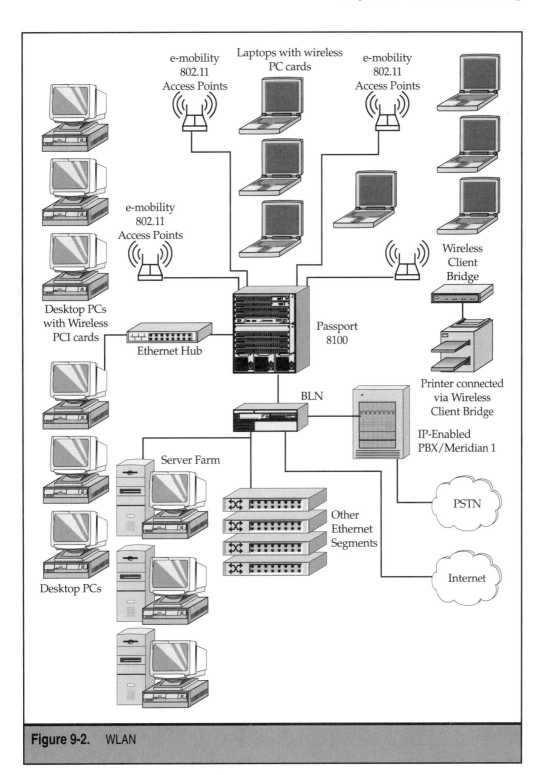

Figure 9-2. WLAN

The e-mobility 802.11 wireless LAN portfolio allows transparent access between wired Ethernet networks and wireless mobile units. Using standardized spread spectrum radios, the e-mobility WLAN products are capable of penetrating walls, doors, floors, and other obstacles to create a seamless wireless network. Using this technology, the e-mobility 802.11 wireless LAN products are able to deliver speeds of up to 11 Mbps.

The e-mobility portfolio includes two primary components: Access Points and wireless PC/PCI cards. An Access Point basically is a wireless hub that connects multiple devices to the Ethernet network. Both components use spread spectrum radios for communication that is not only secure and robust, but also license free worldwide. Each component complies with either the IEEE 802.11 Frequency Hopping Spread Spectrum (FHSS) or the IEEE 802.11b Direct Sequence Spread Spectrum (DSSS) industry standard. The portfolio offers plug and play compatibility, site survey utilities, and management software. The e-mobility 802.11 wireless LAN products provide significant cost savings by eliminating the need to drill holes and run wires throughout buildings and campuses.

It often is thought that wireless LANs are useful only for conference rooms and offices with heavy laptop utilization; this is not true. Nortel lists the following uses for WLANs on its Web site:

▼ **Retail**—Wireless point of sale and real-time inventory access.

■ **Healthcare**—Immediate and access to patient records and data.

■ **Hospitality**—High-speed Internet access for hotel guests, special events, and convention center needs.

■ **Education**—Provides students and staff real-time access to the Internet that extends the learning experience.

■ **Manufacturing**—Real-time transfer of mechanical, flow, operation, and other bandwidth-intensive data files.

■ **Government**—Ad-hoc networks for military and civic support for coordination or tracking efforts.

■ **Internet Service Providers**—High-speed Internet access for public areas and multi-tenant facilities including wireless e-mail and data transfer.

▲ **Corporate Environments**—Provides knowledge workers the ability to access network functions and applications from anywhere in their campus including conference rooms, meeting areas, and customer centers.

E-mobility 802.11 Access Point

The e-mobility Access Point (AP) works with the 802.11 wireless PC cards in portable computers and PCI adapters in desktop PCs to provide users with wireless network access. The Access Point receives data on either its wired or wireless interface and sends that data out the appropriate interface. A mobile unit (MU) or a desktop attached to the network through an Access Point functions as a peer to other network devices; the wireless interface is transparent. Access Points are capable of prioritizing data, voice, and multimedia traffic for uninterrupted, high-quality transmissions. A variety of system management options (see Table 9-1) allows network managers to monitor performance, change configuration, and run diagnostics.

The e-mobility 802.11 Access Point utilizes dynamic rate scaling as defined in the 802.11b standard, always attempting to connect at 11 Mbps; then automatically scaling down to 5.5 Mbps as well as 2 Mbps; and if needed, 1 Mbps. This is done to increase data range and ensure wireless network connectivity. The Access Point is able to trade network speed for greater distance between APs. As the signal strength increases, its speed increases until it reaches an optimal rate of 11 Mbps.

Table 9-1 describes the features of the e-mobility 802.11 Access Point.

Features	Benefits
11 Mbps direct sequence (DS) high data rate transmission	Supports bandwidth-demanding applications and high-speed data transmission
IEEE 802.11b compliant	Fully interoperable wireless networking based on the high rate standard
Mobile IP function	Enables multiple users to roam across routers/subnets and between cells for uninterrupted connectivity
Output up to 100mW Worldwide	Extended high-speed communications indoors and out
Dynamic rate scaling at 11, 5.5, 2, and 1 Mbps	Provides continuous connectivity at the highest rate even in high-interference environments; automatically selects the highest usable rate
System-wide upgrades from a single Access Point using FLASH memory accessible by HTTP, serial, Telnet	Fast and easy access point maintenance and upgrades
Network management, configuration, and diagnostic tools	Straightforward administration of the high-speed wireless network
Wired Equivalent Privacy (WEP) encryption and decryption	Powerful data security

Table 9-1. E-mobility 802.11 Access Point Features

Features	Benefits
Event logging, data packet tracing, SNMP alarm generation, operating statistics, protocol and bandwidth filters for optimum network management	Diagnostic capabilities for simplified, optimal network management
Standards: Commitment to open standards at every hardware and software interface including IEEE 802.11b, HTML user interface, NIC utilities	Bridges communication paths between wired and wireless network segments Uses diverse application tools in the same wireless LAN environment Supports technology that is already installed; integrates seamlessly with existing systems Ensures interoperability with wireless LAN devices from other vendors Protects your investment by ensuring migration path
Scaleable	Adding an access point expands coverage and capacity
Ethernet Access Point supports up to 256 mobile units	Seamlessly connects with all popular host environments
Wi-Fi Certified	Ensures interoperability among other Wi-Fi certified wireless systems for investment protection and system architecture flexibility
Bridge-to-Bridge - mode	Seamless bridging between separate Ethernet networks which enables connectivity without cables
Radio Characteristics	
Frequency Range	Worldwide product covering 2.4–2.5 GHz, programmable for different country regulations
Data Rate	11 Mbps per channel maximum
Output Power	100 mW Worldwide
Power Management	Continuous Aware mode and Power Saving Polling mode

Table 9-1.   E-mobility 802.11 Access Point Features *(continued)*

Features	Benefits
Range	Data throughput scaled to support up to 1,500 ft./450 m outdoors and up to 400 ft./120 m indoors
TX Maximum Radiated EIRP	FCC regulations part 15.247 in U.S.; ETS 300 328 in Europe; RCR STD-33 in Japan
Modulation	Direct Sequence Spread Spectrum (DSSS) with BPSK (1 Mbps), QPSK (2 Mbps), and CCK (5.5 and 11 Mbps)
TX Out-of-Band emissions	FCC regulations part 15.247, 15.205, 15.209 in U.S.; ETS 300 328 in Europe; RCR STD-33 in Japan
Operating Temperature	-20° to 70° C; -4° to 158° F
Storage Temperature	-30° to 80° C; -22° to 176° F
Network Characteristics	
Driver Software Support	Microsoft Windows 95/98, Windows NT 4.0, Windows CE 2.11 (only for Symbol's PPT2740), Windows 2000, NDIS 4 and 5
Access Protocol	CSMA/CA
Roaming	Virtually instantaneous

Table 9-1.   E-mobility 802.11 Access Point Features *(continued)*

Wireless LAN Adapters

The e-mobility 802.11 Wireless LAN adapters allow a host (desktop computer or server) to connect to a Nortel Networks WLAN. The PCI version of the adapter implements the Plug and Play standard. Its features include

▼ Support for Windows 95, 98, NT 4.0, 2000, and CE

■ Standard Network Driver Interface Specification (NDIS)

■ Card and Socket Services support

■ Low-power operation for battery-powered devices with PC card slots

■ Power Management

■ Continuously Aware Mode (CAM)

▲ Power Save Polling (PSP)

802.11 PC Card

The e-mobility 802.11 PC card fits into any laptop or other device with a PC card slot, providing low-maintenance wireless network connectivity. Its integrated antenna supports simultaneous transmit and receive functionality, providing a full duplex network connection. Power management prolongs battery life by ensuring a slower rate of power consumption. Most wireless environments are geared toward laptop and palmtop computers, so this is the component that will be installed most often.

802.11 PCI Adapter

The 802.11 PCI adapter has a semi-slot design that fits PC-compatible devices with a PCI interface. Because of its plug and play interface, the adapter can be configured quickly and connected to the wireless network, saving network managers the time and expense of wiring that should be avoided when network needs are temporary.

802.11 Client Bridge

The e-mobility 802.11 Client Bridge provides a cost-effective interface between Access Points and devices with RS-232 serial or Ethernet ports such as printers. Other possible applications include network devices that are not PC card compatible and other computing platforms.

802.11 Remote Power Interface (RPI)

E-mobility remote power options provide a reliable and economical method for powering Access Points from a remote location. The RPI can provide centralized power for numerous Access Points without installing a power supply at each Access Point location. APs often are installed in locations far from power outlets, such as the ceilings of large rooms or high above a warehouse floor. The RPI allows the Access Point to receive power without a local power source.

802.11 Wireless LAN Antennas

Nortel is able to offer directional or omni-directional antenna (from 20–70 degrees) options for indoor or outdoor use to provide different coverage patterns, depending on site and power requirements. Network administrators can choose from an integrated diversity antenna or an external, high-gain, directional model.

E-MOBILITY 802.11 SERIES CONFIGURATION

The next section covers all but the most advanced configuration options of the Access Point and Mobile Units (the most common components of a wireless network). However, discussion of the RPI and Client Bridge is beyond the scope of this book. The understanding that remote power and serial connectivity is available should suffice; although the technology behind wireless Ethernet is complex, the basic configuration of a wireless network is rather simple.

E-mobility 802.11 Access Point Configuration

In our discussion of Access Point administration we start, as always, with the basic serial connection to begin configuration.

1. Attach a null modem serial cable from the Access Point to the PC or laptop serial port.

2. From the PC, start a communication program such as HyperTerminal in a Windows environment.

3. Select the correct COM port and the following parameters:

   - Emulation: ANSI
   - Baud Rate: 19,200 bps
   - Data Bits: 8
   - Stop Bits: 1
   - Parity: none
   - Flow Control: none

4. Press the ESC key to refresh the display. The AP will display the Access Point main menu, as shown in Figure 9-3.

5. Exit the communication program to terminate the session.

```
                              MAIN MENU
              Symbol Access Point
              Show System Summary        AP Installation
              Show Interface Statistics  Special Functions
              Show Forwarding Counts     Set System Configuration
              Show Mobile Units          Set RF Configuration
              Show Known AP              Set Serial Port Configuration
              Show Ethernet Statistics   Set Access Control List
              Show RF Statistics         Set Address Filtering
              Show Misc. Statistics      Set Type Filtering
              Show Event History         Set SNMP Configuration
              Enter Admin Mode           Set Event Logging Configuration
```

Figure 9-3.   Access Point main menu

Entering Admin Mode

When in Serial mode, the user interface (UI) defaults to user level access allowing read-only functionality on the AP (for example, view statistics). Entering Admin mode allows access to configuration menus and allows an administrator to configure the Access Point. Entering Admin mode requires the administration password.

1. Select Enter Admin Mode from the main menu. The AP will prompt for the administration password:

   ```
   Enter System Password:
   ```

2. Type the default password:

   ```
   Symbol
   ```

NOTE: The password is case sensitive.

If the password is correct, the AP will display the main menu with the Enter Admin Mode menu item changed to Exit Admin mode. If the password is incorrect, the AP will continue to display the main menu with the Enter Admin Mode menu item.

NOTE: System passwords are set in the SET System Configuration screen.

IP Configuration

The AP UI includes an Access Point installation screen supporting additional configuration to set basic parameters for an e-mobility 802.11 wireless network. These parameters include specifying an IP address and designating a gateway address that enables the AP to forward messages across routers on the wired Ethernet.

To install an AP, follow these steps:

1. Enter the Admin mode.

2. Select AP Installation from the main menu. The following screen will display:

   ```
   Symbol Access Point
                         Access Point Installation
   Unit Name             Symbol Access Point    Additional Gateways
   IP Address            10.10.100.45           10.10.100.2
                                                10.10.100.3
   .Gateway IP Address   10.10.100.1            0.0.0.0
                                                0.0.0.0
   .Subnet Mask          255.255.255.0          0.0.0.0
                                                0.0.0.0
   .Net_ID (ESS)         101                    0.0.0.0
   ```

```
.Antenna Selection        Diversity On

.DHCP                     Enabled

OK - [CR]            Save - [F1]        Save All APs - [F2] Cancel - [ESC]
```

where

- ■ **Unit Name** is the name assigned to the AP.

- ■ **IP Address** is the IP address of the AP.

- ■ **Gateway IP Address** is the IP address of a router accessible to the AP on its wired Ethernet interface.

- ■ **Subnet Mask** is the subnet mask on the local network.

- ■ **Net_ID (ESS)** is a unique 32-character, alphanumeric, case-sensitive network identifier of the Access Point.

- ■ **Antenna Selection** enables the selection of antenna diversity.

- ■ **Additional Gateways** are the IP addresses of any additional gateways the Access Point should use. The AP will support up to seven gateways.

- ■ **DHCP** enables the AP's DHCP client to automatically send a DHCP request every XX hours/days to renew the lease as long as the AP is running.

3. Verify that the AP's parameters accurately reflect the network environment. Change them as needed.

4. In the Antenna Selection field, use the space bar or left/right arrow keys to toggle between Primary Only and Diversity On.

5. Select OK or Save to register settings by writing changes to non-volatile memory. Selecting Save displays a confirmation prompt.

6. Select Save All APs—F2—to save the AP installation configuration information to all APs with the same Net_ID (ESS). This option saves the configuration changes for the current AP on the known APs table and tells all other APs to update their configurations and reset after the configuration has been modified.

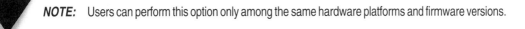

NOTE: Users can perform this option only among the same hardware platforms and firmware versions.

7. Select Cancel | ESC to disregard any changes made to this screen and return to the previous menu.

System Configuration

The AP provides configuration options for how the unit operates, including security access and interface control. Many options do not require modification.

1. Select Set System Configuration from the main menu; the next screen will display the following:

```
Symbol Access Point
                        System Configuration
Channel                 3              .Access Control        Disabled
                                       .Type Filtering        Disabled
.Ethernet Timeout       0
                                       WNMP Functions         Enabled
.Telnet Logins          Enabled        .AP - AP State Xchg
Enabled
.Encryption Admin       Any            Ethernet Interface     On
                                       PPP Interface          Off
.Agent Ad Interval      0              RF Interface           On
.S24 Mobile IP          Disabled
.Mobile-Home MD5 key    *******        Default Interface      Ethernet

.Web Server             Enabled        .MU - MU Disallowed    Off

System Password Admin - [F4]
OK - [CR]        Save - [F1]     Save All APs - [F2]  Cancel - [ESC]
```

2. After any changes have been made, press F1 or F2 depending on whether changes should be saved only to the local AP or to all APs with the same Net_ID (ESS).

3. After modifications have been saved, the AP(s) should be reset for changes to take effect.

4. Configure the country-specific, direct-sequence channel settings.

Frequency	Allowed Channel Range	Country
2412–2470	1–11	United States
2430–2447	5–8	Israel
2457–2463	10–11	Spain
2458–2472	10–13	France
2483–2485	14	Japan

5. Configure the AP system settings as required:

   ■ **Ethernet Timeout**—Disables the radio interface if no activity is detected on the Ethernet line after the seconds indicated (30–255). The Access Point disassociates Mobile Units and prevents further associations until it detects Ethernet activity. This prevents MUs from connecting if the AP has lost its connection to the wired network. The default value 0 disables this feature. The 1 value detects if the 10Base-T line goes down.

When the Ethernet connection is broken, the AP clears the MU table and disables the RF interface until the Ethernet connection comes up.

- **Telnet Logins**—Specifies whether the AP accepts or rejects Telnet logins. The default value is Enabled.

- **Encryption Admin**—Indicates which interface can change the encryption keys and the encryption key index. Without admin privileges, users cannot change this parameter or view the encryption keys. Any allows users with admin privileges to change encryption keys through any interface. Serial allows users with admin privileges to change this parameter and encryption keys only through the Serial port.

- **Agent Ad Interval**—Specifies the interval in seconds between the mobility agent advertisement transmission.

- **S24 Mobile IP**—If enabled, this feature allows MUs to roam across routers.

- **Mobile-Home**—Secret key used for Mobile-Home registration and authentication.

- **MU–MU Disallowed**—If enabled, Mobile Units associated with the same AP are not allowed to communicate with each other.

- **Web Server**—Enables the use of a Web browser to access the UI instead of a HyperTerminal or Telnet application. An Access Point reset is required for this feature to take effect.

- **System Password**—This screen can be accessed only when the AP is in Telnet mode.

- **Admin**—Serial mode provides read-only privileges and does not allow the user to view this screen.

- **Access Control**—Specifies enabling or disabling the access control feature. If enabled, the ACL (Access Control List) specifies the MAC addresses of MUs that can associate with this AP. The default is Disabled.

- **Type Filtering**—Specifies filter type for packets received; either Forward/Discard or Disabled. The default value is Disabled.

- **WNMP Functions**—Specifies whether the AP can perform WNMP functions. The default value is Enabled.

- **AP-AP State Xchg**—Specifies AP-to-AP communication exchanged.

6. To enable or disable interfaces in the AP, modify the following parameters:

- **Ethernet Interface**—Enables or disables wired Ethernet.

- **PPP Interface**—Enables or disables serial PPP. The default value is Off.

- **RF Interface**—Enables or disables radio. The default value is On.

- **Default Interface**—Specifies the default interface (Ethernet, PPP, or WLAP) that the AP forwards a frame to if the AP cannot find the address in its forwarding database. The default interface is Ethernet.

7. Verify that the values set reflect the network environment; change them as needed.

8. Select OK or Save to register settings by writing changes to NVM. Selecting Save displays a confirmation prompt.

9. Select Save All APS –F2—to save the system configuration information to all APs with the same Net_ID (ESS). This option saves the configuration changes for the current AP and sends two WNMP messages to all other APs on the Known APs table to update their configuration and reset after the configuration has been modified. Users can perform this option only among the same hardware platforms and firmware versions.

10. Select Cancel | ESC to disregard any changes made to this screen and return to the previous menu.

E-mobility 802.11 Mobile Unit Configuration

The configuration of the e-mobility 802.11 PC card and PCI card includes the installation of the actual hardware in the laptop or PC. This is covered in this book, as adequate documentation of the installation process is included with the hardware. It is assumed in the following section on software configuration that the hardware has been installed and the drivers loaded on the host machine.

Wireless Adapter Configuration for Windows 95 and 98

To configure the Spectrum24 WLAN adapter in Windows 95/98, follow these steps:

1. Click Start | Settings | Control Panel.

2. Select the Network icon and click the Symbol PC Card/PCI Adapter.

3. Select the Properties button. The Symbol Spectrum24 Easy Setup dialog box will display.

4. Click the Advanced button and scroll through the five Network Control Panel Applet (NCPA) property pages to view the default adapter configuration. Use the Mobile Unit, Power, Mobile IP, Encryption, and WLAN Adapter tabs to view or adjust the adapter configuration settings.

5. Exit and save the configuration settings by clicking OK or Finish. Select Cancel to use the default values.

6. Restart the system for the changes to take effect.

Wireless Adapter Configuration for Windows NT

To configure the Spectrum24 WLAN adapter for Windows NT, follow these steps:

1. Click Start | Settings | Control Panel.

2. Select the Network icon.

3. Select the Adapters tab and click the Symbol PC Card/PCI Adapter.

4. Click the Properties button. The Symbol Easy Setup dialog box displays.

5. Click the Advanced button and scroll through the five Network Control Panel Applet (NCPA) property pages to view the default adapter configuration. Use the Mobile Unit, Power, Mobile IP, Encryption, and WLAN Adapter tabs to view or adjust the adapter configuration settings.

6. Click OK or Close to save the changes to the adapter configuration and exit the Symbol NCPA utility. Select Cancel to use the default values.

7. Restart the computer when prompted by Windows NT.

Wireless Adapter Configuration for Windows 2000

To configure the Spectrum24 WLAN adapter for 2000, follow these steps:

1. Click Start | Settings | Control Panel.

2. Click the System icon and select the Hardware tab.

3. Click the Device Manager button.

4. Double-click Network Adapters.

5. Right-click the Spectrum24 WLAN adapter.

6. Select Properties; the Symbol PC Card Properties dialog box displays.

7. Select the Spectrum24 tab. The Symbol NCPA Easy Setup dialog box displays.

8. Click the Advanced button and scroll through the five Network Control Panel Applet (NCPA) property pages to view the default adapter configuration. Use the Mobile Unit, Power, Mobile IP, Encryption, and WLAN Adapter tabs to view or adjust the adapter configuration settings.

9. Click OK or Close to save the changes to the adapter configuration and exit the Symbol NCPA utility. Select Cancel to use the default values.

10. Restart the computer when prompted by Windows.

Wireless Adapter Configuration for Windows CE

To download the Spectrum24 Windows CE device driver from the driver installation CD-ROM to a handheld computing device:

1. Attach the 9-pin serial cable included with the handheld computer between the desktop computer and the handheld computer.

2. Click Start | Programs.

3. Select Microsoft Windows CE Services.

4. Select Mobile Devices. A listing of supported handheld computing devices is displayed.

5. Select the handheld computing device to be used for the driver download.

6. Click My Computer and select the desktop computer CD-ROM drive.

7. Click on the Spectrum24_DS11.EXE file from the Windows CE subdirectory. The Windows CE driver files install in a temporary directory on the desktop computer. The Spectrum24 for Windows CE 2.x Setup dialog box appears.

8. Click Next.

9. Select the destination (location) to receive the driver files from the desktop computer. Click Next. A Setup Complete dialog box appears. Click Finish.

10. From the Microsoft Windows CE Services dialog box, click Yes to launch the driver download from the desktop computer to the handheld computer. A progress bar appears as the files download from the desktop computer to the handheld computer. The Spectrum24 Easy Setup dialog box appears on the handheld computer when the file download is complete.

11. Enter the network ESSID in the Easy Setup dialog box.

12. Restart and reset the handheld computer and remove and reinsert the PC card for the configuration changes to take effect.

CONCLUSION

The developments of 802.11 wireless LAN products should make the idea of actually deploying wireless LANs more attractive. In fact, the Cahners In-Stat Group predicts dramatic growth in the number of wireless LAN users in the United States, from 2.3 million today to 23 million in the year 2003. This kind of growth potential ensures that companies such as Nortel will continue to develop their wireless products well into the future.

The stated goal of many network hardware vendors is "always on" Internet access capable of connecting the mobile user to both corporate and personal network resources as quickly and seamlessly as possible. Products such as Nortel's e-mobility 802.11 Wireless LAN suite will soon bring that goal within reach.

CHAPTER 10

VPNs and the Contivity Extranet Switch

The Virtual Private Network or VPN is an exciting up-and-coming technology. The market for VPN services has been estimated at over 10 billion dollars in the year 2001 alone! Expected growth rates after 2001 are off the charts. An understanding of the underlying technologies that make up VPNs is vital to any data engineer's future career.

Nortel Networks has developed a market-leading product for the VPN space; one that combines VPN capabilities with remote access and LAN/WAN routing functionality. The Contivity Extranet Switch is one of Nortel's most exciting hardware offerings.

VIRTUAL PRIVATE NETWORKS

A Virtual Private Network makes use of a public network such as the Internet as a secure channel for communicating private information. VPNs allow the creation of a secure link between an organization's local LAN and a remote network or remote user's PC.

A VPN is created using a process known as *tunneling*. Tunneling allows a network transport protocol to carry information for other protocols within its own packets. For example, IPX packets can be encapsulated within IP packets to be transported across the Internet, which is not possible without tunneling. The data can be secured using data encryption, authentication, and integrity functions.

DEFINITIONS: *Encryption* scrambles the contents of a data packet as it travels over a network, making it unintelligible to those who might want to monitor or copy it. Encryption uses a mathematical algorithm and a digital key (or series of bits) based on the algorithm to encode a packet at one end of a transmission and then decode it at the other end.

Authentication is the process of forcing users to prove they are who they say they are before they can gain access to network resources.

Authorization, or access control, is a method of establishing access privileges for users. Access can be granted to all network resources or restricted to specific subnets, network servers, devices, or applications.

EXTRANETS DEFINED

Before extranets became available, a company's geographically dispersed networks existed independently, sometimes connected to each other by Frame Relay or leased lines. The Internet now allows companies to connect multiple local area networks and remote users (such as telecommuters and traveling employees) into their private, internal networks (intranets). The standard protocols of the Internet such as HTTP, TCP/IP, FTP, and so on make it the ideal avenue to support this new paradigm of connectivity for remote employees and customers. This extension of the Internet in conjunction with the intranet is known as an *extranet*. Extranets allow remote users to connect to an Internet service provider and reach corporate headquarters or other branch offices through the Internet from wherever they might be located. The extranet can provide remote users access to any and all resources available to their local peers.

Why Use an Extranet?

Traditionally, remote access solutions have employed modem technology to handle remote connectivity (see Figure 10-1). This type of solution has historically proven problematic for information technology (IT) staffs. The Contivity Extranet Switch removes the need for corporate modem pools. Instead, it utilizes ISPs to provide modem, ISDN, DSL, or cable access. This removes a routine yet time-consuming task from the plates of already overworked IT staffs. The Contivity's extranet access capabilities allow an organization to leverage this new technology, improving performance and lowering overhead. This resource shift can translate into significant cost savings.

More savings can be realized by reducing the number of telephone company T1 lines needed. A traditional channelized T1 can support only 24 modem users per T1; a T1 connected to the Internet on one end and a Contivity Extranet Switch (CES) on the other can service between 800 and 175 remote users, depending upon usage. There also are savings from reduced long-distance calls from an employee's home to corporate modem pools, and from replacing leased lines connecting branch offices to corporate headquarters. CES users dial into a local ISP, which almost always is a free call these days, and branch offices can use DSL or cable services to connect to the Internet for much less than a traditional leased line would cost.

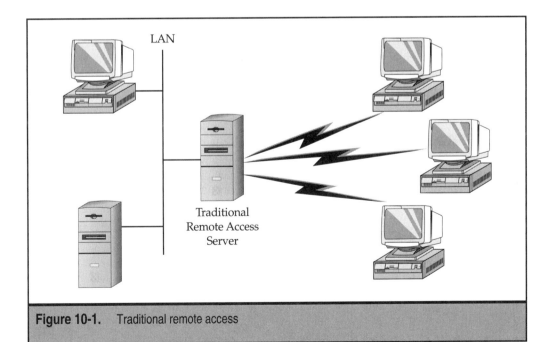

Figure 10-1.   Traditional remote access

THE CONTIVITY EXTRANET SWITCH (CES)

Forward-thinking organizations have been quick to see the potential in VPN services, which use Internet technology to extend their private networks anywhere the Internet can reach. The Contivity Extranet Switch can be used to create highly scalable, secure, and robust VPNs to connect multi-location enterprises and supply chains or for service providers to offer IP VPNs as a managed service. The complete product family includes models designed to serve large corporations, mid-sized companies, remote branches, small offices, and home offices.

Remote Access

The CES uses the Internet and tunneling protocols to create secure extranets. A secure protocol is required for safe transport of data over the Internet. The switch uses the most popular tunneling protocols: IPsec, PPTP, L2TP, and L2F. To form a tunnel, the remote user establishes a connection with an Internet service provider. Once the user is connected to the Internet, a second "dial-up" connection is launched. This second connection uses an IP address instead of a phone number to connect to the Contivity Extranet Switch. It also can use a name if the IP address has been mapped to a domain name in a DNS server.

The second connection can utilize either the IP Security (IPsec) Protocol or Point-to-Point Tunneling Protocol (PPTP). Layer 2 Forwarding Tunneling Protocol (L2TP) and Layer 2 Forwarding (L2F) tunnels are a bit different. These tunnels are not created between the user's PC and an extranet switch; instead they are formed between a piece of equipment located at the ISP and an extranet switch. In this case, the user dials into the ISP with a specific telephone number that causes an L2F or L2TP tunnel to be created directly to a specific organization's extranet switch. This is basically a way for a corporation to outsource modem pool management duties. This method of providing connectivity is quickly being abandoned as it is more expensive than simply using IPsec or PPTP and a standard dial-up connection for remote access. Figure 10-2 demonstrates how data moves from the remote user to the internal network through the Internet.

Software Features

The following table details the software features of the Contivity Extranet Switch. It will serve as a useful tool when evaluating whether the CES is the correct tool for your environment.

Protocols	PPTP, L2F, L2TP, IPsec
Routing Protocols	RIP v1
	RIP v2
	OSPF
	VRRP

Protocols	**PPTP, L2F, L2TP, IPsec**
Authentication Services	Internal or external Lightweight Directory Access Protocol (LDAP) Remote Authentication Dial-In User Service (RADIUS) Token card integration: Security Dynamix and AXENT Digital certificate authentication with Entrust and VeriSign
Encryption	Federal Information Processing Standard 140-1 Level 2 certified IPsec-certified by the International Computer Security Association Up to 128-bit encryption
Filtering Criteria	Individual user or group profile; source and destination IP address; port, service, and protocol type; Synchronize Flag/Acknowledgement (SYN/ACK) bit
Bandwidth Management	Group-level configurable minimum bandwidth settings, priority levels using Random Early Detection (RED); four connection priority levels; differentiated services; code point marking; Quality of Service; Resource Reservation Protocol (RSVP).
Accounting	Internal and external RADIUS accounting; event, system, security, and configuration accounting; automatic archiving to an external system
Management	Full HTML and Java configuration; SNMP alerts; bulk load configuration; NNCLI; four levels of administrator access; role-based management to separate service provider and end user management Optivity VPN Manager, batch configuration and management of multiple Contivity Extranet Switches Preside IP VPN Service Management System
Reliability	Intel processor architecture Multi-level authentication servers Automatic backup of all system data Redundant components on Contivity Extranet Switch 4500

Protocols	**PPTP, L2F, L2TP, IPsec**
Security	Contivity stateful firewall including stateful packet inspection, audit, Network Address Translation (NAT) Berkeley packet filters
Client Software	Runs on Windows 95, 98, 2000, or Windows NT 4.0 or later IPsec Auto-configuration with "one-click" connections Tested with Linux Free S/WAN client IPass dial-up database with more than 8,000 locations (Service requires customer subscription with IPass)
MS Windows 2000	Support for Windows 2000 embedded tunnel protocols; mix and match with existing Nortel Networks clients or other tunnel protocols such as PPTP and L2TP; support configurable to offer end user remote access applications with end user stations and a VPN gateway to Windows 2000 servers

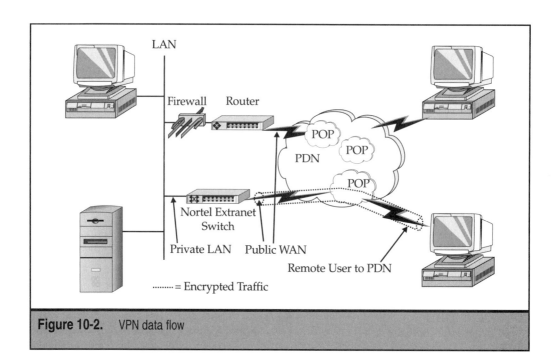

Figure 10-2. VPN data flow

Hardware Features

The Contivity Extranet Switch comes in five hardware versions, each designed to meet the needs of different size organizations; from the CES 4500, designed for the largest of corporations and service providers to the CES 100 intended for the small office/home office (SOHO) market.

NOTE: The only major difference in the product line is the number of tunnels each switch is capable of providing.

Contivity 4500

The Contivity 4500 is the high-end offering in the CES family, providing efficient VPN connectivity for up to 5,000 tunnels. It also has the largest physical footprint. Features include

▼ Up to 5,000 concurrent tunnels

■ Dual 450 MHz Intel Xeon processor

■ 128 MB memory

■ Five PCI expansion slots

■ Optional interfaces:

    ■ 10/100 Ethernet LAN card

    ■ T1 with integrated CSU/DSU

    ■ Single and dual port V.35 WAN card

    ■ High-speed serial interface (HSSI) card

    ■ Encryption card

■ Dual, redundant, auto-switching power supply system with dual line cords

■ Dual, redundant storage system

■ Contivity VPN Switch 4500 Software

■ Contivity VPN Access IPsec client software with unlimited distribution license

■ CD and online HTML documentation

■ Length: 17.0 in. (43.2 cm)

■ Width: 17.0 in. (43.2 cm)

■ Height: 14.0 in. (35.6 cm)

■ Weight: 60.0 lb (27.2 kg)

▲ Electrical: 100–240 VAC, 3.0 A, 50–60 Hz

Contivity 2600

The CES 2600 provides high performance and security for up to 1,000 tunnels. Features include

▼ Up to 1,000 concurrent tunnels

■ 733 MHz Pentium II processor

■ 128 MB memory

■ Three PCI expansion slots

■ Data communication grade 125-watt power supply

■ Optional interfaces:

    ■ 10/100 Ethernet LAN card

    ■ T1 with integrated CSU/DSU

    ■ Single and dual port V.35 WAN card

    ■ High-speed serial interface (HSSI) card

    ■ Encryption card

■ Contivity VPN Switch 2600 Software

■ Contivity VPN Access IPsec client software with unlimited distribution license

■ CD and online HTML documentation

■ Length: 21.0 in. (53.3 cm)

■ Width: 17.25 in. (43.8 cm)

■ Height: 5.25 in. (13.3 cm)

■ Weight: 25.0 lb (11.3 kg)

▲ Electrical: 100–240 VAC, 2.0 A, 50–60 Hz

Contivity 1500 Series

The CES 1510, 1520, and 1530 offer more flexibility for office centers, campuses, or branch offices needing up to 100 tunnels. Features include

▼ Up to 100 concurrent tunnels

■ 400 MHz Celeron processor

■ 64 MB memory

■ Contivity VPN Switch 1510—Dual 10/100 Ethernet LAN ports

■ Contivity VPN Switch 1520—V.35 and 10/100 Ethernet LAN port

■ Contivity VPN Switch 1530—T1 with integrated CSU/DSU and 10/100 Ethernet

■ Contivity VPN Switch 1500 Software

■ Contivity VPN Access IPsec client software with unlimited distribution license

■ CD and online HTML documentation

■ Length: 13.0 in. (33.0 cm)

■ Width: 9.5 in. (24.1 cm)

■ Height: 3.5 in. (8.9 cm)

■ Weight: 10.0 lb (4.5 kg)

▲ Electrical: 100–120/220-240 VAC, 2/1.25 A, 50–60 Hz

Contivity 600

The cost conscious will appreciate the Contivity 600, which is designed for smaller offices requiring up to 30 simultaneous tunnels. Features include

▼ Up to 30 concurrent tunnels

■ 300 MHz Celeron A processor

■ 64 MB memory

■ Dual 10/100 Ethernet

■ Contivity 600 Software

■ Contivity VPN Access IPsec client software with unlimited distribution license

■ CD and online HTML documentation

■ Length: 11.0 in. (27.9 cm)

■ Width: 8.5 in. (21.6 cm)

■ Height: 4.0 in. (10.2 cm)

■ Weight: 6.0 lb (2.9 kg)

▲ Electrical: 90 VAC up to 240 VAC, 50–60 Hz

Contivity 100

The CES 100 provides basic connectivity for small or home offices requiring a limited number of concurrent tunnels. Features include

▼ Up to 5 concurrent tunnels

■ Pentium class 300 MHz processor (expandable)

■ 16 MB memory

■ 8 MB Flash memory (replaceable, expandable)

■ Interfaces

    ■ Two 10/100 Ethernet LAN ports

    ■ Serial port, out-of-band management, or PPP

    ■ Single and dual analog ports

- ■ ISDN
- ■ Dual and triple Ethernet
- ■ 1 Meg Modem (DSL)
- ■ Contivity VPN Switch 100 Software
- ■ Contivity VPN Access IPsec client software with unlimited distribution license
- ■ CD and online HTML documentation
- ■ Depth: 14.5 in. (37 cm)
- ■ Width: 12 in. (30 cm)
- ■ Height: 2.64 in. (6.7 cm)
- ■ Weight: 8 lb (3.6 kg)
- ▲ Electrical: internal 145W, 100–240 VAC

Switch Placement

The Contivity Extranet Switch can be placed into a network in several configurations, depending on an organization's network design and manner of accessing the Internet. The four most commonly used topologies are described here:

- ▼ CES behind an Internet-facing router, in parallel with a firewall
- ■ CES with a direct connection to the Internet (The CES is functioning as the Internet-facing router.)
- ■ CES behind both a firewall and a router
- ▲ LAN-to-LAN connectivity

CES Behind an Internet-Facing Router, in Parallel with a Firewall

Figure 10-3 demonstrates the Contivity Extranet Switch connected behind an Internet-facing router and in parallel with a firewall. This allows an enterprise to integrate a CES with the fewest changes necessary on the preexisting network. This is the least expensive option in terms of man hours needed to get the switch up and running. It also saves money by sharing an Internet connection with the rest of the organization. This type of design is used when extranet traffic is not heavy and available Internet bandwidth is not fully utilized.

CES with a Direct Connection to the Internet

In Figure 10-4 the firewall and router are completely separated from the extranet switch. Their configurations remain unchanged. The CES is placed in the network where a more traditional remote access service (RAS) server would be placed. However, in this case the extranet switch is connected to the Internet rather than to modems. This allows extranet traffic to grow without affecting other Internet services. This is the most expensive option, as a completely new Internet connection is required.

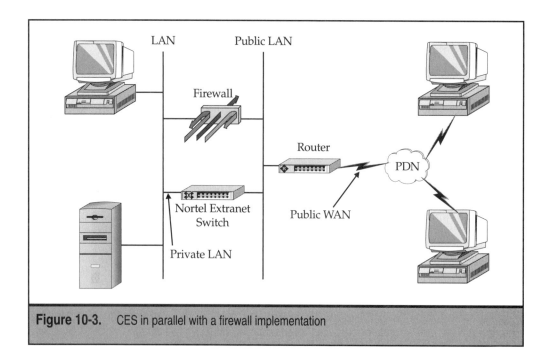

Figure 10-3. CES in parallel with a firewall implementation

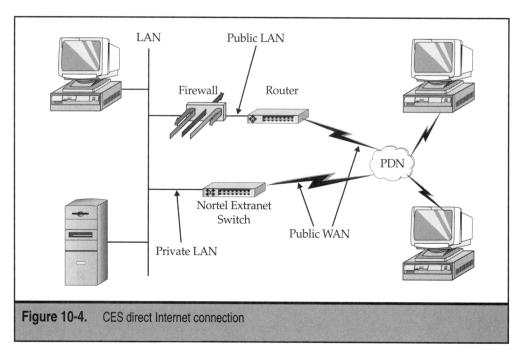

Figure 10-4. CES direct Internet connection

CES Behind Both a Firewall and Router

Figure 10-5 shows the extranet switch placed behind both a firewall and a router. For this configuration to work properly, both the firewall and router allow tunnels to pass through to the switch. This option usually requires changes only on the firewall. Like the first configuration, this option saves money by sharing an Internet connection with the rest of the enterprise; however, it takes more effort to set up initially. Many organizations will feel this is the most secure option as traffic must pass through both the firewall and CES's security criteria.

LAN-to-LAN Connectivity

The branch office feature allows an IPsec tunnel to be configured between two private networks over the public Internet. Usually, one private network is behind a local CES and the other is behind a remote extranet switch. Using the branch office option allows for the configuration of the accessible subnetworks behind each switch. It also contains the information necessary to establish the link, such as the other switch's IP addresses, authentication methods, and encryption types. Limiting connectivity to local subnets can be accomplished by setting policy restrictions such as access hours and filter sets. This design allows for a very inexpensive branch office connection as no leased lines are required; instead, all traffic bound for a remote network is securely routed over the Internet (see Figure 10-6).

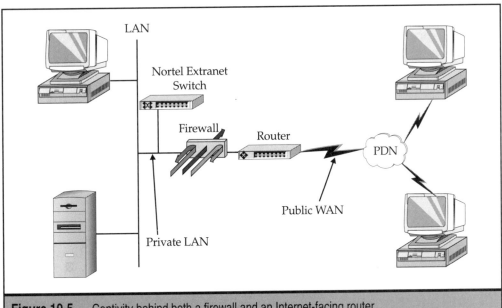

Figure 10-5. Contivity behind both a firewall and an Internet-facing router

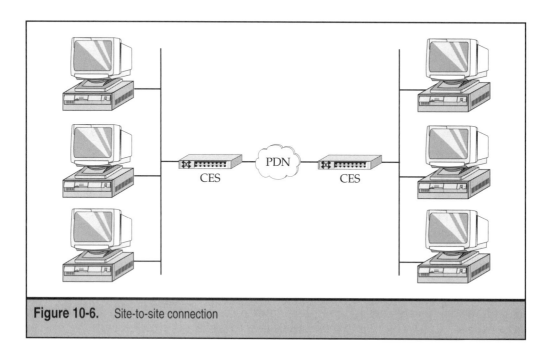

Figure 10-6.   Site-to-site connection

Routing and the CES

The CES is capable of routing authorized traffic both into and out of a private, internal network. The extranet switch also is able to route traffic between two private interfaces and between its public and private interfaces. The CES also can route tunneled traffic from its public interfaces to the Internet. Because of this, the Contivity Extranet Switch can be used to connect the entire organization to the Internet. The extranet switch is capable of providing the following routing capabilities; using these three features, the CES can function as a single device solution for access to the Internet:

▼   **VPN routing**—Routes packets between secure tunnels.

■   **Enhanced routing**—Routes packets between all physical interfaces both public and private. This feature also enables data to flow between a tunnel and a public interface.

▲   **Services routing**—Allows for the routing of data used for the services that the CES provides. This includes support for tunnel protocols such as IPsec, PPTP, L2TP, and L2F.

Initial Configuration

As with most network equipment, to configure the Contivity Extranet Switch a management IP address first must be assigned. The following instructions describe the process by which this is possible.

Serial Interface Configuration

The following procedure should be used to access the CES through its serial interface. The serial interface will allow a manager to assign the extranet switch a management IP address and subnet mask so that a Web browser can be used for management. The serial interface configuration procedure also is useful in a system recovery situation when the switch becomes unreachable because of hardware failure or a configuration mistake.

Terminal Settings   Your terminal emulation program must use the following configuration settings:

▼   9,600 baud

■   8 data bits

■   1 stop bit

■   No parity

▲   No flow control

Procedure   The following instructions should be followed to assign a management IP address to the Contivity Extranet Switch:

1. Connect the serial cable (supplied with your switch) from the switch's serial port to a terminal or a communications port of a PC.

2. Power on the terminal or PC.

3. Using a terminal emulation program on the PC, press the Enter key and you are prompted to supply a user name and password. The factory default user name and password are as follows:

    ```
    User name: admin
    Password: setup
    ```

    A menu appears that allows you to enter the following:

    ■   Management IP address

    ■   Management IP subnet mask

    ■   Gateway IP address (optional)

    ■   Allow HTTP management (check box)

4. Follow the screen prompts. A sample display follows:

    ```
    Main Menu:
    1) Interfaces
    2) Administrator
    3) Private Default Route Gateway* 10.0.0.10
    4) Public Default Route Gateway*
    5) Create A User Management Tunnel (IPsec)
    6) Restricted Management Mode
    ```

```
7) Allow HTTP Management TRUE
8) Firewall
9) Shutdown
P) Configure Serial Port
C) Controlled Crash
R) Reset System to Factory Defaults
E) Exit, Save and Invoke Changes
* Type 0.0.0.0 to delete.
Please select a menu choice (1 - 9,P,C,R,E): 1
5. Select "E" to save your changes and exit.
```

Web-Based Configuration Checklist

The following information should be gathered before beginning the Web-based portion of the configuration:

▼ A management IP address for the system. This address is needed to manage all system services such as HTTP, FTP, and SNMP. This was configured during the serial portion of the installation.

■ An IP address for the LAN port.

■ Any number of public IP addresses; for example, one IP address for each public LAN interface and one IP address for each T1 WAN interface.

■ A plan to distribute IP addresses to clients when connections are requested; for example, through a DHCP server or an internal client address pool (with an address pool you will need a range of IP addresses).

■ An authentication database: If internal authentication through the LDAP database is not being used, you will need an external LDAP or the RADIUS server(s) IP address and password or shared secret (password).

■ An external accounting server, such as RADIUS, with its IP address and shared secret (password).

■ Client dial-in: Prepare the clients for the type of tunneling protocol they will be using. The PPTP client application is available on the Nortel Networks CD for Windows 95; it comes with Windows 98 and Windows NT. Nortel Networks also provides the IPsec client on the Nortel Networks CD.

▲ A complete network topology of the "environment" in which the CES is being tested including the switch, the default router address, and any other IP addresses that might be required.

NOTE: You should begin with either the Quick Start or the Guided Configuration (Preferably Quick Start). Once you are familiar with the switch's navigational menu and capabilities, you will want to select Manage Switch.

Web-Based Configuration

After the Serial Interface Configuration has been completed, open a Web browser and enter the management IP address to load the Contivity Extranet Switch Welcome display. For example, if you entered the management IP address as 154.12.109.52, type the following URL: http://154.12.109.52. At this point you must decide which of the configuration options on the Welcome Display to choose (see Figure 10-7).

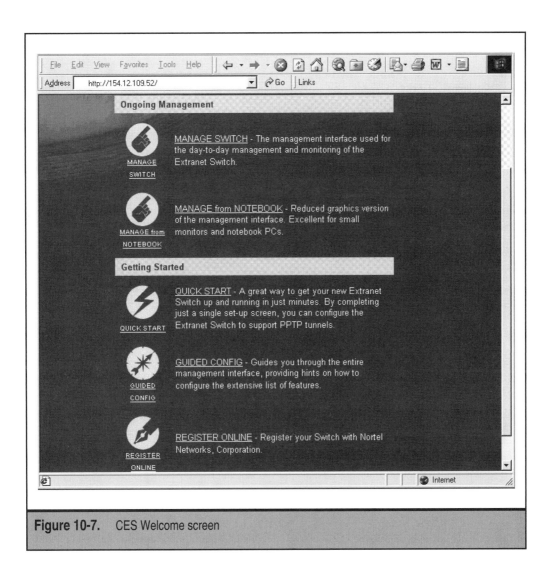

Figure 10-7.   CES Welcome screen

Contivity Extranet Switch Welcome Display

This page allows entry to any of the configuration areas for the Contivity Extranet Switch, including

▼ Manage Switch

■ Manage from Notebook

■ Quick Start

■ Guided Configuration

▲ Register Online

Manage Switch   Click Manage Switch to begin a configuration session. This allows access to all Configuration Management options. For the first configuration, Quick Start or Guided Configuration (preferably Quick Start) should be followed.

Manage from Notebook   This selection activates a notebook display option. The Contivity Extranet Switch Manager then runs in a Java-free display mode, which runs better on slower notebooks. This option is faster over a slow connection, such as a remote VPN connection.

Quick Start   Click here to begin the Quick Start Configuration. For first-time administrators of the Contivity Extranet Switch, this is the recommended option. A configuration can be completed very quickly and the switch can be tested in as little as 15 minutes.

Guided Configuration   Guided Configuration allows access to all Configuration Management functions. This option walks an administrator through the entire navigational menu. Each individual screen begins with a summary of the objectives of the section and then leads the engineer through the setup of the switch through the section (for example, Profiles), one subsection at a time. Context-sensitive help is available in each area in addition to the summary. If the information required to set up the switch is readily available (such as the Web-based Configuration Checklist), the guided configuration should take between two and three hours to complete.

Register Online   Use this option to register the CES with Nortel Networks. It takes only a few minutes and will allow network managers access to the latest software and technical tips. The extranet switch requires Internet access from the private interface for registration to be successful.

Login and Password

Select an option in the navigational menu and submenu; you then are prompted for the login and password.

Enter the system default login and password in lowercase characters, as follows:

```
Login: admin
Password: setup
```

At this point we are going to cover the Quick Start process for configuring the Contivity Extranet Switch. Administrators who would like to be walked through all aspects of the switch's configuration can use the guided configuration procedure.

Requirements for Using Quick Start

This section describes what is needed for the Quick Start configuration option (see Figure 10-8). Guided configuration should be used if the following criteria cannot be met.

Point-to-Point Tunneling Protocol (PPTP)   PPTP is a tunneling protocol supported by Nortel Networks, Microsoft, and other vendors. The PPTP client is available for Windows 95 on the Nortel Networks CD and comes with Windows 98 and Windows NT 4.0 and later.

Static IP Addresses, DHCP, Server Address Allocation, or an Internal Client Address Pool   A DHCP server on the private LAN segment dynamically assigns IP addresses on behalf of remote users. The DHCP server is automatically discovered through broadcasting on the private interface that is associated with the management IP address. With an Internal Client Address Pool you will need a range of IP addresses.

Local Lightweight Directory Access Protocol (LDAP) Database Authentication   LDAP is a standard protocol for Internet directory services that is based on directory entries. A *directory service* is a central repository of user information. The local database is internal to the switch. An LDAP server and associated database will be set up locally on the switch for the Quick Start procedure. Later, you can switch to a network-available external LDAP server using the LDAP Intermediate File (LDIF) data format.

Configuration

This display allows an administrator to add an IP address and subnet mask to the LAN port, establish the tunnel as private (your private LAN) or public (the Internet), and

Figure 10-8. CES Welcome to Quick Start

configure up to three PPTP users and an administrator with user IDs and passwords. The system's date and time also can be configured here. Figure 10-9 displays the top half of the Quick Start Configuration screen; Figure 10-10 displays the bottom half.

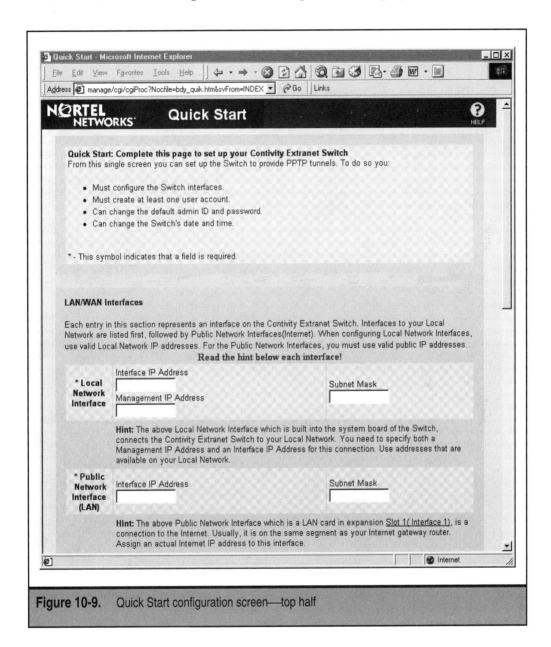

Figure 10-9.   Quick Start configuration screen—top half

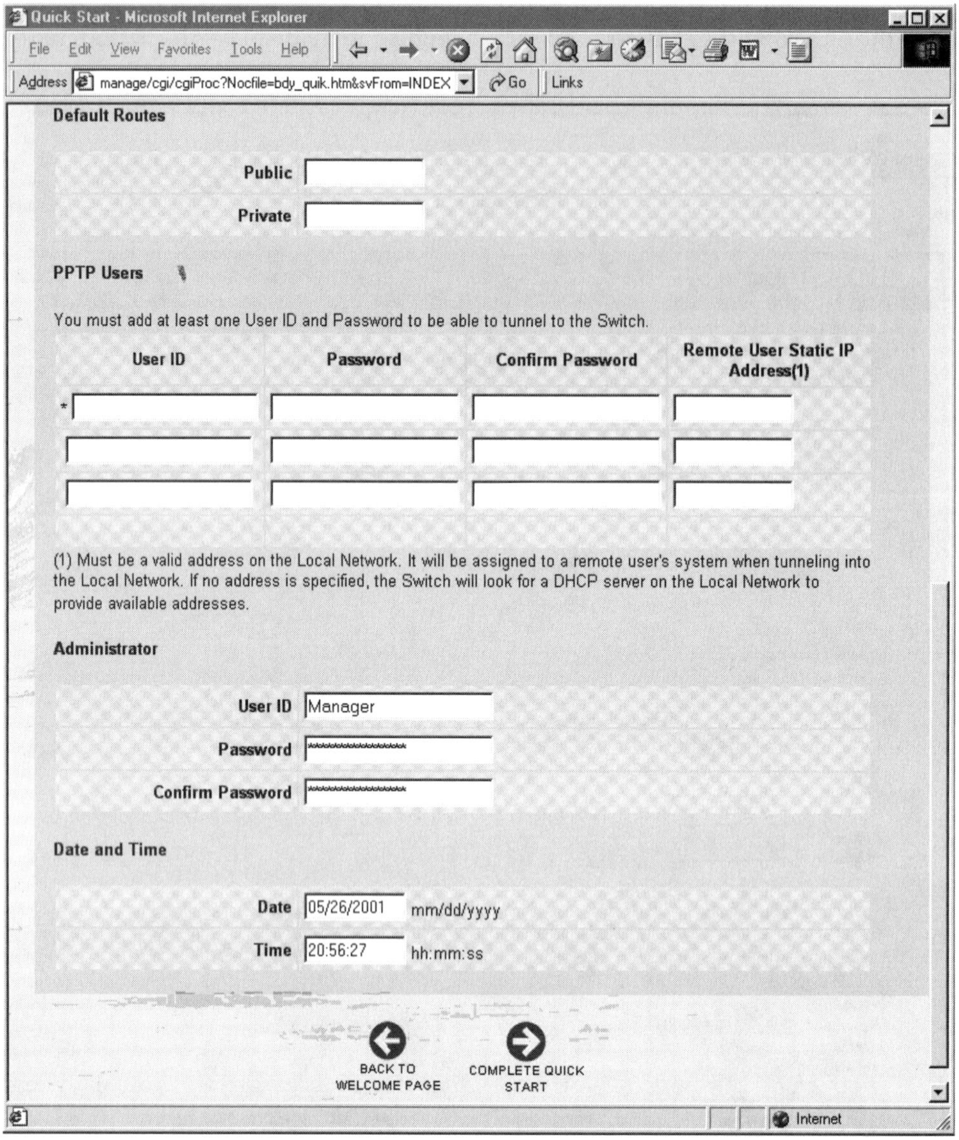

Figure 10-10. Quick Start configuration screen—bottom half

LAN/WAN Interfaces

The following sections allow configuration of all interfaces on the Contivity Extranet Switch.

Interfaces   Displays the switch's management IP address, LAN/WAN port, and any additional LAN or WAN cards.

IP Address   Enter an IP address for all interfaces on the switch, including the LAN port. These IP addresses are used for tunnel creation.

> **NOTE:**   The interface IP address information is required, not the management IP address, which was already set during the initial IP configuration.

Subnet Mask   Enter a subnet mask in dotted-decimal notation; for example, 255.255.0.0.

Default Gateway   A *default gateway* is where packets are sent if there is not a specific route in the routing table to the packet's destination. Enter a default gateway to LAN or WAN interfaces as needed.

Type-Public   Indicates that this interface is attached to a public (external) network such as the Internet. On a public interface, the switch accepts only tunneled protocols such as IPsec, PPTP, L2TP, L2F, and the diagnostic protocol PING; all other protocols are ignored. For security reasons, an external host can send only enough packets to the switch's external interface to establish an encrypted tunnel. If the tunnel is not established before the maximum-number-of-packets-allowed counter is reached, any packets from that host will be ignored.

Type-Private   Indicates that this interface is attached to the private (internal) network and is able to accept nontunneled network protocols such as TCP/IP, FTP, HTTP, and so on. The private interface also is capable of accepting tunneled protocols, such as IPsec and PPTP, which can be used for secure access to manage the switch.

PPTP Users

The following options allow for the creation of a simple PPTP configuration.

User ID   Enter a user ID. The user ID works with the password as the authentication mechanism when attempting to access the local LAN through the Contivity Extranet Switch.

Password   Type the user's password. A minimum of eight characters should be used, preferably using both letters and numbers for better security.

Confirm Password   Retype the user's password to verify that it was typed correctly.

Remote User Static IP Address   If a user will have a static IP address when logging into the Extranet Switch, enter the statically assigned address here. This is unnecessary if you will be assigning addresses through DHCP or an internal address pool.

Administrator

The Administrator settings allow a network manager to set or change the primary administrator user ID and password. This user ID and password combination always has access to all displays and controls. The primary administrator user ID also is used to access the serial port and the recovery disk. Access to the switch through the serial port or a Web browser is allowed using this password. There can be only one primary administrator. This obviously is an important user ID and password; thus it is important to record and save it in a safe place.

User ID   Type a user ID for the primary administrator. This primary administrator user ID has the power to modify and view all settings in the switch.

Password   Type a user password for the primary administrator.

Confirm Password   Retype the password for the primary administrator to verify that it has been typed correctly.

Date and Time

The following three sections allow an engineer to configure date and time parameters for the switch.

Date   Enter the current month, day, and year in the following format: mm/dd/yyyy.

Time   Enter the current hour, minute, and seconds (hh:mm:ss) as shown on a 24-hour clock; for example, 00:00:00 to 23:59:59.

Time Zone   Set the proper time zone. Time zones are important when using digital certificates.

Automatic Backup

The automatic backup display allows an administrator to configure the intervals at which system files will be saved to designated backup servers. Automatic backups should be configured immediately so that system or configuration information will not be lost in case of problems. Automatic backup servers are configured from the Admin/Automatic Backup display page.

The Extranet Access Client (EAC)

The Extranet Access Client (EAC) is the software that allows a remote user, connected to the Internet, to establish an encrypted tunnel into a private network (see Figure 10-11).

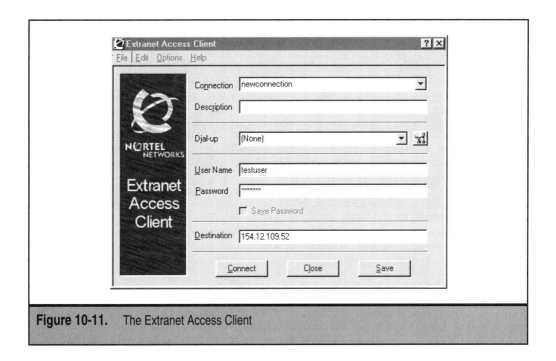

Figure 10-11. The Extranet Access Client

The EAC currently supports only the IPsec protocol. Users wishing to use PPTP should utilize the PPTP client that is included with Windows 95 and higher. There also are many PPTP clients available for the Linux operating system.

Installing the Extranet Access Client on Windows 95

To install the Nortel Networks Extranet Access Client onto a Windows 95 PC, copy the four files from the Client folder on the Nortel Networks Extranet CD onto your hard drive, and install them. International software users must go to the Microsoft Web site (http://support.microsoft.com/support) to get the MSDUN13 patch.

1. First, install Msdun13.exe (Microsoft Dial-up Networking update) by double-clicking the file name. The installation is self-explanatory. You might need your Windows 95 CD (if the CD was not copied onto your drive). During the installation, you will be asked to reboot your system twice.

2. Next, install Wsockupd.exe (Winsock update) if you are using the retail version of Windows 95. Reboot your system after installing the update. You now have the Microsoft PPTP tunneling client installed.

3. Complete the IPsec installation by running the Eac_25d.exe (Nortel Networks Extranet Access Client). The installation is self-explanatory. You might need your Windows 95 CD-ROM (if the CD was not copied onto your drive). When prompted at the end of the installation, reboot your system.

4. If you do not care about operating within the Network Neighborhood, skip this step. To operate within the Network Neighborhood, enable the following items under the Network Control Panel (click the Start | Setting | Control Panel and then double-click the Network icon to open the Network Control Panel).

   a. Under the box titled, "The following network components are installed," verify that the Client for Microsoft Networks is listed. If it is not, click on Add, then select CLIENT, and then click Add again. Select Microsoft followed by Client for Microsoft Networks and click the OK button. You will need your Windows 95 CD if it is not already copied onto your system.

   b. Under the same box titled, "The following network components are installed," make sure NetBEUI is not installed. To verify this, scroll down through the list box and look for any lines that have NetBEUI in them. If there are any lines that include NetBEUI, click on the line, and then click the Remove button. This forces the Network Neighborhood to use NetBIOS over TCP/IP, which is compatible with the extranet switch.

   c. Under the Identity tab, configure the workgroup to be the same as your company's internal workgroup. For example, "Nortelnetworks."

   d. Next under the Identity tab, verify that the computer name is different from your PC at work. Otherwise, you will be attempting to log a second unit with the same name onto the network.

   e. If you have made any changes in the Network Control Panel, click OK, and reboot the system.

   f. Double-click the Extranet Connection Manager icon.

   g. Enter a new connection profile name.

   h. Create a new dial-up connection.

   i. Click the Tool button (next to the Dial-up Connection list box), select New, and follow the wizard.

   j. Create a new extranet connection.

   k. Click the Tool button (next to the Extranet Connection list box), select New IPsec Connection, and follow the wizard.

   l. Click the Connect button.

Installing the Extranet Access Client on Windows 98 and Windows NT

To install the Nortel Networks Extranet Access Client onto a Windows 98 PC or Windows NT 4.0 workstation, you must copy the Extranet Access Client (Eac_25d.exe) that is on the Contivity Extranet Switch CD in the Client folder onto your hard drive.

1. Install Eac_25d.exe by double-clicking the program name. The installation is self-explanatory. When prompted at the end of the installation, reboot your system.

2. If using the Extranet Access Client over a dial-up connection

   ■ In Windows 98: Under the Network Control Panel (from the Start menu, select Settings | Control Panel), select Add | Adapter | Microsoft | Dial-up Adapter.

   ■ In Windows NT: Install the Remote Access Service under the Network Control Panel (from the Start menu, select Setting | Control Panel, and then double-click the Network icon to open the Network Control Panel). Select the Services tab and click Add. Scroll down to select Remote Access Service and click OK.

3. Under the Protocols tab for Windows NT or under the Network Control Panel for Windows 98, verify that NetBEUI is not installed. If NetBEUI is listed, click on it, and then click the Remove button. This will force the Network Neighborhood to use NetBIOS over TCP/IP, which is compatible with the switch. Click the OK button and reboot your system.

4 Double-click the Extranet Connection Manager icon.

   a. Enter a new profile name.

   b. Create a new dial-up connection.

   c. Click the Tool button (next to the Dial-up Connection list box), select New, and follow the wizard.

   d. Create a new extranet connection.

   e. Click the Tool button (next to the Extranet Connection list box), select New IPsec Connection, and follow the wizard.

   f. Click the Connect button.

With the Extranet Access Client properly installed and a CES waiting to receive a connection, you are ready to experience the power of an inexpensive, high-speed remote access solution.

CONCLUSION

It is a widely held belief in the networking industry that VPNs will gradually replace Frame Relay and Point-to-Point WAN links. The cost savings available from VPN offerings will see to this. Many Frame Relay circuits are fully utilized only a fraction of the time, but organizations must pay for these connections whether they are fully utilized or not. By being able to connect to remote sites over the Internet, costs can be driven down significantly. The Contivity Extranet Switch is at the forefront of the VPN boom, and with the features to be added in future releases and the dedication Nortel Networks has shown to the platform, it is sure to remain there.

CHAPTER 11

An Introduction to Network Troubleshooting

We have introduced the concept of networks and networking with Nortel Networks enterprise products. We have discussed the multitude of networking protocols in use today. We have discussed the commands and interfaces used to monitor and configure a Nortel Networks router and switch. We now introduce tools and methods of troubleshooting the network.

Troubleshooting often can be very time-consuming and frustrating. The end user feels frustration when he or she is unable to open a network application needed to do the job. The networking support staff feels frustration because they are trying to discover the cause of a very complex situation and trying to convince the end user they actually are working on the problem. An issue can become even more complex when there are multiple vendors involved (no one is willing to admit their product is the cause of a problem).

Network problems can be discovered and resolved very quickly as well. Often the device's light-emitting diodes (LEDs) can provide a clue as to whether a device is functioning or not. One quick check is the network ping, which will provide response time, reachability, and connectivity information. Many network nodes also contain a log file, which will provide information that at the very least will point you to the protocol or device that might not be functioning correctly.

In a perfect world, there would be no reason for this chapter. Networks are for the most part very stable and reliable, but there are things that can cause a network to go awry; therefore, you must have an understanding of how to discover the problem. Keep in mind that troubleshooting also takes years of experience and a lot of patience. It also is important to understand the needs of the network you are working on. If you are a support engineer for multiple corporate networks, you often are required to prioritize your workload to give attention to the most important issues. If you support a single network, prioritization is still very important. No matter what your position, the needs of the end user should always be the main concern when an issue—even within your network—arises.

Every business has networking needs—from the video shop down the road with a small database that is accessed by the two checkout registers to the major financial institution that must process transactions within milliseconds. When their networking needs are not being serviced, they lose money. Understanding the network and being able to use the tools provided for troubleshooting can ease the problems they encounter.

There are many different troubleshooting approaches in use today. Each one can be very successful. When learning how to troubleshoot, it is recommended that you simply develop a method that helps you to understand the problem. It usually does not matter how you reach a conclusion; just that you are able to reach it.

This chapter is just an introduction to troubleshooting. There are some very good books on the market today that provide in-depth troubleshooting advice and information. *The Network Troubleshooting Handbook* and *Nortel Networks: Troubleshooting and Optimization*, both published by Osborne/McGraw-Hill, are excellent resources, and are a must for the library of any networking professional who supports Nortel Networks equipment.

OVERVIEW OF NETWORK TROUBLESHOOTING

There are many different ways a network problem can be discovered. The most common way a problem is found is by using a network monitoring or a network management station within the network. Also, a problem often is brought to your attention by the end user when they call to report difficulty connecting to the network. Problems also can be discovered when viewing logs or performing routine maintenance on the network.

When tackling any type of network problem, it is important to collect and assemble the information necessary to start troubleshooting. Once the information is gathered to begin troubleshooting, you will need to obtain symptom data and evaluate symptom information. It is very important to gather and understand any network problem as completely as possible before attempting to perform any network troubleshooting.

There are many different diagnostic tools that can be used to assist you in determining your problem. There are some very helpful software applications, system logs, and visual aids. Once a problem has been narrowed down to a particular point within the network, these system logs can be extremely helpful in many problems in today's network.

Finally, experience will play a big part in resolving a problem. It is important to understand all parts of your network. Understand the code revisions, protocols, and nodes that are running in and changing within your network. Knowing your network and its normal operation goes a long way toward determining an issue.

Assembling Information

Regardless of how the problem is discovered, it is always important to assemble as much information as possible. It often is a good idea to keep a checklist nearby to ensure that all the information that needs to be collected for troubleshooting can be gathered. Table 11-1 is an example of the type of checklist you can develop. In the example, assume you have discovered that there are no lights on one of your switches.

Question to Ask	Response
What is the problem?	No lights are on the BayStack 450 switch
Is the network down?	No
When did the problem first occur?	This morning
Is this a recurring problem?	No, just this morning, lights have not returned.
Is this a new installation?	No
Is this an existing network?	Yes
Does the problem occur only during certain conditions? If so, what are they?	Possible—power went off last night.
Other information:	

Table 11-1. An example of a network troubleshooting checklist

In the example, you can see that having a checklist of information that needs to be gathered can be extremely helpful when trying to determine the root of the problem. The following information is helpful and should be considered when developing your information gathering checklist:

▼ What is the problem? (Try to document the problem as exactly as possible. Collect as much information as you can—information that appears insignificant might turn out to be the key point leading to the problem's resolution.)

■ Can the problem be reproduced?

■ What are the configuration parameters used in the system?

■ Is the network down? (This is a very important point. If the network is down, a contingency plan probably needs to be implemented.)

■ When did the problem first occur?

■ Is the problem a recurring problem?

■ Is the problem possibly related to a new installation?

■ Is the problem related to an existing network?

■ Under what conditions does the problem occur?

■ Have there been any recent changes to the network?

■ Have there been any changes to the environment where the network nodes are located? (Environmental changes can be any changes in the environment within the proximity of the network nodes.)

■ How are the network users being affected?

■ How is the network being affected?

■ Has anything been attempted to rectify the problem? (If the answer to this question is yes, get as much information as possible about what has been done. If any configuration changes have occurred, try to obtain a copy of the original configuration file).

■ What version of software code is being used?

■ What version of hardware is being used?

▲ Obtain contact information for the person reporting the problem, or an affected user. (This will allow you an avenue to later verify whether or not the problem is still being exhibited.)

Obtain Symptom Data

Once you have gathered the information on the checklist, you must gather supporting information on the symptoms that are associated with the problem. Most of the symptom data you will collect directly stems from the responses you received when you were gathering information about the problem.

▼ **Obtain detailed symptom information**   Gather as many details about the specific symptoms as possible. To find out that "50 users are unable to establish a PPP connection when trying to dial in to the 5399 located in the MIS closet at 151 nonesuch road" is much more helpful than finding out "Some people cannot dial in." Obtain the specific symptoms that are being experienced. Get as much information as you can about these symptoms. Always remember, there is no such thing as irrelevant information, nor is there such a thing as too much information.

■ **Find out if there have been any changes introduced into the network**   Many problems discovered within networks are due to some changes that have been introduced into the network. Quite often changes do not show up immediately, so never assume that because something does not change "right now" there is no possibility of a delayed adverse effect stemming from a change that was made previously. One important part of troubleshooting would be to obtain a sequence of events in reverse chronological order.

■ **Find out if there are any possible environmental issues**   Weather changes, changes in the climate, and electrical issues all are possible culprits that can and do introduce problems within a network.

■ **Determine a timeline**   Try to determine whether there is any time relationship in the symptoms' recurrence. Try to determine the frequency at which a problem occurs within a particular time frame, or whether there is a specific time that the problem occurs; all very helpful information to gather and analyze.

▲ **Determine how widespread the issue is within the network**   To fully understand what the impact of the problem is, you must try to determine the extent of the network problem. The following must be taken into consideration:

■ Are users in different subnets experiencing the problem, or are users of only a particular subnet being affected?

■ Are there many different groups affected?

■ Is the problem only affecting one network node or multiple network nodes?

■ Is the problem only affecting one protocol, or many protocols?

■ Is the problem associated with only one port, or multiple ports?

Evaluate the Data

Evaluating the data is simply taking the information you have obtained and logically considering what the normal operation should be, and what might be hindering the network from its normal operations. It is helpful when evaluating the problem to take a pencil and a piece of paper and document your findings. You can draw the physical topology to help you to collect your thoughts during the evaluation period. Sometimes it helps to discuss things with a coworker, if one is nearby. Research is key when performing troubleshooting; at times it is helpful to see if you can find any information that might tell you if the issue you are having is a common one.

When evaluating, first consider the normal network operation and how it differs from its current operation. You should be able to compare the normal network operation with the current network operation and discover a discrepancy along the way. Once you have determined a discrepancy, you should troubleshoot further to see what might be generating it.

Determining Where to Start

The complexity of a network can make diagnosing a problem difficult at times. Once you have gathered all the information you can and have collected and evaluated the symptom data, you need to determine where you want to start.

Often it is a good idea to begin at the bottom of the OSI reference model and work your way up. This will allow you to quickly determine whether the problem is a physical one or one that is more operational in nature.

Physical Media Problems

A problem that is related to a physical problem normally is one of the quickest to discover. For instance, an LED that is out, or a frayed or disconnected cable, normally will identify a physical problem. It could be a module that is not seated well or possibly a power cord that has been disconnected.

A physical issue might not be so easy to discover at times. Company XYZ kept reporting to their MIS department that at around 2:00 AM every morning, the users of a particular department report that they are losing complete connectivity to the network. The outage would last for 15–20 minutes, and then their connections would be restored. The network engineer for the company spent several days trying to determine what was wrong. He analyzed logs, performed multiple tests, and verified all physical media connections were made. Still, he was unable to prove that anything was wrong, other than at around 2:00 AM the connection went down. He verified with the electric company and checked the security log; nothing abnormal had been logged or reported.

After a week of trying to see what was happening, he decided to sit by the switch that the users were connected to. He sat in the closet where the switch was located. He watched the time and at 1:59, the janitor came into the closet, reached down, unplugged the switch and plugged his radio in. The engineer asked the janitor what he was doing. The janitor reported that he was taking a break, and as this was the only air-conditioned room in the building to break, he always took his break in the closet.

Problems with Cables   Checking and verifying that your network cables are operational is one important troubleshooting step. Cables are very reliable and do not fail frequently, but should always be considered when a connectivity problem exists in your network. Often it is environmental issues that will lead to problems with your existing network cabling. If you are having problems with a new install, it is important to verify that you are using the correct cable.

When diagnosing problems with cables and cable connections, a visual inspection can let you know whether the cabling has gone bad. Always check for broken pins, cuts in the cable, frayed cabling, loose cabling, and so forth. Another common mistake is using the wrong cable interface connector. Always re-verify that the connector you have chosen is the correct one for the application you are working with.

Problems with the Link Module   The link modules require some visual checks as well when troubleshooting. The first thing you should check is the status of the LEDs on the link module. Each link module will provide an LED that will indicate the current state of the link module. The LEDs on the link module you are connected to might indicate that there is a bad connection on a single port. It also might indicate that the link module is not connected correctly, might need to be reset, or has failed.

Nortel Networks enterprise products do ship with a manual that indicates what each status LED means. It is important to always refer to these manuals when performing any troubleshooting.

Operational Problems

An operational problem is one that encompasses several nodes on the network. It is a problem that could affect multiple protocols on multiple ports on these nodes. Some of the more common operational problems are

▼   Environmental

■   Hardware

■   Memory

- Power
- ▲ Booting

When trying to determine the source of an operational issue, you should try to obtain access to your Nortel Networks router or switch that is exhibiting the symptoms. Once you have connected to the device through the console, try to cold boot the device (provided you are able). The diagnostic tests that are performed during boot-up might indicate where your problem resides.

Also knowing whether there have been any changes in the environment, electrical problems, or changes in the network topology can provide hints to the cause of your operational issue. Always verify that power to the devices in the network is being supplied by a reliable source. Make sure there have been no recent changes in temperature or climate where the devices are physically located. Through the command line and the device event logs, try to determine if there are any problems with the device handling the traffic that is being generated within the network.

Environmental Problems   Environmental issues might be one of the hardest problems to diagnose. Intermittent connectivity problems often are associated with environmental issues, but environmental issues are the problem that is most frequently overlooked.

Changes in temperature can cause problems within some network nodes. An increase in humidity might cause problems as well. Always find out information about the room in which the equipment is located and see if there are any possible environmental concerns that might relate to the problem you are working on.

Hardware Problems   Most hardware problems can be discovered viewing the LEDs. If a module has a problem, the software will ensure that a light changes (or goes out) to bring attention to the problem. Additionally, hardware problems can be discovered through the diagnostic report that is generated during boot-up. Remember, to view the boot-up diagnostics, you need to be connected to the device through the console.

Memory Issues   Memory problems that occur often are the result of network growth or a configuration error, although there are other events that might cause memory problems within a network. Some possible causes are

- ▼ Network growth that leads to large routing tables
- Allocating too much available memory to other resources
- Poor network design
- ▲ Misconfiguration

Memory problems are a very frequent issue in networks today. Even though memory issues are very common, the symptoms of a memory issue are not always the same. Event logs are a good tool to use to see if any memory issues are being reported. In BayRS, the MIBs are extremely helpful when trying to determine problems with memory.

Power Problems   Another common network problem is associated with bad fuses or unreliable power sources. Regardless of where the network node is located physically in your network, there must be a reliable power source; preferably a redundant backup power source.

It also is also preferable that all devices be connected to their power sources through a surge protector to protect against spikes in voltage and use conditioners where possible. If you are using a backup power source, it is recommended that you source the primary power and the backup power from different circuits. Some even source their backup power to a UPS for contingency.

Boot Problems   To determine whether you are having problems during device boot-up, you should console connect to the device and then cold boot the device. Make sure to watch the boot diagnostic process for information.

The diagnostic process will inform you if there is a problem with a link module, images, CPU information, and so forth. The following is an example of a successful diagnostic boot-up message string:

```
BLN Power-up Diagnostics:  Name:  bndiag, Revision 12.05
Approximate Test Time 1 minute 30 seconds or less.
It is Fri, 10/13/2000, 14:17:33 (PM)

Testing Slot 1
Testing..............CPPASSED
Testing I/O Module in Position 2..............PASSED
Testing I/O Module in Position 3..............PASSED
Testing I/O Module in Position 4..............PASSED
Testing I/O Module in Position 5..............PASSED
Invoking Bootstrap...
```

TROUBLESHOOTING TOOLS

There are many software programs and applications that can be used to assist in troubleshooting. The event log is an application that is provided in many of the Nortel Networks enterprise products. The command-line interfaces also are helpful when troubleshooting issues. The MS-DOS commands "ping" and "tracert" can help determine trouble within the network. There also are some very useful programs available through multiple vendors; some excellent shareware and freeware, as well as free evaluations. A sniffer, which can be a device or a software application that analyzes and gathers statistical information on the network, is useful in gathering symptom information.

Event Logs

The event log will provide a detailed description of milestones within the network node. Some of the milestone data contained in the event log are as follows:

- ▼ Boot-up information
- ■ Authentication failures
- ■ Operation exception messages
- ▲ Error reporting

The event log itself often is very cryptic and might require some research to understand it. The following screen capture gives an example of four lines of an event log taken from a BayRS router:

```
#   25: 03/03/2000 09:00:25.507  DEBUG     SLOT  4  GAME    Code:    44
self-mapping of gid=0x08120 @ 0x3164f524 pended

#   26: 03/03/2000 09:00:25.531  DEBUG     SLOT  4  MIB     Code:  76
MIB manager discarding request with op_code=0x146 from dead gid=0x8120

#   27: 03/03/2000 09:00:25.535  INFO      SLOT  4  NAT     Code:  17
NAT Forward up on 192.168.16.110.6

#   28: 03/03/2000 09:00:25.843  DEBUG     SLOT  2  IP      Code:   8
RTM self map old bc000049,  new b4000049
RTM up self map old 3c00014b,  new 3400014b
```

Packet Internet Groper (Ping)

Ping is a program that is used to test and debug networks. The ping command will send an echo request to a specified destination and wait for a response. Once complete, the ping will report to the screen whether it was successful. If successful, the ping will report statistical information relative to its operation.

Ping is supported in the Nortel Networks routers and within the 450 switches as of the 3.0 image release. Ping also is supported by any operating system that supports TCP/IP. An IP ping command is issued by typing **ping**, followed by the IP address for the destination node. An example of a ping issued in MS-DOS is shown here:

```
C:\Ping 211.11.11.99
Pinging 211.11.11.99 with 32 bytes of data:
Reply from 211.11.11.99: bytes=32 time=92ms TTL=241
Reply from 211.11.11.99: bytes=32 time=92ms TTL=241
Reply from 211.11.11.99: bytes=32 time=91ms TTL=241
Reply from 211.11.11.99: bytes=32 time=98ms TTL=241
```

```
Ping statistics for 211.11.11.99:
Packets: Sent = 4, Received = 4, Lost = 0 (0% loss),
Approximate round trip times in milli-seconds:
Minimum = 91ms, Maximum =  98ms, Average =  93ms
```

As you can see in the example, the ping that was requested for IP address 211.11.11.99 was successful. The output that was returned shows the packet size of the ping request, the round trip time in milliseconds for the ping to reach its destination, and the time to live (TTL), which represents the maximum number of hops that an IP data packet can traverse the network before it is discarded. The ping response also provides statistical information.

There are some optional switches that are available in MS-DOS to assist in troubleshooting. These optional switches allow you to specify certain conditions for your ping. The following example is taken from the help feature in MS-DOS:

```
C:\ping
Usage: ping [-t] [-a] [-n count] [-l size] [-f] [-i TTL]
[-v TOS][-r count] [-s count] [[-j host-list] |
[-k host-list]][-w timeout] destination-list
Options:
    -t              Ping the specified host until stopped.
                    To see statistics and continue – type
                    Control-Break;  To stop - type Control-C.
    -a              Resolve addresses to hostnames.
    -n count        Number of echo requests to send.
    -l size         Send buffer size.
    -f              Set Don't Fragment flag in packet.
    -i TTL          Time To Live.
    -v TOS          Type Of Service.
    -r count        Record route for count hops.
    -s count        Timestamp for count hops.
    -j host-list    Loose source route along host-list.
    -k host-list    Strict source route along host-list.
    -w timeout      Timeout in milliseconds to wait for each
                    reply.
```

TROUBLESHOOTING NORTEL NETWORKS DEVICES

Keep in mind that this chapter is an overview of troubleshooting Nortel Networks products. As an introduction, we are covering the basics. There are some very good resources for network professionals out there. Many of these are discussed at the end of this chapter, under the section titled "Resources and Available Services."

There are different approaches to take when troubleshooting different node types. Although the steps remain basically the same for a switch as they do for a router, the function each node performs is very different by design. Therefore, you must make sure you understand the device you are working on when you are troubleshooting.

In the next section, we discuss the BayRS routers and the Passport 1000 and 8000. Some of the tools used to troubleshoot each one of these devices, and some suggestions are provided as well.

Troubleshooting the Nortel Networks Router

Routers operate at layer 3 of the OSI reference model. Routers direct information for the upper-layer protocols. Remember that routers can perform different functions; therefore you must keep in mind the purposes of the router that is being examined during troubleshooting.

Router operations are based on tables of possible networks and routes to those networks. Some routers are very simple and are single-protocol routers; some are much more complex, supporting multiple protocols. These multiprotocol routers can offer many challenges to network troubleshooting. Multiprotocol routers will support various upper- and lower-layer protocols. These routers are performing a very complex task and therefore must be robust enough to handle the workload.

No matter what type of router you are troubleshooting, the basic information for troubleshooting must be gathered. The BayRS routers provide some useful tools to assist with troubleshooting and network monitoring.

Router Troubleshooting Tools

As was mentioned at the beginning of this chapter, there are a lot of tools available for troubleshooting. Some products such as sniffers, network and protocol analyzers, and symptom analysis applications are very helpful and advanced. There also are some useful tools available within the BayRS routers. These include

▼ Router event log

■ Packet capture (PCAP)

▲ Technician Interface (TI)/Management Information Base (MIB)

The tools you need for network monitoring and troubleshooting are entirely up to you. Many software vendors provide evaluation copies of their applications for you to test to see if you want to purchase the full version. There also are some helpful and inexpensive applications that are worth purchasing. This section discusses only those tools that are already available within the BayRS router.

Router Event Log   The most useful troubleshooting tool available in the BayRS routers is the event log. The event log keeps track of events that occur on a router and preserves this information in a first in, first out (FIFO) basis.

The event logged is stored in a memory buffer that is either 32k or 64k, depending on which router you are using. Once the buffer has been filled, it will overwrite information. Because of this, it is a good idea to get in the habit of saving your logs periodically, or invoking the log's AutoSave feature.

A lot of information can be obtained from the event log, including

▼ Dynamic changes

■ Faults

■ Hog buffs

■ Slot reset

■ Slot disconnect

▲ System information

How to View the Event Log   The event log is viewed through the TI. There are several parameters, known as switches, which can narrow down the output to specific event occurrences. The log command is used to view the log. The following switches are optional:

▼ **-c**   The code switch. This switch will display all of the events logged with a specific event code.

■ **-d**   The date switch. This switch allows the user to view events that have been logged from a particular date to the current period of time. The syntax for this command is listed here. In the example, we are asking to view the log from October 11, 2000 to present.

```
[x:y]$  log -d 10/11/00
```

■ **-e**   The entity switch. This switch allows the user to view all the events that have been logged against a specific entity. A couple of examples of the syntax for this switch are listed here. In the first example, we have asked to view all NAT-related events that have been logged. In the second example, we have asked to view all the ATM events that have been logged.

```
[x:y]$  log -eNAT
```

```
[x:y]$  log -eATM
```

■ **-f**   The severity switch. This switch will allow the user to indicate the level of severity they want to view. There are several different severity flags:

■ **w**   (warning)

■ **i**   (informational)

■ **t**   (trace)

■ **d**   (debug)

The correct syntax for this switch is the switch followed by the flag. In the following example, we have asked to view all the logged faults:

```
[x:y]$ log -ff
```

In the following example, we have asked to view all the events that are logged with the warning and debug severities:

```
[x:y]$ log -fwd
```

In the following example, we have asked to view the events that have been logged for all the severities:

```
[x:y]$ log -ffdwit
```

■ **-p** The rate switch. This switch will allow you to poll information from the log. If implemented, this switch will monitor the log and will display new information every 5 seconds, which is the default value. If you want to adjust the interval time between the displays, just input the new value after the switch. In the following example, we have asked to see all of the logged GAME entity events with a severity level of fault, and have asked the log to be polled every 15 seconds.

```
[x:y]$ log -eGAME -ff -p15
```

■ **-s** The slot switch. This switch allows the user to obtain information on the events logged to a particular slot. In the following example, we have asked to see all of the events logged on slot 2 with the severity of warning and fault:

```
[x:y]$ log -ffw -s2
```

▲ **-t** The time switch. This switch allows the user to view events that have been logged from a particular time to the present. The syntax for this command is listed here. In this example, we are asking to view the log from October 12 at 1:30 AM to present:

```
[x:y]$ log -d10/12/2000 -t01:30:00
```

An example of the output of an event log command is as follows:

```
[x:y]$log -fdi
#   25: 03/03/2000 09:00:25.507  DEBUG    SLOT  4  GAME        Code:   44
self-mapping of gid=0x08120 @ 0x3164f524 pended

#   26: 03/03/2000 09:00:25.531  DEBUG    SLOT  4  MIB         Code:   76
MIB manager discarding request with op_code=0x146 from dead gid=0x8120

#   27: 03/03/2000 09:00:25.535  INFO     SLOT  4  NAT         Code:   17
```

```
NAT Forward up on 192.168.16.110.6


#  28: 03/03/2000 09:00:25.843  DEBUG    SLOT  2  IP         Code:   8
RTM self map old bc000049,  new b4000049
RTM up self map old 3c00014b,  new 3400014b
```

As you probably noticed, you can specify multiple switches and flags in your log request command. An error will be provided to you if there are any problems with your command syntax. If your return is blank, there were no events logged that matched your command criteria.

AutoSave   When you suspect you have a problem that is associated with your Nortel Networks router, you should save the log immediately. If the log exceeds the storage space allotted, it will wrap and all event information will be lost. It is possible to invoke the AutoSave feature on your router. The AutoSave feature will write the log to a file and save it each time it is full. You must be certain that you have enough available flash space to save the log each time it is rewritten.

By default, AutoSave is disabled. Only setting the wfSerialPortAutoSaveNumFiles to a value between 1 and 99 can enable AutoSave. AutoSave can be implemented only through the MIBs. The value that is assigned is the number of times you wish the log to be saved.

If the flash you have chosen to AutoSave your files to runs out of room, the AutoSave feature will not be successful in save attempts until additional space is provided onto the flash card. Some have suggested having an additional flash provided solely for the purposes of gathering logs saved in the AutoSave process. However, with routine maintenance, you should never run out of room.

Files that have been AutoSaved will be stored onto the designated flash with the file name autox.log. The x designates the file number in chronological order. The next example shows the directory output for a flash that is being used to save logs.

```
[x:y]$  dir
Volume in drive 2:  is
Directory of 2:
File Name Size Date Day Time
Auto1.log 26011     12/01/99 Wed. 10:01:21
Auto2.log 26732     12/13/99 Mon. 23:21:09
Auto3.log 25768     01/12/00 Wed. 15:17:23
...
...
Auto69.log 261623    03/03/00 Fri. 01:24:24
16777216 bytes – Total size
260868      -   Available free space
230000      -   Available contiguous space
```

Packet Capture (PCAP)   A packet is defined as a group of bits that are arranged in a specified format and then transmitted as a whole. Its structure is dependent on the protocol type that it belongs to. The packet capture (PCAP) application is a utility that is used to collect, or capture, packets on a specified interface.

Usually, the information that needs to be gathered to determine network abnormalities can be obtained through the TI or event log. There are times when the information gathered in the event log and TI is not enough. The PCAP application allows you to obtain the exact protocol frames to be analyzed. Using PCAP, one can gather information from a specific interface and then save the data to be viewed later.

The use of PCAP does not require any downtime to install or tools to facilitate the data gathering. PCAP can be run without affecting network operations. PCAP does require a small amount of local memory to operate. Once you have allocated the local memory to PCAP, you must still have at least 200k of local memory remaining, or the PCAP application will be shut down.

PCAP performs some very specific functions. It will replicate frames, assign a timestamp to those frames, and then pass the frame to the appropriate destination.

NOTE: If the frame is an inbound frame, it will be passed to the data link and the network layer; if it is an outbound frame, it will be passed to the line driver.

When performing a PCAP, it is not necessary to capture everything contained within a specific frame. Usually all that is required to be captured are the data link and network layer headers, which will be present in the first 64 bytes of the frame. You can set the PCAP to conclude when the PCAP buffer is full, when a pattern match is discovered, or manually.

Configuring PCAP with TI   PCAP is set up and run from TI. The commands used to set up the PCAP can be issued through the TI or the MIBs. The actual PCAP begins and ends through the appropriate MIB strings.

In TI, the command to set up your PCAP is the config packet command. The pktdump command in TI will be used to display the captured frames in hexadecimal format. Information gathered in a PCAP cannot be viewed dynamically. Once you have terminated the PCAP and have performed the pktdump command, you can review your PCAP frame data offline. You must have an understanding of frame formats to understand the information that has been captured. The following is an example of the pktdump command and its output:

```
[x:y]#  pktdump  102101

Pkt#  1  11/11/00  09:12:10.230  CSMACD  60  Rx
00000000:  80 02 c3 00 00 00 00 00 00 a2 00 0c 00 00 23 32 c7
00000010:  02 00 00 00 00 00 00 00 00 c4 00 c3 01 21 42 42 00
00000020:  80 00 00 00 00 00 00 00 00 00 07 60 07 c2 00 00 00
00000030:  03 00 00 00 00 00 80 00 00 00 a3 14 42 42 00 51 5
```

There are a few steps to be taken to set up and configure the PCAP application:

1. Load the PCAP application on the slot. In TI, this is done with the config packet load command. If you do not specify the slot number when you enter the config packet load command, you will be prompted for a slot number.

2. Get the line number (physical or logical) of the port on which the capture is to be enabled; the config packet line command is used to do this. Using this command, you will be prompted to specify the line number, capture buffer size, packet capture size, and the capture direction.

3. Begin the PCAP via the MIBs. The following shows the MIB string that starts the PCAP. The committed value of 1 starts the PCAP, whereas the committed value of 2 stops the PCAP. The item number 102101 is the calculated line number that was provided in your output in step 2.

```
[x:y]# set wfPktCapture Entry.wfPktCaptureControl.102101 1; commit
[x:y]# set wfPktCapture Entry.wfPktCaptureControl.102101 2; commit
```

   During packet capture, the show packet status command will allow you to check the current status of the PCAP and total number of packets captured.

4. Save and view your PCAP using the pktdump command.

Configuring PCAP with MIBs   Many network engineers prefer to use the appropriate MIB strings to configure the PCAP application. The method you choose depends on your preference. Either method will provide the same information. The steps to configure the PCAP application through the MIBs are listed here:

1. Load the PCAP application on the slot that it will be run on. This is accomplished through the following MIB string:

```
[x:y]$  set wfProtocols.wfPktCaptureLoad.0 0x78000000
```

NOTE: The preceding example loads the software onto slots 2, 3, 4, and 5. To determine how to include a lost, follow this formula: 7 = 0111 and 8 = 1000. Slots are read from left to right, with each slot specified by a single bit. Therefore, 78=0111 1000 means that 1, 6, 7, and 8 are not included, but 2, 3, 4, and 5 are.

2. Get the line number (physical or logical) of the port that the capture is to be enabled on. This is accomplished using the following MIB string:

```
[x:y]$  get wfCSMACDEntry.wfCSMACDLine Number.2.1
```

NOTE: This example shows that you are getting the line number from port 1 on slot 2.

Your output from the get request in this example should read:

```
[x:y]$  wfCSMACDEntry.wfCSMACDLineNumber.2.1=102101
```

3. Form the instance of the PCAP with the line number you just generated.

```
[x:y]$ set wfPktCaptureEntry.wfPktCaptureDelete.102101 1; commit
```

4. Establish the amount of memory that will be used by PCAP.

```
[x:y]$  set wfPktCaptureEntry.wfPktCaptureBufSize.102101 2000; commit
```

5. Allocate resources to the PCAP instance that has been created.

```
[x:y]$  set wfPktCaptureEntry.wfPktCaptureDisable.102101 1; commit
```

6. Set the number of bytes to be captured and the direction in which the capture will occur.

```
[x:y]$  set wfPktCaptureEntry.wfPktCaptureSize
[x:y]$  set wfPktCaptureEntry.wfPktCaptureDirection
```

7. Begin the PCAP. The following shows the MIB string that starts the PCAP. The committed value of 1 starts the PCAP, whereas the committed value of 2 stops the PCAP. The item number 102101 is the calculated line number that was provided in your output in step 2.

```
[x:y]# set wfPktCapture Entry.wfPktCaptureControl.102101 1; commit
[x:y]# set wfPktCapture Entry.wfPktCaptureControl.102101 2; commit
```

Troubleshooting the Nortel Networks Passport 1000 and 8000

Troubleshooting the Nortel Networks Passport 1000 and 8000 series routing switches is very similar to troubleshooting the BayRS routers. Most of the troubleshooting tools used by the BayRS routers also are available with the Passport routing switches. The Passport contains an event log that is helpful in obtaining symptom data. There also are some very helpful CLI commands that can aid in obtaining operating information.

Boot Process Diagnostics

Another helpful resource when troubleshooting the Passport 1000 and 8000 routing switches is to view system diagnostic messages that are available during the system boot process. Some of the information that can be gathered in the boot process output includes

▼ Dynamic Random Access Memory information

■ File location

- Boot image version
- Memory diagnostic check information
- ▲ Slot initialization information

An example of the system boot output is shown here:

```
Checking system DRAM
Bank 5 (DRAM): 16 MB Addr: 0x01000000
Bank 7 (DRAM): 16 MB Addr: 0x00000000
Installed DRAM: 32 MB
Checking DRAM between 0x80000000 and 0x82000000
80220000          <-hit spacebar to stop memory scan
System DRAM Test terminated by user
System DRAM Check complete
User Selected Boot Sources
 Primary   = flash:acc2.0.5.7
 Secondary = skip
 Tertiary  = net
 Config    = flash:4
Booting from [flash:acc2.0.5.7] on-board flash memory
Configuration from [nvram] ...
Unzipping file acc2.0.5.7
Details /rel2.0.5.7/acc2.0.5.7.st on
Thu Dec  7 23:16:18 PST 2000
from 0x760000b0 to 0x80010000 1877739 to 9331288 bytes
Attaching network interface nicEvb0... done.
Attaching network interface lo0... done.
Accelar System Software Release 2.0.5.7
Copyright (c) 1996-1999 Bay Networks, Inc.
[000 00:00:00:633]   INTERPRET FOLLOWING TIMESTAMPS AS TIME SINCE BOOT
[000 00:00:00:900]   System boot
[000 00:00:01:166]   Accelar System Software Release 2.0.5.7
[000 00:00:01:433]   System log file flash:syslog:1:70
[000 00:00:03:100]   INTERPRET FOLLOWING TIMESTAMPS AS ACTUAL DATES
[07/21/1998 16:59:02]  Card Inserted: Slot#=2, Serial#=TB1H5,
Version=v5.0
** Loading configuration from flash:5 **
Initializing card in slot #2 ... OK
[07/21/1998 16:59:11]  Global filters are not supported in this
release.
[07/21/1998 16:59:11]  System is ready
*******************************
* Bay Networks,Inc.                 *
```

```
* Copyright (c) 1996-1999      *
* All Rights Reserved          *
* Accelar 1200                 *
* Software Release 2.0.5.7     *
*******************************
Login: rwa
Password: ***
Passport_Test#
```

The Passport Event Log

The Passport routing switches contain an event log. To view the event log, issue the following command:

```
Passport_Test# show log file
```

This command will output the log file in its entirety. If you would like to view the event log in reverse chronological order, you will need to issue the following command:

```
Passport_Test#  show log file tail
```

The Passport 1000 and 8000 event logs will capture and store the following information:

▼ Console information

■ Error messages

▲ Warning messages

All logged events are stored in the system flash. If there is not enough space available on the system flash during the initialization of the Passport, the log file is created on the PCMCIA. Log files are divided into two 64k banks, for a total of 128k of storage space for event information. Once the first log bank is full, the information will be recorded in the second bank. Once the second bank is full, the events will be logged onto the first bank, overwriting any information contained there.

CLI Commands

There are some commands in the Passport 1000 and 8000 routing switches that are helpful in gathering information for troubleshooting. The show log file is only one CLI command used to gather information for troubleshooting.

In this section, we will introduce the show config and the show tech commands. The CLI help feature also will assist you with other show commands.

▼ **show config**   This command will display the current switch configuration. During troubleshooting, this command can be useful when trying to replicate and issue, verify configuration integrity, and compare with original configuration status. The output response to this command is very lengthy. Some of the information that is provided in response to this command includes

- The type of Passport chassis
- Software and boot monitor version
- Hardware configuration information
- System configuration information
- STG configuration information
- MLT configuration information
- Access policy information
- Traffic filter information
- Port configuration information
- VLAN information
- Routing protocol information

▲ **show tech**   This command will display technical information relevant to the current system status. The output response to this command is very lengthy. The information contained in the output includes

- System information
- Information about the chassis
- Hardware peripheral information
- Boot source information
- Priority information
- Performance
- VLAN
- Port information
- Routing information
- Memory allocation information
- Interface information
- Log files
- Trace files

RESOURCES AND AVAILABLE SERVICES

Nortel Networks provides various information and services to assist in configuring and maintaining your Nortel Networks product. There also are several public newsgroups available to discuss networking technologies. In this section, we briefly discuss the following services:

- ▼ Documentation
- ■ Online resources
- ▲ Global Customer Care Services (GCCS)

Documentation

Nortel Networks products normally are shipped with soft copy documentation that is useful in configuring, maintaining, and troubleshooting your Nortel Networks device. The documentation describes protocol configuration and management, product-specific information, and so forth. Hard copy documentation can be ordered as well.

Online Resources

The Nortel Networks Web site contains some very good Nortel Networks corporate information and information about the Nortel Network products. The Nortel Networks Web site URL is http://www.nortelnetworks.com. Another good technical online resource is the Nortel Networks online library. The online library contains documentation that is published by Nortel Networks. The online library's URL is http://support.baynetworks.com. The online library also is provided to customers who have a valid software contract with Nortel Networks.

Global Customer Care Services (GCCS)

Nortel Networks customers with a valid service and support contract are able to call the Global Customer Care Services for assistance with problems that are not easy to resolve. The GCCS will open a case and will work with the customer and higher-level support and development engineers to help reach a resolution.

CONCLUSION

In this chapter we discussed only a small amount of the troubleshooting tools and techniques that can be used to discover and resolve problems that might occur within your network.

Networks are evolving, standards are changing, and new technologies are being introduced daily. It is important to understand every inch of your network; to understand its topology and fully research any changes made to it. With this understanding, you will be much better prepared when a problem does arise.

Keep documentation, save your configuration files, and back up your log files. Introduce changes subtly. Following some of the suggestions in this chapter will greatly reduce downtime when an issue occurs.

APPENDIX A

Glossary

This glossary lists many of the networking terms that are introduced in this book. This is not a complete listing of all the networking terms in use today. For a detailed listing, there are many excellent resources available. We recommend the following Web sites for a detailed description of networking terms that are not introduced in this beginner's guide.

▼ The Bay Networks Guide to networking terms online:
http://support.baynetworks.com/library/tpubs/terms

▲ The IT-specific encyclopedia (an online reference):
http://www.whatis.com

GLOSSARY

ACL *Access Control List.* The usual means by which access to and denial of network services is controlled by network security systems.

AP *Access Point.* Wireless equipment analogous to a hub.

ARE *ATM Routing Engine.* The ARE is a Nortel Networks processor module that, together with a high-performance link module, is capable of providing high-level routing between LANs.

AS *Autonomous System.* A group of routers maintained by a single organization.

ASIC *Application-Specific Integrated Circuit.* A silicon chip that is designed to support specific applications.

AUI *Attached Unit Interface.* A network adapter connector. Sometimes referred to as an attachment unit interface.

BayRS *Bay Networks Routing Services.* Nortel Networks router services that support all major protocols.

BCC *Bay Command Console.* A CLI for the BayRS.

BGP *Border Gateway Protocol.* A routing protocol used mostly by ISPs or in very large networks.

BPDU *Bridge Protocol Data Unit.* Information contained within a data unit that provides connectivity information between connected nodes.

BRI *Basic Rate Interface.* An integrated services digital network (ISDN) service. Sometimes referred to as an *Basic Rate ISDN.*

CCNA *Cisco Certified Network Associate.* A Cisco networking certification.

CES *Contivity Extranet Switch.* Bay Networks product family providing secure and reliable extranet access over public networks; that is, Virtual Private Networks (VPNs).

CNE *Certified NetWare Engineer.* A Novell networking certification.

CSMA/CA *Carrier Sense Multiple Access/Collision Avoidance.* A method of contention arbitration in wireless networks.

CSMA/CD *Carrier Sense Multiple Access/Collision Detection.* An Ethernet LAN access method used by stations to access shared media to transmit packets.

CSU *Channel Service Unit.* A device that works as a buffer to prevent faulty equipment from affecting network performance. The CSU is placed between the corporate LAN and a public WAN.

DCE *Data Communication Equipment.* The DCE is a device, such as a modem, that will establish and maintain a network connection with a DTE device.

DNS *Domain Name Service.* Addressing system that translates a name into an IP address.

DRAM *Dynamic Random Access Memory.* Computer memory that uses electronic charges to represent memory.

DSSS *Direct Sequence Spread Spectrum.* A wireless communications method.

DSU *Digital Service Unit.* A device that connects the DTE equipment to communication lines, ensuring that data is formatted for transmission. Sometimes referred to as a *Data Service Unit.*

DTE *Data Terminal Equipment.* The DTE is a device that normally acts as an end node (such as a server or a workstation). The DTE normally is attached to a DCE.

EAC *Extranet Access Client.* Software used to create secure connections over the Internet between a workstation and a Contivity Extranet Switch.

EGP *Exterior Gateway Protocol.* A protocol in the IP suite used to exchange network reachability information between routers in different autonomous systems. Routers establish EGP neighbor relationships to periodically exchange reliable reachability information.

FHSS *Frequency Hopping Spread Spectrum.* A wireless communications method.

Frame An OSI layer 2 data unit that contains information to be transmitted through the network. The minimum size of a frame is 64 bytes, and the maximum size is 1,518 bytes.

FRE   *Fast Routing Engine.* A processor module that is used with the link modules and the Nortel Networks routers. The standard FRE is a 32 MHz processor module.

FRE-2   *Fast Routing Engine type 2.* A processor module that is used with the link modules and the Nortel Networks routers. The FRE-2 is either a 32 MHz or 60 MHz processor module.

GBIC   *Gigabit Interface Converter.* Allows different types of fiber connections into the same switch by simply changing the GBIC.

Hot-Swappable   A device component that can be removed and replaced without causing disruption to the current operating status of the device in which it is being installed.

HSSI   *High-Speed Serial Interface.* High-level serial interface supporting up to 52 Mb/s and offering LAN-like performance over a wide area.

IGP   *Interior Gateway Protocol.* The term applied to any protocol used to increase network reachability and distribute routing information within an autonomous system. Routing Information Protocol (RIP) and Open Shortest Path First (OSPF) protocols are common IGPs.

IISP   *Interim Inter-Switch Protocol.* A standardized signaling protocol to enable switched virtual circuits (SVCs) between switches in a private ATM network using static routes.

ILI   *Intelligent Link Interface.* The combination of a link module and a processor module within the BN routers.

IOS   *Internetwork Operating System.* Cisco's routing software.

IPsec   *IP security.* An emerging standard, this Bay Networks–supported tunneling protocol offers strong encryption, support for IP address translation, and packet-by-packet authentication.

ISDN   *Integrated Services Digital Network.* A global telecommunications network that provides for the transmission of digital data.

ISM   *Industry, Science, and Medical* band for wireless communications.

L2F   *Layer 2 Forwarding.* A tunneling protocol enabling remote access to corporate networks across the public Internet.

L2TP   *Layer 2 Forwarding Tunneling Protocol.* A tunneling protocol enabling remote access to corporate networks across the public Internet.

LAN   *Local Area Network.* A network of digital communication users that comprises a limited geographical area.

LDAP *Lightweight Directory Access Protocol.* An IEEE protocol for accessing certain online services such as searching directories over TCP/IP.

LECS *LAN Emulation Configuration Server.* A portion of ATM Multicast Server (MCS) software that maintains tables of information such as virtual LAN membership and addresses.

LES/BUS *LAN Emulation Server* and *Broadcast Unknown Server.* A portion of ATM multicast server (MCS) software that provides LAN Emulation Address Resolution Protocol for a virtual LAN.

LSDB *Link State Database.* A database that contains the state of connections in an OSPF network.

MAC *Media Access Control.* The address of an individual network interface.

MAN *Metropolitan Area Network.* A network of digital communication users that comprises a medium-size geographical area.

MCP *Master Control Processor.* A feature on the switch modules for the Nortel Networks Centillion and BH 5000 switches.

MCSE *Microsoft Certified Systems Engineer.* A Microsoft networking certification.

MDA *Media Dependent Adapter.* An adapter used to add functionality to a switch.

MIB *Management Information Base.* A database that contains MIB objects and instances that allow the configuration of a network device and provide a vehicle to obtain network information.

MLT *Multilink Trunking.* A method of combining multiple links for greater bandwidth.

MMF *Multimode Fiber.* A fiber-optic cable that is able to transmit communication signals over a distance of 2 kilometers or less. The signals that are carried might consist of multiple frequencies.

MU *Mobile unit.* Any mobile device connected to a wireless network.

NDIS *Network Driver Interface Specification.* Also sometimes called network device interface specification. A device driver specification developed by Microsoft and 3Com that is independent of the NIC hardware and the network protocol.

NMS *Network Management System.* A system or application used to monitor the status of your network. An example is Optivity.

NNI *Network-to-Network Interface.* An interface connecting private or public switches.

OID *Object identifier.* An integer, separated by dots, that is used by the MIB to set the path to a specified object.

OIT *Optivity Integration Toolkit.* The toolkit that allows new hardware to be integrated into Optivity without recompiling the entire network management system.

OSPF *Open Shortest Path First.* A routing protocol designed for use in larger networks.

Packet A block that is used to transport information in an OSI layer 3 environment.

PDU *Protocol Data Unit.* The unit of data in the OSI reference model containing both protocol-control information and user data from the layer above.

PNNI *Private Network-to-Network Interface.* A standard that is used to establish point-to-point and point-to-multipoint connections between networks.

PPS *Packets per Second.* A measurement of network speed.

PPTP *Point-to-Point Tunneling Protocol.* A tunneling protocol using existing Internet protocols of PPP and TCP/IP to create Virtual Private Networks (VPNs).

PPX *Parallel Packet Express.* The processors that interconnect in the BN routers to distribute data.

PRI *Primary Rate Interface.* An Integrated Services Digital Network (ISDN) service. Sometimes referred to as a *primary rate ISDN.*

PROM *Programmable read-only memory.* Memory that is read-only and programmed for a specific node.

PSTN *Public Switched Telephone Network.* The network that connects regular voice calls.

PVC *Permanent Virtual Circuit.* Dedicated connection between devices manually set up to be used for a single purpose.

QoS *Quality of Service.* A method of measuring the quality of a transaction over a network.

RADIUS *Remote Authentication Dial-In User Service.* Provides authentication, authorization, and accounting for remote dial access users.

RAM *Random access memory.* Memory that is read/write and is directly accessible by the CPU.

RAS   *Remote Access Service.* A method of accessing a network through a modem.

Redundancy   A secondary or backup software or hardware device that acts as a primary if the primary fails.

RIF   *Routing information field.* A field within a network node that contains routing information.

RIP   *Routing Information Protocol.* A routing protocol designed for use in smaller networks.

RPI   *Remote Power Interface.* The piece of hardware that is capable of powering an AP remotely.

RSVP   *Resource Reservation Protocol.* Provides a method for real-time applications to communicate requirements to network elements along the data path. RSVP conveys quality of service (QoS) information between network elements and the application.

RTS/CTS   *Request to Send/Clear to Send.* RS-232-C standard hardware signal requesting permission to transmit and the "all clear" reply.

SMF   *Single-mode fiber.* An optical fiber cable that is capable of transmitting communications signals over three miles. The signals are limited to a single frequency.

SNMP   *Simple Network Management Protocol.* An IP-based protocol for network management.

SRM-F   *System Resource Module-Front.* An optional module that allows for double the bandwidth in the BN routers and provides for PPX redundancy.

SRM-L   *System Resource Module-Link.* A required module that provides bandwidth and terminal access within the BN routers.

SSF   *Silicon Switch Fabric.* This is part of the Passport routing switches. In the Passport 1100/1150 models, the SSF is built in. The SSF is a module for the remainder of the Passport routing switch. The SSF contains the switch fabric and the CPU subsystem.

STP   *Sales, Technology, and Product* exams. Web-based Nortel certification exams.

SVC   *Switched Virtual Circuit.* A connection between a Frame Relay or ATM source node and destination node that is established and maintained on an as-needed connection.

TFTP   *Trivial File Transport Protocol.* Used to upgrade software over the network.

TI   *Technician Interface.* A command-line interface for the BayRS.

TTL   *Time to Live.* A counter that specifies the maximum hops that a packet can travel before it is discarded.

UNI   *User-to-Network Interface.* Term used to describe the interface between end nodes to either a public or private Frame Relay or ATM network.

URL   *Uniform resource locator.* An Internet address.

UTP   *Unshielded twisted pair.* A type of cable that contains one or more pairs of copper conductors twisted together.

VoIP   *Voice-over IP.* A method of routing voice phone calls over an IP network.

VPN   *Virtual Private Network.* An encrypted data stream that travels over a public network.

WAN   *Wide Area Network.* Two or more geographically dispersed LANs connected to each other through a WAN protocol such as Frame Relay.

APPENDIX B

Passport CLI Overview

The following pages illustrate the command-line structure of the Passport series switches.

Passport Command-Line Interface -Login

```
********************************
* Nortel Networks, Inc.         *
* Copyright (c) 1996-2000        *
* All Rights Reserved           *
* Accelar 8010                   *
* Software Release 2.0.0.0       *
********************************

Login: rw
Password: *****
8000Edge03:5# ?

Sub-Context: clear config dump monitor show
Current Context:

    attribute <file> <attributes>
    back
    boot [<file>] [config <value>] [-y]
    box
    cd <dir>
    convert-11-config <devfile> [standby <value>] [backup <value>]
    copy <srcfile> <destfile>
    cp <srcfile> <destfile>
    cwc [..]
    date
    directory [<dir>] [-l]
    exit
    help [<command>]
    history
    login
    logout
    ls [<dir>] [-r]
    mkdir <dir>
    mv <old> <new>
    peer <operation>
    ping <ipaddr> [datasize <value>] [count <value>] [-s] [-I <value>]
    [-t <value>] [-d]
    pwc
```

```
pwd
quit
remove <file>
rename <old> <new>
rlogin <ipaddr>
rm <file>
rsh <ipaddr> -l <value> <cmd>
save <savetype> [file <value>] [verbose] [standby <value>]
[backup <value>]
source <file> [stop] [debug] [syntax]
telnet [<ipaddr>]
top
traceroute <ipaddr> [<datasize>] [-m <value>] [-p <value>] [
-q <value>] [-w <value>] [-v]
```

Config Subprompt

```
8000Edge03:5# config
8000Edge03:5/config# ?
```

```
Sub-Context: bootconfig cli diag ethernet log mlt rmon stg sys vlan
web-server Current Context:
```

```
    info
```

Bootconfig Subprompt

```
8000Edge03:5/config# bootconfig
8000Edge03:5/config/bootconfig# ?
```

```
Sub-Context: choice cli flags net show sio tz
Current Context:
```

```
    delay <seconds>
    master <cpu-slot>
    multicast <value>
```

```
8000Edge03:5/config/bootconfig# flags
8000Edge03:5/config/bootconfig/flags# ?
```

```
Sub-Context:
Current Context:
```

```
    accelar-8100-mode <true|false>
```

```
    autoboot <true|false>
    egress-mirror <true|false>
    factorydefaults <true|false>
    ftpd <true|false>
    info
    machine-check <true|false>
    logging <true|false>
    reboot <true|false>
    rlogind <true|false>
    telnetd <true|false>
    tftpd <true|false>
    trace-logging <true|false>
    verify-config <true|false>
    wdt <true|false>

8000Edge03:5/config/bootconfig/flags# back
8000Edge03:5/config/bootconfig# ?

Sub-Context: choice cli flags net show sio tz
Current Context:

    delay <seconds>
    master <cpu-slot>
    multicast <value>

8000Edge03:5/config/bootconfig# show
8000Edge03:5/config/bootconfig/show# ?

Sub-Context:
Current Context:

    choice
    cli
    config [verbose]
    flags
    host
    info
    master
    net
    sio
    tz

8000Edge03:5/config/bootconfig/show# net
net mgmt autonegotiate true
```

```
net mgmt bootp false
net mgmt enable true
net mgmt fullduplex false
net mgmt ip 10.10.56.73/255.255.248.0
net mgmt route net 0.0.0.0 10.10.56.1
net mgmt speed 10
net mgmt tftp 192.0.0.2
net cpu2cpu autonegotiate false
net cpu2cpu bootp true
net cpu2cpu enable true
net cpu2cpu fullduplex true
net cpu2cpu ip 127.0.0.5/255.0.0.0
net cpu2cpu route net 0.0.0.0 0.0.0.0
net cpu2cpu speed 100
net cpu2cpu tftp 0.0.0.0
net pccard autonegotiate true
net pccard bootp true
net pccard enable true
net pccard fullduplex false
net pccard ip 0.0.0.0/0.0.0.0
net pccard route net 0.0.0.0 0.0.0.0
net pccard speed 10
net pccard tftp 0.0.0.0
8000Edge03:5/config/bootconfig/show# back
8000Edge03:5/config/bootconfig# back
```

Diag Subprompt

```
8000EDGE03:5/CONFIG# ?

SUB-CONTEXT: BOOTCONFIG CLI DIAG ETHERNET LOG MLT RMON STG SYS VLAN
WEB-SERVER
CURRENT CONTEXT:

INFO

8000EDGE03:5/CONFIG# diag
8000EDGE03:5/CONFIG/DIAG# ?

SUB-CONTEXT: MIRROR-BY-PORT
CURRENT CONTEXT:

INFO
```

```
8000EDGE03:5/CONFIG/DIAG# info

SUB-CONTEXT: MIRROR-BY-PORT
CURRENT CONTEXT:

8000EDGE03:5/CONFIG/DIAG# back
```

Ethernet Subprompt

```
8000Edge03:5/config# ?

Sub-Context: bootconfig cli diag ethernet log mlt rmon
stg sys vlan web-server
Current Context:

    info

8000Edge03:5/config# ethernet
object <ports> not entered
<ports>            = portlist {slot/port[-slot/port][,...]}
8000Edge03:5/config# eth 1/2-1/33
8000Edge03:5/config/ethernet/1/2-1/33# ?

Sub-Context: stg
Current Context:

    action <action choice>
    auto-negotiate <enable|disable>
    default-vlan-id <vid>
    duplex <half|full>
    qos-level <0...7>
    info
    linktrap <enable|disable>
    lock <true|false>
    perform-tagging <enable|disable>
    speed <10|100>
    state <enable|disable|test>
    tagged-frames-discard <enable|disable>
    untagged-frames-discard <enable|disable>

8000Edge03:5/config/ethernet/1/2-1/33# back
```

MLT Subprompt

```
8000Edge03:5/config# ?

Sub-Context: bootconfig cli diag ethernet log mlt rmon stg
sys vlan web-server
Current Context:

    info

8000Edge03:5/config# mlt
object <mid> not entered
<mid>              = mlt id {1..32}
8000Edge03:5/config# mlt 1
8000Edge03:5/config/mlt/1# info

Sub-Context: add remove
Current Context:

        Mlt 1 is not created

8000Edge03:5/config/mlt/1# mlt 2
8000Edge03:5/config/mlt/2# info

Sub-Context: add remove
Current Context:

                    create : 2
                    delete : N/A
                      name : To_8000Core02
            perform-tagging : enable

8000Edge03:5/config/mlt/2# add
8000Edge03:5/config/mlt/2/add# info

Sub-Context:
Current Context:

                    ports : 1/33,2/33
                     vlan :  1
```

```
8000Edge03:5/config/mlt/2/add# back
8000Edge03:5/config/mlt/2# back
```

VLAN Subprompt

```
8000Edge03:5/config# ?

Sub-Context: bootconfig cli diag ethernet log mlt rmon
stg sys vlan web-server
Current Context:

    info

8000Edge03:5/config# vlan
object <vid> not entered
<vid>             = vlan id {1..4094}
8000Edge03:5/config# vlan 1
8000Edge03:5/config/vlan/1# ?

Sub-Context: create fdb-entry fdb-static igmp-snoop ip ports
Current Context:

    action <action choice>
    add-mlt <integer>
    agetime <10..1000000>
    delete
    qos-level <integer>
    info
    name <vname>

8000Edge03:5/config/vlan/1# back
```

CLI Subprompt

```
8000Edge03:5/config# ?

Sub-Context: bootconfig cli diag ethernet log mlt rmon
stg sys vlan web-server
Current Context:

    info

8000Edge03:5/config# info

Sub-Context: bootconfig cli diag ethernet log mlt rmon
```

```
stg sys vlan web-server
Current Context:

                         setdate : N/A

8000Edge03:5/config# cli
8000Edge03:5/config/cli# ?

Sub-Context: monitor
Current Context:

    info
    more <true|false>
    prompt <prompt>
    rlogin-sessions <nsessions>
    screenlines <nlines>
    telnet-sessions <nsessions>
    timeout <seconds>

8000Edge03:5/config/cli# back
```

Log Subprompt

```
8000Edge03:5/config# log
8000Edge03:5/config/log# ?

Sub-Context:
Current Context:

    clear
    info
    level [<level>]
    screen [<setting>]
    write <str>

8000Edge03:5/config/log# back
(2) Show Commands
8000EDGE03:5# show
8000EDGE03:5/SHOW# ?

SUB-CONTEXT: BOOTCONFIG CLI DIAG IP LOG MLT PORTS RMON STG SYS
TEST VLAN
CURRENT CONTEXT:
```

```
CONFIG [VERBOSE] [MODULE <VALUE>]
WEB-SERVER
```

Config Subcommand

```
8000Edge03:5/show# config
#
# THU JAN 04 14:19:23 2001 UTC
# box type           : Accelar-8010
# software version   : 2.0.0.0
# monitor version    : 1.0.0.0/0
#

#
# Asic Info :
# SlotNum|Name   |CardType|MdaType |Parts Description
#
# Slot  1 8132TX 30211120 30320201
# Slot  2 8132TX 30211120 30320201
# Slot  3 8148TX 30210130 00000000
# Slot  4 8148TX 30210130 00000000
# Slot  5 8190SM 200e0100 00000000 CPU: CPLD=14
# Slot  6   --   00000001 00000000
# Slot  7 8148TX 30210130 00000000
# Slot  8 8148TX 30210130 00000000
# Slot  9 8148TX 30210130 00000000
# Slot 10 8148TX 30210130 00000000
config

#
# CLI CONFIGURATION
#

cli prompt "8000Edge03"

#
# SYSTEM CONFIGURATION
#

sys set contact "System Contact Here"
sys set location ""8000ha"
sys set snmp trap-recv 10.10.56.254 v2c public
sys syslog host 1 create
```

```
sys syslog host 1 address 10.10.56.254
sys syslog host 1 facility local2
sys syslog host 1 host enable
sys syslog host 1 severity info warning error fatal


#
# LINK-FLAP-DETECT CONFIGURATION
#



#
# ACCESS-POLICY CONFIGURATION
#



#
# WEB CONFIGURATION
#



#
# RMON CONFIGURATION
#



#
# PORT CONFIGURATION - PHASE I
#



#
# MLT CONFIGURATION
#

mlt 2 create
mlt 2 name "To_8000Core02"
mlt 2 perform-tagging enable
mlt 2 add ports 1/33,2/33

#
# STG CONFIGURATION
#
```

```
stg 1  add ports 1/33,2/33

#
# VLAN CONFIGURATION
#

vlan 1 add-mlt 2
vlan 1 ports remove 3/45 member portmember
vlan 2 create byport 1 name "Corpnet" color 3
vlan 2 ports remove 1/1-1/33,2/1-2/33,3/1-3/44,3/46-3/48,4/1-4/48,
7/1-7/48,8/1-8
/48,9/1-9/48,10/1-10/48 member portmember
vlan 2 ports add 3/45 member portmember

#
# PORT CONFIGURATION - PHASE II
#

ethernet 1/1 qos-level 0
ethernet 1/1 stg 1 faststart enable
ethernet 1/2 qos-level 0
ethernet 1/2 stg 1 faststart enable
ethernet 1/3 qos-level 0
ethernet 1/3 stg 1 faststart enable
ethernet 1/4 qos-level 0
ethernet 1/4 stg 1 faststart enable
ethernet 1/5 qos-level 0
ethernet 1/5 stg 1 faststart enable
ethernet 1/6 qos-level 0
ethernet 1/6 stg 1 faststart enable
ethernet 1/7 qos-level 0
ethernet 1/7 stg 1 faststart enable
ethernet 1/8 qos-level 0
ethernet 1/8 stg 1 faststart enable
ethernet 1/9 qos-level 0
ethernet 1/9 stg 1 faststart enable
ethernet 1/10 qos-level 0
ethernet 1/10 stg 1 faststart enable
ethernet 1/11 qos-level 0
ethernet 1/11 stg 1 faststart enable
ethernet 1/12 qos-level 0
ethernet 1/12 stg 1 faststart enable
ethernet 1/13 qos-level 0
ethernet 1/13 stg 1 faststart enable
```

```
ethernet 1/14 qos-level 0
ethernet 1/14 stg 1 faststart enable
ethernet 1/15 qos-level 0
ethernet 1/15 stg 1 faststart enable
ethernet 1/16 qos-level 0
ethernet 1/16 stg 1 faststart enable
ethernet 1/17 qos-level 0
ethernet 1/17 stg 1 faststart enable
ethernet 1/18 qos-level 0
ethernet 1/18 stg 1 faststart enable
ethernet 1/19 qos-level 0
ethernet 1/19 stg 1 faststart enable
ethernet 1/20 qos-level 0
ethernet 1/20 stg 1 faststart enable
ethernet 1/21 qos-level 0
ethernet 1/21 stg 1 faststart enable
ethernet 1/22 qos-level 0
ethernet 1/22 stg 1 faststart enable
ethernet 1/23 qos-level 0
ethernet 1/23 stg 1 faststart enable
ethernet 1/24 qos-level 0
ethernet 1/24 stg 1 faststart enable
ethernet 1/25 qos-level 0
ethernet 1/25 stg 1 faststart enable
ethernet 1/26 qos-level 0
ethernet 1/26 stg 1 faststart enable
ethernet 1/27 qos-level 0
ethernet 1/27 stg 1 faststart enable
ethernet 1/28 qos-level 0
ethernet 1/28 stg 1 faststart enable
ethernet 1/29 qos-level 0
ethernet 1/29 stg 1 faststart enable
ethernet 1/30 qos-level 0
ethernet 1/30 stg 1 faststart enable
ethernet 1/31 qos-level 0
ethernet 1/31 stg 1 faststart enable
ethernet 1/32 qos-level 0
ethernet 1/32 stg 1 faststart enable
ethernet 1/33 qos-level 0
```
**Lines deleted for cards 2 - 9, so that this appendix remains
readable.**
```
ethernet 10/1 qos-level 0
ethernet 10/1 stg 1 faststart enable
ethernet 10/2 qos-level 0
```

```
ethernet 10/2 stg 1 faststart enable
ethernet 10/3 qos-level 0
ethernet 10/3 stg 1 faststart enable
ethernet 10/4 qos-level 0
ethernet 10/4 stg 1 faststart enable
ethernet 10/5 qos-level 0
ethernet 10/5 stg 1 faststart enable
ethernet 10/6 qos-level 0
ethernet 10/6 stg 1 faststart enable
ethernet 10/7 qos-level 0
ethernet 10/7 stg 1 faststart enable
ethernet 10/8 qos-level 0
ethernet 10/8 stg 1 faststart enable
ethernet 10/9 qos-level 0
ethernet 10/9 stg 1 faststart enable
ethernet 10/10 qos-level 0
ethernet 10/10 stg 1 faststart enable
ethernet 10/11 qos-level 0
ethernet 10/11 stg 1 faststart enable
ethernet 10/12 qos-level 0
ethernet 10/12 stg 1 faststart enable
ethernet 10/13 qos-level 0
ethernet 10/13 stg 1 faststart enable
ethernet 10/14 qos-level 0
ethernet 10/14 stg 1 faststart enable
ethernet 10/15 qos-level 0
ethernet 10/15 stg 1 faststart enable
ethernet 10/16 qos-level 0
ethernet 10/16 stg 1 faststart enable
ethernet 10/17 qos-level 0
ethernet 10/17 stg 1 faststart enable
ethernet 10/18 qos-level 0
ethernet 10/18 stg 1 faststart enable
ethernet 10/19 qos-level 0
ethernet 10/19 stg 1 faststart enable
ethernet 10/20 qos-level 0
ethernet 10/20 stg 1 faststart enable
ethernet 10/21 qos-level 0
ethernet 10/21 stg 1 faststart enable
ethernet 10/22 qos-level 0
ethernet 10/22 stg 1 faststart enable
ethernet 10/23 qos-level 0
ethernet 10/23 stg 1 faststart enable
```

```
ethernet 10/24 qos-level 0
ethernet 10/24 stg 1 faststart enable
ethernet 10/25 qos-level 0
ethernet 10/25 stg 1 faststart enable
ethernet 10/26 qos-level 0
ethernet 10/26 stg 1 faststart enable
ethernet 10/27 qos-level 0
ethernet 10/27 stg 1 faststart enable
ethernet 10/28 qos-level 0
ethernet 10/28 stg 1 faststart enable
ethernet 10/29 qos-level 0
ethernet 10/29 stg 1 faststart enable
ethernet 10/30 qos-level 0
ethernet 10/30 stg 1 faststart enable
ethernet 10/31 qos-level 0
ethernet 10/31 stg 1 faststart enable
ethernet 10/32 qos-level 0
ethernet 10/32 stg 1 faststart enable
ethernet 10/33 qos-level 0
ethernet 10/33 stg 1 faststart enable
ethernet 10/34 qos-level 0
ethernet 10/34 stg 1 faststart enable
ethernet 10/35 qos-level 0
ethernet 10/35 stg 1 faststart enable
ethernet 10/36 qos-level 0
ethernet 10/36 stg 1 faststart enable
ethernet 10/37 qos-level 0
ethernet 10/37 stg 1 faststart enable
ethernet 10/38 qos-level 0
ethernet 10/38 stg 1 faststart enable
ethernet 10/39 qos-level 0
ethernet 10/39 stg 1 faststart enable
ethernet 10/40 qos-level 0
ethernet 10/40 stg 1 faststart enable
ethernet 10/41 qos-level 0
ethernet 10/41 stg 1 faststart enable
ethernet 10/42 qos-level 0
ethernet 10/42 stg 1 faststart enable
ethernet 10/43 qos-level 0
ethernet 10/43 stg 1 faststart enable
ethernet 10/44 qos-level 0
ethernet 10/44 stg 1 faststart enable
ethernet 10/45 qos-level 0
```

```
ethernet 10/45 stg 1 faststart enable
ethernet 10/46 qos-level 0
ethernet 10/46 stg 1 faststart enable
ethernet 10/47 qos-level 0
ethernet 10/47 stg 1 faststart enable
ethernet 10/48 qos-level 0
ethernet 10/48 stg 1 faststart enable

#
# DIAG CONFIGURATION
#


back
```

Bootconfig Subcommand

```
8000Edge03:5/show# ?

Sub-Context: bootconfig cli diag ip log mlt ports rmon stg sys
test vlan
Current Context:

    config [verbose] [module <value>]
    web-server

8000Edge03:5/show# bootconfig
8000Edge03:5/show/bootconfig# ?

Sub-Context:
Current Context:

    choice
    cli
    config [verbose]
    flags
    host
    info
    master
    net
    sio
    tz


8000Edge03:5/show/bootconfig# back
```

CLI Subcommand

```
8000Edge03:5/show# cli
8000Edge03:5/show/cli# ?

Sub-Context:
Current Context:

    info
    who

8000Edge03:5/show/cli# back
```

IP Subcommand

```
8000Edge03:5/show# ?

Sub-Context: bootconfig cli diag ip log mlt ports rmon stg sys
test vlan
Current Context:

    config [verbose] [module <value>]
    web-server

8000Edge03:5/show# ip
8000Edge03:5/show/ip# ?

Sub-Context: arp
Current Context:

    interface

8000Edge03:5/show/ip# interface
```

```
================================================================
                        Ip Interface
================================================================
INTERFACE IP        NET      BCASTADDR    REASM    VLAN    BROUTER

ADDRESS             MASK     FORMAT       MAXSIZE  ID      PORT
----------------------------------------------------------------
Port5/1 16.80.56.73  255.255.248.0 ones    1500     0       false

8000Edge03:5/show/ip# back
```

MLT Subcommand

```
8000Edge03:5/show# ?

Sub-Context: bootconfig cli diag ip log mlt ports rmon stg sys
test vlan
Current Context:

    config [verbose] [module <value>]
    web-server

8000Edge03:5/show# mlt
8000Edge03:5/show/mlt# ?

Sub-Context: error
Current Context:

    info [<mid>]
    stats [<mid>]

8000Edge03:5/show/mlt# stats


================================================================
                                              Mlt Interface
================================================================
MLT    IN      OUT      IN      OUT      IN      OUT      IN
OUT
ID    OCTETS  OCTETS   UNICST  UNICST   MULTICST MULTICST BROADCST
BROADCST
----------------------------------------------------------------
2     5468745432965 125416807456 68494990482 27127450015 5743632
1049977   27475044 526309

8000Edge03:5/show/mlt# info


================================================================
                                              Mlt Info
================================================================
                     PORT         PORT         VLAN
MLTID     IFINDEX    NAME         TYPE         MEMBERS      IDS
----------------------------------------------------------------
2         4097       To_8000Core02   trunk        1/33,2/33    1

8000Edge03:5/show/mlt# back
```

Ports Subcommand

```
8000Edge03:5/show# ?

Sub-Context: bootconfig cli diag ip log mlt ports rmon stg sys
test vlan

Current Context:

    config [verbose] [module <value>]
    web-server

8000Edge03:5/show# ports
8000Edge03:5/show/ports# ?

Sub-Context: error info stats
Current Context:


8000Edge03:5/show/ports# stats
8000Edge03:5/show/ports/stats# ?

Sub-Context: interface
Current Context:

    bridging [<ports>]
    rmon [<ports>]
    stg [<ports>]

8000Edge03:5/show/ports/stats# back
8000Edge03:5/show/ports# info
8000Edge03:5/show/ports/info# ?

Sub-Context: stg
Current Context:

    all [<ports>] [by <value>]
    arp [<ports>]
    config [<ports>]
    interface [<ports>]
    vlans [<ports>]

8000Edge03:5/show/ports/info# back
8000Edge03:5/show/ports# back
```

SYS Subcommand

```
8000Edge03:5/show# ?

ext: bootconfig cli diag ip log mlt ports rmon stg sys
test vlan
Current Context:

    config [verbose] [module <value>]
    web-server

8000Edge03:5/show# sys
8000Edge03:5/show/sys# ?

Sub-Context: access-policy link-flap-detect syslog
Current Context:

    info [card] [asic] [mda]
    msg-control
    perf
    sw
    topology

8000Edge03:5/show/sys# back
```

VLAN Subcommand

```
8000Edge03:5/show# vlan
8000Edge03:5/show/vlan# ?

Sub-Context: info igmp-snoop
Current Context:


8000Edge03:5/show/vlan# info
8000Edge03:5/show/vlan/info# ?

Sub-Context:
Current Context:

    advance [<vid>]
    all [<vid>] [by <value>]
    arp [<vid>]
    basic [<vid>]
    fdb-entry <vid>
```

```
    fdb-static <vid>
    ip [<vid>]
    ports [<vid>]
    snoop [<vid>]
```

```
8000Edge03:5/show/vlan/info# back
8000Edge03:5/show/vlan# back
8000Edge03:5/show# back
```

Save Commands

```
8000Edge03:5# save bootconfig
8000Edge03:5# save config standby config
standby cpu not present
8000Edge03:5# save bootconfig standby bootconfig
standby cpu not present
```

Logout

```
8000Edge3:5# logout
```

APPENDIX C

TI and BCC Command Reference

TI COMMAND USAGE

```
[x:y] $help
```

```
!                    [<repeat count>]
alias                [<name> [["]<alias_value>["]]]
arrayenv             [-a] <variable name> "<string1>" ["<string2>" ...]
atmarp               table [<options>] <IP address>
bcc
bconfig              <image | config> <local | network> [<IP address>
                     <pathname>]
bconfig              -d <image | config>
boot                 [<vol>:<image_name>|- <vol>:<config_name>|-]
cd                   [<vol>:] [<directory>]
clear                <sub_commands> <flags>
clearlog             [<slot ID>]
commit
compact              <volume>:
copy                 <vol>:<filename1> <vol>:<filename2>
cutenv               -s -d<delimiter> [-f<list>|-c<list>] <variable>
date                 [<mm/dd/yy>] [<hh:mm:ss>] [<+|-><hh:mm>]
delete               <vol>:<filename>
diags                [<slot ID>]
dinfo
dir                  <vol:>
disable              <entity> <option>
echo                 [["]<string>["]]
enable               <entity> <option>
enumenv              <start #> [+<incr.> <variable name>
exec                 [-load|-unload] <command name>
export               {<variable name> ...}
firewall             <sub_command>
format               <volume>:
fwputkey             [<key_string> <ip_address>] | [clearkey]
get                  {<obj_name>|<obj_id>}.{<attr_name>|<attr_id>|*}
getcfg
getenv               [<variable name>]
gosub                :<label name>:
goto                 :<label name>:
help                 [-all|<command>]
history              [n]
if                   "<string1>" [<=>|<!=>] "<string2>"
```

	[then]; command(s) ;
ifconfig	[-s] [-d|-enable|-disable] <xcvr>|[-r4|-r16] <mau> [<IP addr> <mask> [<Next Hop>]]
ifconfig	[-s] [-fr [-annexd|-lmi|-annexa]] | [-int_clk] | [-d|-enable| -disable] <com> [<IP addr> <mask> [<Next Hop>]]
instenv	<variable prefix> <mib-object name> [<mib-instance- pattern>]
ip	<sub_command> <flags>
ip6	<sub_command> [<options>]
ipsec	<sub_command> [<options>]
isdb	<sub_command> [-s<slot>] [-c<connector>] [-p<port>] [<vol>:<filename>]
kexit	
kget	<sub_command>
kpassword	
kseed	
ksession	
kset	<sub_command> [<flags>]
ktranslate	<old_npk>
let	<var. name> = <expression>
list	[[<instances> [<obj_name>]]]
loadmap	[<slot list> | all] [<filepath>]
log	[<vol>:<logfile>] [-d<date>] [-t<time>] [-e"<entity>"] [-f<severity>] [-s<slot ID>] [-p[<rate]] [-c<code #>] [-x|-i] [-e"<entity>"] [-f<severity>] [-s<slot ID>] -z [-s<slot ID>]
logout	
mibget	[-n] [-p <pattern>] <object> <attribute var. array> <inst. id> <value var. array> <next_inst var.>
more	[on | off] [# of lines per screen]
mrinfo	[-r retry_count] [-t timeout_count] multicast_router
mtrace	[-M] [-O] [-U] [-s] [-w wait] [-m max_hops] [-q nqueries] [-g gateway] [-e extrahops] [-S statint] [-t ttl] [-r resp_dest] [-i if_addr] source [receiver] [group]
octetfmt	<variable name> <format option> <MIB object>
on	ERROR :<label name>:
osi	<subcommand> [<options>]
osidata	-s <SLOT> -t <lsp_l1 | lsp_L2 | path_L1 | path_L2 | adj_L1 | adj_L2 | adj_ES> -i <ID>

```
partition       create|delete [<vol>:]
password        [<login-id>]
pause           <seconds>
permit          [ -file    [<vol>:]<filename> ] |
                [  <command>    [<attribute>] ] |
                [  <mib object> ]
ping            <-IP| -IPV6| -IPX|-OSI|-VINES|-AT|-APPN>
                <hostname|address>
                [-t<timeout>] [-r<repeat count>] [-s<size>] [-p]
                [-a<address>]
                [-m<mode_name>] [-iifindex] [-v] [-n]
pktdump         <linenumber> [-s<start>] [-c<count>]
printf          <format string>  <p1> <p2> ... <pN>
prom            [-v|-w] <vol>:<ROM Update File> <slot ID>
                [<slot ID> ...]
readexe         <vol>:<filename>
record          open [-fileonly] [-pause]  <vol>:<filename>
                record pause [on|off]
                record close
reset           [<slot ID>]
restart         [<slot ID>]
return          :<label name>:
revoke          <command> [<attribute>]
rsvp            <sub_command>
run             <vol>:<filename> [<p1> [... <p9>]]
save            {config|aliases|perm} <vol>:<filename>
save            log [<vol>:<logfile>] [-d<date>] [-t<time>]
                [-e"<entity>"]
                [-f<severity>] [-s<slot ID>]
                securelogin
set             {<obj_name>|<obj_id>}.{<attr_name>|<attr_id>}.
                <inst_id> <value>
setenv          <variable name> "<text string>"
show            <entity> <option>
snmpserver      view [view-name] [oid-tree] [included | excluded |
                list | delete]
                community [community-name] view [view-name]
                [RO | RW | list | delete]

source          {aliases|env|perm} <vol>:<filename>
sprintf         <variable name> <format string>  <p1> <p2> ... <pN>
stamp
```

```
stop              <slot ID>
string            load|unload
system
tarp              <sub_command> <flags>
telnet            [-d] [-e escape_char] [hostname|address [port]]
tftp              {get|put} <name|address> <vol>:<file_spec>
                  [<vol>:<file_spec>]
type              [-x] <vol>:<filename>
unalias           {<alias name>|*}
unmount           <volume>:
unsetenv          [<variable name> ...| [-l] [-g] *]
verbose           [on | off]
xmodem            rb|sb [ylwpn] filename...
wfsnmpkey         <key_string> [encryption_alg_id]
wfsnmpmode        <proprietary(3) | trivial(1)>
wfsnmpseed        <community> <manager> [-|<val1>] [-|<val2>]
                  [-|<val3>]
                  [-|<val4>][-|<val5>]
```

TI COMMAND LISTING

alias	arrayenv	atmarp	bcc	bconfig	boot
cd	clearlog	commit	compact	copy	cutenv
date	delete	diags	dinfo	dir	disable
echo	enable	enumenv	exec	export	firewall
format	fwputkey	get	getcfg	getenv	gosub
goto	help	history	if	ifconfig	instenv
ip	ip6	isdb	kexit	kget	kpassword
kseed	ksession	kset	ktranslate	let	list
loadmap	log	logout	mibget	more	mrinfo
mtrace	octetfmt	on	osi	osidata	partition
password	ping	pktdump	printf	prom	readexe
record	reset	restart	return	run	save
set	setenv	show	source	sprintf	stamp
stop	securelogin	snmpserver	string	system	telnet
tftp	type	unalias	unmount	wfsnmpkey	wfsnmpmode
wfsnmpseed	unsetenv	verbose	xmodem		

TI SUBCOMMAND EXAMPLES

This section exhibits some frequently used TI *show* subcommands. To obtain menu options for subcommands, simply type in the command and a syntax screen will list subcommand options and the appropriate syntax.

```
[x:y]$show

Show Command Script
-------------------

show <command>
    Where <command> is one of the following:

ahb       console   hifn      mpr       rredund   sync
aot       copsc     hssi      nat       rsc       syslog
appn      csmacd    http      nbip      rsvp      system
asr       date      hwcomp    nhrp      srsvp     t1
at        decnet    igmp      gre       pim       tag1q
atm       diffserv  ip        nml       radius    tcp
atmarp    dls       ip6       osi       sdlc      telnet
atmdxi    drivers   ipsec     ospf      smds      tftp
atmsig    ds1e1     ipx       ping      snmp      token_ring
aurp      dsx3      iredund   packet    sonet     vines
autoneg   dvmrp     isdn      ppp       span      wcp
bgp       e1        l2tp      process   sr        wep
bisync    egp       lane      protocols srspan    x25
bootp     fddi      lnm       protopri  st2       xb
bot       fr        memory    rarp      sta       xns
bridge    frsw      mospf     rip6      state     dcmmw
buffers   ftp       mpls      rptr      sws       ntp
circuits  hardware  mpoa


[x:y]$show hardware


Hardware Show Command Help
--------------------------

show hardware <option>
    Where <option> is one of the following:
```

```
    ?                        - show this help message
    backplane                - show backplane information
    config_file              - show config. file used during boot
    image                    - show active image information
    memory           [<slot#>]    - show memory information
    proms            [<slot#>]    - show PROM information
    slots            [<slot#>]    - show slot information
    daug_cards       [<slot#>]     - show daughter cards information
    version                  - show version of this script


[x:y]$show buffers

Buffer Usage Statistics:
-----------------------


Slot      Total     Used        Free       %Free
----      -----     -----       -----      -----
   1       761       389         372        48 %
   2       761       387         374        49 %
   4      1144       231         913        79 %
   8       761       238         523        68 %
  12      3263       260        3003        92 %
  13      3263       260        3003        92 %
  14      1527       653         874        57 %


 [x:y]$show telnet

Telnet Server enabled.
    TI/Telnet Prompt: "[%slot%:N01FX1]$"
    Screen Size: 24
    Max. Login Retries: 3
    Login Time Out: 1 minutes
    Password Time Out: 1 minutes
    Command Time Out:  15 minutes
    TI/Telnet Prompt: "[%slot%:N01FX1]$"
    Screen Size: 24
    Max. Login Retries: 3
    Login Time Out: 1 minutes
    Password Time Out: 1 minutes
    Command Time Out:  15 minutes
Telnet In-bound sessions:
```

```
Telnet Client enabled.
    Telnet Command Prompt: ""
    Remote Telnet/Tcp Port: 23


 [x:y]$show circuits


show circuits  <option>
    Where <option> is one of the following:
    ?
    alerts
    base              [<circuit name>]
    configuration     [<circuit name>]
    disabled
    enabled
    hwfilters
    receive  errors   [<circuit name>]
    stats             [<circuit name>]
    system   errors   [<circuit name>]
    transmit errors   [<circuit name>]
    version




 [x:y]$show circuits stats


CSMACD Module I/O Statistics:

                  Received   Received  Transmit   Transmit   Total
   Slot Conn Circuit Bytes    Frames    Bytes      Frames     Errors
   ---- ---- ------- ---------- --------- ---------- ---------- ---------
   1    1    E11_1s- 45291591  189702    758415     6191       5
   1    2    E12_2E- 0         0         0          0          2
   1    3    E13_2W- 0         0         0          0          2
   ...
   ...
   ...
   14   1    E141_D  0         0         0          0          0


   12 entry(s) found
```

```
[x:y]$show ip

Usage: show ip <option>
where <option> is one of the following:
    ?
    adjacent hosts
    alerts
    arp
    base
    circuits          [<circuit_name>]
    disabled
    enabled
    rfilters          [<export | import>] [<PROTO>]
    rip
    rip alerts
    rip disabled
    rip enabled
    rip timers
    rip auth
    routes            [type [local|bgp|rip|egp|ospf|<etc.>] |
                      <ip address> | find <search pattern>]
    static
    stats
    stats datagrams   [<circuit_name>]
    stats cache       [<circuit_name>]
    stats fragments   [<circuit_name>]
    stats icmp client [<circuit_name>]
    stats icmp in     [<circuit_name>]
    stats icmp misc   [<circuit_name>]
    stats icmp out    [<circuit_name>]
    stats icmp server [<circuit_name>]
    stats security in [<circuit_name>]
    stats security out[<circuit_name>]
    traffic filters
```

```
[x:y]$show ip rip
                             RIP      Def.Rt      Poison    RIP    Trig
IP Interface  Ckt# State  Sup/Lis Sup/Lis      Reverse   Mode   Updt TTL
------------  ---- -----  ------- -------      -------   ----   --- ---
10.10.10.10   1    Up     En /En  Dis/Dis      Poison    RIP1   Dis  1
19.19.19.19   6    Up     En /En  Dis/Dis      Poison    RIP1   Dis  1
2 entries found
```

```
[x:y]$show system


System Show Command Help
------------------------

show system <option>
    Where <option> is one of the following:
    ?
    buffers
    drivers
    information
    memory
    protocols
    tasks
    version



[x:y]$show system buffers


Buffer Usage Statistics:
------------------------

Slot   Total   Used    Free   %Free
----   -----   -----   -----  -----
  1     761     388     373   49 %
  2     761     387     374   49 %
  4    1144     231     913   79 %
  8     761     281     480   63 %
 12    3263     260    3003   92 %
 13    3263     260    3003   92 %
 14    1527     653     874   57 %


[x:y]$show protocols
```

```
Dynamically Loadable Protocols Configuration
-------------------------------------------

          Protocol:   Slots:
          ---------   ------
                IP:   _1__2__3__4__5__6_____8__9_10_11_12_13_14_
       Frame Relay:                         8__9_10_
               DLS:                  5__6_
            TELNET:   _1__2__3__4__5__6_____8__9_10_11_12_13_14_
              TFTP:   _1__2__3__4__5__6_____8__9_10_11_12_13_14_
              SNMP:   _1__2__3__4__5__6_____8__9_10_11_12_13_14_
               TCP:   _1__2__3__4__5__6_____8__9_10_11_12_13_14_
              OSPF:           3__4_____6_____9_10_
              LLC2:                  5__6_
               PPP:                            9_10_
               FTP:   _1__2__3__4__5__6_____8__9_10_11_12_13_14_
               WCP:                            9_10_
```

```
[x:y]$show tftp

TFTP protocol is enabled.
    The Default Volume: 2
    Retransmit Timeout Value: 5 Seconds
    Max Number of Retransmits: 5
    Number of Writes Received: 0
    Number of Reads Received: 0
    Number of Retransmits: 0
```

```
[x:y]$show memory


Memory Usage Statistics (Megabytes):
------------------------------------

Slot  Total  Used     Free    %Free
----  -----  -----    -----   -----
   1   32 M   16 M     16 M    50%
   2   16 M    8 M      8 M    50%
```

```
[x:y]$show snmp
Snmp protocol is enabled.
    Authentication Type: Trivial
    Received PDUs: 4400
    Transmitted PDUs: 4400
    MIB Objects Retrieved: 7735
    MIB Objects Set: 192
    Get Request PDUs Accepted & Processed: 2397
    Get Next Request PDUs Accepted & Processed: 1907
    Get Response PDUs Generated: 4400
    Set Request PDUs Accepted & Processed: 96
    Trap PDUs Generated: 0
    Decoding ANS.1 Parsing Errors: 0
    Received Bad Community Name PDUs: 0
    Received Unsupported Operation PDUs: 0
    Generated PDUs with "tobig" Error: 0
    Generated PDUs with "noSuchName" Error: 809
    Generated PDUs with "badValue" Error: 0
    Generated PDUs with "readOnly" Error: 0
    Generated PDUs with "genErr" Error: 0
```

BCC COMMAND LISTING

This section contains commands that are used in the Bay Command Console mode of TI. You will notice as you look through these that most of the commands are similar to commands used in TI. The output is different, as can be seen in the following examples:

System Commands

?	exit	pktdump
back	format	prom
bccExit	getcfg	pwc
bconfig	help	readexe
boot	help-file-version	record
cd	history	reset
check	ifconfig	restart
clear	info	rm
clearlog	loadmap	save
commit	log	securelogin
compact	logout	show
config	lso	snmpserver
cp	mbulk	stamp
cwc	mdump	stop
date	mget	system

delete	mlist	telnet
diags	mnext	tftp
dinfo	more	type
dir	mset	unmount
disable	partition	xmodem
display	password	
enable	ping	

USING BCC SUBCOMMANDS

This section contains some examples of BCC subcommands. To list subcommand options, type in the parent command and a listing will be shown with the available subcommands to the parent command.

bcc> show

access	hardware	ppp
atm	hifn	process
bgp	hssi	radius
bri	http	rarp-server
bridge	hwcomp	sdlc
classical-ip	igmp	serial
config	instance	snmp
console	interface	sonet
dial	ip	span
dlsw	ipx	srb
dns	isdn-switch	syslog
dsucsu	lane	system
dsx3	llc2	tcp
dvmrp	mct1e1	telnet
ethernet	modem	tftp
fddi	mpoa	token-ring
firewall	mtm	translation-bridge
frame-relay	nat	vrrp
ft1e1	nhrp	wcp
ftp	ntp	
gre	ospf	

bcc> show ip

adjacent-hosts	enabled	routes	traffic-filter
alerts	icmp	static	
arp	interfaces	stats	
disabled	rip	summary	

```
bcc> show ip rip
alerts           disabled        summary
auth             enabled         timers

bcc> show ip interfaces
show ip interfaces                          Jul 03, 2000 15:54:51 [GMT]

Circuit   Cct #   State    IP Address     Mask             MAC Address
-----------------------------------------------------------------------------
S1_SS             down     10.1.1.1       255.255.255.0
E12_Dino          down     10.10.10.10    255.255.255.0
...


E51_fred          up       10.0.0.1       255.255.255.0    00.00.A2.CB.FE.D4
ATM_wilma         up       192.13.9.1     255.255.255.0
ATMbarney         up       192.11.10.1    255.255.255.0

bcc> show ip routes
show ip routes                              Jun 13, 2001 15:54:58 [GMT]

Network/Mask           Proto       Age  Slot      Cost  NextHop Address
------------------     ------  ---------- ----  ---------  ------------------
4.0.0.0/8              RIP         29   1         2     112.247.126.7
10.0.0.0/8             RIP         25   1         3     112.247.126.5
...
...

...
10.0.0.0/24            RIP         25   1         6     112.247.126.15
10.0.1.0/24            RIP         25   1         2     112.247.126.5
10.0.1.1/24            RIP         25   1         2     112.247.126.35

   Total Networks on Slot 1 = 212

bcc> show hardware
backplane        daughter_card   memory          slots
config_file      image           prom
```

INDEX

B

D

E

K

L

S

U

V

W

INTERNATIONAL CONTACT INFORMATION

AUSTRALIA
McGraw-Hill Book Company Australia Pty. Ltd.
TEL +61-2-9417-9899
FAX +61-2-9417-5687
http://www.mcgraw-hill.com.au
books-it_sydney@mcgraw-hill.com

CANADA
McGraw-Hill Ryerson Ltd.
TEL +905-430-5000
FAX +905-430-5020
http://www.mcgrawhill.ca

**GREECE, MIDDLE EAST,
NORTHERN AFRICA**
McGraw-Hill Hellas
TEL +30-1-656-0990-3-4
FAX +30-1-654-5525

MEXICO (Also serving Latin America)
McGraw-Hill Interamericana Editores S.A. de C.V.
TEL +525-117-1583
FAX +525-117-1589
http://www.mcgraw-hill.com.mx
fernando_castellanos@mcgraw-hill.com

SINGAPORE (Serving Asia)
McGraw-Hill Book Company
TEL +65-863-1580
FAX +65-862-3354
http://www.mcgraw-hill.com.sg
mghasia@mcgraw-hill.com

SOUTH AFRICA
McGraw-Hill South Africa
TEL +27-11-622-7512
FAX +27-11-622-9045
robyn_swanepoel@mcgraw-hill.com

**UNITED KINGDOM & EUROPE
(Excluding Southern Europe)**
McGraw-Hill Education Europe
TEL +44-1-628-502500
FAX +44-1-628-770224
http://www.mcgraw-hill.co.uk
computing_neurope@mcgraw-hill.com

ALL OTHER INQUIRIES Contact:
Osborne/McGraw-Hill
TEL +1-510-549-6600
FAX +1-510-883-7600
http://www.osborne.com
omg_international@mcgraw-hill.com